NVQ/SVQ  Level **4**

# Children's Care, Learning & Development

**www.heinemann.co.uk**

✓ Free online support
✓ Useful weblinks
✓ 24 hour online ordering

**01865 888118**

Sharina Forbes • Lianne Blake • Kelly Hill

Part of Pearson

Heinemann is an imprint of Pearson Education Limited, a company incorporated in England and Wales, having its registered office at Edinburgh Gate, Harlow, Essex, CM20 2JE. Registered company number: 872828

www.heinemann.co.uk
Heinemann is a registered trademark of Pearson Education Limited

Text © Sharina Forbes, Lianne Blake, Kelly Hill

First published 2009

12 11 10 09 08
10 9 8 7 6 5 4 3 2 1

**British Library Cataloguing in Publication Data**
A catalogue record for this book is available from the British Library.

ISBN 978 0 435448 55 4

Edited by Caroline Broughton
Designed by Hicks Design
Typeset by Phoenix Photosetting
Original illustrations © Pearson 2009
Illustrated by Jo Goodberry and TekArt
Cover design by Pearson Education
Cover photo/illustration © Digital Vision/Punchstock
Printed in Spain

Every effort has been made to contact copyright holders of material reproduced in this book. Any omissions will be rectified in subsequent printings if notice is given to the publishers.

**p29** Extract from www.standards.dfes.gov.uk/eyfs/site/about/index.htm, EYFS principles © Crown copyright. Reproduced under the terms of the Click-Use Licence
**p70** Flowchart from 'What to do if you're worried a child is being abused', DFES publications. © Crown copyright. Reproduced under the terms of the Click-Use Licence
**p71** Extract from www.nspcc.org.uk/whatwedo/aboutthenspcc/keyfactsandfigures/keyfacts_wda33645.html reproduced by kind permission from the NSPCC
**p80** The eatwell plate, from www.eatwell.gov.uk © Crown copyright material is reproduced with the permission of the Controller of HMSO and Queen's Printer for Scotland.
**p83** Extract from www.hse.gov.uk © Crown copyright. Reproduced under the terms of the Click-Use Licence
**p85** Extract from www.hse.gov.uk © Crown copyright. Reproduced under the terms of the Click-Use Licence
**p134** Extract from Kolb's Four Learning Styles. Reproduced by kind permission of Hay Group, Transforming Learning
**p136** Extract from 'Learning Style Inventory' 1986 Honey and Mumford, reproduced by kind permission of Peter Honey and Alan Mumford
**p144** Extract from www.ofsted.gov.uk © Crown copyright. Reproduced under the terms of the Click-Use Licence
**p144–5** Extract from www.surestart.gov.uk © Crown copyright. Reproduced under the terms of the Click-Use Licence
**p145–6** Extract from www.scotland.gov.uk © Crown copyright. Reproduced under the terms of the Click-Use Licence
**p146** Extract from www.everychildmatters.gov.uk © Crown copyright. Reproduced under the terms of the Click-Use Licence
**p146** Extract from www.scotland.gov.uk © Crown copyright. Reproduced under the terms of the Click-Use Licence
**p147** Extract from www.scotland.gov.uk © Crown copyright material is reproduced with the permission of the Controller of HMSO and Queen's Printer for Scotland.
**p170** Extract from www.ofsted.gov.uk on Ofsted gradings © Crown copyright. Reproduced under the terms of the Click-Use Licence
**p188** Extract from http://www.mindtools.com/pages/article/newLDR_84.htm © Mind Tools Ltd, 1995–2009, All Rights Reserved, reproduced with kind permission
**p277** Extract from the SEN Code of Practice, DFES, 2001 SEN definition © Crown copyright. Reproduced under the terms of the Click-Use Licence
**p277** Extract from www.additionalsupportneeds.org.uk is used by kind permission of Copyright of Govan Law Centre, Education Law Unit (www.edlaw.org.uk)
**p277–8** Extract from www.deni.gov.uk SENDO 2005 © Crown copyright. Reproduced under the terms of the Click-Use Licence

The websites used in this book were correct and up-to-date at the time of publication. It is essential for tutors to preview each website before using it in class so as to ensure that the URL is still accurate, relevant and appropriate. We suggest that tutors bookmark useful websites and consider enabling students to access them through the school/college intranet.

# Contents

| | | |
|---|---|---|
| Introduction | | v |
| Features of this book | | vi |
| About the authors | | viii |
| **Part One: The NVQ/SVQ – A Survival Guide** | | I |
| | National Occupational Standards for Children's Care, Learning and Development | 4 |
| | The Units and elements for NVQ and SVQ Level 4 CCLD | 4 |
| | The Principles and Values | 6 |
| | Assessment processes | 7 |
| **Part Two: Mandatory Units** | | 23 |
| 401 | Establish and develop working relationships | 25 |
| 402 | Support policies, procedures and practice to safeguard children and ensure their inclusion and well being | 54 |
| 403 | Support programmes for the promotion of children's development | 90 |
| 404 | Reflect on, review and develop own practice | 132 |
| **Part Three: Optional Units** | | 157 |
| | **Leadership and management of the setting** | 159 |
| 413 | Develop and implement operational plans for your area of responsibility | 160 |
| 418 | Coordinate and support the revision of policies, procedures and practice for registration and inspection | 166 |
| 424 | Obtain additional finance for the organisation | 171 |
| 430 | Manage finance for your area of responsibility | 174 |
| 420 | Research and develop an area of practice | 178 |
| 428 | Ensure health and safety requirements are met in your area of responsibility | 181 |

**Leadership and management of staff and colleagues** 185

425 Provide leadership in your area of responsibility 186

426 Encourage innovation in your area of responsibility 191

427 Allocate and monitor the progress and quality of work in your area of responsibility 195

429 Provide learning opportunities for colleagues 199

333 Recruit, select and keep colleagues 204

**Learning and curriculum development** 212

405 Coordinate provision for babies and children under 3 years in partnership with their families 213

406 Develop and support children's early learning in partnership with teachers 217

407 Support and evaluate the curriculum for children's early learning 221

408 Evaluate, assess and support the physical, intellectual, emotional and social development of children 226

409 Evaluate, assess and support children's communication 232

410 Evaluate, assess and support children's creativity 236

411 Evaluate, assess and support children's mathematical learning, exploration and problem solving 240

419 Contribute to the enhancement of early education for children 245

**Working in partnership** 249

412 Evaluate and coordinate the environment for children and families 250

416 Assess quality assurance schemes against agreed criteria 255

417 Establish and sustain relationships with providers of services to children and families 259

421 Provide information about children's and families' services 261

422 Coordinate work with families 264

423 Manage multi-agency working arrangements 268

431 Contribute to the leadership and management of integrated childcare provision 271

**Coordinating special educational needs and safeguarding children** 275

414 Coordinate and support provision for disabled children and those with special educational needs 276

415 Coordinate special educational needs for early education within a local area 276

326 Safeguard children from harm 287

Index 291

**W**elcome to the Candidate Handbook for NVQ/SVQ Children's Care, Learning and Development Level 4. This book has been developed for Early Years professionals by Early Years professionals who have much experience and knowledge of Early Years and the NVQ assessment processes.

Up until now those of you working towards your NVQ CCLD Level 4 have not had a textbook that specifically links to the requirements of the National Occupational Standards, so here it is. We hope you find this textbook a very useful tool to help you navigate your way through your NVQ.

Much consideration has been given to the layout of this book so that, whatever job role you are in, you can quickly find all the information that is relevant to you. As you have an initial 'flick' through this book you will see that it has been split into three parts.

Part One gives information about the NVQ process and will help you gain a greater understanding of ways in which you can present your evidence and prepare for assessments. Those of you who are new to the NVQ process will find this very valuable, and for those of you already familiar with the NVQ route it will help refresh your memory. You will also find a useful reference chart showing all the unit and element numbers for both the NVQ and the SVQ Level 4 CCLD.

Part Two focuses on the mandatory Units of the CCLD Level 4 framework and will help you in building your knowledge and understanding. Part Three looks at all of the 29 optional Units in the CCLD Level 4 framework. This is a feature the authors felt was important in developing this book to ensure that there is enough information in this single source to help you with the entire qualification, regardless of your choice of option Units.

Within Part Three the optional Units have been grouped into five sections which present the 29 optional Units in the most logical way, linking wherever possible any Units that have similar or related content. These groupings are not representative of any awarding body requirements, but will help you to navigate your way around the book more effectively.

At the end of each optional Unit you will find a unique learning feature entitled 'Can't find what you were looking for?' which directs you to sections of the book where you can find related information.

As you look at Parts Two and Three you will see that information relating to the Units of study is clearly presented in bite-size text with many learning features designed to get you thinking about elements of your own practice. Each of the following learning features is presented in a separate box near the section of text it relates to. They have been designed to help you improve your knowledge and understanding, reflect on your own practice and help you put the information you have read into context.

# Features of this book

Throughout the book there are a number of features which are designed to encourage reflection, discussion, or to help you in your professional development. These are shown below.

In addition to the learning features, the authors have endeavoured to create clear links to the knowledge statements of the National Occupational Standards so that the book can fit your personal learning needs and enable you to find and pick out specific statements that you require further information or guidance on.

We hope you enjoy reading this book and wish you every success in your NVQ or SVQ Level 4.

## Case studies

Examples of real situations taken from the Early Years sector to help link theory to practice, followed by one or two questions to help you check your understanding and explore concepts and ideas

## Key terms

Concise definitions of key words or phrases located adjacent to where the phrase appears in a Unit

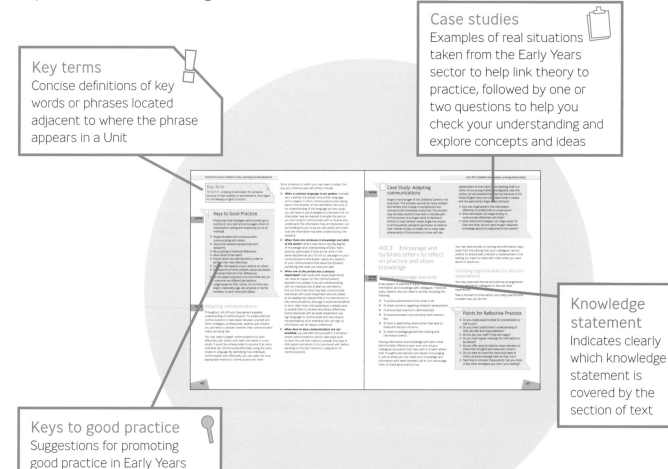

## Knowledge statement

Indicates clearly which knowledge statement is covered by the section of text

## Keys to good practice

Suggestions for promoting good practice in Early Years management

## Find it out
Promoting you to embark on further research or a fact-finding mission

## Did you know?
Short feature boxes including interesting facts about children's care, learning and development

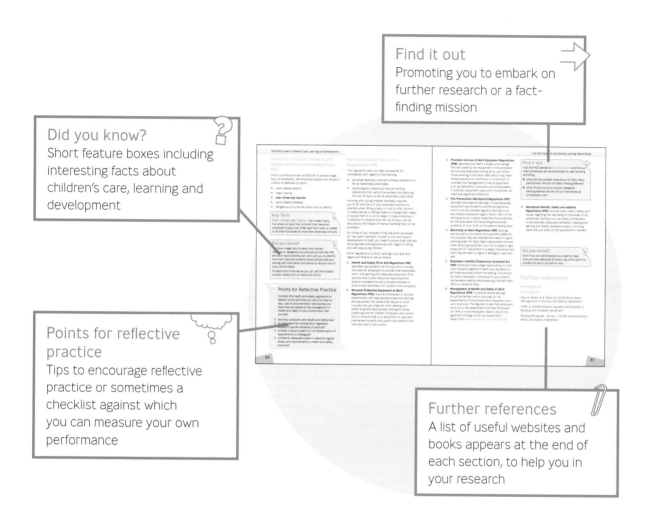

## Points for reflective practice
Tips to encourage reflective practice or sometimes a checklist against which you can measure your own performance

## Further references
A list of useful websites and books appears at the end of each section, to help you in your research

# About the authors

**Sharina Forbes** has been working in the Early Years sector since qualifying as a nursery nurse in 1990. Having worked in a variety of settings both in England and Europe, she has gained a wealth of knowledge and experience which she has been fortunate enough to share with the adult learners that she has been teaching for the last 10 years on a number of Early Years programmes. Sharina was an active childminder until recently and received the accolade of being recognised as 'outstanding' by Ofsted during this time. In 2007, Sharina set up her owning training company and now delivers NVQs in Children's care, Learning and Development to learners across the Midlands.

Sharina Forbes would like to thank everyone who had the belief in her to take on this project and see it through, including Virginia Carter at Heinemann who never doubted her ability, even when she doubted herself. Her deepest thanks go to her husband, John, who supported her throughout and kept the house in order! And finally her two children, Jessica and Lewis, for keeping it real!

**Lianne Blake** is NNEB qualified and has worked in a variety of childcare settings with children from birth to 5 years. She has worked her way up from Nursery Assistant to Manager, and is also a qualified NVQ assessor, internal verifier and lecturer. She has trained and taught NVQ levels 2, 3 and 4 to many new childcare staff who work in nurseries, preschools and as childminders. She currently works as a freelance writer.

Lianne Blake would like to thank her husband Jeremy for all his support, and her 2-year old daughter Bethan for her help pressing the buttons on the computer! She would also like to thank Bethan's Nonna, Pops and Gran for all their help with childcare and looking after Beth at a moment's notice. Thanks also go to the co-writers on this project for their help and support.

**Kelly Hill** has been working in the Early Years sector for over 15 years in a range of roles from nursery nursing to running her own successful Early Years training company. Kelly has worked as an assessor, internal verifier and external verifier for a number of awarding bodies. As a freelance training consultant she has advised many centres on the development of their awards, and supported hundreds of learners through the NVQ system. Kelly is also a Quality Assured Network childminder.

Kelly would like to thank her children for putting up with her hogging the computer! She would also like to thank the children and families she works with for being such inspirations.

## Acknowledgements

The author and publisher would like to thank the following individuals and organisations for permission to reproduce photographs:
© Albert Bandura p126; © Alamy/Janine Wiedel Photolibrary p224; © Alamy/Anne Barber p269; © Alamy/Christina Kennedy p58; © Alamy/David Wall p281; © Bananastock/Imagestate p157; © Corbis/Jim Craigmyle p150; ©Corbis/Najlah Feanny p208; © Ian Sanderson/Getty Images p269; © Ian Wedgewood/Pearson Education p36; © Masterfile p1; © Pearson Education Ltd/Arnos Design Ltd p164; © Pearson Education Ltd/Gareth Boden p168; © Pearson Education Ltd/Jules Selmes pp46, 98, 145, 189, 227, 265, 280, 265; © Photolibrary p23; © Shutterstock p81; © Shutterstock/Fred Goldstein p40; © The Food Standards Agency p80.

# Part One

## The NVQ/SVQ – A Survival Guide

- National Occupational Standards for Children's Care, Learning and Development
- The Units and Elements for NVQ and SVQ Level 4 CCLD
- The Principles and Values
- Assessment Processes

# The NVQ/SVQ – A Survival Guide

Over recent years, the National Occupational Standards (NOS) for the childcare sector have been developed, resulting in the current NVQ/SVQ in Children's Care, Learning and Development. As a candidate working towards this qualification, you need to be familiar with the content and layout of the NOS, and how to use them to support and guide you through the assessment process. You will find the information within this chapter will be relevant to you whether you are new to the NVQ/SVQ system, working within the NOS for the first time, or have previously completed an NVQ/SVQ and making the transition from the Early Years Care and Education (EYCE) to the new CCLD NOS. This section will encourage you to work through the NOS, ensuring you are familiar with their arrangement and feel confident to use them productively throughout the course.

## Learning Outcomes

This section will help you to understand:

- The National Occupational Standards (including SVQ) for CCLD and how to use them effectively.
- The organisation of the Units and elements.
- Assessment methods and how to plan for them.
- The importance of the Principles and Values.
- How to implement effective study skills.

# National Occupational Standards for Children's Care, Learning and Development

The introduction of the National Occupational Standards (NOS) in Children's Care, Learning and Development, was generally well received, with the majority of practitioners feeling that a redevelopment of the award was necessary.

You may be familiar with the old Early Years Care and Education NOS, through your previous studies, and as you work though this book and use your NOS you will no doubt see many differences and variations.

After consultation with practitioners in the Early Years and Childcare sector various changes were made, including making the NOS easier to follow, jargon free and easily accessible.

Another important change was the recognition that practitioners often carry out a variety of job roles, working within a range of settings with a diverse cross section of families. The decision to increase the age range from 0–8 years to 0–16 years allowed the standards to become accessible to more practitioners, and designing a wider selection of optional Units helped to make the NVQ/SVQ more accessible to practitioners from many settings.

For example, practitioners working with children in after-school clubs or youth clubs may have traditionally opted for the 'playwork' NVQ/SVQ, which was a sufficient qualification for that job role. However, it left them with little scope to move into other areas of childcare, and meant that should they wish to work with younger children, they would have to retrain. The CCLD NOS have addressed this issue, and the range of optional Units that are available are more accessible and achievable for practitioners across the field, whilst being flexible enough to see them through their current and prospective job roles.

## So, what exactly are the National Occupational Standards?

The NOS define the outcomes that you are expected to reach. They show what skills, knowledge and understanding you will need for employment within the sector, and guide you towards the expected level of skill which you will be demonstrating to your assessor. It is essential that you understand that the NOS are not specific training courses. They are a set of criteria to clearly demonstrate what you need to achieve and the levels of competence that you are required to reach; they also set a benchmark for best practice, and indicate acceptable levels of service. The NOS also ensure that both you and your assessor are clear about the range and depth of the competence and knowledge you need to demonstrate.

## The Units and elements for NVQ and SVQ Level 4 CCLD

The National Occupational Standards for Children's Care, Learning and Development, Level 4, are broken down into **Units**. The Units are individually numbered, and at level 4 there are 4 mandatory Units and 29 optional Units from which you should chose 5.

> ## Key Term
> Unit – describes a particular function within a job role and breaks it down to list the specific activities or duties this comprises. Indicates the functions that that you are required to carry out in the workplace, forming the building blocks that make up the qualification.

All four mandatory Units have to be completed to gain the qualification, regardless of your job role or setting.

The optional Unit choices will depend upon your current job role and/or future career goals. Each Unit consists of a range of elements, which will be discussed later in this section.

The Units and elements for the NVQ/SVQ level 4 Children's Care, Learning and Development are given on pages 18–22.

At the beginning of each Unit in the standards, you will find a page that gives you the information about the content of that particular Unit. It acts as a summary for the Unit, identifying what the Unit is about and whom it is for. This information will be particularly useful to you when choosing your optional Units, so it is important that you read this information.

Following on from this information is 'Key Words and Concepts'. This section explains and defines key words used within the Unit, as they may be used or interpreted in a particular way.

It is important that you do not miss out on this information by moving directly to the main Performance Criteria, as this summary can be extremely useful in understanding the main points of the Unit before you begin.

Now that you understand the Units, let's look at the elements within the Units.

Each Unit is divided into **elements**. The elements demonstrate particular aspects of that Unit. It is up to you to show competence in *all* elements to complete the qualification. The number of elements within each Unit will vary.

Elements are broken down further into **performance criteria (PCs)**. This list of PCs identifies several criteria which you must be familiar with in order to demonstrate competence. Whilst they demonstrate to you the specific aim of the criteria, they don't tell you exactly how you should do it. For example, in Unit 401, performance criteria 1 says 'Initiate relationships with colleagues that help them adjust to and develop their roles and responsibilities'. There are a number of ways you can chose to demonstrate your ability to do this. You might choose take responsibility for a new member of staff, becoming their mentor/buddy and supporting them through their induction period. Alternatively, a colleague may be moving into a different age group within your setting and you need to develop the relationship you have with them in order to support their transition. The important factor here is that the NOS identify key skills for work-based practice; how these are demonstrated will be up to you and your assessor.

At the end of each Unit, the NOS provide a list of **knowledge specifications**. These indicators identify the knowledge and understanding that is required to carry out competent practice in the performance described in the Unit. In essence, the PCs are about *what* you do, the knowledge specifications are about *why* you do it.

At this point, it may help to clarify all that you have learnt so far. It is important to take the time to look through your NOS, identifying the Units, elements, performance criteria, and knowledge specifications. Familiarise yourself with the layout of the NOS and the language used. They may seem confusing at first, but the more you work with them, the more they will

become useable. If you have any questions regarding the National Occupational Standards, talk them through with your assessor.

## Key Terms

**Element** – describes one distinct aspect of the function depicted by the Unit. Identifies one particular aspect of the work that you must be able to do.

**Performance criteria** – describes one distinct aspect of the function depicted by the Unit. Identifies one particular aspect of the work that you must be able to do.

**Knowledge specification** – describes a particular function within a job role and breaks it down to list the specific activities or duties this compromises. Indicates the functions that that you are required to carry out in the workplace, forming the building blocks that make up the qualification.

## Age ranges within the NOS

As you have previously read, the CCLD NOS are designed for practitioners working with children from 0–16. Throughout the NOS, you will find that the context, rather than the age of the child, is highlighted, stressing the importance of working within an individual child's developmental capacity rather than chronological age bands.

You are required to have a sound knowledge and understanding of the 0–16 age range, regardless of which age group you actually work with. This knowledge and understanding gives you flexibility, offering transferable skills should you wish to work with a different age range in the future. However, when demonstrating your real work practice, you will only need to cover the age group you are actually working with. You will find out more about this later in this section.

The CCLD NOS consist of 87 Units of competence. 22 of these Units have been imported from other awards: Playwork, Health and Social Care, Management and Leadership, Teaching Assistants, and Learning and Development. Again, this is a great way to widen the opportunities available to you, and offers flexible career routes.

If you have already completed any imported Units through previous study, you will not be required to repeat them. It is possible for you to be fully accredited

## Case Study: Flexibility of the NOS

Sarah Major, a childminder for over 7 years, has seen how the extended age range has offered her greater choice and flexibility in her future career path. She says:

'Having the age range up to 16 years now means that I have more choice in the type of setting I work and practise in, in the future. I enjoy working with the under 5s in my home setting, but the studying across the 0–16 age range has meant that I have a deeper understanding of the older children in my care, and I feel I can provide more balanced learning opportunities for them. It also means that if I decide to change my job, I can look into different settings, such as after-school clubs, youth clubs and holiday play schemes.'

through a direct transfer via your awarding body. If you think this applies to you, you should speak to your assessor, who will let you know the procedure you need to follow.

You should now have a good understanding of how the NOS for CCLD are designed and be able to find your way around them. It is worth taking the time to familiarise yourself with the layout and terminology.

# The Principles and Values

When working with children and young people within the childcare sector, there are certain basic principles and values that affect everything you believe and guide everything you do. These principles and values permeate every area of practice, and impact on your work, your colleagues and the families and children you have contact with. There are three principles that underpin everything you do, and alongside these principles are nine values.

## Principles

1. The welfare of the child is paramount.
2. Practitioners contribute to children's care, learning and development and this is reflected in every aspect of practice and service provision.
3. Practitioners work with parents and families who are partners in the care, learning and development of their children, and are the child's first and most enduring educators.

## Values

1. The needs, rights and views of the child are at the centre of all practice and provision.
2. Individuality, difference and diversity are valued and celebrated.
3. Equality of opportunity and anti-discriminatory practice are actively promoted.
4. Children's health and well being are actively promoted.
5. Children's personal and physical safety is safeguarded, whilst allowing for risk and challenge as appropriate to the capabilities of the child.
6. Self-esteem, resilience and a positive self-image are recognised as essential to child's development.
7. Confidentiality and agreements about confidential information are respected as appropriate unless a child's protection and well being are at stake.
8. Professional knowledge, skills and values are shared appropriately in order to enrich the experience of children more widely.
9. Best practice requires reflection and a continuous search for improvement.

These principles and values form the foundations of the NVQ/SVQ and, as such, you need to have a full understanding of how they impact on your practice in order for you to correctly interpret and understand the NOS. As you progress through this qualification, your assessor will be looking for evidence of **competency**. For your assessor to assess you as competent within aspects of your job role, you must demonstrate that you work within the framework of these principles and values.

## Key Term

Competency – having the necessary skill or knowledge to do something successfully.

# Assessment processes

## Introduction

As you progress through your NVQ/SVQ, you will hear terms such as 'collecting evidence' or 'evidence gathering', particularly from your assessor. It is important, however, not to take this too literally. Your portfolio is much more than a 'folder of evidence'. It should demonstrate your abilities, skills, knowledge and competencies as required by the National Occupational Standards.

Your assessor will guide and support you in building your portfolio, mainly by observing your practice within your setting, and writing or typing these observations, and by discussing your practice with you through what is known as a 'professional discussion'. Your portfolio will predominantly be made up of these observations of actual work practice and discussion, and your assessor will support and guide you through the whole process of putting your portfolio together, offering you ideas of how you might demonstrate your competence, and evidencing your skills and abilities.

Within your NOS for CCLD, you will find a list of 'Evidence Gathering Methods', describing the ways in which you can demonstrate your competence for the award. These are shown in Figure I.

## Direct observation

You may hear your assessor use the term 'holistic observation', which is a term used describe the way your performance is assessed in the workplace. **Holistic assessment** involves both you and your assessor looking at a forthcoming event within your work place, and considering where this evidence may fit into a range of the Units and elements within the NOS. Working in this holistic manner allows the evidence to be generated from real work situations, rather than relying on you 'setting up' activities with the children to cover a particular Unit or element.

> ### Key Term
> **Holistic assessment** – observing real work situations as they happen with a view to covering a range of Units and elements.

An example of holistic assessment might be during outside play. The assessor might arrange to see you supporting children during the outside play session, with an idea of the kind of evidence she might observe. They may, for example, hope to see some physical play, maybe you organising some group games, or action games. They may anticipate that you will have

**Figure I:** Evidence-gathering methods

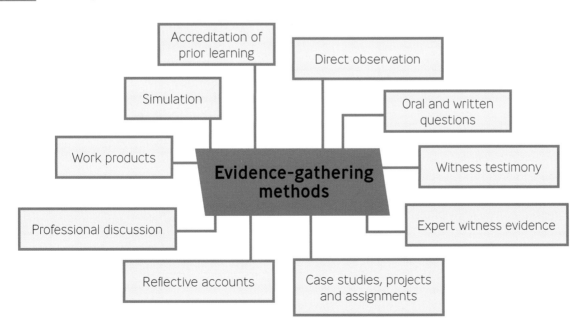

to organise the staffing to ensure ratios are met, and hopefully they will see you following health and safety guidelines.

They will bear all of this in mind as they observe you during your work with the children. However, your assessor will not prescribe to you exactly what you should do, but allow the situation to develop as it normally would. By working in this manner, your assessor might observe you carrying out a range of activities with the children, for example if a child has an accident, or struggles to catch a ball, or if you have to deal with another member of staff who is not working in an appropriate manner.

The opposite to this holistic approach would be for your assessor to prescribe to you exactly what it is they want to see you perform. For example, the assessor might ask you to play a game of 'Farmer's in the Den' with a group of children. By doing this, other sources of observational evidence might be missed. Holistic direct observation should be the primary source of evidence within your portfolio. During direct observations, your assessor will be observing you carrying out your normal duties within your setting, and writing the observation as she sees it happen; often referred to as 'naturally occurring evidence'. Assessing holistically means looking at the whole picture of what you are doing, rather than focusing on a particular task, activity or Unit of the NOS. A holistic observation will detail how you have shown competency, covering a range of PCs within a variety of Units and elements, whilst demonstrating your commitment to the principles and values.

Once the observation has been written, your assessor will then cross reference it, by identifying which PCs and knowledge statements have been demonstrated from which Units, and referencing them onto the NOS. Cross referencing is something which gets easier with practice, and your assessor may carry out the referencing with you, to enable you to see how your evidence is meeting the standards.

Referencing is a means of relating the practice that your assessor has observed to the requirements of the NOS.

For example, your assessor may have written the following statement within an observation:

'. . . Steph then encouraged the member of staff (J) to consider how her late time keeping had impacted on the children and their families, her colleagues and the nursery as a whole, and encouraged J to think about how she could change her morning routine to ensure she arrived at work on time. She set time scales for these improvements and suggested that they meet again in two weeks to see how the changes were working and to hopefully close the matter. Steph ensured that J understood her lateness could not continue and that if changes weren't made, she would have to follow the disciplinary procedure . . .'

The assessor would then reference the observation onto the NOS, picking out PC and KS that had been observed. For example:

| Unit | Element | PC/Knowledge Specification |
|------|---------|----------------------------|
| 401 | I | 2. Identify and agree with colleagues ways in which you can support each other's roles and responsibilities to maintain and improve provision to children |
| | | K4C749 The processes you should follow to help colleagues adjust to and develop their roles and responsibilities |

Your assessor may also observe work products as evidence (**product evidence**). For example, while carrying out a **direct observation**, you may show your assessor an accident record book, demonstrating and discussing how you have previously dealt with an accident and recorded it according to the polices and procedures of your setting. Your assessor should then write this within the direct observation, stating that she has seen the document, and that it was completed accurately. It would not be necessary for you to then include copies of this document as evidence within your portfolio, as your assessor has stated that she has seen it, and used her professional judgement to decide its value as evidence.

## Key Terms

**Product evidence** – products derived from real work situations, such as fire drill records, accident books, stationery orders etc.

**Direct observation** – a record of the actions you carry out under real work situations, written by the assessor.

# Professional discussion

The CCLD NVQ/SVQ lends itself very well to the use of **professional discussion**. By offering an alternative method to present evidence, it will enable you to discuss with your assessor why you performed in a particular way. Professional discussions are a useful tool for drawing out depth and breadth of knowledge and will help you to reflect on your practice, providing an opportunity for you to discuss how you feel your practice and evidence meets the NOS. As an assessment process, it can be one of the most effective ways of demonstrating your abilities, knowledge and skills.

The professional discussion can be recorded in a range of formats, including on tape or in writing, and should be in the form of a structured review of your practice. They are particularly useful in demonstrating your knowledge and understanding, and how well you understand the principles and values of the childcare sector.

There are three key stages to professional discussion.

1. Planning the discussion.
2. Carrying out the discussion.
3. Recording and evidencing the discussion.

## Key Term

**Professional discussion** – a discussion between you and the assessor, to draw out your depth and breadth of knowledge and understanding, establishing the rationale behind your actions.

## Planning

The planning of the professional discussion should be two-way, between you and your assessor. There may be gaps in your evidence which need to be filled by discussion, or your assessor may want to probe deeper into your understanding of a particular subject. Being clear about the aims of the discussion is important, so that your can research any necessary information, and bring to the discussion any visual evidence to support what you are saying.

How this plan is presented will vary from centre to centre, but it may look something like Figure 2 (page 10).

## Carrying out the discussion

It is important that you should feel comfortable and at ease during the discussion, and being well prepared will help you to settle into the discussion. Your assessor will allow you plenty of time to discuss your views, and express your opinions, as well as explaining how your practice meets the standards and requirements of both your setting and national guidelines. You will also be given opportunities to ask questions about anything you are unsure of, and comment accordingly. Your assessor's role will be to facilitate the discussion, prompting you when necessary, and helping to draw out your knowledge and understanding. It should not be a question and answer session, but a conversation led by you in order to demonstrate your knowledge and understanding.

## Recording

It is a requirement that your assessor makes an audio recording of the professional discussion, as this will ensure that nothing is missed when referencing the evidence. The referencing of a professional discussion needs to be clear and accurate. Recording may be through any audio route.

Using digital recordings may allow for further accuracy in the referencing of the discussion, and make the sourcing of the evidence easier. Of course this doesn't have to be with an MP3 player; voice recording and burning onto a CD may be just as effective.

## Oral and written questions

**Questioning** can be used as an effective way to for your assessor to check your understanding of a subject. For example, during a direct observation, you may do something in particular which your assessor would like to clarify your understanding on. An example of this may be during an observation of sand play where you ask one child to wear gloves. This is common practice for that child in your setting. It would not be

## Case Study: Using an MP3

Recently, many colleges and training providers have introduced the use of MP3 players to record professional discussions. As training providers endeavour to bring their delivery up to date with new technology, the use of MP3 players is one step closer to this aim, and has been well received by many candidates.

When a candidate and assessor have a professional discussion, it is recorded via the MP3 player. The assessor will then upload the recording onto a PC and it will remain saved there to be verified by the Internal Verifier or External Verifier if required. The assessor will then reference the discussion onto the NOS as they normally would. This method enables the assessor to be clear about the candidate's knowledge and skills, and releases them from the time spent writing the discussion down as they have previously.

**Figure 2:** Example of an assessment plan

## Forbes Training

Candidate's Name:

| Assessment Method/Description | PCs, Knowledge and scope | |
|---|---|---|
| | | |

| Considerations for Assessment/Feedback | By Candidate | By Assessor |
|---|---|---|
| | | |

| Date and Time of Next Assessment |
|---|
| |

| Candidate's Signature: | Assessor's Signature |
|---|---|
| Date: | Date: |

Top copy: Candidate     2nd Copy: Assessor     3rd Copy: Centre File

appropriate for your assessor to interrupt you during the observation to ask why you have done this, so your assessor may make a note to ask this question at the end. If your response was appropriate, for example, if the child had a skin complaint that was aggravated by the sand, your assessor would be able to reference your understanding accordingly. However, if you answered that you didn't know why, and only did it because you saw other practitioners doing so, this would not show your competency, and your assessor may set you a task or ask you to research this information further. Questions may also be used where direct observations are not available, for example to clarify your understanding of emergency evacuation, or in a medical emergency. In these situations, your assessor may ask 'what if' questions to check that you have the knowledge required.

Questions can be asked verbally and written down by your assessor as the questioning is taking place, or taped in similar ways to the professional discussion.

## Key Term

Questioning – using questions to clarify your knowledge and understanding.

## Witness testimonies

**Witness testimonies** are written by witnesses who were present at a particular time, and can confirm the consistency of your practice, but are not expert witnesses (see below). Practitioners who write witness testimonies must only write what they have witnessed, and the testimony must be written by the witness themselves.

Some training centres have their own format for writing witness testimonies, and will supply witnesses with printed sheets to write their testimony on. Alternatively, a testimony on a piece of headed paper should be fine, as long as it is signed and dated appropriately. If witness testimonies are used within your portfolio as evidence, you must also provide a witness status list. A witness status list identifies the names, status and signature of anyone involved within your portfolio, such as a teacher who writes a witness statement, or the expert witness. A pro-forma of this can be found within your NOS, and should state clearly the name and status of the witness, along with their signature. Your assessor may wish to clarify the authenticity of a random selection of witness testimonies as part of the training centre's quality assurance procedures.

Again, witness testimonies can be useful for Units that are particularly difficult to directly observe, such as outings with children, however it is important to remember that direct observation should take place wherever possible and be the main process of evidence gathering within your portfolio.

## Key Term

Witness testimony – an account of your performance, written by another person who is not your assessor.

## Expert witness evidence

This type of evidence is very similar to direct observation, however it is written by the expert witness, not your assessor. **Expert witness** evidence is used primarily where there are no occupationally competent assessors for occupationally specific Units. Expert witnesses are employed within your setting, must be approved and trained by your training centre, and records of expert witnesses must be kept up-to-date. Expert witness evidence is extremely valuable for providing evidence on confidential matters, where an assessor's presence may be inappropriate.

The CCLD assessment strategy states that expert witnesses must demonstrate the following.

- A working knowledge of the relevant National Occupational Standards.
- Current or recent (within the last 2 years) experience of working at or above the level for which they are attesting competence.
- Demonstration of appropriate, continuous professional development relevant to the sector for which they are attesting competence.
- That they have no conflict of interest in the outcome of their evidence.

It is not necessary for expert witnesses to hold an assessor qualification, as a qualified assessor must assess the contribution of performance evidence drawn from an expert witness to the overall evidence of competence.

**Key Term**

**Expert witness** – an approved practitioner, inducted by your training centre, who carries out observations on you in order to provide written evidence.

## Case studies, projects and assignments

Previously, **case studies, projects and assignments** have been relied on too heavily, with candidates producing masses of written evidence and huge portfolios. The NVQ/SVQ process is all about real work evidence, and you should not be producing written evidence for each Unit of the NOS. This type of evidence should be used sparingly where there is no naturally occurring evidence available, or where knowledge evidence cannot be observed or discussed. For example, you may demonstrate competence in working with children within a particular age range through direct observation, but use case studies, projects or assignments to demonstrate knowledge of other age ranges. For example, you may be directly observed by your assessor working with children aged 3–5, and, during your professional discussion, demonstrate knowledge for the 5–7 age range. Your assessor may ask you to work with some case studies or produce an assignment to demonstrate your knowledge for the 0–3 and 8–16 age group, to ensure that you can fully meet the knowledge specifications.

**Key Term**

**Case studies, projects and assignments** – used to provide evidence where no naturally occurring evidence is available.

## Reflective accounts

**Reflective accounts** provide evidence from you, and should be a detailed account of your practice within your setting. These accounts should give you the opportunity to think through your practice, consider your progression and identify any future development needs. By reflecting on your practice in this way you can identify how your practice has improved as a result of your training and developing skills and knowledge. You can also provide reflective accounts orally to your assessor, which they would record either on tape, in writing or on videotape. Your training centre may have its own format for recording reflective accounts.

Reflective accounts should demonstrate the points in Figure 3.

**Key Term**

**Reflective accounts** – a written or oral account reflecting on your practice

**Figure 3:** What reflective accounts should demonstrate

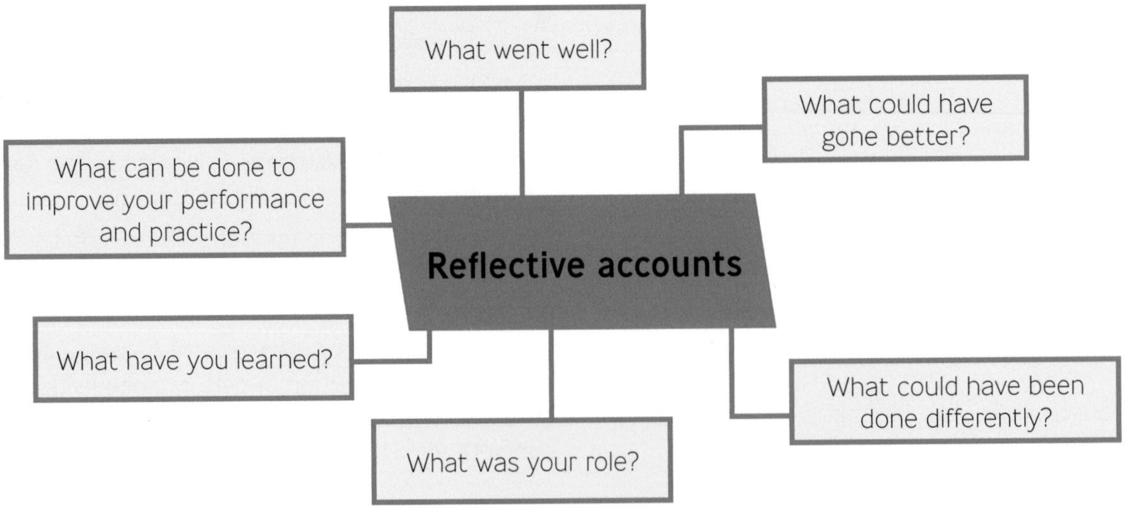
What went well?
What could have gone better?
What can be done to improve your performance and practice?
Reflective accounts
What have you learned?
What could have been done differently?
What was your role?

## Work products

Throughout the duration of the course, you may produce **work products**, both from your working practice and any training sessions you attend. These may be minutes from meetings, leaflets, child observation, curriculum plans etc. It is important that you realise that whilst these products are worthwhile for your practice, learning, development and as reference material, they may not be necessary to have in your portfolio as evidence. Your assessor may suggest that you have a 'working file' in which you can keep all of this supplementary evidence. Should any of these products be required for evidence, they can be put into the portfolio, or better still observed by the assessor, referenced into the NOS and kept in the working file. In accordance with children's safety, you should not include photographs or any personal details of children within your setting. You should also be aware that work products must have been produced by you, and not by someone else within the setting.

### Key Term
Work products – evidence produced by you during work practice.

## Simulation

This type of evidence should only be used as directed by the NOS. **Simulation** can only be used if no other evidence is available and only where it is stated within the NOS. Where there is no alternative, your assessor must endeavour to make the simulation as realistic as possible, and you must demonstrate your competency in the same manner as you would in a real work situation, including following all policies and procedures of your setting. Simulation may never be the sole source of evidence within an element.

### Key Term
Simulation – to 'set up' an observation that is not within a real work situation. Only to be used where clearly indicated within the NOS.

## Accreditation of prior learning (APL)

This evidence type can be used when you have prior learning experiences, which have been certificated. For example, you may have been on a first aid course or behaviour management course, and therefore your assessor will reference this evidence accordingly. Your training centre should have an **accreditation of prior learning** policy, outlining how accreditation of prior learning should be carried out, but if you are unsure if a course you have been on can be accredited, speak to your assessor. Your assessor will need to see original copies of certificates, and may put copies of these certificates in the portfolio, although this is not necessary as the assessor can write an observation of the product. Your assessor may also wish to clarify the knowledge you have actually gained from this APL during a professional discussion.

The stages to APL are:

1. identify what you can do or have learnt
2. identify how those silks and knowledge relate to the CCLD NOS
3. reference accordingly.

As you can see, there are a range of possible assessment opportunities available to you, in order for you to demonstrate your competence, skills, knowledge and understanding. To ensure that you use these opportunities effectively, the assessments must be well planned and scheduled, detailing how the assessments will support and enhance the achievement of the award. Therefore, it is essential that you work in cooperation with your assessor to make the most of observational opportunities and gather the very best evidence.

### Key Term
Accreditation of prior learning – identifying your previous learning experiences and referencing them accordingly into the NOS.

## Assessment planning

Forward planning is essential in our daily lives. From planning holidays and trips to managing day-to-day tasks, we all need to plan in order to effectively achieve our goals and ambitions. The same planning principles you use personally can be put into practice when working with your assessor to plan your learning and assessment opportunities.

By taking responsibility for assessment planning, you can lead the assessment process and provide your assessor with all the information they need to assess your progress. Planning assessments will ensure that you are aware of your goals and targets, which will in turn help you to achieve your qualification and plan any further training you may wish to do. By taking ownership of your qualification in this way, you will find the process much more satisfying, rewarding and clear. Planning will provide you with a clear sense of direction and enable you to assess your own progress.

There are many methods for planning, and your assessor will use a combination of planning methods, being led by your individual needs. Arranging appropriate assessment opportunities is central to the success of NVQ/SVQ training and will do the following.

- Help identify the opportunities for collecting evidence efficiently across a range of elements.
- Ensure that the evidence collected is authentic, valid and reliable.
- Encourage you to take ownership of your learning and assessment.
- Help you to see how your work practice relates to the NOS.
- Help to avoid the collection of too much evidence.

## Preparing for an assessor visit

If you have never experienced direct observation before you might find the idea of your first observation very daunting. Your assessor will put you at ease, and help you to understand that all you need to do is whatever you would do normally in your day-to-day work. You will probably find that your first one or two observations have very little planning, as your assessor will just observe whatever happens naturally, which is usually quite a lot, so you should not feel under any pressure to 'perform'. You may be quite shocked at the amount of evidence your assessor can gather through watching your normal daily practice. However, as you progress through the qualification, the observations

will become more planned, and certain aspects of the NOS need to be evidenced. In this event, it is important that both you and your assessor discuss how best to observe these parts. When thinking about observation assessment opportunities within your setting, consider how holistic the observation could be. For example, you might think about asking your assessor to observe you during a staff meeting within your setting. Consider how much evidence from the NOS can be demonstrated, and what you might want to have prepared to show your assessor at the end of the meeting, such as minutes and agendas. You may also plan a professional discussion with your assessor at the end of the staff meeting to discuss why you did or said certain things and reflect on how the meeting went and how it may have been improved. Consider where you have gaps in your evidence, and try to plan observations that will meet those gaps.

Before any assessment, your assessor will discuss with you the shift patterns you may be working, the ages of the children you will be working with, and agree a date and time for the observation to take place. Your assessor will write an assessment plan, which will detail how, when and where the assessment will take place. During the observation, the assessor will sit quietly somewhere where they can observe your practice, without being intrusive or obstructing you. They will watch as you carry out your tasks within the setting, and may follow you if you move into another area or room. Your assessor will try to be as inconspicuous as possible, subtly noting down what you say and do. This may feel odd at first; however, you will get used to it and eventually forget they are even there!

Once the observation is over, your assessor will feedback to you about the observation and give you the opportunity to think over how things went, what you might have done differently etc. The review will allow you to reflect on your practice, and consider how you might improve your knowledge or practice in the future. During the review, you will discuss your progress with your assessor and think about further assessment opportunities. You may also have planned to have a professional discussion at this time. Once this is all over, your assessor will reference the assessment into the NOS and you can then discuss the next assessment opportunity, making a plan as to how you will move forward in the qualification.

## Case Study: E-portfolios

When Chesna enrolled at her local college, she was informed that they were introducing E-portfolios. Chesna said: 'I was nervous at first. I wondered if my IT skills would be good enough to do everything electronically. But to be honest, I had nothing to worry about. My tutor in college showed me how to use the system, and we had workshops to make sure we were all OK with it. Then, each observation was uploaded onto it, so everything was accessible whenever I wanted to view it.' Chesna was able to log on to her portfolio and view her progress, observations and feedback at a time that suited her, and didn't have to carry heavy portfolios around with her. Having a secure log-in meant that she could work from anywhere: her home, the library, college or her workplace. She was even able to access her learning when travelling to visit her family.

## E-portfolios

E-portfolios do the same job as your standard portfolio, except that they are electronic versions as opposed to paper based, holding the evidence electronically.

E-portfolios are becoming increasingly popular within centres as they strive to provide high-class training and keep up to date with modern technology. They allow flexibility for candidates like yourself, as you can access them at any time, as well as contacting your assessor and viewing your progress. Table 1 on page 16 identifies the advantages of the e-portfolio system for all involved.

## Planning your studies

The NVQ system is designed to allow practitioners to demonstrate their competence through real work situations. However, there will be times where you will need to show your assessor that you have sufficient knowledge as well as skills for a managerial role. Being able to manage your studies effectively will enable you to produce evidence that demonstrates your knowledge.

For example, you may need to demonstrate that you have knowledge of differing psychological or developmental theories, and therefore you will have to research theorists to gain that knowledge.

## Carrying out research

Sometimes it can be difficult to know where to start, but many people now use the Internet as a starting point for their research. You can use the Internet in a variety of ways, to search for the work of a particular person, to access libraries from around the world, research local and international news, or access magazines and journals. You may even access chat rooms and use email to discuss your ideas and research with other students. The Internet is accessible to most people, and fairly straightforward to use. However, the sheer amount of information accessible through the Internet can be mind-blowing, and how can you be sure that the information you are finding is relevant and credible?

Entering keywords into a search engine will provide you with a 'hit list' of sites that are relevant to the key word you entered. They should be ordered according to relevance and will provide you with a link to the site. It is important only to use credible sites, and you may want to check that your findings match with findings on other sites.

It is important to remember that much of the information on the Internet is also available in libraries, and you may find it easier to use books and journals; these have the added advantage that you can see exactly what the source of the information is and how credible it is.

However you gather your information, there are a few techniques which you can use to make your studies more effective.

- ■ Make notes of exactly what you want to research. You may find that writing down a few definitive questions will help you to focus on what it is you want to find out.
- ■ Try to define the scope of your research, such as time scales, publication dates or geographical areas.
- ■ Make a list of potential key search words to use when searching the Internet or library catalogue.

**Table I:** Advantages of E-portfolios

| | Advantages of E-portfolios |
|---|---|
| **Candidate** | ■ identifies to the candidate what needs to be done in order to proceed to the next stage of the assessment process<br>■ candidate can send a message to their assessor for further assistance<br>■ candidate has the opportunity to be proactive in the assessment process<br>■ instant charts, diagrams and reports can show the candidate exactly how far they have progressed in their Units<br>■ encourages motivation by providing an easy-to-use and stimulating point-and-click interface<br>■ no need to carry a large and heavy portfolio around<br>■ portfolio can be viewed over the Internet from any number of locations at any time of day<br>■ can be worked on at the same time by both learner and assessor even without them being in the same room<br>■ ability to use more diverse assessment methods such as sound wave files or with visual digital photos or video recordings |
| **Assessor** | ■ able to assess criteria-based qualifications such as NVQ/SVQs, Key Skills, Basic Skills<br>■ time-saving benefits such as cross referencing and instant progress reporting<br>■ both the learner and assessor are able to access the portfolio simultaneously<br>■ hard copies of written work completed offline can be scanned and uploaded as an image attachment, as can other media files such as audio ('wave' files) and visual (pictures and movie clips).<br>■ less to carry around and less storage required<br>■ enforces a training centre's assessment consistency by implementing customised rules and procedures |
| **Internal Verifier** | ■ Internal Verifiers (IVs) are sent a task to complete as soon as a Unit has been signed off by an assessor<br>■ the Unit or the entire portfolio can be verified remotely meaning a faster verification time and feedback to the assessor<br>■ assessors are peripatetic; there is no travel time wasted in picking up or dropping off portfolios<br>■ IV database automatically generates a matrix of anticipated completion dates set against learners and the Units they are studying. From this the IV can set their sampling plan without having to wait for information from the centre or the assessor<br>■ a verifier can access any page of a learner's portfolio directly using hyperlinks without having to search through a paper-based portfolio or struggle with plastic wallets |
| **Centre** | ■ can be used to assess any criteria based qualification such as NVQ/SVQ, Key Skills, Basic Skills and Technical Certificates<br>■ assessment Units can be individually standardised for consistency and any assessment methods<br>■ detailed audit trail is provided to track learner, assessor and verifier productivity<br>■ built-in security to ensure that each user login only has access to the pages and processes that should be available to them<br>■ wide range of reports on the different aspects of the assessment process, for example, learner progress, visits made by assessors, placement efficiency and time spent logged in<br>■ no paperwork involved and no storage is required for portfolios<br>■ savings should be made in many areas such as manpower, purchase of portfolios, paper, photocopying, postage and petrol<br>■ with increased learner motivation, the learner should progress quicker and therefore finish sooner. This will mean higher achievement rates and higher retention rates, as with a quicker completion the learners will have less time to leave |

## Recording your findings

At all stages of any research, you should record your findings, to make the job of putting your research together easier. For example, you may wish to keep a note of:

- details of the books and journals used
- details of effective searches used
- website addresses
- libraries visited.

As you gather the information you require, you will need to make notes of your research, and one effective way to do this is mind mapping. Keeping your initial question in the centre of the page, make notes all around, indicating all the snippets of information you are gathering. If you are reading material that belongs to you, you might wish to highlight specific pieces of information as you read them. However you choose to record your findings, remember to keep a note of the source of the information to enable you to reference it appropriately at the end.

## Presenting your research findings

How you choose to present your evidence will depend on what it is you have to present. For example, you may have been asked to show how you plan for continuous provision in your setting, so you may include a copy of the planning sheet and reflect on your role in its creation and how you evaluated the plan – this should be directly observed. Before embarking on the task of researching, your assessor will advise you on the best way to present your evidence. Planning a professional discussion to talk about what you have found out can be a very beneficial way of demonstrating your new found knowledge. You can complement your discussion using some of the suggestions below:

- diagram
- mind map
- chart
- graph
- essay
- report
- presentation
- leaflet
- poster.

## Referencing

All of the resources you use in your evidence need to be referenced. This allows the reader to find the resource should they wish to and also acknowledges the original work of the author. The most commonly used reference system is the Harvard reference system, which uses the author and date in the main body of the writing and then has a reference list at the end of the work. There are variations of the system, some more complicated than others, and therefore it is essential that you check with your assessor to find out the referencing policies of your centre.

**Table 2:** The Units and Elements for NVQ and SVQ Level 4 CCLD

## Mandatory Units

| NVQ Unit | SVQ Unit | NVQ/SVQ CCLD Level 4 Unit Title | Knowledge Specifications | | | | | | | |
|---|---|---|---|---|---|---|---|---|---|---|
| | | | NVQ | SVQ | NVQ | SVQ | NVQ | SVQ | NVQ | SVQ |
| 401 | DR7L 04 | Establish and develop working relationships | K4M746<br>K4M747<br>K4P748<br>K4C749<br>K4C750<br>K4C751<br>K4C752<br>K4C753 | 1<br>2<br>3<br>4<br>5<br>6<br>7<br>8 | K4P754<br>K4C755<br>K4M756<br>K4M757<br>K4C758<br>K4M759<br>K4C760 | 9<br>10<br>11<br>12<br>13<br>14<br>15 | K4M761<br>K4C762<br>K4M763<br>K4M764<br>K4P765<br>K4C766<br>K4C767 | 16<br>17<br>18<br>19<br>20<br>21<br>22 | K4M768<br>K4M769<br>K4C770<br>K4C771<br>K4P772<br>K4M773<br>K4C774 | 23<br>24<br>25<br>26<br>27<br>28<br>29 |
| 402 | DTIL 04 | Support policies, procedures and practice to safeguard children and ensure their inclusion and well being | K4P775<br>K4H776<br>K4H777<br>K4P778<br>K4S779<br>K4S780<br>K4P781<br>K4P782 | 1<br>2<br>3<br>4<br>5<br>6<br>7<br>8 | K4DlII6<br>K4D783<br>K4P784<br>K4P785<br>K4P786<br>K4M787<br>K4H788<br>K4H789 | 9<br>10<br>11<br>12<br>13<br>14<br>15<br>16 | K4H790<br>K4H791<br>K4H792<br>K4D793<br>K4S794<br>K4S795<br>K4S796 | 17<br>18<br>19<br>20<br>21<br>22<br>23 | K4M797<br>K4M798<br>K4H799<br>K4D800<br>K4P801<br>K4SlI20 | 24<br>25<br>26<br>27<br>28<br>29 |
| 403 | DTIM 04 | Support programmes for the promotion of children's development | K4M802<br>K4M797<br>K4D804<br>K4D805<br>K4D374<br>K4D375 | 1<br>2<br>3<br>4<br>5<br>6 | K4D376<br>K4P377<br>K4M378<br>K4M379<br>K4D380<br>K4M381 | 7<br>8<br>9<br>10<br>11<br>12 | K4M382<br>K4D383<br>K4D384<br>K4D385<br>K4D806<br>K4D807 | 13<br>14<br>15<br>16<br>17<br>18 | K4D808<br>K4D809<br>K4D810<br>K4D811<br>K4TlII3<br>K4DlII4 | 19<br>19<br>19<br>19<br>20<br>21 |
| 404 | DTIO 04 | Reflect on, review and develop own practice | K4P812<br>K4P813<br>K4P814 | 1<br>2<br>3 | K4D815<br>K4P816<br>K4P817 | 4<br>5<br>6 | K4P818<br>K4P819<br>K4D820 | 7<br>8<br>9 | K4P821<br>K4P822<br>K4M823 | 10<br>11<br>12 |

## Optional Units

| NVQ Unit | SVQ Unit | NVQ/SVQ CCLD Level 4 Unit Title | Knowledge Specifications | | | | | | | |
|---|---|---|---|---|---|---|---|---|---|---|
| | | | NVQ | SVQ | NVQ | SVQ | NVQ | SVQ | NVQ | SVQ |
| 405 | DR6X 04 | Coordinate provision for babies and children under 3 years in partnership with their families | K4P824<br>K4M825<br>K4D826<br>K4D827<br>K4M828<br>K4D829 | 1<br>2<br>3<br>4<br>5<br>6 | K4M830<br>K4D831<br>K4D832<br>K4P833<br>K4D834 | 7<br>8<br>9<br>10<br>11 | K4M835<br>K4D836<br>K4D837<br>K4D838<br>K4D839 | 12<br>13<br>14<br>15<br>16 | K4P840<br>K4P841<br>K4H842<br>K4DlII5 | 17<br>18<br>19<br>20 |
| 406 | DR7E 04 | Develop and support children's early learning in partnership with teachers | K4D836<br>K4D843<br>K4D844 | 1<br>2<br>3 | K4D845<br>K4D847<br>K4D848 | 4<br>5<br>6 | K4D849<br>K4D850 | 7<br>8 | K4D851<br>K4M797 | 9<br>10 |

| NVQ Unit | SVQ Unit | NVQ/SVQ CCLD Level 4 Unit Title | Knowledge Specifications | | | | | | | |
|---|---|---|---|---|---|---|---|---|---|---|
| | | | NVQ | SVQ | NVQ | SVQ | NVQ | SVQ | NVQ | SVQ |
| 407 | DTIC 04 | Support and evaluate the curriculum for children's early learning | K4D853<br>K4D854<br>K4D855<br>K4D856<br>K4D857 | 1<br>2<br>3<br>4<br>5 | K4D858<br>K4D859<br>K4C860<br>K4D861 | 6<br>7<br>8<br>9 | K4D862<br>K4D863<br>K4D864<br>K4D865 | 10<br>11<br>12<br>13 | K4P866<br>K4P867<br>K4D868 | 14<br>15<br>16 |
| 408 | DR88 04 | Evaluate, assess and support the physical, intellectual, emotional and social development of children | K4M802<br>K4M797<br>K4D804<br>K4D872<br>K4D873<br>K4D374<br>K4D375 | 1<br>2<br>3<br>4<br>5<br>6<br>7 | K4D376<br>K4M378<br>K4M379<br>K4D1122<br>K4D380<br>K4M381<br>K4M382 | 8<br>9<br>10<br>11<br>12<br>13<br>14 | K4D383<br>K4D806<br>K4D885<br>K4D385<br>K4D887<br>K4D888<br>K4H889 | 15<br>16<br>17<br>18<br>19<br>20<br>21 | K4D890<br>K4D891<br>K4D892<br>K4D893<br>K4M894<br>K4D895 | 22<br>23<br>24<br>25<br>26<br>27 |
| 409 | DR82 04 | Evaluate, assess and support children's communication | K4M802<br>K4M797<br>K4D804<br>K4D873<br>K4D374<br>K4D375<br>K4D902 | 1<br>2<br>3<br>4<br>5<br>6<br>7 | K4D903<br>K4D904<br>K4M905<br>K4D1122<br>K4M381<br>K4M382<br>K4D383<br>K4D910 | 8<br>9<br>10<br>11<br>12<br>13<br>14<br>15 | K4C911<br>K4D912<br>K4D913<br>K4D914<br>K4C915<br>K4D916<br>K4D917 | 16<br>17<br>18<br>19<br>20<br>21<br>22 | K4D918<br>K4D919<br>K4D920<br>K4M921<br>K4D922<br>K4D923<br>K4D924 | 23<br>24<br>25<br>26<br>27<br>28<br>29 |
| 410 | DR84 04 | Evaluate, support and assess children's creativity | K4M802<br>K4D926<br>K4M797<br>K4D804<br>K4D873<br>K4D374<br>K4D375 | 1<br>2<br>3<br>4<br>5<br>6<br>7 | K4D932<br>K4D376<br>K4M378<br>K4M379<br>K4D936<br>K4M381<br>K4M938 | 8<br>9<br>10<br>11<br>12<br>13<br>14 | K4D383<br>K4D940<br>K4D385<br>K4D942<br>K4D943<br>K4D944 | 15<br>16<br>17<br>18<br>19<br>20 | K4D945<br>K4D946<br>K4D947<br>K4D948<br>K4M949<br>K4D950 | 21<br>22<br>23<br>24<br>25<br>26 |
| 411 | DR86 04 | Evaluate, assess and support children's mathematical learning, exploration and problem solving | K4M802<br>K4D952<br>K4M797<br>K4D804<br>K4D374 | 1<br>2<br>3<br>4<br>5 | K4D375<br>K4D957<br>K4M958<br>K4M381<br>K4M938 | 6<br>7<br>8<br>9<br>10 | K4D890<br>K4D962<br>K4D1122<br>K4D964<br>K4D965 | 11<br>12<br>13<br>14<br>15 | K4D966<br>K4D967<br>K4M949<br>K4D969<br>K4D970 | 16<br>17<br>18<br>19<br>20 |
| 412 | DR80 04 | Evaluate and coordinate the environment for children and families | K4D971<br>K4D972<br>K4D973 | 1<br>2<br>3 | K4D974<br>K4D975<br>K4H976 | 4<br>5<br>6 | K4H977<br>K4D978<br>K4P979 | 7<br>8<br>9 | K4P980<br>K4P981 | 10<br>11 |
| 413 | DR47 04 | Develop and implement operational plans for your area of responsibility | 413K001<br>413K002<br>413K003<br>413K004<br>413K005<br>413K006<br>413K007 | 1<br>2<br>3<br>4<br>5<br>6<br>7 | 413K008<br>413K009<br>413K010<br>413K011<br>413K012<br>413K013<br>413K014 | 8<br>9<br>10<br>11<br>12<br>13<br>14 | 413K015<br>413K016<br>413K017<br>413K018<br>413K019<br>413K020 | 15<br>16<br>17<br>18<br>19<br>20 | 413K021<br>413K022<br>413K023<br>413K024<br>413K025<br>413K026 | 21<br>22<br>23<br>24<br>25<br>26 |

| NVQ Unit | SVQ Unit | NVQ/SVQ CCLD Level 4 Unit Title | Knowledge Specifications | | | | | | | |
|----------|----------|----------------------------------|------|-----|------|-----|------|-----|------|-----|
| | | | NVQ | SVQ | NVQ | SVQ | NVQ | SVQ | NVQ | SVQ |
| 414 | DR63 04 | Coordinate and support provision for disabled children and those with special educational needs | K4D982 K4D857 K4D984 K4M985 K4D859 | 1 2 3 4 5 | K4D987 K4D988 K4D989 K4D990 | 6 7 8 9 | K4C991 K4D1122 K4D993 K4D994 | 10 11 12 13 | K4D995 K4C996 K4M997 K4M998 | 14 15 16 17 |
| 415 | DR71 04 | Coordinate special educational needs for early education within a local area | K4D982 K4PI000 K4MI001 K4SI002 K4DI003 | 1 2 3 4 5 | K4MI004 K4PI005 K4DI006 K4DI007 K4CI008 | 6 7 8 9 10 | K4DI009 K4DI010 K4DI011 K4PI012 K4PI013 | 11 12 13 14 15 | K4PI014 K4MI015 K4MI016 K4DI017 K4MI018 | 16 17 18 19 20 |
| 416 | DR59 04 | Assess quality assurance schemes against agreed criteria | K4PI019 K4PI020 K4PI021 | 1 2 3 | K4PI022 K4PI023 | 4 5 | K4PI024 K4PI025 | 6 7 | K4CI026 K4CI027 | 8 9 |
| 417 | DR7V 04 | Establish and sustain relationships with providers of services to children and families | K4MI028 K4CI029 K4PI030 | 1 2 3 | K4MI031 K4PI032 K4MI033 | 4 5 6 | K4CI034 K4CI035 | 7 8 | K4PI036 K4PI037 | 9 10 |
| 418 | DR66 04 | Coordinate and support the revision of policies, procedures and practice for registration and inspection | K4PI038 K4PI039 K4PI040 | 1 2 3 | K4MI041 K4PI042 K4PI043 | 4 5 6 | K4PI044 K4DI045 K4PI046 | 7 8 9 | K4PI047 K4M797 | 10 11 |
| 419 | DR5V 04 | Contribute to the enhancement of early education for children | K4D853 K4DI050 K4D856 K4D857 | 1 2 3 4 | K4DI053 K4D859 K4C860 K4D861 | 5 6 7 8 | K4D863 K4D864 K4DI059 K4D865 | 9 10 11 12 | K4DI122 K4P866 K4P867 K4DI064 | 13 14 15 16 |
| 420 | DTI8 04 | Research and develop an area of practice | K4PI065 K4MI066 K4PI067 | 1 2 3 | K4PI068 K4PI069 K4PI070 | 4 5 6 | K4MI071 K4PI072 | 7 8 | K4PI073 K4PI074 | 9 10 |
| 421 | DT0M 04 | Provide information about children's and families' services | K4MI075 K4MI076 K4PI077 | 1 2 3 | K4MI078 K4MI079 | 4 5 | K4PI080 K4MI081 | 6 7 | K4MI082 K4MI083 | 8 9 |
| 422 | DR74 04 | Coordinate work with families | K4DI084 K4PI085 | 1 2 | K4DI086 K4CI087 | 3 4 | K4CI088 K4CI089 | 5 6 | K4PI090 K4DI091 | 7 8 |
| 423 | DR8H 04 | Manage multi-agency working arrangements | K4MI092 K4MI093 K4SI094 | 1 2 3 | K4M797 K4MI096 K4MI097 | 4 5 6 | K4MI098 K4CI099 | 7 8 | K4MI100 K4PI101 | 9 10 |

| NVQ Unit | SVQ Unit | NVQ/SVQ CCLD Level 4 Unit Title | Knowledge Specifications | | | | | | | |
|---|---|---|---|---|---|---|---|---|---|---|
| | | | NVQ | SVQ | NVQ | SVQ | NVQ | SVQ | NVQ | SVQ |
| 424 | DR6E 04 | Obtain additional finance for the organisation | 424K0I<br>424K02<br>424K03<br>424K04<br>424K05<br>424K06<br>424K07<br>424K08 | I<br>2<br>3<br>4<br>5<br>6<br>7<br>8 | 424K09<br>424KI0<br>424KII<br>424KI2<br>424KI3<br>424KI4<br>424KI5 | 9<br>I0<br>II<br>I2<br>I3<br>I4<br>I5 | 424KI6<br>424KI7<br>424KI8<br>424KI9<br>424K20<br>424K2I<br>424K22 | I6<br>I7<br>I8<br>I9<br>20<br>2I<br>22 | 424K23<br>424K24<br>424K25<br>424K26<br>424K27<br>424K28<br>424K29 | 23<br>24<br>25<br>26<br>27<br>28<br>29 |
| 425 | DR75 04 | Provide leadership in your area of responsibility | 425K0I<br>425K02<br>425K03<br>425K04<br>425K05 | I<br>2<br>3<br>4<br>5 | 425K06<br>425K07<br>425K08<br>425K09<br>425KI0 | 6<br>7<br>8<br>9<br>I0 | 425KII<br>425KI2<br>425KI3<br>425KI4<br>425KI5 | II<br>I2<br>I3<br>I4<br>I5 | 425KI6<br>425KI7<br>425KI8<br>425KI9<br>4I5K20 | I6<br>I7<br>I8<br>I9<br>20 |
| 426 | DR4N 04 | Encourage innovation in your area of responsibility | 426K0I<br>426K02<br>426K03<br>426K04<br>426K05<br>426K06<br>426K07<br>426K08 | I<br>2<br>3<br>4<br>5<br>6<br>7<br>8 | 426K09<br>426KI0<br>426KII<br>426KI2<br>426KI3<br>426KI4<br>426KI5 | 9<br>I0<br>II<br>I2<br>I3<br>I4<br>I5 | 426KI6<br>426KI7<br>426KI8<br>426KI9<br>426K20<br>426K2I<br>426K22 | I6<br>I7<br>I8<br>I9<br>20<br>2I<br>22 | 426K23<br>426K24<br>426K25<br>426K26<br>426K27<br>426K28<br>426K29 | 23<br>24<br>25<br>26<br>27<br>28<br>29 |
| 427 | DR3Y 04 | Allocate and monitor the progress and quality of work in your area of responsibility | 427K0I<br>427K02<br>427K03<br>427K04<br>427K05<br>427K06<br>427K07<br>427K08 | I<br>2<br>3<br>4<br>5<br>6<br>7<br>8 | 427K09<br>427KI0<br>427KII<br>427KI2<br>427KI3<br>427KI4<br>427KI5<br>427KI6 | 9<br>I0<br>II<br>I2<br>I3<br>I4<br>I5<br>I6 | 427KI7<br>427KI8<br>427KI9<br>427K20<br>427K2I<br>427K22<br>427K23<br>427K24 | I7<br>I8<br>I9<br>20<br>2I<br>22<br>23<br>24 | 427K25<br>427K26<br>427K27<br>427K28<br>427K29<br>427K30<br>427K3I<br>427K32 | 25<br>26<br>27<br>28<br>29<br>30<br>3I<br>32 |
| 428 | DR52 04 | Ensure health and safety requirements are met in your area of responsibility | 428K0I<br>428K02<br>428K03<br>428K04<br>428K05<br>428K06 | I<br>2<br>3<br>4<br>5<br>6 | 428K07<br>428K08<br>428K09<br>428KI0<br>428KII<br>428KI2 | 7<br>8<br>9<br>I0<br>II<br>I2 | 428KI3<br>428KI4<br>428KI5<br>428KI6<br>428KI7<br>428KI8 | I3<br>I4<br>I5<br>I6<br>I7<br>I8 | 428KI9<br>428K20<br>428K2I<br>428K22<br>428K23<br>428K24 | I9<br>20<br>2I<br>22<br>23<br>24 |
| 429 | DR7C 04 | Provide learning opportunities for colleagues | 429K0I<br>429K02<br>429K03<br>429K04<br>429K05<br>429K06<br>429K07<br>429K08 | I<br>2<br>3<br>4<br>5<br>6<br>7<br>8 | 429K09<br>429KI0<br>429KII<br>429KI2<br>429KI3<br>429KI4<br>429KI5<br>429KI6 | 9<br>I0<br>II<br>I2<br>I3<br>I4<br>I5<br>I6 | 429KI7<br>429KI8<br>429KI9<br>429K20<br>429K2I<br>429K22<br>429K23<br>429K24 | I7<br>I8<br>I9<br>20<br>2I<br>22<br>23<br>24 | 429K25<br>429K26<br>429K27<br>429K28<br>429K29<br>429K30<br>429K3I | 25<br>26<br>27<br>28<br>29<br>30<br>3I |

| NVQ Unit | SVQ Unit | NVQ/SVQ CCLD Level 4 Unit Title | Knowledge Specifications | | | | | | | |
|---|---|---|---|---|---|---|---|---|---|---|
| | | | NVQ | SVQ | NVQ | SVQ | NVQ | SVQ | NVQ | SVQ |
| 430 | DR5T 04 | Manage finance for your area of responsibility | 430K0I 430K02 430K03 430K04 430K05 430K06 430K07 430K08 | I 2 3 4 5 6 7 8 | 430K09 430KI0 430KII 430KI2 430KI3 430KI4 430KI5 430KI6 | 9 I0 II I2 I3 I4 I5 I6 | 430KI7 430KI8 430KI9 430K20 430K2I 430K22 430K23 | I6 I7 I8 I9 20 2I 23 | 430K24 430K25 430K26 430K27 430K28 430K29 430K30 | 24 25 26 27 28 29 30 |
| 43I | DR5Y 04 | Contribute to the leadership and management of integrated childcare provision | K4CII02 K4PII03 K4PII04 | I 2 3 | K4PII05 K4PII06 | 4 5 | K4PII07 K4MII08 | 6 7 | K4PII09 K4CI099 | 8 9 |
| 326 | DTI9 04 | Safeguard children from harm | K3S344 K3S345 K3S346 K3S347 K3S348 | I 2 3 4 5 | K3S349 K3S350 K3M35I K3C352 K3S353 | 6 7 8 9 I0 | K3M354 K3S355 K3S356 K3S357 | II I2 I3 I4 | K3D358 K3D359 K3S360 K3S36I | I5 I6 I7 I8 |
| 333 | DP6X 04 | Recruit, select and keep colleagues | 333K0I 333K02 333K03 333K04 333K05 333K06 333K07 | I 2 3 4 5 6 7 | 333K08 333K09 333KI0 333KII 333KI2 333KI3 333KI4 | 8 9 I0 II I2 I3 I4 | 333KI5 333KI6 333KI7 333KI8 333KI9 333K20 333K2I | I5 I6 I7 I8 I9 20 2I | 333K22 333K23 333K24 333K25 333K26 333K27 | 22 23 24 25 26 27 |

# Part Two

## Mandatory Units

Unit 401
Unit 402
Unit 403
Unit 404

# Unit 401

## Establish and develop working relationships

In this Unit you will learn about the importance of effective working relationships, working with other professionals and agencies and encouraging others to reflect on practice and share knowledge.

Effective working relationships with colleagues, parents and other agencies are a vital part of any practitioner's role and particularly those in senior positions. Taking time to develop working relationships with your colleagues and others will help encourage a culture of team work and open and honest communications which can enhance your working environment. Working with children is a rewarding yet highly demanding profession where team work and communication help build your own confidence and ability to contribute to the team effectively.

Working with colleagues requires you to communicate in a variety of ways, ensuring you understand the reasons for these communications. Throughout this Unit you will discover practical ways in which you should be seeking to communicate effectively and understand the potential issues that may arise and how these may be overcome.

The elements for Unit 401 are:

401.1    Establish and develop working relationships with colleagues.
401.2    Establish and develop working relationships with other professionals and agencies.
401.3    Encourage and facilitate others to reflect on practice and share knowledge.

# Learning Outcomes

After reading this Unit you will be able to:

- Understand responsibilities regarding confidentiality and the disclosure of information.
- Understand and apply anti-discriminatory/inclusive practices in the work place.
- Recognise the importance of supporting colleagues in adjusting to their roles and responsibilities and the role of the team within this.
- Identify methods of effective communications with all types of colleagues and understand the importance of these.
- Identify and implement effective strategies for conflict management and resolution.
- Clearly define the role of yourself and other professionals in building and maintaining effective working relationships.
- Reflect on the benefits of learning from others and how this can be achieved.
- Understand the importance of all professionals working with children to share knowledge and skills.
- Adopt essential skills in encouraging colleagues to share knowledge and skills and reflect on practice.

This Unit includes the following themes and covers the knowledge statements listed below:

- Confidentiality
  **K4M746, K4M747, K4P748**
- Working together
  **K4C749, K4C750, K4C75I, K4C752, K4C753, K4P754, K4C755, K4C767**
- Working with other professionals
  **K4M756, K4M757, K4C758, K4M759, K4C760, K4M76I, K4C762, K4M763, K4M764, K4P765, K4C766**
- Sharing knowledge and skills
  **K4M768, K4M769, K4C770, K4C77I, K4P772, K4M773, K4C774**

# 401.1 Establish and develop working relationships with colleagues

## Confidentiality

## Information sharing

K4M746

Regardless of the setting you work in you will need to share information to ensure the provision you make meets the needs of the children and families using them.

Shared information could include the examples in Figure 1. Examples of the ways in which this information could be shared are shown in Figure 2.

**Figure 1:** What information can be shared?

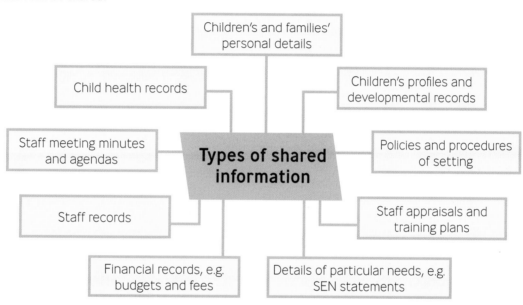

**Figure 2:** How can information be shared?

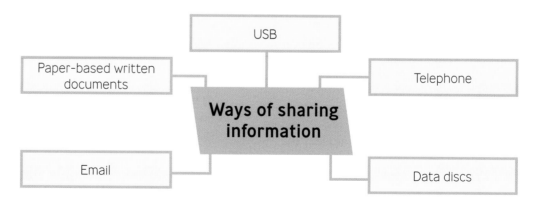

# Confidentiality and the disclosure of information

Within any Early Years setting much consideration needs to be given to the appropriate storage of information to ensure confidentiality.

Under the Data Protection Act all settings have a responsibility to handle information appropriately.

## Keys to Good Practice

So, what do you need to know about the Data Protection Act?

- Personal data must be obtained fairly and lawfully.
- The data subject should be informed of the purpose or purposes for which the data are intended to be processed; and to whom the data will be disclosed.
- Personal data processing may only take place if specific conditions have been met; these include the subject having given consent or the processing being necessary.
- Additional conditions must be satisfied for the processing of sensitive personal data that relate to the ethnicity, political opinion, religion, trade union membership, health, sexuality or criminal record of the data subject.
- The new Act covers personal data in both electronic form and manual form (e.g. paper files, card indices).
- Personal data must be kept accurate and up-to-date and shall not be kept for longer than is necessary.
- Appropriate security measures must be taken against unlawful or unauthorised processing of personal data and against accidental loss of, or damage to, personal data. These include both technical measures, e.g. data encryption and the regular backing-up of data files and organisational measures, e.g. staff, data protection, training.
- Personal data shall not be transferred to a country outside the European Economic Area unless specific exemptions apply (e.g. if the data subject has given consent); this includes the publication of personal data on the Internet.

It is important to remember that information should only be shared on a 'need to know' basis. This is applicable for all types of information shared about children, families, staff and the setting.

Ensuring that only the relevant personnel are included in information exchanges will ensure confidentiality procedures are followed.

## Keys to Good Practice

Consider the systems in your own setting: do they meet Data Protection requirements?

## Find it out

Is your setting required to be registered with the information commissioner's office? For further guidance visit www.ico.org.uk.

## Points for Reflective Practice

- What information should be treated confidentially within your setting?
- What type of information will you need to share with colleagues in the setting?
- What information may need to be shared with other professionals?
- When might you be unable to ensure confidentiality of information?

## Confidentiality – written policies and procedures

All Early Years settings in the UK should ensure that a robust written procedure exists for handling and processing information that is both verbal and written. It is good practice to have a written policy if you work in a setting such as a nursery or if you work alone as a childminder.

Written policies enable guidelines to be drawn up and administered ensuring that all staff members are acting in accordance with the setting's requirements.

Parents and other professionals should have access to such policies to ensure that they are well informed of the setting's procedures with regard to the handling of information and ensure that they fulfil any obligations within these.

Policy reviews are important and as a senior practitioner your role is to ensure these occur. The benefits of policy reviews are to ensure: staff are coherent and compliant, information is current and valid and that amendments can be made in the 'here and now' context.

## Find it out

Look at the welfare requirements of the Early Years Foundation Stage. Do the policies and procedures of your setting/practice meet these requirements?

## Keys to Good Practice

You can demonstrate through everyday opportunities that you work in an inclusive manner. Think about the opportunities you provide for the children in your care or in the care of your team.

- Do you ensure the setting is accessible to all who do or may use it?
- Do you ensure their varying needs are met through differentiation of activities?
- Do you ensure that you value and respect colleagues' individual needs and preferences and provide equality of opportunity within the setting with regard to training and development?
- Do you support your colleagues, children and families in identifying and valuing the views, wishes and individuality of others?
- Do you provide resources, planned activities/experiences to demonstrate this and opportunities for parental engagement with the setting?
- Do you ensure specific care and/or learning needs are identified and provided for within the setting to best meet the child's needs and balance these effectively with the group as a whole?
  Through these we can ensure issues of **inclusive** and **anti-discriminatory practice** can be addressed.

You can find out more about guidance on policies and policy reviews in Unit 402.

## Anti-discriminatory and inclusive practice

K4P748

Inclusive practice is extremely important in service delivery. As an advanced practitioner you need to ensure that you are working with both children and adults in an environment which meets the needs of all.

## Key Terms

**Anti-discriminatory** – taking positive action to counter discrimination. This will involve identifying and challenging discrimination and being positive in your practice about differences and similarities between people.

**Inclusive practice** – a process of identifying, understanding and breaking down barriers to participation and belonging and implementing these principles in your practice.

## Did you know?

The Early Years Foundation Stage must be complied with by all maintained and registered Early Years settings in England from September 2008. You will need to ensure that your setting complies with the framework requirements and demonstrates a commitment to implementing the welfare and learning and development requirements. When ensuring inclusive and anti-discriminatory practice you will need to consider your setting's approach.

The Early Years Foundation Stage states:

'The EYFS is based on principles of inclusion which means that early years providers oppose discrimination and prejudice and welcome all families and children. They provide care and education for a wide range of children in environments that enable children to feel safe and supported and which extend their learning and development.'

(Taken from www.standards.dfes.gov.uk/eyfs/site/about/index.htm.)

You can find out more about the EYFS and its implications for practice in Unit 403.

K4P748

## Points for Reflective Practice

Think about why inclusive practice is important in the workplace.

Think about the main themes and principles of the EYFS.

- How could you demonstrate to your assessor that your practice is anti-discriminatory and inclusive?
- How can you show your assessor how this is implemented in your setting in accordance with requirements of EYFS?

K4C749
K4C750

## Working together

### Team work

Working within the Early Years sector will require a strong element of team work. Effective team work is essential for the success of any setting, as you will already know from your own experiences. It would be impossible for one person to fulfil every role and responsibility within the setting due to the sheer volume of requirements within the sector; even for those working independently of a setting at a senior level there will be an infrastructure in place that requires the involvement of other 'team' members from the sector.

## Roles and responsibilities

All Early Years practitioners need to be well informed of their roles and responsibilities within the setting/ sector, ensuring that a duty of care is central to this. Effective communication between practitioners and managers is essential from the beginning of any term of employment so that practitioners are aware of what is expected of them.

When dealing with interviews, employment and probationary periods clear and concise person specifications must be created. These should be determined in principle when vacancies go to press, so you can attract appropriately qualified and/or experienced practitioners to the post.

## Points for Reflective Practice

Look at a recent vacancy you have advertised.

- Was the job description informative and relevant to the post advertised?
- Was there any vital information missing?
- Could any improvements have been made to the content?

**Figure 3:** Key strategies for effective team work

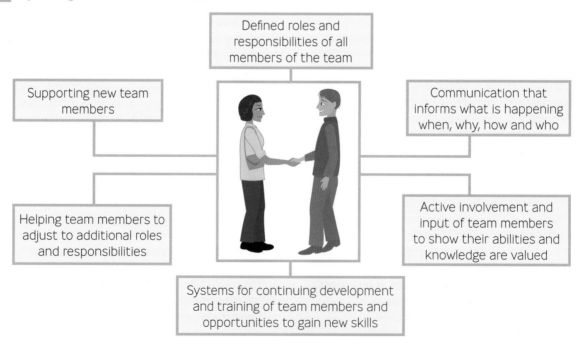

## Clarifying expectations

Time spent carrying out robust interview processes (including working interviews where appropriate) will enable potential employees to gain a greater understanding of the role and the setting's expectations before an offer of employment is taken up. Giving potential employees written information about the job role is vital in ensuring they are fully informed of the post they have applied for. Job descriptions and person specifications should give clear guidance to the candidate about the skills and attributes required for the post. Outline contracts so they know the day-to-day logistics of what they would be potentially committing to. A prospectus and the policies of the setting will also enable them to gather vital information about the setting, its aims, objectives and ethos, so they can make informed choices about potential offers of employment in line with their own requirements and expectations.

## Keys to Good Practice

When interviewing candidates for positions in your setting it is always a good idea to have a pre-determined list of questions, discussion points and scenarios which each interviewee is scored against. This enables a fair assessment of all the potential candidates and eliminates bias for or against any individual.

## Helping colleagues to adjust to roles and responsibilities

The next step in the employment process is ensuring practitioners are well supported in their adjustment to their role throughout their probationary period of employment. You may have your own internal processes that prove effective, such as a mentoring/buddy system and regular reviews of practice throughout the probationary period.

The level of support and or mentoring needed by a new team member will be totally dependent on their prior knowledge and experience. Practitioners who have come from other settings may have a different perspective and attitude to their job role than a newly qualified practitioner. Whilst many settings would consider the value of someone with experience, it is also worth considering what attributes a newly qualified

team member can bring. As Early Years professionals are always striving to maintain best practice, a newly qualified practitioner may bring a wealth of understanding regarding current legislation that could be extremely beneficial to the setting.

Practitioners who are new to Early Years will be enthusiastic about the career they are embarking on and may have a very open-minded approach to their work as they do not have any prior experiences to relate it to.

More experienced practitioners will have a wealth of knowledge and experience. Their own experiences in previous settings may be useful to your setting, particularly when considering alternatives to the current ways of thinking and doing.

Although a setting may have procedures in place for supporting team members adjusting to their roles and responsibilities, it is also important to ensure the needs of the individual are identified and met. Some practitioners may be happy with a general discussion about how they are getting along whereas others may feel a more formal approach would better suit their needs, such as a one-to-one discussion with the manager at the end of their shift.

Strategies to support team members adjusting to their roles could include a combination of the following.

### Comprehensive induction programme

It is amazing how many practitioners start a new job and don't go to the toilet at all on their first day. Why? Because nobody has told them where it is and they don't feel able to ask. This is one of the many reasons why an induction programme is beneficial to new team members and indeed to the setting and others.

During the first few days of employment it would be useful to ensure that the logistics of the job and setting are communicated to the new team member, including where the toilet is, where to go for lunch, break times and lengths, and where to find resources for the children. Ensuring such information is given will mean that they will not have to keep on asking, which could make them feel very awkward and uncomfortable.

### Job shadowing

This is a useful tool to enable a practitioner to adjust to their roles and responsibilities and may be particularly beneficial when there is an overlap in employment as one practitioner leaves and another takes their place.

Shadowing gives practitioners a 'real view' of what the job entails and allows them time to absorb information fully without having to worry about the responsibility of the job at this stage.

## Mentor or buddy system

Having someone who is a constant source of support when starting a new job can really help with the transition into a setting. A 'point of contact' gives a new practitioner peace of mind that there is someone they can turn to if they need to ask questions or clarify any elements of their practice. Implementing the buddy system will also ensure that a new practitioner will not get any conflicting ideas or answers as they may do if they needed to approach a different person each time they had a query.

## Being available

Being available to colleagues and always providing them with opportunities to speak to you will help you to ensure practitioners are adjusting to the roles and responsibilities of the job and will enable all parties to identify any problems or potential problems. Identifying problems is important; for example, early identification of gaps in a practitioner's knowledge can lead to training and development programmes for them to build their understanding of early years and the job they are doing. Practitioners who are supported effectively through their probationary period are more likely to continue their employment with you than those who feel 'thrown in at the deep end'. Remember: people do not know what is expected of them unless you tell them.

## Considering group dynamics

This is key when introducing new members to the team, as are the dynamics of the overall team, room or setting. If you have had the opportunity to conduct a working interview you will be able to see if the potential candidate could work well in this environment and if their attributes can make a positive contribution to the setting.

We are all individuals and our perceptions can be similar or can differ greatly; this does not mean that people should not be working together just because their perceptions, views or practice vary, but it is important that all team members feel able and supported to contribute to the team for the benefit of the children.

## Supporting colleagues in taking on additional roles and responsibilities

It is also important to consider that you may need to help colleagues adjust to roles and responsibilities when they have been at the setting for a while.

They may need support when taking a promotion or additional responsibilities, changing their hours of work or moving from working with one age group to another.

When colleagues are established within the setting you may wish to allocate them additional job roles and responsibilities. Figure 4 summarises a few examples.

**Figure 4:** Examples of additional roles and responsibilities for practitioners

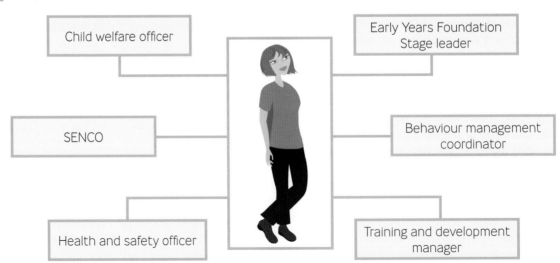

Child welfare officer

Early Years Foundation Stage leader

SENCO

Behaviour management coordinator

Health and safety officer

Training and development manager

## Points for Reflective Practice

Think about how you support new team members adjusting to their role.

- Do you use any of the strategies mentioned?
- Discuss your induction processes with your assessor.

Before assigning such responsibilities to individuals you should think about their ability to perform the task requested of them and their level of knowledge and skill. In all disciplines individuals strive to work to their strengths and at elements of practice they enjoy and are good at.

In-depth discussions with individuals will ascertain their capabilities to manage additional responsibilities in the setting and will confirm if they actually want to take on an additional workload.

In addition you will need to consider how you are going to support individuals to develop their added responsibilities. Practitioners with responsibility for specific elements of practice or service delivery will need access to ongoing training and support to ensure they are up to date with current guidelines and legislation. As a manager, your duty of care to your team means that you should facilitate continuous learning opportunities and provide time both in and out of the setting for them to develop their role.

Ongoing support from you will ensure they are happy in their role and fully equipped to perform their duties to the best of their ability.

You can offer your support through the following.

- ***Talking regularly to them about their role:*** providing time to discuss what they are doing and demonstrating that you care about how they are getting along can prove to be very valuable in building their self-esteem and confidence to do their job, knowing that you are available should they have any problems.

- ***Asking them how you can be of use:*** after all, team work is the key focus and if you help others out they are more likely to want to help you.

- ***Informing them of training events being offered:*** keep colleagues well informed of opportunities available; it may not necessarily be an element of practice you see as a priority, but people need to attend courses that engage their personal interests too. Colleagues may tell you about an assertiveness course they wish to attend or a time management event which will build on their personal skills as well as enhance their professional development.

- ***Allowing time to attend training events:*** training events and information days are valuable tools in enabling practitioners to build on their knowledge and skills, ensuring that they have the support and opportunity to do this is essential if you want them to put maximum effort and ability into the job role they have been given. Supporting colleagues to update skills is essential in meeting best practice benchmarks.

- ***Allowing time in the working day for them to complete paperwork relevant to job role:*** there is a lot of pressure on practitioners these days to complete paperwork and audit trails of all aspects

## Case Study: EYFS Coordinator

Emma works in a day nursery with children aged 2 to 3 years. She has always been quite forward thinking in her approach to providing activities and experiences for the children in her care. She has attended information days about the Early Years Foundation Stage and has begun to implement the principles of this in her everyday practice. The manager of the setting has noticed that Emma has a good grasp of the requirements and feels that it would be appropriate to give her the lead responsibility for

the implementation of the EYFS in the setting. The manager has asked Emma to attend a one-to-one meeting with her at the end of her shift to discuss the possibilities of taking on additional responsibilities within the setting.

- How can the manager ensure that Emma is fully informed of the expectations of the role?
- How can the manager ensure that Emma has the time to fulfil these additional responsibilities?
- What other practical ways can the manager support Emma in this role?

of service. This can be both time consuming and brain taxing; by allowing colleagues time away from their duties with the children they will be able to focus and concentrate on their paper-based tasks and accurately record what is necessary. Sitting in a room with the children can be distracting as they will always need to supervise the children first and foremost. Paperwork can then become a secondary concern so mistakes are made and inaccuracies become regular. Some practitioners prefer to do paperwork at home in their own time where there are few distractions. However, if you allow colleagues to do this you will need to think about the types of documentation being taken off the premises and any implications for confidentiality of information and data protection requirements. It is safer to ensure all records relating to children and families remain on the registered premises so that confidentiality cannot be compromised.

**K4C750**

## Points for Reflective Practice

Ask each of your colleagues and/or team members to write down the ways in which they feel they are supported in their job. Whilst they do this, write down the ways in which you feel you support your team. This can be done as an exercise during a staff meeting.

Bring everyone's thoughts together. Did everyone come up with the same answers? Did theirs match yours?

**K4C751**

## The importance of communication and information sharing

Communication is extremely important in effective and efficient service delivery. Effective communication is essential for a team to work successfully together. Good teamwork creates an enjoyable working environment for all involved including staff, children, parents and visitors.

Settings are not only judged on their appearance but on the 'feel' of the place when people walk in. Human instinct can often tell an individual if the working atmosphere is positive. People can pick up on and tune in to a range of communications and can often gauge the relationships between practitioners by watching

how individuals engage and communicate with each other.

When a team of people work well together this makes for a positive and pleasant working environment which has a direct impact on the children they are caring for. This in itself has implications for the emotional well being and security of the children.

In addition to this, you will be encouraging effective communication. Other team members will look to you to model good practice and the children will look to you and your team members as good role models for communication skills.

Good communication certainly gets things done, and when things are going well in a setting everyone involved feels a lot more at ease in their role and can perform effectively, rather than chasing their tails when a lack of communication and information sharing means delivery of provision is affected and things start to go wrong.

Later on in this Unit we will explore what to do when things go wrong and how to manage conflict in the workplace. Prevention is most definitely better than cure and good team work and good team management will hopefully ensure that such issues are rarely encountered.

## Effective communication methods

Today there are many ways in which we communicate with our colleagues and other professionals. With the increasing use of modern technology communications are no longer limited. Methods such as telephone and video conferencing have liberated the way in which meetings are conducted and mean that people in locations all over the country, or indeed all over the world, can be in attendance. If you work in an organisation that has several locations, meetings can now be conducted with relative ease thanks to the technology.

Other forms of communication have revolutionised the way in which we converse and share information. With email and attachments individuals can send lengthy communications and documentation at the touch of a button, making things happen much faster and getting tasks done more efficiently.

However, there are still downsides to such innovative forms of communication and, as explored earlier in this Unit, you do need to think about the implications

**Table 1:** Methods of communication

| Communication method | Advantages | Disadvantages |
|---|---|---|
| **Face-to-face** <br> **One-to-one** | Shows the person you are communicating with you have time for them | Can be difficult when dealing with issues of a sensitive nature |
| **Face-to-face** <br> **Group meetings** | Can share and cascade information without having to repeat it | Can be difficult to gauge everyone's understanding of information received |
| **By phone** | Easy to contact and communicate out of office hours | Information can be misinterpreted or forgotten |
| **Email** | Information is recorded and is therefore easy to revisit and comprehend <br> Can be done any time day or night <br> Can be traced or saved | Toneless, can cause discord when meaning is misinterpreted <br> Can be ignored <br> Could be read by unauthorised personnel |
| **Letter** | Gives written details of necessary information exchange <br> Can be kept on file | Can be ignored <br> Not immediate |

for confidentiality and data protection when sharing information in this way.

Methods of communication will be determined by the type of information you are sharing or giving. You will need to consider the most appropriate form of communication prior to information exchanges taking place. Look at the communication methods listed in Table 1 and their associated advantages and disadvantages.

## Points for Reflective Practice

Think about the methods of communication you use in your setting.

- Which methods of communication are effective in your practice?
- When might your methods of communication be ineffective?

## Styles of communication

As well as understanding the variety of communication methods, it is also important to consider the styles of communication.

Look at Table 2 on page 36, which details three key communication styles and the key features of behaviour linked to these.

Behaviour plays an important part in information exchanges and it is our behaviour that will determined if the communication is successful.

The following are strategies for effective communication.

- Ensure those who wish to speak to you have your full attention. You can minimise distractions by closing the office door or diverting the phone.
- Demonstrate that you are a good listener by giving time for others to talk and communicate without interrupting them.
- Make sure information has been clearly understood by both parties, clarifying key points if necessary.
- Share appropriate information with relevant personnel 'first hand'.
- Pick the right time to communicate.
- Be aware of your roles and responsibilities in the team.
- Respect confidentiality of information at all times.

**Table 2:** Communication styles and linked behaviour

| | You do | You don't |
|---|---|---|
| **Passive** | Put up with things<br><br>Give in easily to others<br><br>Do things that you don't really want to but go along with others | Stand up for yourself<br><br>Deal directly with problems<br><br>Ask for what you want |
| **Assertive** | Stand up for your own rights but respect other people's rights at the same time<br><br>Express your own views but also listen to other people<br><br>Stay calm and polite even when you disagree with other people<br><br>Accept no for an answer without being resentful<br><br>Negotiate rather than try to dominate or give in<br><br>Can give no for an answer without blame | Expect others to know what you want without telling them |
| **Aggressive** | Dominate others<br><br>Be rude, sarcastic, abusive<br><br>Try to get your own way regardless of what other people want<br><br>Express your own views without listening to others | Understand the needs of others<br><br>Look for compromise |

**Figure 5:** Effective communication is crucial

## Maintaining agreements

A key feature of effective communications in the workplace is to ensure you maintain agreements, or to put it another way, do what you say you are going to do.

If for any reason you are unable to keep to a work agreement you must let those it affects know at the earliest opportunity; this saves any unnecessary disruption to services or any embarrassment on your part. For example, it would be bad to leave 20 people waiting for you in a meeting when you have forgotten to let them know you cannot attend. Colleagues will not take too kindly to you if you promise to cover their lunch break and then don't turn up because you were busy with paperwork.

Your ability to maintain agreements not only impacts on the running of the provision but also models good practice for your colleagues.

There are situations in any work environment where you may not be able to fulfil commitments you have made as other duties or responsibilities have to take priority.

### Points for Reflective Practice

Sometimes agreements cannot be maintained. What should you do?

- Make a list (mental or written) of all commitments to be fulfilled.
- Prioritise these by level of urgency.
- Make constructive decisions about which commitments will be fulfilled and which will need to be rescheduled.
- Act immediately to ensure those commitments/ agreements that cannot be maintained can be assigned to an alternative time or alternative member of the team.

## The importance of sharing information and how to do this

Information sharing is an essential part of everyday practice in the Early Years. Information is shared with colleagues, parents, children and other professionals to ensure the smooth and effective running and management of the setting. On a day-to-day basis information is shared between individuals about the children and the provision.

The most common way of sharing information with others in the setting on a day-to-day basis is verbally, face-to-face, which is ideal for cascading small amounts of information needed in the 'here and now' context. More complex information exchanges would be best supported with written documentation.

Written information exchanges can include the following.

- *Policies and procedures of the setting:* policy documents are usually deep in content and require individuals to take on board a large amount of information relating to the procedures for practice. As practitioners endeavour to uphold the principles of these in their every day practice it is important that the information be shared in a written format so they can have the time to read and understand the setting's policies.
- *Planning of provision and meeting the needs of young children:* the aims and objectives of the setting's planned provision will cover many aspects of the EYFS that need to be evidenced for the purpose of providing for the children's care, learning and development needs on a daily basis.
- *Daily events:* on a day-to-day basis colleagues will need to be informed of 'the diary for the day'. This will include information such as the number of children booked in for the day, who needs lunch, which children have a sleep, visitors coming to look round the setting, staff shift patterns and lunch and break rotas.

All of the above information exchanges ensure that the setting can run smoothly day-to-day. When information is not communicated to individuals correctly it can result in chaos. Routines of children can be severely disrupted as can the routines of staff, who will be particularly disgruntled if they have not been covered to go for their lunch.

### Points for Reflective Practice

Think about how information is shared in your setting.

- What types of informal methods do you implement on a daily basis?
- What formal arrangements do you have for information sharing?

**K4P754**

## Getting feedback

As the manager, deputy or team leader of a setting it is important that you encourage colleagues to give you feedback on your own performance.

Comments and feedback may come more readily from some than others. Colleagues can and will criticise elements of your practice or judgements and decisions you have made if they feel these are inadequate or inappropriate.

Most practitioners can communicate their thoughts and opinions regarding your practice constructively. For others this may be difficult to do as they feel anxious about a particular issue. Creating a culture where colleagues are regularly encouraged to comment on your performance will lessen the impact of criticism as they will not have been left to stew about things AND, if you have demonstrated that you have taken on board their concerns and grievances with adequate outcomes, they are more likely to present concerns in a positive light.

Consider the feedback very carefully before responding. You should employ your powers of reflection and ask yourself a number of questions; for example, how you handled a situation or made a decision.

### Keys to Good Practice

There are other points to be considered when your own practice is challenged.

- Always explain to colleagues the reasons for decisions and justify them.
- Explain the reasons why these may or may not be changed.
- Always acknowledge what others have to say; listen carefully to show you value their feedback, even if it is not what you wanted to hear.
- Ask them for their suggestions: this demonstrates that you value them as a practitioner and shows you can learn from them too.

It is important for your colleagues to give *you* feedback on positive elements of your practice. Everyone benefits from praise, so it is vital that you know what you are good at too!

## Conflict in the workplace

Conflicts can arise and occur for different reasons and between a variety of people and situations, such as between you and a team member, team members, other practitioners or professionals from other agencies you work with.

Whatever the case, it is important that conflicts are resolved at the earliest opportunity to restore harmony in the team and indeed in the setting.

### Reasons for conflicts

Situations that may cause conflict include the following.

#### Difference of opinions

Practitioners working together may have mixed and varied views about the way something should be done. Their interpretation of what they see or think will determine their response.

#### Breakdown in communication

Conflicts can occur when communications are ineffective; this includes not telling someone something vital about a child that could impact on their care and development. In settings where practitioners are on shift pattern there is a need for effective communication to ensure the needs of children and parents are met. Settings need to have robust systems for sharing, passing on and disseminating information.

#### Clash of personalities

Despite all practitioners understanding and knowing the importance of working together and acting in a professional manner at all times, there are times when people just 'don't get along'. Instead of insisting that every one think from the same perspective you need to identify the individuality of all practitioners and accept people for their differences, which may result in ensuring some practitioners don't work together.

#### Promotion of colleagues

When a team have worked together effectively it can be difficult for some to accept the promotion of a colleague, particularly when the focus shifts from them being a member of the team to perhaps being a leader who now has to have some authority over those they work with. Others within the team may not find it easy to adjust to the change in group dynamics.

Distorted views of roles and responsibilities.

Practitioners who have not received adequate guidance during initial induction may not know what is required of them, as discussed earlier in this Unit. This may be interpreted by others as not pulling their weight in the setting, when in actual fact they don't have a clue about what is expected of them.

Team members not complying with job role and requirements

Complacency and a laid-back approach to their roles and responsibilities can cause friction between these and other practitioners. Some practitioners may fail to see how their lack of team work can have an impact on others within the team.

Unwillingness to take direction from others

It is inevitable that at some point in your career you will come across a practitioner who feels they do not have to do what others tell them to do and think that they can please themselves in their job role. People with this outlook cannot be classed as team players and their unwillingness should be addressed.

Not being receptive to other people's thoughts, opinions and feelings

Outspoken individuals with strong personalities in the workplace may be so consumed by their own thoughts, opinions and feelings that they give little regard to the feelings of others. This may not be a conscious process, but either way practitioners need to be aware of the need to embrace what others think, say and feel.

Bullying and harassment

Whilst individuals may not respect the feelings of others, and this in itself is an issue to be addressed, to subject another to any kind of bullying or harassment in the workplace is totally unacceptable practice and needs immediate action.

Bullying in the workplace is not alien to the sector of Early Years and may not be apparent to you or others in the first instance.

It has been estimated that workplace bullying affects up to 50 per cent of the UK workforce at some time in their working lives, with annual prevalences of around 40 per cent. (Field, T. (2003) 'Workplace bullying: the silent epidemic'. *BMJ* 326: 776–7.)

According to one estimate, workplace bullying and harassment costs employers 80 million lost working days and up to £2 billion in lost revenue each year. It also accounts for around 50 per cent of stress-related workplace illnesses. (Chartered Institute of Personnel and Development (2004) *Managing Conflict at Work: A Survey of the UK and Ireland*. London: CIPD.)

Bullying and harassment can present in many forms including the following.

- Unwarranted or humiliating offensive behaviour towards an individual or groups of individuals. Such persistently negative malicious attacks on personal or professional performance are typically unpredictable, unfair, irrational and often unseen .

- An abuse of power or position that can cause such anxiety that people gradually lose all belief in themselves, suffering physical ill health and mental distress as a direct result.

- The use of power or position to coerce others by fear, persecution or to oppress them by force or threat.

Workplace bullying and harassment can range from extreme forms, such as violence and intimidation, to less obvious actions such as deliberately ignoring someone at work. (Chartered Institute of Personnel and Development (2004) *Managing Conflict at Work: A Survey of the UK and Ireland*. London: CIPD.)

Bullying and harassment can impact on the victim in many ways, including:

- low morale
- mental stress
- lack of confidence and lowered self-esteem
- illness
- absenteeism
- lack of motivation.

## Grievance procedures

On occasions it will be necessary to implement your setting's grievance procedure if there is a case for a colleague to answer to. When doing this it is important to follow the rules of practice and not deviate because of instinct or emotion. Managers need to send a clear message to all practitioners in the setting about the setting's 'zero tolerance' approach to bullying and harassment.

K4C767

**Figure 6:** Harassment can result in a great deal of mental stress

K4C755

## Points for Reflective Practice

Reflect on a situation in your setting that has involved conflict management. Discuss this with your assessor. Then look at the keys to good practice below. How many of these strategies did you employ?

■ From the outset ensure that factual reliable evidence is gathered and recorded about the issue or conflict.

■ Indulge in face-to-face discussions with the relevant people about the conflict that has occurred.

■ Ensure all individuals have time to put across their point of view and that sufficient time is made to listen.

■ Always take the issues away from the children; discussions should be held in confidence with the support of an advocate if necessary.

■ Ensure that as a manager you not only listen but that you are heard; be assertive, decisive and diplomatic.

■ Ensure all people involved understand the possible or decided outcomes.

■ Clarify that the desired outcome or resolution is achievable.

■ Allocate time to monitor the conflict resolution and progress made.

■ Ensure progress is acknowledged by holding a review meeting or taking time to talk to the individuals involved.

It is important that all parties involved work collaboratively in resolving any conflicts and work issues.

## Case Study: Complacent practice

Belinda has been a member of the toddler room team for a year, having successfully completed her work-based training placement with the setting. Since being employed, Belinda has become quite laid back in terms of her time-keeping and dress code. When she is on an early shift she is often late – with no apology or explanation. She also neglects to wear the nursery uniform on occasion, stating it is in the wash.

The room leader has tried to approach this informally, reminding her of her responsibilities. Now the room leader has brought the matter to the attention of the nursery manager as she feels she is not being heard and other members of the team are becoming fed up and think she is 'getting away with it'.

- How should the manager approach Belinda about these issues?
- What can the manager do to ensure these matters are resolved?

## Conflicts with other adults

You need to consider conflicts that may occur between the setting and those from external agencies, and indeed parents. Many of the strategies you employ when dealing with conflict with colleagues can be used when dealing with conflicts with other adults.

You will need to be careful with your approach to conflict management and be assured that you have relevant information and evidence to enable you to resolve such conflicts effectively whilst maintaining working relationships with those involved.

Parents may raise a concern, issue or grievance with you which may be aimed at a member of your team. Concerns and issues may come in the form of informal grievances or more formal complaints about the member of staff. It is your duty to respond efficiently to any complaints or grievances raised by parents and inform them fully of your setting's procedures in responding to these, with proposed outcomes and within an allocated time frame. Parents will want to know if you have responded to their complaint and, if founded, sought appropriate solutions. If parent's grievances are unfounded you will need to ensure that the reasons for your decided outcome are clearly communicated to the parents involved. When dealing with conflict where the concerns are clearly founded, you will need to discuss this in detail with the team member in question and the parent. The best outcome will be one where both parties can resolve the conflict and restore harmony in their professional working relationship.

Conflicts with other professionals can occur when working in a multi-agency situation and, very much like all conflicts, need a rapid response to ensure such professional relationships can be maintained. Later in this Unit you will find out about managing disagreements with other agencies.

Colleagues who have been subject to grievances or conflicts with parents may need emotional support from you in order to understand why the situation occurred or how they can avoid such incidents in the future. It is important to affirm with colleagues that it is normal to be upset when involved in these situations and knowing that you are there to listen and support them can often be enough for many to come to terms with the situation and close on it.

## Points for Reflective Practice

Consider a situation where you have managed conflict between a colleague and another adult.

- What strategies did you employ?
- How did you ensure a successful conflict resolution?
- Did your colleague require any emotional support during this time?

If you have been fortunate enough not to have had to deal with such a situation, then consider how you would approach this and respond.

THE LIBRARY
NORTH WEST KENT COLLEGE
DERING WAY, GRAVESEND

# 401.2 Establish and develop working relationships with other professionals and agencies

## Working with other professionals

In your job role you will on occasion work with professionals from a variety of disciplines and external agencies. Representatives from various organisations may be involved in your setting for a variety of reasons including the following.

### To support the setting

A range of professionals may work within your setting to help support you in service delivery, meet inspection requirements and meet principles of delivery of learning. Professionals involved in this type of support include:

- regulatory bodies
- Early Years advisory teachers
- registration advisors
- qualified teachers.

### To support staff and their development

As well as delivering your own in-service training you may engage the support of other agencies in developing staff skills and knowledge. These professionals include:

- first aid trainers
- health and safety trainers
- basic food hygiene specialists.

### To benefit the children's care, learning and development

Liaising with external sources is a valuable tool in providing for children's needs. Some are specific, such as an identified need for support with language or physical development. Professionals you may liaise with in these situations include:

- speech therapists
- physiotherapists
- educational psychologists.

Professionals may also attend your setting to enhance the learning of the children in your care. Some of these experiences will take place in the setting, while others will involve a visit for the children, which is always an exciting prospect. These professionals include:

- parents and carers with specific skills to talk about their job
- people in the community who help us (police officer, crossing patrol, vet, dentist)
- theatre production companies
- out of school services (football coaching, gymnastics, music and language lessons).

### To support trainees

Professionals will visit to mentor and support any trainees undertaking formal qualifications, and work with you to ensure trainees are consolidating knowledge and practice to demonstrate their ability and achieve their qualification. These include:

- college tutors
- learning mentors
- NVQ assessors.

## Points for Reflective Practice

Think about the range of professionals you liaise with.

- Do you have networks with a variety of professionals to benefit all aspects of provision?
- Are there any other agencies and professionals you can engage with to support you and your colleagues with any aspects of service delivery?

## Establishing roles and responsibilities with other professionals

When working with professionals from any discipline it is essential to develop effective working relationships from the outset. It is important to establish each person's roles and responsibilities and agree the limitations of these.

When attending meetings for the first time you will often be asked to introduce yourself and tell others

## Case Study: Establishing roles with other professionals

Jacki is an accredited childminder who is working with her local Inclusion and Disability Service (IDS) team to provide inclusive practice in her setting for children who she cares for with physical impairments. Jacki is keen to ensure that she is meeting their daily care needs and would like to access additional equipment to ensure they can participate fully in the setting. To find out more about how this can be done, she has set up a meeting with a professional from the team so they can advise her on support and equipment available.

- What should Jacki do to prepare for this meeting?
- What information should Jacki make accessible for this meeting?
- How can Jacki establish the roles of each party in service delivery?
- What information might Jacki require from the IDS team?

in attendance what setting you are from and your job role. Although this activity is traditionally viewed as unnecessary and laborious it can be extremely beneficial in giving you an insight into the roles and responsibilities of others in attendance. Pay careful attention to what others say in introductory meetings, as your perception of their job role may differ greatly from what it actually is.

Meetings are generally recorded and well documented so that you can re-visit what has been said, done and decided. By ensuring you keep records of minutes of meetings you attend you can be certain that you have the information readily available should you need to re-visit it to establish the responsibilities placed on yourself and others in the meeting and beyond.

Professionals from all disciplines will bring a level of expertise with them. However, all professionals should acknowledge the input, knowledge and skills of others as these will be instrumental in meeting the objectives of multi-disciplinary work. You may be involved in meetings, discussions and case conferences with a range of professionals.

During meetings you may be presented with the opportunity to assert your own expertise, particularly where you have a sound understanding of your provision or the development of a child in your care. Equally it is important to value the expertise of others as they may have skills they wish to share to benefit your setting and/or the children you work with.

## Common objectives

When working with other agencies and professionals from other disciplines it is important that everyone works to a common objective; after all you all want the best outcomes for the children and the sector you represent.

Establishing common objectives will give all those involved a clear vision of the outcomes.

Where teams of people, or individuals working with a team of professionals, are carrying out the same roles or working towards a common purpose it may be most effective to set objectives with and for the work group as a whole.

Your objectives and those of others need to be clear, consistently applied and known to everyone involved.

Where a number of people from your setting are involved in reaching these objectives, it is important that they understand what these are and that their input will be monitored and reviewed to ensure the key objectives have been met.

## Keys to Good Practice

When working as part of a team, it is important to ask yourself the following questions.

- What are the reasons for this collaboration?
- How will it benefit my practice?
- How will it benefit the children in my care?
- How will it benefit other colleagues and professionals I work with?
- How will the outcomes be measured?

# Respecting professional boundaries

When you discuss professional boundaries it can be quite difficult to visualise what these are, as professional boundaries are not a physical or tangible concept.

Professional boundaries are present whenever you communicate with colleagues, parents and other professionals: it is the unspoken acceptance of knowing where your responsibilities end and the responsibilities of another begin.

Professional boundaries are important in relationships with other professionals as they help to agree limits of roles, responsibilities and duties and can help to clearly define who is responsible and for what. Professional boundaries can make for an efficient and effective working environment where tasks and duties are completed fully and on time.

Your own professional boundaries are established from the outset of employment. This may differ slightly if you are a childminder working independently, as you may have less contact with other professionals on a day-to-day basis.

Job contracts and descriptions will give an indication as to the limits of your roles and responsibilities, but further information will come from your first days in the post as discussed earlier in this Unit.

You will need to consider your role beyond the immediate work environment when liaising with other professionals. Sometimes you may question yourself about how far you should go when communicating and working with other professionals.

Ask yourself the following questions to see if you are aware of the boundaries of your roles and responsibilities.

- Who do I answer to on a daily basis?
- Who determines my roles and responsibilities?
- Do I have the authority to share information about children with other professionals?
- Do I make decisions for the setting?
- Who is responsible for creating and developing working relationships in the setting?

If you know the answers to these questions then this shows that you have a good understanding of your own professional boundaries. You will need to remember what these are to ensure effective relationships are maintained with other professionals.

When working with other professionals, meetings are a useful way to understand and negotiate professional boundaries. Well organised meetings will have an agenda so that all in attendance will know the sequence of events and running order, which may also give those involved information about where they fit in to the meeting or where they will be required to contribute.

During meetings, allotted time frames will help with keeping the content or subject matter on track allowing the meeting to run efficiently. As matters are discussed it is important for those involved to establish who is responsible for 'actioning' these and

## Case Study: Case review

Dawn is the manager of Little Stars pre-school and has been asked to attend a speech and language review of a child in her care to be held at the local child development centre. Dawn has asked if the child's key worker, Meena, can attend as she has built a close relationship with the child and understands his speech and language needs. Dawn tells Meena on the morning of the review that she will be accompanying her to the meeting to listen to what will be said.

During the meeting Dawn is asked by the speech therapist if she would like to add comments about the setting's observations and understanding of the child in question. Dawn looks at Meena and asks her to comment on her observations. Meena is totally unprepared for this and begins to waffle about the child saying what a lovely boy he is.

As they head back to pre-school Meena tells Dawn how frustrated she feels because the speech and language team never got to find out how much the little boy in her care had progressed.

- What professional boundaries had been set for this meeting?
- How could Dawn have prepared Meena for the meeting?
- Why did Meena not give the other professionals the information they required?

the time frame in which this is going to happen. As part of this team you may or may not be assigned actions depending on your overall role and reason for attendance. If you are, it is important that you act within your professional boundaries and seek to do what you said you were going to do in the time you said you were going to do it.

Being able to maintain professional boundaries successfully demonstrates to other professionals your ability to do a job well, and when you work well with others this will build the trust and faith in you that is required for professional relationships to continue.

## Effective communications and communication methods with other professionals

Unlike your colleagues, you may not have the opportunity to communicate with other professionals on a day-to-day basis. In fact, you may have very limited opportunity to have face-to-face contact with other professionals.

The way in which you communicate with other professionals will be dependent on their role in their relationships with you and/or the setting. Due to the restrictive nature of many relationships you will have with other professionals it is extremely important that communications are robust and efficient.

Communications with other professionals may take place inside or outside the setting and may be regular or one-offs. Whatever the reason for the communication or the methods used it is important that they suit the purpose for which they are intended.

## Limitations and extent of expertise

It is important that you understand and acknowledge the expertise you have in the Early Years field. After all, you will have spent many years in practice and in developing your skills and knowledge of the sector. Hands-on experience is crucial to understanding the needs of the children in your care and it is an understanding of these needs and the ability to effectively meet these needs that makes you the practitioner you are. Whilst other professionals you work with will bring much in the way of knowledge and skills to the table, you must not underestimate your skills and abilities.

Your expertise in your role will undoubtedly be proven in situations where others require information about the children in your care or about the service and provision you are involved in, and it is in situations such as forums, case conferences and reviews that other professionals will seek to draw on your knowledge and experience.

When embarking on professional relationships with others from varying disciplines it is only natural to feel daunted by their expertise. But it is important to remember that others will seek your viewpoint in ensuring that all parties involved are working to the common objective of meeting children's and families' needs in which you play a crucial role.

Of equal importance is to understand the limitations of your own expertise and how to recognise the value that others bring. It is necessary for you to be mindful of this during communications with other professionals to ensure you contribute within the boundaries of your capabilities.

## Points for Reflective Practice

Look at the communication methods identified in Table 1 on page 35 and consider how effective each of these are when communicating with other professionals.

Which communication methods work best with the professionals you liaise with? Why?

Figure 7: Childcare practitioners have a key role in promoting self-esteem, resilience and a positive self-image in children

## Keys to Good Practice

How should you seek to understand the limits of your expertise?

- Acknowledge your own expertise.
- Have belief in your knowledge and skills but also belief in those of others.
- Share your expertise in an appropriate and constructive way.
- Don't be afraid to admit that you don't understand something and ask for clarification from others.
- Respect and value other expertise.
- Learn from what others say or do.
- Embrace further development and learning to extend your expertise.
- Don't undermine the expertise of others.
- Identify ways in which yours and others' expertise can complement one another.

## Good practice, values and ethical requirements

Having undertaken your NVQ you will already be aware of and endeavour to uphold the values and principles of the sector but, just to remind you, these are the 'foundation stones' of the NVQ and a thorough understanding of these is necessary to properly interpret the occupational standards.

Principles and Values can be found on page 6.

Values form the bedrock of practice and the importance of these when liaising with other professionals should never be undermined.

Your values and ethical codes of practice will not only come from the principles of the NVQ standards but also from your own setting's policies and procedures

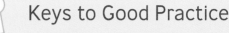

for practice, including meeting children's needs, working in partnership with parents and working in partnership with other professionals.

Policies can be seen as predetermined 'guidelines' for practice and it is these that you should uphold when working with others.

## Points for Reflective Practice

Think about the ethics of your practice that may need consideration when working with other professionals.

Do they include:

- Confidentiality procedures – guidelines for sharing information about the setting, children and families?
- Partnership with parents policy – ensuring that parents' needs and wishes are considered when working with other professionals?
- Equal Opportunities policy – maintaining the needs of all children as being central to any collaboration with other professionals?

## Handling disagreements with other agencies

There will be occasions through your career when you have disagreements with others or occasions when information has been misunderstood. Misunderstandings can occur when your perceptions vary. Everyone will view the world from differing perspectives and have their own viewpoints on various issues in Early Years. Working in a setting, you would have a greater understanding of the inner workings of the establishment than someone coming in to advise the setting. They may view what they see in a very different light to you. This can also happen with communications and the way in which information is put across. You may interpret the information in one way and someone else may interpret the information to mean and to represent something totally different. This is where disagreements and misunderstandings can occur.

## Keys to Good Practice

K4M764

Sometimes you may find yourself in a situation where there is an interagency misunderstanding. To avoid this happening, think about these key points for good practice.

- Listen to others, carefully ensuring you have received relevant information and are fully informed.
- Step out of your own shoes and try to view things from a different angle.
- Seek further clarification from other professionals which will help in understanding their viewpoint.
- Examine your own perceptions again. Once somebody shares their thoughts and feelings your perception may change.

If you still feel there is a disagreement or misunderstanding it is essential to handle it in a sensitive and professional manner.

The checklist that follows helps you to avoid misunderstandings.

## Keys to Good Practice

K4M764

How to avoid misunderstandings:

- Do not let disagreements become personal.
- Challenge the comment or opinion and not the individual.
- Allow opportunity for both parties to put their point across.
- Gain the involvement of an impartial third party to come to a constructive resolution.
- Ensure strategies are explored to avoid further misunderstandings.

## Respecting others

Being able to make choices in everyday life is a fundamental part of being recognised and respected as an individual. Such choices enable people to have control of their lives. Respecting the choices of others is crucial if you want **respect** from others.

## Key Term

Respect – a feeling of admiration for someone because of their qualities or achievements. Due regard for the feelings or rights of others.

K4P765

## Keys to Good Practice

Employing these strategies demonstrates good practice on your part and encourages others to reciprocate in valuing and respecting you as an individual.

- Always be polite and courteous when communicating with others.
- Value other people's perspectives and viewpoints.
- Be accepting of individual differences.
- Allow others to be heard.
- Ensure others are well informed in order to perform their roles effectively.
- Consider the impacts of your actions on others.
- Be respectful of other people's values and beliefs and accept them for their differences.
- Do not expect everyone to act and think like you – everyone has different perceptions.
- Judge people on their merits, not on their race, religion, nationality, age, sex, physical or mental condition, or socio-economic status.

K4C766

## Adapting communications

Throughout Unit 401 you have gained a greater understanding of communication. To enable effective communications to take place between yourself and other colleagues, professionals, parents and children you will need to consider whether their communication needs are being met.

You may need to adapt communications to work effectively with others and meet the needs of other adults. It would be unreasonable to assume that every individual can communicate effectively using the same modes or language. By identifying how individuals communicate most effectively you can seek the most appropriate method to communicate with them.

Some situations in which you may need to adapt the way you communicate with others include:

- ***When a common language is not spoken:*** consider very carefully the spoken and written language and or dialect in which communications are taking place if the receiver of the information has little or no understanding of the language you are using; you will have to use strategies to overcome this. An interpreter may be required to enable the person you are trying to communicate with to receive and understand the information fully. An interpreter can be beneficial to you to as you can clarify with them that the information has been understood by the recipient.

- ***When there are variances in knowledge and skills of the sector:*** others may have a varying degree of knowledge and understanding of Early Years practice, particularly if they do not work in the same discipline as you. Try not to use jargon in your communications and explain clearly any aspects of your communication that leave the recipient pondering over what you have just said.

- ***When one of the parties has a sensory impairment:*** both audio and visual impairments can have an impact on the communications between two people. If you are communicating with an individual who is deaf you will need to find out from them how they best communicate. Individuals with audio impairment who are skilled at lip reading may require little or no intervention in the communications, although it would be beneficial to be in clear vision and speaking at a steady pace to enable them to receive information effectively. Some individuals with an audio impairment use sign language to communicate and may require the attendance of an individual who can sign so information can be clearly understood.

- ***When face-to-face communications are not available:*** you will often find yourself in a situation where communications cannot take place face-to-face. You will then need to consider the type of information and whom it is to be shared with before deciding on the best method or adaptation to communications.

## Case Study: Adapting communications

Angie is the manager of the Children's Centre in her local town. This provides services for many children and families from a range of backgrounds and cultures in the immediate community. The centre's stay and play sessions have been a valuable part of this provision and Angie wants to develop it further to meet families' needs. Angie has written to all the parents asking for permission to observe their children at play to enable her to make valid assessments of the provision to share with key stakeholders at their next forum meeting. Erek is a father of two young children and regularly uses the centre; he has received the letter but because of his limited English does not understand what it means and has approached Angie quite confused.

- How can Angie present this information differently to enable Erek to understand?
- What techniques can Angie employ to communicate effectively with Erek?
- What additional strategies can Angie adopt for Erek and other service users to gain maximum knowledge about the objectives of the centre?

# 401.3 Encourage and facilitate others to reflect on practice and share knowledge

## Sharing knowledge and skills

A key aspect of practice in Early Years is sharing information and knowledge with colleagues. There are many reasons why you need to do this, including the following.

- To ensure practitioners know what to do.
- To share concerns regarding children's development.
- To ensure best practice is demonstrated.
- To ensure provision runs smoothly each session/day.
- To build a relationship where others feel able to share and discuss concerns.
- To share knowledge gained from training and information events.

Sharing information and knowledge with each other demonstrates effective team work and will give colleagues assurance that they work in a team where their thoughts and opinions are valued. Encouraging a culture where you can share your knowledge and information with team members will in turn encourage them to share good practice too.

You may have access to training and information days away from the setting that your colleagues cannot attend; to ensure best practice is implemented in the setting you need to share with them what you have learnt or found out.

## Creating opportunities to discuss experiences

You may have both formal and informal arrangements in your setting for colleagues to discuss their experiences.

Take a moment to think about your daily practice and consider how you do this.

## Points for Reflective Practice

- Do you create opportunities for practitioners to talk to you?
- Do you check practitioners' understanding of their job roles and responsibilities?
- Do you ask your staff if they are happy?
- Do you have regular meetings for information to be shared?
- Do you offer opportunities for team members to share their thoughts and ideas with others?
- Do you take on board the views and ideas of others and acknowledge them as their own?
- Take time to consider these points. Can you think of any other strategies you use in your setting?

**Figure 8:** Listening requires the use of your whole body

## Encouraging environment

There are many ways in which you can foster an environment in which others are happy to discuss their experiences and the work that they do, and throughout this Unit communication has been shown to be a key factor in this.

As a manager or someone in a role supporting others you need to think of the practical ways in which you can demonstrate an open approach to others' thoughts, opinions and reflections. Being open, honest and approachable enables colleagues to come to you when they need to discuss elements of their practice or seek answers to difficulties or challenges they face.

K4C77I
## Essential listening skills

Being a good listener is an essential skill and key aspect of effective communication. To fully understand information being conveyed to you requires your full attention. Listening not only requires the use of your ears but your whole body.

- **Eye contact:** is important when listening to others as it shows that you are paying attention and that your mind is not elsewhere. By making eye contact you are telling the person who is communicating with you 'I am taking time to listen to what you have to say'.

- **Posture:** can influence a talking and listening situation greatly. If you sit in a chair angled forward in the direction of the person talking to you it will show that you are listening to them and them

alone. Your body language tells them that there are only two people in this conversation. Sitting back or to the side can give the impression that you are not bothered about what they have to say.

- **Facial expressions:** can often be a give away when you are listening to someone (or not listening, as the case may be). If a colleague is sharing information of a sensitive nature and wants an impartial listening ear then it would be wholly inappropriate to look shocked or gasp when they talk. Be aware of how you use your face to express your opinion as sometimes it isn't an opinion that people want.

In this busy world people feel the need to multi-task many elements of their life to get things done faster, and while this may be appropriate for some tasks it is not best practice when others are seeking to communicate and share information with you.

You can show that you are listening to colleagues by making time to listen; time is valuable in ensuring that others are heard and that you value their input.

By actively listening you can encourage others to think reflectively. Reflection enables colleagues to:

- maximise their professional potential
- utilise their knowledge and skills
- create opportunities for lifelong learning
- analyse practice
- investigate and implement alternative strategies for practice.

## Keys to Good Practice

Strategies for encouraging reflection amongst colleagues include:

- self-assessment
- appraisals and development reviews
- peer assessment
- team meetings
- ongoing professional development.

# The importance of learning from others

From the moment you were born you began to learn about the world around you by exploring your environment and 'learning' behaviour from your primary care givers. Throughout your life you seek out new information, try out new ideas and ask many questions to make sense of the information you have. You learn from what you see and hear others do. You develop your own understanding, thoughts and perceptions of the world by watching and learning from those around you: those who have cared for you, educated you and watched you grow.

As most adults know, learning doesn't end the minute you leave education or training; the journey of learning continues throughout your life. Everyday you learn something new about yourself, your job or the world around you. You need to learn from your experiences to develop on both a personal and professional level.

Your colleagues can play a key part in your learning and development and their skills and knowledge can teach you much about yourself, your work and the world.

## Keys to Good Practice

Ask a colleague to observe your practice and give you feedback on your performance.

- Did their perception of your practice differ from yours?
- Did their observation help to analyse any aspects of your practice?
- How would you use this observation exercise to benefit future practice?

When team work was discussed earlier in this Unit, we identified how people bring with them many attributes. Some may be similar to yours and others will differ greatly. That doesn't stop you learning from others; in fact it can reinforce your own beliefs and self perceptions. Equally, it can make you examine your own beliefs and values and this can, in some instances, bring about change that can benefit you and your practice.

Learning from your colleagues can be an essential tool for effective team work, as discussed earlier. Everyone's experiences differ in life and your own background and experiences, and indeed those of other practitioners, play a vital role in this. By taking on board others' skills and abilities you can view practice from a varying perspective and may seek alternative routes to achievable outcomes. Practitioners will feel their knowledge and expertise is valued if you are able to say 'I didn't know that, thanks for sharing that with me' or 'I hadn't thought about doing it like that – let's see if that method works.' This demonstrates your ability to take on board what others have to contribute and shows that you value such contributions.

## Keys to Good Practice

How can you learn from others?

- Observe practice.
- Ask them questions.
- Listen to their reflections, thoughts and ideas.
- Encourage them to share skills and knowledge.

# Exceeding your expertise

It is important that as a manager or a team leader you can identify and acknowledge the strengths and weaknesses of your own skills and knowledge. You also need to be honest with your team members about your understanding or level of **expertise** in certain areas and the limitations of these.

To say 'I don't know the answer but I will find out for you' or 'perhaps we need to source additional support because this is beyond my capabilities' is definitely a more professional approach than second guessing a solution by saying 'I don't know but I assume this is right' or 'I won't bother contacting other professionals, anyone can do what they do!'.

To try and deal with challenges beyond your own level of expertise without the input of additional support can have detrimental consequences for your service and its users. It also sends out the wrong messages to your team, giving them the overall impression that you just 'muddle along' or 'do things your own way' and in turn can set a negative precedent for practice.

By involving other agencies and professionals and by accessing further training and development you can show that you deal with challenges in an appropriate manner by 'finding out' rather than 'assuming'.

## Key Term

Expertise – great skill or knowledge in a particular field.

## Keys to Good Practice

- Be honest with colleagues and tell them if you don't know the answer to their question or enquiry.
- Ask them to clarify exactly what it is they want to know.
- Explain you will find the answer or the appropriate person to give them the answer.
- Follow through, ensuring you carry out what you said you would.

## Encouraging colleagues to share knowledge and skills

Your colleagues have varying abilities, skills and knowledge. Their experiences prior to working in your setting may prove valuable to their current job role.

There is no one route to achieving a qualification in Early Years and every individual's learning experiences will differ, enabling a wide range of skills and knowledge to be brought into the setting.

When interviewing prospective employees you will have the opportunity to explore their current knowledge and skills, and it is at this stage that you may be able to see how they can have a positive effect on the setting.

Cascading information down is a valuable tool in enabling others to share knowledge and experience, particularly new knowledge and skills gained from their attendance at information days and training programmes.

Whilst settings would like to send all practitioners on training and development opportunities and information days, this can prove to be a logistical nightmare on a day-to-day basis, especially when such opportunities arise within the working day. You cannot feasibly send everyone to find out the information. This is where you rely on those that you have enabled to attend to gather the relevant information and cascade it down to others on their return to the setting.

## Case Study: Information day

Katja, who is the manager of a pre-school setting, has received information from her local authority about an information day that will help practitioners in Early Years settings understand the requirements of the EYFS statutory framework. The course is running from 9 am until 1 pm on a Thursday. Katja is aware that she can only send one or possibly two members of staff to this, as it is during the time the setting is open. She has decided that Tom should attend as he has been the leader of the curriculum planning for the last three years in the setting. Katja ensures that Tom is happy to attend and represent the pre-school.

- Why has Katja chosen Tom to attend the information day?
- How can Katja ensure that Tom gathers relevant information for the setting?
- How can Katja ensure the information gathered is cascaded down to other members of the team?

K4M773

K4M769
K4C774

You will find that there are opportunities for team members to share their skills and knowledge on a daily basis.

## Keys to Good Practice

Opportunities to share skills and knowledge include the following.

- When planning provision and experiences for children.
- When reflecting on practice in staff meetings.
- When involving team members in policy reviews.
- When conducting appraisals and development reviews.

# Check Your Understanding

1. What information needs to be stored confidentially in the setting?
2. What does the term 'inclusive practice' mean to you?
3. List some strategies you can adopt to help colleagues adjust to their roles and responsibilities.
4. List ways in which information is effectively shared in your setting and with other professionals.
5. Can you think of some examples of conflicts that can occur in the setting?
6. How do you ensure effective working relationships with other professionals?
7. How do you respect professional boundaries?
8. Why is it important to be aware of the boundaries of your own expertise?
9. What are the benefits of those working with children sharing knowledge and skills?
10. Why is it important to encourage practitioners to reflect on practice and how can you learn from this?

# Further references

www.dcsf.gov.uk

www.ico.gov.uk

Daly, M., Byers, E. & Taylor, W. (2009) *Early Years Management in Practice,* 2nd edition, Heinemann

Griffin, S. (2008) *Inclusion, Equality and Diversity in Working with Children*, Heinemann

Macleod-Brudenell, I. & Kay, J. (2008) *Advanced Early Years,* 2nd edition, Heinemann

# Unit 402

## Support policies, procedures and practice to safeguard children and ensure their inclusion and well being

In this Unit you will think about the policies, practices and procedures that underpin an effective service within your setting. You will be considering how to ensure the equality of access, inclusion and participation of all users of your setting, and the importance of maintaining a safe environment for all concerned. This Unit also looks at the policies, practices and procedures regarding safeguarding children.

Ensuring your setting is fully inclusive, and open to all users is an important part of your role. Whilst some elements of inclusive practice are fairly easy to implement, others may be more difficult, but still as important. This Unit will help you to look at your setting objectively, and consider the changes you could make to become more inclusive.

This Unit will encourage you to consider your role in developing the policies, procedures and practices of your setting, and reflect on how you might make improvements to ensure the safety and well being of both children and adult users. Without consistent, reliable and coherent guidelines to follow, children may be at risk, and this Unit will provide you with practical ways to ensure risks are minimised.

The elements for Unit 402 are:

402.1 Protect children's rights to equality of access, inclusion and participation.

402.2 Support the maintenance of policies and procedures for safeguarding children.

402.3 Support the integration of procedures for safeguarding children into systems and practices.

402.4 Support the maintenance of policies, procedures and practice for the well being of children.

## Learning Outcomes

After reading this Unit you will be able to:

- Understand the policies, practices and procedures that underpin an effective service.
- Apply and encourage anti-discriminatory and inclusive practice in your work setting.
- Recognise the importance of your role in safeguarding and maintaining a safe and healthy environment.
- Identify and implement effective strategies to support children in empowering themselves and keeping safe.
- Clearly define your role and those of others in relation to multi-agency working.
- Adopt essential skills in encouraging colleagues to share knowledge and experience, and reflect on practice.
- Understand the importance of healthy eating and exercise in improving chidren's health and well being.
- Support and implement practices that encourage healthy eating and exercise.

This Unit includes the following themes and covers the knowledge statements listed below:

- Inclusion and participation
  **K4P775, K4P78I, K4P782, K4DIII6, K4D783, K4P784, K4P785, K4P786**
- Safeguarding children
  **K4H776, K4P778, K4S779, K4S780, K4S794, K4S795, K4S796, K4D800, K4SII20**
- Working in partnership
  **K4M787, K4P789, K4M797, K4M798, K4P80I**
- Positive health and well being
  **K4H777, K4H788, K4H790, K4H79I, K4H792, K4D793, K4H799**

# 402.1 Protect children's rights to equality of access, inclusion and participation

## Inclusion and participation

Every child has the right to belong, and to be valued as an individual. **Inclusion** is about more than making children feel welcome. It is more than treating children fairly. Inclusion is about looking critically at how you can ensure each and every child can access appropriate education and care. As a practitioner, it is your responsibility to strive for inclusive education and care for all children, and to celebrate the diversity of children, families and communities. This is not only so that every child is included and not disadvantaged, but also so that they learn to value diversity in others.

### Key Term

Inclusion – identifying, understanding and breaking down barriers to participation and belonging.

### Points for Reflective Practice

Before you read through the rest of this Unit, take time to consider your setting. How inclusive is it? Consider the following scenarios.

- A child from the travelling community, accessing the provision for short periods of time.
- A child whose parents are profoundly deaf.
- A child with cystic fibrosis, requiring daily physiotherapy.
- A child whose mother is an alcoholic.

What potential barriers to access can you imagine for the children described above? How inclusive would your setting be to them and their families? Consider access to the setting, access to resources, sharing information with parents, providing for essential medical needs etc. You may find it useful to note down your thoughts on this reflection, as we will refer back to them later in the Unit. You may also find it helpful to familiarise yourself with the Common Assessment Framework (CAF). The CAF is used to carry out assessments of children's needs and to help decide how these needs should be met. You can download further information at www.everychildmatters.gov.uk.

Further information about the CAF can be found in Part 3, Units 414/415, on pages 276–78.

## Legislation

'Legislation', or 'Statutory Law', are both terms that describe laws that have been enacted by a governing body. There is a huge array of legislation covering all aspects of our daily lives, to which we adhere without even thinking about it, such as stopping at red traffic lights. In the Early Years sector, a range of legislation is in place in order to safeguard children's safety, well being and development. With so much legislation in place, it is essential that you keep up-to-date with changes and amendments so that your practice is always in line with statutory law. You can keep abreast of any changes to legislation at www.everychildmatters. gov.uk.

## United Nations Convention on the Rights of the Child

There is a huge amount of legislation governing settings, to ensure that all children are treated fairly, and given equal access to care and education. A major part of this legislation is the United Nations Convention on the Rights of the Child. This is an international treaty that determines the human rights of children, and to which the UK is a signatory. The treaty applies to all children and young people aged 17 and under, providing them with a set of comprehensive rights. Table 1 on page 57 shows some of the main rights set out in the treaty.

## Race Relations (Amendment) Act 2000

This Act amends the 1976 Act, which outlawed racial discrimination, requiring named public authorities to review their policies and procedures. It places responsibility onto public organisations to take account of the need to:

- eliminate unlawful racial discrimination
- promote equality of opportunity
- promote good relations between people of different racial groups
- prepare and publish a race equality policy
- monitor and assess the effect of their policies.

Table I: Some key rights set out in the UN Convention on the Rights of the Child (taken from G. Squire, 2007, *BTEC National Children's Care, Learning & Development*, Heinemann)

| Article | Essential features |
|---|---|
| Article 3 | ■ In all actions concerning children, whether undertaken by public or private social welfare institutions, the best interests of the child shall be a primary consideration.<br>■ The government must ensure the child such protection and care as are necessary for his or her well being.<br>■ All services and facilities responsible for the care or protection of children shall conform with the requirements of safety, health, number and suitability of staff. |
| Article 6 | Every child has the inherent right to life. |
| Article 7 | A child has the right to a name, a nationality and, as far as possible, the right to know and be cared for by his or her parents. |
| Article 9 | ■ Children shall not be separated from their parents against their will, except when such separation is necessary for the best interests of the child (for example, where there is abuse or neglect of the child by the parents).<br>■ A child who is separated from one or both parents must be able to maintain regular personal relations and direct contact with both parents, except if this is contrary to the child's best interests. |
| Article 12 | Children who are capable of forming their own views have the right to express those views freely in all matters affecting them, and these views should be given due weight in accordance with the age and maturity of the child. |
| Article 13 | A child has the right to freedom of expression; including freedom to seek, receive and impart information and ideas of all kinds, orally, in writing or in print, in the form of art, or through any other media of the child's choice. |
| Article 14 | A child has the right to freedom of thought, conscience and religion. |
| Article 15 | A child has the right to freedom of association and to freedom of peaceful assembly. |
| Article 18 | Both parents have common and primary responsibilities for the upbringing and development of the child. |
| Article 19 | Government must take all appropriate measures to protect a child from all forms of physical or mental violence, injury or abuse, neglect or negligent treatment, maltreatment or exploitation, including sexual abuse, while in the care of parent(s), legal guardian(s) or any other person who has the care of the child. |
| Article 23 | ■ All mentally or physically disabled children should enjoy a full and decent life, in conditions which ensure dignity, promote self-reliance and facilitate the child's active participation in the community.<br>■ Disabled children have the right to special care with assistance appropriate to the child's condition and to the circumstances of the parents or others caring for the child. |
| Article 24 | Children have the right to the highest attainable standard of health and facilities for the treatment of illness and rehabilitation of health. |
| Article 26 | Every child has the right to benefit from social security, including social insurance. |
| Article 27 | ■ Every child has the right to a standard of living adequate for the child's physical, mental, spiritual, moral and social development<br>■ The parent(s) or others responsible for the child have the primary responsibility to provide, with government help if necessary, within their abilities and financial capacities, the conditions of living necessary for the child's development. |
| Article 28 | All children have the right to free primary education and secondary and higher education should be available to all. |
| Article 32 | Children must be protected from economic exploitation and from performing any work that is likely to be hazardous or to interfere with the child's education, or to be harmful to the child's health or physical, mental spiritual, moral or social development. |
| Article 37 | ■ No child shall be subjected to torture or other cruel, inhuman or degrading treatment or punishment. Neither capital punishment nor life imprisonment without possibility of release shall be imposed for offences committed by persons below 18 years of age.<br>■ No child shall be deprived of his or her liberty unlawfully. |

**Figure 1:** It is vital to break down barriers to access

## Special Educational Needs and Disability Act 2001 (SENDA)

K4P775

This Act ensures the right for disabled children and young people to access education and training without being discriminated against. It makes it unlawful for any educational setting, including a childminder, to treat a person with a disability less favourably than a non-disabled person because of their disability.

For example, if a child is refused a place within a setting because they have a visual impairment, the setting is likely to be acting unlawfully. It is the setting's responsibility to take reasonable steps to prevent disadvantaging and discriminating against the child and their family. This may require the manager of the setting to do the following.

- Make changes to the setting's policies and procedures.
- Gain information, advice, training and support on how to fully include the child into the setting.

- Make changes to the physical layout of the setting.
- Work with other professionals who support the family.
- Make changes to planning.
- Provide activities in alternative formats.

## Disability Discrimination Act 1995 (DDA)

This Act is intended to prevent the discrimination that many disabled children and young people face. In 2005 it was significantly extended, giving disabled people extended rights. It defines a disabled person as 'someone who has a physical or mental impairment which has a substantial and long-term adverse effect on his or her ability to carry out normal day-to-day activities'.

All schools are covered by this Act, including independent and publicly funded schools, mainstream and special schools, nursery, primary and secondary schools, non-maintained special schools and pupil referral units.

It is unlawful under the DDA for settings to discriminate in admissions, education and associated services, and exclusions.

The duties under the Disability Discrimination Act are designed to join together with existing duties under the Special Educational Needs (SEN) framework. The purpose of the SEN framework is to ensure provision to meet the individual special educational needs of children. It states that: 'A child has special educational needs if he or she has a learning difficulty that calls for special educational provision.'

Many children who have SEN will be defined as having a disability under the DDA. However, the reverse of this is not always true, not all children who are defined as disabled under the DDA will have SEN. For example, a child with chronic arthritis may have rights under the DDA, but may not have SEN.

## The Children Act 2004/Every Child Matters

The 1989 Act was enforced in October 1991, and was hailed as the most important reform of the law concerning children over the last century. In 2004 it was updated, building on the 1989 principles and encompassing the government's wider agenda and programme of change set out in the Green Paper, Every Child Matters. This reform put the following aims at the heart of the Children Act 2004:

- be healthy
- stay safe
- enjoy and achieve
- make a positive contribution
- achieve economic well being.

Chapter 2 of the Green Paper confirmed the government's commitment to:

- ensure children are safe from bullying and homelessness
- the **Sure Start project**
- tackling child poverty
- raising school standards
- improving children's access to health services
- more investment in services for young people.

## Key Term

**Sure Start project** – government programme to deliver the best start in life for every child, by bringing together early education, childcare, health and family support.

## The Human Rights Act 1998

K4P781

This Act outlines the basic rights of everyone in our society. These include:

- the right to life
- protection from slavery
- the right to education
- the right to marriage.

This Act is essential in keeping our society fair, equal and evenly balanced. Without this Act, our society would be very different. Consider countries where there are no freedoms or rights, where education is not allowed and opinions are forbidden. In such countries slavery is widespread, health unimportant and lives insignificant. We often take our human rights for granted, however, without them, our lives would be very different.

## Points for Reflective Practice

Consider the information you have read about legislation, particularly children's rights.

- How might you empower children and young people to understand and exercise their rights?
- How might this vary according to the ages of the children in your setting?

## Discrimination

In Unit 401, we looked at ways to establish and develop working relationships with colleagues and other professionals. The Unit discussed how to ensure that your **practice** was **anti-discriminatory** and how to ensure your relationships were inclusive. This is also important in your direct work with children.

You can find out more about establishing and developing working relationships with colleagues in Unit 401.

Even with legislation, rights laws and governmental reform to combat it, **discrimination** is still something that children and young people have to live with every day. Working so closely with children means that you are ideally placed to support them in working through discriminatory experiences and to model good practice. Setting high standards and demonstrating how to deal with discriminatory experiences can help children and young people to grow up with an understanding of inclusivity and the importance of anti-discrimination. Using play and learning resources to think about discrimination can encourage children and young people to consider their feelings, thoughts and prejudices in a safe way, and supports them in reflecting on the consequences of discrimination.

## Key Terms

**Anti-discriminatory practice** - taking positive action to counter discrimination.

**Discrimination** - treating someone less favourably than someone else because they or their family are seen as belonging to a particular group in society.

K4P782
K4DII6

## Direct and indirect discrimination

Direct discrimination tends to be obvious discriminatory behaviour, such as not accepting a child into a setting on the basis that they belong to a particular religious group. This kind of discrimination is less prevalent in today's society. This may be because we have become more aware of anti-discriminatory behaviour, the effects of our actions, and also as a result of legislation. However, indirect discrimination is more difficult to observe. Indirect discrimination is when policies, procedures and practices discriminate against particular groups inadvertently. For example, a nursery might have a local food policy, where the ingredients for provided meals are sourced locally, including the local butcher for meat products. Whilst the nursery manager may have designed this policy to demonstrate a commitment to local sustainability, and to keeping food fresh and healthy for the children, the policy may be indirectly discriminating against Jewish and Muslim groups, who would require their meat to be Halal or Kosher.

Discrimination can come in many forms such as:

- racial discrimination, including colour, race, nationality, citizenship, and ethnic and national origins
- gender discrimination
- age discrimination
- religious discrimination
- disability discrimination
- language discrimination
- sexuality discrimination.

All groups of children and young people may face discrimination, however this is more likely for some groups than others. For example, an Afro-Caribbean male may face racial and gender discrimination, and if he has a disability, he may face further discrimination because of his disability. Discrimination in any form can lead to a variety of self-esteem and confidence problems, leading to feelings of worthlessness and insignificance. Discriminatory attitudes can lead to exclusion and isolation, which in turn may lead to erratic attendance, resulting in under-achievement and children not reaching their full potential.

The experiences of parents are also significant to a child's well being. If a parent feels excluded from a setting due to a disability or language barrier, for example, their contribution to the setting may be significantly reduced.

The damaging consequences of discrimination can also affect children and young people, even when they themselves are not experiencing the inequality directly. Observing another child, peer or friend being bullied, abused or excluded can be devastating. A child may feel guilt for not intervening or helping a friend who is being discriminated against. Witnessing discrimination can build prejudice, as children learn from what they see and hear in their communities. Belonging to a school or setting where diversity is not celebrated or valued can lead to a misunderstanding of a child's community and the values they hold dear. By recognising and celebrating the social and cultural capital of the child and their community, practitioners, children and families can learn about their communities, and begin to understand and welcome the diversity within their neighbourhood.

There are many barriers to participation that you may not have thought about

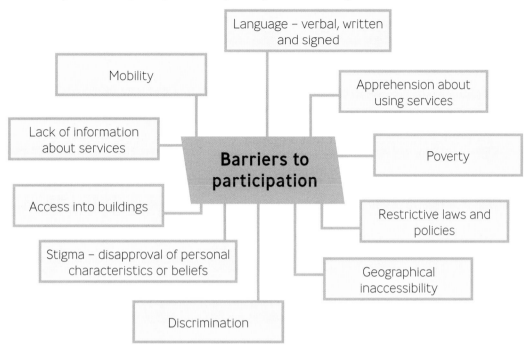

## Barriers to participation

Exclusion and inequality are mainly due to the barriers created within society. Many advocates for disabled people argue that is not the person's impairment that is disabling, but the environment around them. For example, a child who uses a wheelchair due to a physical impairment may argue that it is not the impairment that prevents access to a building, but the lack of ramps and wider doors.

All children, including those with special needs or disabilities, those from disadvantaged or minority ethnic backgrounds, and their families, have the right to access provision and services, but will face many barriers to this access, as shown in Figure 2.

It is important, therefore, that the policies and procedures of your setting ensure these barriers are recognised and addressed.

## Policies and procedures

Table 2 on pages 62–64 describes how policies and procedures can support anti-discrimination, inclusion and participation for children. Although there are many more policies and procedures implemented by settings, the following policies and procedures adhere to the specific requirements of the EYFS.

> You can find out more about the policies and procedures of the setting in the optional Units 413, 418 and 428.

Table 2: Policies and rights

| Policy/ procedure | EYFS specific requirement | Implementation |
|---|---|---|
| **Safeguarding children policy** | An effective safeguarding children policy and procedure are implemented.<br><br>All registered providers inform Ofsted and other required statutory bodies of any allegations of serious harm or abuse by any person living, working, or looking after children at the premises (whether that allegation relates to harm or abuse committed on the premises or elsewhere), or any abuse which is alleged to have taken place on the premise.<br><br>In group settings, a practitioner is designated to take lead responsibility for safeguarding children within the setting, attend a child protection training course, and to liaise with local statutory children's services agencies (the local authority's children's social care department, the police, the NSPCC). | Ensuring your setting has an effective safeguarding policy will make sure all staff are aware of their duties and responsibilities. It is important that all staff have an up-to-date understanding of safeguarding children issues and are able to implement the safeguarding children policy and procedure appropriately. The designated safeguarding practitioner should ensure that all staff know how to implement this policy efficiently. This policy should be shared with parents and carers. |
| **Equality of opportunity policy** | All providers must have and implement an effective policy about equal opportunities and for supporting children with learning difficulties and disabilities.<br><br>The policy includes:<br>▪ information about how the individual needs of all children will be met<br>▪ information about how all children, including those who are disabled or have special educational needs, will be included valued and supported, and how reasonable adjustments will be made for them<br>▪ a commitment to working with parents and other agencies<br>▪ information about how the Special Educational Needs Code of Practice is put into practice in the setting<br>▪ the name of the Special Educational Needs Coordinator (in group settings)<br>▪ how all children will be included and valued<br>▪ arrangements for reviewing, monitoring and evaluating the effectiveness of inclusive practices<br>▪ how the setting will promote and value diversity<br>▪ how inappropriate attitudes and practices will be challenged<br>▪ how the setting will encourage children to value and respect others. | An equal opportunities policy is essential to ensure that all children and users of the setting are treated with equal regard. The policy should be explicit in how the setting will care for individual children, and should be shared with parents before the child attends. The policy should allow parents and carers to feel confident in the inclusive practices of the setting, and should demonstrate how the setting values the diversity of the community. It is also important to set out how the setting will challenge inappropriate attitudes and practices from both practitioners and users of the setting. The policy may also set out guidelines for displays in the settings, indicating the importance of depicting diversity and inclusion. |

| Policy/ procedure | EYFS specific requirement | Implementation |
|---|---|---|
| Medication policy and procedure | Providers must implement an effective policy on administering medicines. The policy must include effective management systems to support individual children with medical needs.<br><br>Providers must keep written records of all prescribed medicines administered to children, and inform parents.<br><br>Providers must obtain prior written permission for each and every medicine from parents before any medication is given. | It is important that children requiring medication whilst at the setting feel respected and included. Some children with medical needs may need support to administer their medication, but it important that their privacy is also respected. It is important that children are not excluded because of any medical needs they have, and that practitioners are trained and supported to assist the child with dignity and care.<br><br>It is for the registered person to arrange who should administer medicines within a setting, either on a voluntary basis or as part of a contract of employment. |
| Behaviour management policy | Providers must have an effective behaviour management policy which is adhered to by all members of staff. | A child must not be excluded due to special educational needs, including challenging behaviour. This policy will set out the strategies to be used where a child is demonstrating unwanted behaviour, and will ensure that practitioners feel supported and have a procedure to follow during this difficult time. Physical intervention is only used to manage a child's behaviour if it is necessary to prevent personal injury to the child, other children or an adult or to prevent serious damage to property. Any occasion where physical intervention is used to manage a child's behaviour is recorded and parents are informed about it on the day.<br><br>Training in behaviour management strategies is also good practice, and will lead to all children, parents, carers and practitioners knowing what is and isn't acceptable.<br><br>Where a child has a behavioural support need, this should be discussed with parents, to ensure strategies are in place to effectively include the child, and practitioners and parents should work together to support the child during any transitional or difficult periods. |
| Risk assessment procedure | The provider must conduct a risk assessment and review it regularly – annually at a minimum and/or where the need arises.<br><br>The risk assessment will identify aspects of the environment which need to be checked on a regular basis – providers must maintain a record of these particular aspects and when and by whom they have been checked. Providers must determine the regularity of these checks according to their assessment of the significance of individual risks.<br><br>The provider must take reasonable steps to ensure that hazards to children – both indoors and outdoors – are minimised. | When a child with a special educational need or disability is due to attend the setting, the risk assessment must be reviewed to take account of their individual needs. For example, tables may need to be moved further apart for a wheelchair user, of the room re-arranged for a visually impaired child. The risk assessment should cover anything which a child may come into contact with.<br><br>. |

| Policy/ procedure | EYFS specific requirement | Implementation |
|---|---|---|
| **Health and safety policy** | A health and safety policy should be in place and includes procedures for identifying, reporting and dealing with accidents, hazards and faulty equipment. (EYFS states this is guidance to which providers should have regard, not a specific requirement.) | This policy should inform the risk assessment, in that any hazards could become part of the risk assessment. Sharing this policy with parents and carers ensures that they understand their responsibility in keeping children safe. It also supports practitioners in knowing their role and responsibilities regarding their own and the children's health and safety. This policy should identify any adaptations which need to be made, or particular items to which practitioners should pay regard when a child with a special need enters the setting. Children must not be excluded on the grounds of health and safety. |
| **Anti-bullying policy** | No specific requirement | Bullying can be a particular concern for children with special needs and their families, and families from marginalised groups. The anti-bullying policy needs to address how children will be encouraged to value diversity within their setting and their community, and should also detail how inappropriate responses and practices by adults and practitioners will be challenged. |

There are a variety of resources and information available within local communities to support equality of access, inclusion and participation (Figure 3).

K4P784 **Figure 3:** There are many resources to support equality, inclusion and participation

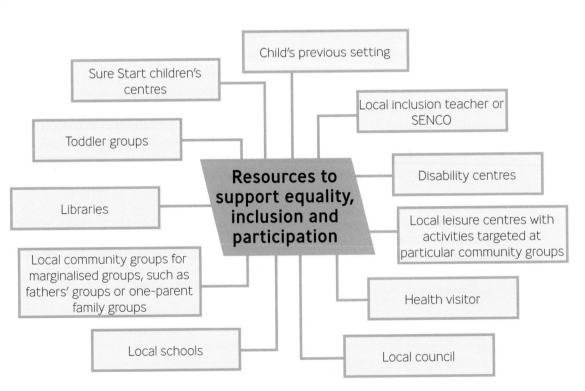

## Case Study: Community support

Raj is a manager of a local private daycare setting. Over recent years he has seen a rise in the number of ethnic minority children attending the setting, particularly children and families from the Middle East. Raj considered how he and his colleagues could effectively meet the diverse needs of the children, and contacted the local primary school. He found out that they ran support groups for ethnic minority children and met with the head teacher of the school to discuss how they could work together and pool resources. The outcome of the meeting led to Raj being introduced to a range of support agencies, and meant Raj could offer additional support to the children in his setting though an external agency. He built relationships with the school, and was invited to attend integration training with them. As a result, both children and parents from this marginalised group were included fully into the setting, with one parent volunteering in the setting to support the children through the language barriers. Parents felt valued in the setting, and set up a support group for new refugee families in the community.

- What personal skills did Raj draw on to develop the relationship with the school?
- How have Raj's actions impacted on the children in the setting?
- What might the impact be on the community?
- What follow-on work might Raj consider?
- How could you develop relationships with other organisations to make your setting more inclusive?

**A child's previous setting** will be able to provide you with information regarding the child's needs and how they ensured the child was included in all activities. This can assist you in doing the same, and will help you to reassure the family that the child's individual needs can be met.

**Sure Start children's centres** can support practitioners with advice, guidance, funding and a range of services to ensure that your setting is fully inclusive.

**Toddler groups** are attended by children and their parents, and who better than parents to inform practitioners of their family's needs? By attending toddler groups, you can begin to get to know children and families on neutral territory, and get an understanding of the barriers they face, and how you can help to overcome them

**Local community groups for marginalised groups, such as fathers' groups or one-parent family groups** can again lead you directly to the very people you are trying to support. By getting involved with the community, practitioners can be better placed to understand the needs of the community.

**Libraries** will have resources and material to support your personal development, and may hold training for the local community. This development will be valuable in meeting the needs of the community and ensuring your methods are up-to-date.

**Local schools and local inclusion teacher or SENCO** will be able to support the transition of children and young people into the settings in which you work. They can offer support, resources and guidance to ensure that the transitions involved are smooth and seamless.

**Disability centres and local leisure centres** may target a specific marginalised group and can allow you access to qualified and experienced practitioners who can offer support and advice. You may be able to spend time with those affected by discrimination, and attempt to fully understand the barriers they encounter.

**Health visitors** have an understanding of the issues faced by the community you are working with, and can be valuable in imparting knowledge, advice and support. They will have lots of experience of the community and this can be useful in understanding inclusion concerns.

**Local councils** will have a designated inclusion officer, who can again offer support and advice, and may have knowledge of the needs of the local neighbourhood.

Being aware of the resources and information available to you locally opens up a new level of support. It has been said that no-one knows more about a community's needs than those living in the community, and this is very true.

Gathering data regarding the backgrounds of the children in your setting can support you in ensuring that your policies and practices are inclusive to all members of your local community. It will also help in the review and evaluation of your policies and procedures.

## Points for Reflective Practice

Consider the diversity of your community and identify any marginalised groups.

- How does your setting work to ensure these groups are encouraged into your setting?
- What local resources and information are available to you to support equality of access, inclusion and participation?

## Strategies and practice

As service providers, it is essential that all settings implement organisational strategies and good practice to ensure equal access and compliance with legislation for disabled children and children with special educational needs. Earlier in this Unit we looked at the legislation covering children's rights, equality and inclusion, and we have the different policies and procedures required by the EYFS framework to ensure good practice. But putting all of this into place, and using it as a good practice framework, can be more difficult.

It is essential that all practitioners within the setting know exactly what their roles and responsibilities are in

relation to each policy. They need to understand how the policy or procedure should be implemented, why it should be implemented in this way, and who they can go to for support. Policies and procedures should inform good practice, and form the basis of all the work carried out within the setting.

One effective means of ensuring each practitioner understands their role is to use their induction period. Providing each new practitioner with a comprehensive set of policies and procedures, which are clearly written, before they begin their role, allows them time to read through and fully understand the policies and procedures they must follow. Practitioners need to be given time to digest the written information, and consider how they should implement the policies and procedures in their working day. They should be given the opportunity to reflect on the policies and procedures, and to ask questions, clarifying any concerns.

It is essential that all policies and procedures are reviewed and assessed regularly, and meet the changing and developing needs of the service. This assessment may take place during staff meetings, as in the following case study.

## Evaluation

It is important to have a strategy to evaluate the impact of the policies and procedures. For example, if all practitioners in the setting are following the behaviour management policy of the setting, but the behaviour being displayed by the children is getting worse, then something needs to change. Having an

## Case Study: 'Little Ones' policy review

Little Ones is a toddler group offering sessional educational care in an industrial town. In May 2008, a new manager took over, and felt it was important to reflect on the current policies and procedures, which had been in place for a number of years. It was agreed that they would review one policy or procedure at each staff meeting, which took place monthly. The manager prioritised the policies and procedures so that the most important ones were reviewed first. All practitioners were made aware of which policy was to be addressed at the next meeting, to give them the opportunity to consider what changes or

adaptations they felt were necessary to bring the policy up-to-date and to meet current standards and legislation. This strategy proved very effective as the whole team had an input and made a contribution to the implementation of the policies and procedures. It ensured that all practitioners were valued and gave them the opportunity to work together to promote best practice.

- Which policies or procedures should have been reviewed first?
- Why do you think the manager carried out reviews at the team meetings?
- Are there any negatives to the approach the manager used?

approach in place to monitor the effectiveness of the policies and procedures will ensure that the children and families receive the best possible care and learning, in a supportive environment.

For example, we have seen many cases in the news recently where young people feel excluded or discriminated against because of strict uniform policies. The DCSF strongly encourages schools to have a uniform, believing that it can promote positive behaviour and discipline, ensure pupils of all races and backgrounds feel welcome, and protect children from social pressures to dress in a particular way. Whilst all of this may be true, strict policies on uniform may disadvantage ethnic minority groups, who for faith and culture reasons would wish to dress in another manner. It can also serve to exclude families who are living in poverty as the cost of the uniform may be too much for them to readily afford.

It is vital, therefore, that policy and procedures are evaluated to address the impact on all children and their families in the area and whether they might advantage or disadvantage families from particular marginalised groups.

Using the time spent planning developments in the setting to consider improvements to the services provided can also be successful. For example, a childminder may be planning changes to her outside space, incorporating a vegetable patch for the children to learn about growing. During this planning cycle, she might come across ways she can improve other areas of her service, such as supporting parents with healthy eating by suggesting recipes to enjoy the vegetables the children are growing. The childminder may consider taking the children to the local allotment to see larger vegetable plots, which might lead her to consider the access for a child in her care who uses a walking frame due to a physical impairment. This cycle of planning and reflection is important to developing an inclusive service.

Working in a managerial role within a setting requires you to be aware of changes in legislation and reflect on how this impacts on the policies and procedures of your setting. By keeping abreast of local and national changes, you will be in a position to adjust your policies and procedures accordingly and deliver best practice at all times.

# 402.2 Support the maintenance of policies and procedures for safeguarding children

## Safeguarding children

As a practitioner, working closely with children and young people and their families, you have a duty to ensure their safety and promote their welfare. Parents and carers need to feel sure that the people in charge of settings are trustworthy, responsible and will do everything they can to keep the vulnerable adult or child safe from harm. The EYFS guidance states: 'The provider must take necessary steps to safeguard and promote the welfare of children', and therefore you are responsible for ensuring that your policies, procedures and practices effectively safeguard each child in your care, and that the staff you are responsible for also understand their responsibility for **safeguarding**.

> **Key Term**
> Safeguarding – includes protecting children from abuse and neglect, alongside supporting their welfare.

## Statutory requirements and legislation

K4S779
K4S780
K4SII2O

As we discussed earlier in this Unit, legislation is essential in order to effectively safeguard children's safety, well being and development. Managers have a responsibility under this legislation to ensure that those working with children are safe to do so, by following vetting procedures and legislation. The Acts that follow outline such legislation, and as you read through them you should consider how your setting ensures compliance with the each statutory law.

## The Rehabilitation of Offenders Act (1974)

K3S344

This Act made any convictions 'spent' after a certain period, meaning that the convicted person would not normally have to reveal or admit the existence of a spent conviction.

This means that, in most circumstances, an employer cannot refuse to employ someone, or dismiss them, on the basis of a 'spent' conviction.

However under the Rehabilitation of Offenders Act (1974) all applicants for positions which give them 'substantial, unsupervised access on a sustained or regular basis' to children, must declare all previous convictions whether spent or unspent, and all pending cases against them. In practice, all Early Years settings are eligible to carry out 'enhanced' disclosures, which will detail all convictions, giving you, as manager, a more robust system to ensure the suitability of potential employees.

## The Police Act 1997

This Act facilitated the set up of the Criminal Records Bureau (CRB) for England and Wales. The CRB provides access to criminal record information through its 'Disclosure Service'. This service assists organisations to recognise potential employees who may be unsuitable for work with children or vulnerable adults. The potential employee completes a 'disclosure' form, giving personal details, and provides the employer with a range of evidence, proving their name, date of birth and address. Once all the forms are complete, and sufficient evidence is gathered, the forms can be submitted to the CRB who will carry out the checks. Once the checks have been processed, a copy of the disclosure will be sent to the employee and the employer.

Under this Act it is a criminal offence for an employer to:

■ not check an employee working with children or vulnerable adults

■ give a job to someone who is inappropriate to work with children or vulnerable adults when they know this to be case.

### Find it out

You can find out more about the CRB procedure by visiting www.crb.gov.uk.

## The Protection of Children Act 1999

Under this Act, childcare organisations must make use of the Disclosure Service in their recruitment and reporting processes, and advises other organisations working with children to also do so.

## Criminal Justice and Court Services Act 2000

This Act covers issues surrounding disclosures and safeguarding children. It contains the list of convictions that bar offenders from working with children in 'regulated positions', such as the following.

■ Employment in schools, children's homes and daycare premises where children are present.

■ Caring for, training, supervising or being in sole charge of children.

■ Unsupervised contact with children.

■ Other positions which give the kind of access or influence which could put children at risk if held by a disqualified person (e.g. management committee members).

## Every Child Matters and the Children Act 2004

Within the Green Paper, Every Child Matters, local authorities are required to set up statutory Local Safeguarding Children Boards which replace the non-statutory Area Child Protection Committees. The children's trusts are a direct response to Lord Laming's report of the inquiry into the death of Victoria Climbié, which highlighted the extent to which better working together and better communication were crucial.

### Local Safeguarding Children Boards (LSCB)

LSCBs have been designed to help to ensure that agencies work together effectively to keep children safe. LSCBs include local authorities, health bodies, the police and others, with further information being set out in the Children Act 2004.

LSCBs have one main objective – 'to coordinate and ensure the effectiveness of their member agencies in safeguarding and promoting the welfare of children.'

The Department for Children, Schools and Families (DCSF) supports the development of LSCBs, preparing a core guidance on how agencies should work together in safeguarding children.

You will find further information about working together and working practices later in this Unit (see pages 76–78).

## Did you know?

You can access a copy of 'Working Together to Safeguard Children' at www.everychildmatters.gov.uk/resources-and-practice/IG00060/.

# Safeguarding children: policy and procedure

It is essential that all settings implement an effective safeguarding children policy and procedure. This is to ensure that all practitioners are completely aware of the procedure they must follow should they be part of a safeguarding concern. The policy and procedure should be explicit in detailing the procedures practitioners should follow when there are safeguarding concerns. When preparing or evaluating your procedure, you should consider the following.

- Why is this policy important?
- How inclusive is the procedure?
- Does it make it clear that all practitioners must follow it?
- What is abuse, and how might certain areas of the work of your setting make children more vulnerable?
- What to do if there is a suspicion of abuse? Consider what to do if a vulnerable person reports abuse happening at home or elsewhere, and how to get in touch with local authority social services, in case a concern needs to be reported.
- What safeguards are or will be put in place to protect children? How will the children or vulnerable adults be informed about their rights and what to do if they have any concerns?
- The procedure to be followed if a practitioner is implicated in an allegation of abuse.
- What sort of training will be provided to practitioners to support them in the use of the policy and procedure?
- How will the policy be monitored, reviewed and evaluated?
- How will confidentiality be kept should an allegation be made, e.g. how will records be kept and who will have access to them?
- How will other sensitive or potentially sensitive information be handled, e.g. web-based materials and activities?

Settings should designate a practitioner who is responsible for safeguarding children within the setting. This practitioner should be fully trained, and take charge during safeguarding concerns. They will be responsible for contacting the Local Safeguarding Children Board or the police if necessary. This person can also ensure that the policy and procedures are implemented.

The policy should illustrate the good working practices that should be followed by practitioners to ensure their own protection.

## What to do if you are worried a child is being abused

K3S346

Having concerns about the safety and well being of a child can cause alarm, and it is essential that every practitioner is fully aware of their roles and responsibilities regarding safeguarding. If you are concerned about the welfare of a child, the first thing you should do is discuss these concerns with your line manager, designated health professional or designated member of staff. It is essential that confidentiality is maintained at all times, and the safety and well being of the child is at the forefront of the discussion. The outcome of the discussion may be to keep an account of concerns for an agreed time scale, and review again at the end of the agreed time. Alternatively, you may still have concerns, and feel that the child and family would benefit from further services and, as a result, make a referral to an appropriate agency, such as speech and language therapy or parenting support groups. You may, however, feel that the child is at risk of suffering significant harm, and therefore an immediate referral to the child's social worker, the police or the NSPCC would be appropriate.

The DCSF has produced a document which provides best practice guidance for those who work with children in order to safeguard their welfare. The document provides a clear flow chart, illustrating the process for safeguarding children.

In addition to the safeguarding children policy and procedure, settings should have a **whistle-blowing** policy in place, to enable practitioners to disclose confidential information relating to unacceptable behaviour by another member of staff. This process should be confidential to allow practitioners to feel completely confident in the policy.

Figure 4: What to do if you suspect a child is being abused

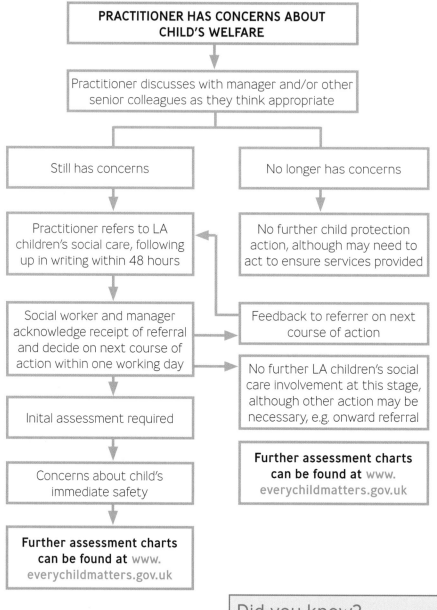

## Data Protection

The Data Protection Act 1998 prevents confidential and personal information from being passed on without a person's consent. This includes information stored electronically, on video, on film, and tape recorded as well as on paper. Under the Act any organisation that collects and stores information must register with the Data Protection Commission. There are eight enforceable

principles of practice. Information must be: processed for limited purposes; adequate, relevant and not excessive; accurate; not kept longer than necessary; processed in accordance with the data subject's rights; secure; not transferred to countries that do not have adequate protection; fairly and lawfully processed.

When working with children and young people, most of the information collected will be confidential. Passing

## Key Term

Whistle-blowing – reporting the misconduct of a colleague to another member of staff.

## Did you know?

You can access a copy of 'What to do if you are worried a child is being abused' at www. everychildmatters.gov.uk.

# Case Study: Whistle blowing

James Dowt worked as a Family Support Worker in his local Children's Centre. His role was to encourage local families to access support services, and to become involved in community development activities. As part of his role, James worked alongside families in the centre's Stay and Play sessions, modelling play techniques and behaviour management strategies. Whilst at the session one afternoon, James witnessed a member of staff, Bal, physically restraining a child on a chair. The child was obviously in distress, but Bal continued to restrain the child, stating that it was for the child's own good, and that she had to learn to control her temper. James was horrified by the situation as he knew that restraining the child in such a manner was against the policies and procedures of the setting.

After some consideration, James decided to go through the procedure of the whistle-blowing policy and report Bal's misconduct.

The manager of the children's centre discussed the incident with Bal, giving her a formal warning.

- What exactly was Bal doing wrong?
- How might James have handled the situation differently?
- How might the manager have prevented the situation from arising in the first place?
- What else might the manager have done to ensure that the situation doesn't happen again?
- What might be the wider impact of the situation?

any of this information on to others without consent would be a breech of this Act. This is one reason why consent has to be given by parents before you can make contact with external agencies on their behalf.

# Keys to Good Practice

- Always have the consent of the parent or carer when collecting personal data.
- Only collect the information you justifiably need.
- Ensure all data is recorded accurately.
- Ensure all data is stored securely.
- Use the data appropriately, only sharing data with permission.
- Dispose of data safely.
- Ensure parents know that confidentiality is respected.
- Ensure all practitioners in the setting are aware of the rules of confidentiality.
- Let parents know that there may be circumstances where confidential information may be shared without their knowledge, such as in a safeguarding concern.
- Never gossip about parents, children or practitioners.

## Concepts of child abuse

Consider these facts, from the NSPCC.

- Every ten days in England and Wales one child is killed at the hands of their parent. In half (52 per cent) of all cases of children killed at the hands of another person, the parent is the principal suspect.
- More than one third (36 per cent) of all rapes recorded by the police are committed against children under 16 years of age.
- Six per cent of children experienced frequent and severe emotional maltreatment during childhood.
- Three-quarters (72 per cent) of sexually abused children did not tell anyone about the abuse at the time; 27 per cent told someone later. Around a third (31 per cent) still had not told anyone about their experience(s) by early adulthood.
- A quarter (25 per cent) of children experienced one or more forms of physical violence during childhood. This includes being hit with an implement, being hit with a fist or kicked, shaken, thrown or knocked down, beaten up, choked, burned or scalded on purpose, or threatened with a knife or gun. Of this 25 per cent of children, the majority had experienced 'some degree of physical abuse' by parents or carers.
- Almost two thirds of children killed at the hands of another person in England and Wales are aged under 5.

(Taken from www.nspcc.org.uk.)

With so many children in need of safeguarding intervention, it is essential that practitioners are able to spot the signs and indicators of abuse and follow procedures to ensure that children and their families get all the intervention and support they need.

Some children have an increased risk, and are more vulnerable to abuse and exploitation. There are a range of **pre-disposing factors** that may make a child more vulnerable to abuse – see Table 3 for examples.

### Key Term

Pre-disposing factors – factors in a child's background which may make them more vulnerable or susceptible to abuse.

K4S794

**Table 3:** Pre-disposing factors for abuse

| Pre-disposing factor | Examples and indicators |
|---|---|
| **Looked-after children** | Children who are looked after in local authority care are cared for in a 'closed' environment. They may experience abusive carers, who abuse their trusted position. This may lead to feelings of isolation as the child may already have low self-esteem and a lack trust in adults. They may find it difficult to disclose this information |
| **A child with a disability** | Caring for a child with a disability can be extremely tiring, isolating and frustrating. A parent who has responsibility for significant physical care of a child with a disability might find it increasingly difficult to manage, and take their frustration and anger out on the child. As with looked after children, children with disabilities may be cared for by trusted adults in closed environments, leaving them more vulnerable to abusive carers |
| **A loner** | Children who spend lots of time alone, and who have few friends or social activities, may be more vulnerable than their peers |
| **An eldest child** | Children who are the eldest child in their family are often given higher levels of responsibility, which can in turn lead to stress. Children may take out their anger on younger siblings, or may look for comfort or friendship in older adults who may prey on their vulnerability |
| **A very young, difficult child** | A child who is difficult to care for, such as a child who cries a lot, or a child who won't eat/sleep, can lead to stress and exhaustion for parents and carers. This may lead to the parent or carer losing their temper or taking their frustration out on the child |
| **A child who has communication difficulties** | Children who have difficulties communicating may find they are unable to disclose the abuse that is happening to them |
| **Parents who have been abused** | Although many parents who were abused themselves are able to overcome childhood adversity, some are unable to protect their own children from abuse |

K4D800

## Empowering children

Empowering children is a key area of your work. Children who feel confident and self-assured are more likely to be able to keep themselves safe. As a practitioner, you are responsible for helping the children in your care to feel empowered to protect themselves. There are many ways you can do this within your setting. The following are examples.

- Teaching children it is OK to say 'No' to people they know, as well as to strangers.
- Helping children to understand the difference between good and bad touching.
- Discussing what are good and bad secrets.

- Helping children to understand that their body belongs to them and they have a right to privacy.
- Actively listening to children and taking their concerns seriously.
- Helping children to understand their rights.
- Giving children strategies to use to get help and support.
- Involving children and young people in the development of practices and systems which affect their safety, well being and safeguarding.

Table 4 on page 73 illustrates strategies that you may use to enable children to protect themselves.

**Table 4:** Strategies to enable children to protect themselves (taken from G. Squire, 2007, *BTEC National Children's Care, Learning & Development*, Heinemann)

| Concept | Strategies |
|---|---|
| **Good and bad touches**<br>Children should be able to identify good and bad touches. Touches that hurt, are rude or make them feel uncomfortable are not acceptable | Promote through appropriate daily physical care routines<br>Support children who say 'No' to tickling games, hugs or kisses<br>For older children, discussions such as 'I like hugs from . . . I would not like a hug from . . .' |
| **To say 'No' to adults they know as well as to strangers**<br>Although it is important to promote the concept of 'stranger danger', more children are at risk from adults that they know well | Role play<br>Books and videos, for example the NSPCC's *Emily and the Stranger* or Rolf Harris's *Say No* video<br>Visits from a police officer<br>Discussion about people you trust |
| **Good and bad secrets**<br>You can provide opportunities for children to discuss good and bad secrets | Discussion about good and bad secrets. No one should ever ask children to keep a hug, touch or smack secret<br>'Don't tell Mummy what we have bought for her birthday' = good secret<br>'Don't tell Mummy that I hit you' = bad secret |
| **That their body belongs to them**<br>Children should be encouraged to know that their body belongs to them and that they have control over what happens to it | Young children can be helped by learning body vocabulary<br>Songs such as 'Head, shoulders, knees and toes . . .'<br>Books such as *My First Body Book* (Early Learning Centre)<br>Appropriate physical care routines<br>Draw a picture of a body and discuss which parts of the body are the 'private' parts<br>Body 'beetle game' |
| **That they have the right to privacy**<br>Children have the right to their own privacy | Physical care routines |
| **Getting help**<br>There are some situations where children can help themselves by getting help | Children should be taught their address and phone number in case they get lost<br>Learning about which adults they can go to for help, for example the police, the person at the shop till, a lollipop lady, a mother with a pram or school teacher<br>Visits from a police officer<br>Shouting 'No!' |

## Keys to Good Practice

- Teach children how to keep themselves protected and safe.
- Empower them with strategies to enable them to tell someone if they are being abused.
- Ensure they know that abuse is never their fault.
- Promote external service, such as Childline or the NSPCC.

## Indicators of abuse

Table 5 on page 74 shows possible indicators that might suggest abuse. This should be used only as a guide, and it is essential that you follow all protocols of your setting, and local and national guidance.

K3S348
K4S795
K3S349

Table 5: Indicators of abuse

| Category of abuse | Definition | Physical indicators | Behavioural indicators |
|---|---|---|---|
| **Physical abuse** | Causing physical harm or non-accidental injury to a child or young person. May include shaking, hitting, poisoning, suffocating, biting | Unexplained multiple bruises in unusual places, such as thighs, back, back of legs, upper and inner arms<br>Multiple and frequent bruises, all at differing stages of healing. This is indicated by the colour of the bruise, from dark purple to yellow/green<br>Cigarette burns<br>Bruises consistent with the shape of an object, such as rope or slipper<br>Bruises consistent with the shape of fingertips<br>Bite marks<br>Unexplained burns and scalds<br>Internal injuries<br>Unexplained fractures<br>Bruising on a baby who is not yet mobile | Giving explanations that seem unlikely<br>Changing explanations for physical indicator<br>Being withdrawn and submissive<br>Cowering from a parent or carer or being unusually fearful<br>Poor social skills and aggression<br>Low confidence and self-esteem<br>Inappropriate play<br>Reluctant to change for physical activities or swimming |
| **Emotional abuse** | Withdrawal of emotion and love towards a child, persistent emotional ill-treatment, such as name-calling, humiliating, and threatening | | Demonstrating attention-seeking behaviour<br>Poor concentration<br>Thumb sucking or rocking for comfort<br>Reluctant to go home or fearful of parents<br>Withdrawn and isolated<br>Low self-esteem<br>Over-reacting, and having tantrums which are inappropriate for age<br>Developmental delay<br>Problems making friends and cooperating with peers<br>Self-harm<br>Toileting accidents |
| **Sexual abuse** | Forcing or coercing a child or young person to take part in sexual activities, whether or not the child is aware of what is happening. This may include incest, buggery, rape, oral sex, the use of sexually explicit language, exposure to pornographic material and pressuring children to witness such acts | Pain and discomfort in the genital area<br>Semen on skin, clothes or genital area<br>Pregnancy or sexually transmitted infections<br>Promiscuity<br>Underwear which is stained, bloody or torn<br>Bruising to the breast, buttock, genital and anal area | Nightmares<br>Attention-seeking behaviour<br>Poor relationships with peers<br>Inappropriate sexual knowledge<br>Inappropriate sexual play<br>Using sexual language<br>Anti-social behaviour<br>Frequent lying<br>Unusually secretive<br>'Special' relationship with an older person |
| **Neglect** | The persistent failure to meet the needs of the child or young person. This may include, lack of food, not being kept clean, unwashed clothes, not being bathed or washed | Poor hygiene<br>Inadequate clothing for time or year/weather conditions<br>Untreated medical problems and illnesses<br>Persistent nappy rash<br>Emaciation | Difficult to stimulate the interests of the child or young person<br>Low confidence and self-esteem<br>Withdrawn<br>Late for setting or school<br>Inappropriate affection towards others |

## Responding to disclosures

Working closely with children and young people puts you in a position of trust and confidence. There may come a time when a child makes a **disclosure** to you.

There are two types of disclosure.

- *A direct disclosure:* when a child or young person explains to an adult or older child that they are being or have been abused in some way.
- *An indirect disclosure:* when a professional becomes aware of possible indicators of abuse, or a child's indirect attempts to disclose.

Should a child make a disclosure to you, it is essential that you follow the policies and procedures of your setting. You should report your concerns to the person in charge of safeguarding children within your setting, and follow the protocols set out within the safeguarding children document 'What to do if you are worried a child is being abused'.

> You can find the flow chart to guide you through the process on page 70.

## Safe working practices

We have looked in detail at how to support children who make disclosures, or who are the victim of abuse, but how can you ensure good working practices to keep children in your care and other practitioners safe?

## Key Term

Disclosure – when a child informs you that they are being or have been abused.

---

### Keys to Good Practice

If a child makes a disclosure:

- Always ensure that the child's needs are paramount when developing and embedding systems for safeguarding children.
- Always listen calmly and openly, without asking questions, prompting or investigating.
- Tell the child they have been very brave and have done the right thing by telling you.
- Tell them that you believe them.
- Tell the child that none of what has happened is their fault; do not say things which might make the child feel they are responsible.
- Reassure the child that they are not the only child to go through this.
- Do not promise the child that you will keep their disclosure a secret, tell them who you will need to speak to and why.
- Always keep the child informed about what is happening.
- Provide the child with other sources of support such as the NSPCC or Childline.
- Always keep calm, and keep any personal feelings of shock or anger to yourself whilst talking to the child. You can discuss your emotions with your line manager at a later date.

---

**Figure 5:** Ensuring safe working practices

Adhere to the staffing ratios of your setting members

Be alert to signs of stress and concern from other practitioners

Check the qualifications, experience and references of employees

Strive to maintain high standards of care and service

Maintain confidentiality at all times

Ensure that all practitioners are trained in the implementation of your setting's Safeguarding Children Policy

Make sure staff are not left alone with children

K4P789

## Training and support

It is essential that you keep up to date with changes in legislation and protocols regarding safeguarding children. You can do this through accessing training from local colleges or training providers.

The NSPCC offers training to organisations 'to meet the changing needs of children, families and professionals'.

You can also access online and paper-based training, written by the NSPCC at www.educare.co.uk.

Keeping up to date with current guidance and legislation enables you deliver the best possible care for the children in your setting, and ensures that you are fully informed about your roles and responsibilities.

---

## Case Study: Cloverdale Children's Centre

Children's Centres offer a wide range of services for children and their families, and as such employ a diverse team. The Centre manager at Cloverdale Children's Centre wanted to ensure that all employees were up-to-date with guidance and legislation relating to safeguarding children, but acknowledged that each practitioner would need a differing degree of knowledge depending upon their role and responsibilities. The manager was also keen to allow practitioners choice in the way they participated in training. After some investigation, the manager offered each practitioner a range of ways they might undertake training, and discussed with each of them how the training could support their role. The training offered was as follows.

- Direct childcare practitioners, level 2: online basic awareness training course to be carried out independently.
- Direct childcare practitioners; level 3: two-day intermediate training course.
- Family support practitioners: intermediate two-day training course, plus Common Assessment Framework Training.
- All other practitioners: basic online training course.

Consider:

- How effective do you think the manager's strategy will be?
- How might the employees react to this differentiation?
- How might you tackle this differently?

---

## 402.3 Support the integration of procedures for safeguarding children into systems and practices

K4P801

### Working in partnership

Working together to safeguard children and ensure their inclusion and well being requires you to develop and maintain sound working practices. By working together, you can ensure that the children and families you work with can receive seamless support from a variety of agencies and professionals. As noted earlier in this Unit, the document 'Working Together to Safeguard Children' sets out how agencies should work together to safeguard children. The document acts as a guide for interagency working and good practice and illustrates the processes involved in safeguarding

through clear flow charts. These guidelines also include definitions and indicators of abuse. The key principle within the document is that the best way of protecting children is through cooperation between different agencies and professionals involved with the child and family.

There is a huge range of support services, agencies and professionals that may be involved in safeguarding children, such as the following:

- Special Educational Needs Coordinators (SENCOs)
- Social Workers
- Educational Psychologists
- Police
- Local Authorities
- Speech and Language Therapists
- Teachers
- Local Safeguarding Children Boards
- Family Support Workers

- Maternity Services
- Addiction Counsellors
- Social Services
- National Health Services
- Prison and probation services
- Housing Authorities
- Youth Services
- Primary Care Trusts (PCTs)
- Paediatricians
- Obstetrics and gynaecological staff
- GPs
- The children and family court advisory and support services (CAFCASS).

## Why work collaboratively?

There are lots of reasons why working together is important in safeguarding children and the list below shows some examples.

- To learn from each other.
- To avoid failures in communication.
- To disseminate and share good practice.
- To ensure resources are used to their maximum effect and prevent duplicating services.
- To support children and families, working to help them out of poverty and prevent social disadvantage.
- To safeguard children and reduce the number of abuse cases.

Working within an **interagency** approach, or in multi-disciplinary teams, can be very difficult to manage;

however, it is important to remember that all practitioners are working towards the same goal of improving outcomes for children. Successful interagency working requires all partners to work cooperatively together in a sustainable way. It is essential that all partners share a set of common commitments and objectives and are well supported with resources.

One key factor for successful partnership working is the establishing of each other's roles and responsibilities, accountabilities and the decision-making process. By understanding the role each partner plays, each practitioner will feel able to offer support, and guidance, and know who to discuss certain matters with. It is also important that each partner understands how they add value to a meeting, the purpose of the meeting, and how the partnership will enable the delivery of better outcomes for children and young people. Being clear and concise from the beginning will facilitate a smooth seamless process.

During interagency working, it is essential that the lines of communication are open, and positive communication skills are developed. Having clear communication will make meetings run more effectively, and ensure that the viewpoints of everyone involved are listened to. It is also important during such meetings that good practice ethics and values are considered, such as those shown in Figure 6.

> ### Key Term
> **Interagency working** – sharing information and decision-making between agencies to meet the needs of children, young people and their families.

Figure 6: Good practice in interagency working

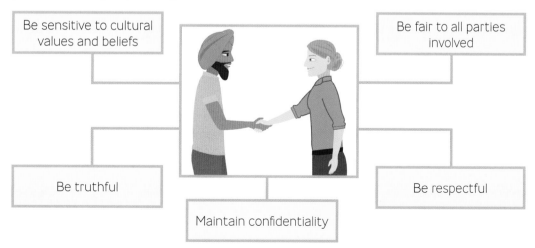

Working together in this collaborative manner improves professional relationships, and therefore improves outcomes for children and their families. However, many professionals hold an intrinsic approach to their work – working for the good of the outcome rather than reward – and may find interagency work difficult, as they have the desire to get results from their individual work. Working hard with a family for a long time can make it difficult to let go when other professionals need to become involved. Professional differences, such as approaches to work and differences in pay and training, can lead to the child and their family receiving inadequate support, thus leaving the child at risk.

Tragic consequences can result from the failure of various agencies to collaborate effectively. This was evident in the case of Victoria Climbié, whose death in 2000 prompted a public inquiry into the British child protection system. This inquiry, the Laming Report, identified 12 separate occasions where professionals had the opportunity to take action to protect Victoria from further abuse. However, distinct flaws in the child protection system, particularly where professionals had failed to work together and share information, lead to the failure to protect the child. More recently, the Green Paper Every Child Matters (DoH, September 2003), and its sister report Keeping Children Safe, address the recommendations of the Laming report, and offer a number of common threads linking the findings of child death inquiries, as illustrated below.

- Lack of coordination between agencies.
- Failure to share information.
- Absence of an individual with a strong sense of accountability.
- Frontline workers coping with vacancies and stress at work.
- Poor management.
- Lack of effective training.

(Reference: Every Child Matters, DoH, 2003.)

Sadly, the case of 'Baby P', who died in 2007 at the hands of his main carers, demonstrates that there is still a long way to go and that all professionals must strive to collaborate fully in instances where children are deemed to be at risk.

# 402.4 Support the maintenance of policies, procedures and practice for the well being of children

## Positive health and well being

Working closely with children and their families allows practitioners to be directly involved in a child's health and well being. Understanding the impact of nutrition and exercise on a child's well being will help you to reflect upon how your practice can make a difference to the health and well being of each and every child.

## Current research and best practice

Over the last decade, there has been much interest in the health and well being of children. Rises in childhood obesity have prompted much media interest as well as research and development.

In 2004, the government launched Every Child Matters: Change for Children, placing emphasis on the health of children and young people. The document recognised that in order to achieve positive health and well being for children, the health provision needed to improve.

## Healthy Schools

The national Healthy Schools Programme began in 1999, with the aim of promoting a whole school approach to health and its benefits in the following areas.

- Improvement in health and reduced health inequalities.
- Raised pupil achievement.
- More social inclusion.
- Closer working between health promotion providers and education establishments.

The government set a target of 75 per cent of schools to achieve 'healthy schools' status by 2009, and demonstrated a commitment to include Early Years settings and Further Education settings in this approach. At the time of writing, 95 per cent of schools were involved in the programme, with 60 per cent having achieved the healthy schools status.

## Nutritional requirements and healthy eating

For children to thrive and grow they require a balanced diet that contains foods from all the essential food groups. The nutrients within these foods perform different functions in meeting the body's needs.

These essential nutrients are found in a mixture of foods and are not just from one food source. The government's guidelines for healthy eating uses food groups rather than nutrients as this is a clearer basis on which to build a healthy and well balanced diet. The five food groups are defined in Table 7, along with food sources and the nutrients they contain.

**Table 6:** Nutrients and their functions

| Nutrient | Functions |
|---|---|
| Protein | Helps to build and replace all body cells, assists with repairing the body. Also a good source of energy |
| Carbohydrate | An energy provider essential for activity and growth; fuel for the heart and circulation. Helps with the digestion of other nutrients and aids the production of all body cells |
| Fats | Provide fuel for energy, body heat and insulation, some can contain vitamins (A, D, E) |
| Vitamins | Perform many roles in helping the growth and function of the body, the skeletal system, blood formation and clotting. Also essential for growth, repair and prevention of disease |
| Minerals | Aid the production of energy, essential for the metabolism, development of skeletal system and control of muscles and nerves |
| Fibre | Helps the body move food through its digestive system; makes you feel full by adding 'bulk' to food |
| Water | Essential for life and the prevention of dehydration. Can also prevent kidney problems and constipation |

**Table 7:** The five food groups

| Food group | Food sources | Main nutrients |
|---|---|---|
| Bread, rice, potatoes, pasta and other starchy foods | Pasta, rice, noodles, oats, maize, millet, cornmeal and breakfast cereal. Includes yams and plantains, beans and pulses | Carbohydrate (starch), fibre, B vitamins<br>Some calcium and iron |
| Fruit and vegetables | Fresh, canned, frozen fruit and vegetables, dried fruit, fruit juice, beans and pulses | Carotenes, vitamin C, folates, fibre, some carbohydrate |
| Milk and dairy foods | Cheese, milk, yogurt, fromage frais | Protein, calcium, vitamins A and D, vitamin B12 |
| Meat, fish, eggs, beans and other non-dairy sources of protein | Meat, poultry, fish, eggs, nuts, beans and pulses | Iron, protein, B vitamins, zinc, magnesium |
| Foods drinks high in fat and/or sugar | Foods containing fat:<br>Margarine, butter other spreading fats and low fat spreads, cooking oils, oil based salad dressing, mayonnaise, cream, chocolate, crisps, biscuits, rich sauces and gravies, puddings, ice cream<br>Food and drink containing sugar:<br>Soft drinks, sweets, jams, cakes, pastries puddings, biscuits, ice cream | Fat, including some essential fatty acids, some vitamins<br>Some products contain sugar and salt<br>Some sugar products contain minerals whilst others contain fat |

# The eatwell plate

Use the eatwell plate to help you get the balance right. It shows how much of what you eat should come from each food group.

Figure 7: The 'eatwell plate' provides a visual summary of guidance from the Food Standards Agency

## The 'eatwell plate'

The 'eatwell plate', based on the five food groups listed above, summarises the latest guidance from the Food Standards Agency. It provides guidance for healthy eating, giving a visual representation of what makes a balanced diet – and clearly shows how much of people's daily food should come from each food group. The messages from the government are clear and have been placed in the public domain to promote healthy living and eating in the UK.

The guidelines are as follows.

- Enjoy your food.
- Eat a variety of different foods.
- Eat the right amount to be a healthy weight.
- Eat plenty of foods rich in starch and fibre.
- Eat plenty of fruit and vegetables.
- Don't eat too many foods that contain a lot of fat.
- Don't have sugary foods and drinks too often.
- Drink alcohol sensibly and in moderation.

The above principles do not apply to children under the age of 2 years as they require a diet that contains full-fat dairy produce and milk.

## Find it out

The information above has been sourced from the food standards agency guidelines for 'the eatwell plate'; for further reading visit www.food.gov.uk.

## Points for Reflective Practice

All childcare settings work hard in providing children with a nutritious menu of foods for their consumption. Some settings, however, only provide children with fruit-based products for dessert or pudding!

- What is your view on this?
- Do you think children need pastries, puddings and cakes for a healthy balanced diet?

Take a look at the range of snacks and meals you offer the children in your setting.

- Do they contain a range of nutrients?
- Do they contain foods from all the identified foods groups?
- Is there anything lacking within the diet offered?
- If so, how can you ensure this is addressed?

## The role of physical exercise

In today's society there is much focus and media attention on children's weight and the increasing levels of childhood obesity in the UK. Much research is underway into the causes and effects of childhood obesity and the implications this has for children as they grow up, including the increased risk of other conditions such as type-2 diabetes, high blood pressure and heart disease.

Modern technology plays an increasing role in children's play. In previous decades much play took place in the great outdoors with little more than the imagination as a tool, whereas now children have a vast range of computer-related gizmos available to them which can restrict time spent outside or indeed discourage them from engaging in direct play and exercise with their peers.

Many schools and Early Years settings recognise the sometimes limited access children have to outdoor play and exercise, and put in place adequate provision within the day for this to take place. Practitioners should not be put off taking children outside if the weather is cold or it is a blustery day. As long as children are adequately dressed for the weather conditions, time spent outdoors can be both refreshing and invigorating. Of course there is an exception to the rule: practitioners would not be expected to take children outside in gale force winds or storms!

As children can spend many hours indoors during the day it is important they are able, where possible, to get outdoors to 'let off steam' and release any pent-up energy. Having a good run around increases the heart rate, which is good for physical well being and can help burn excess calories.

In addition to the health benefits, physical exercise and outdoor play can provide a great opportunity for children to socialise with their peers. Activities that increase stamina and endurance, such as football, can also increase children's ability to cooperate in play and build friendships with others through common interests.

## Why exercise?

The information below is taken from www.bupa.co.uk.

Physical activity can prevent many major illnesses. Evidence shows that regular exercise can:

- promote healthy blood sugar levels to prevent or control diabetes
- promote bone density to protect against osteoporosis
- reduce the overall risk of cancer
- increase levels of HDL or 'good' cholesterol – reducing the risk of developing heart disease
- lower high blood pressure – reducing the risk of developing heart disease
- boost the immune system
- boost self-confidence and help prevent depression

**Figure 8:** Healthy eating and exercise are vital to a child's well being

■ in combination with a balanced diet, help to maintain a healthy weight.

Visit BUPA's website for more information on the benefits of physical exercise.

## Points for Reflective Practice

Consider your setting's approach to physical exercise and activity.

■ How do you encourage practitioners to provide outdoor activities and experiences for the children in their care?

■ What activities and experiences can children be provided with to increase their physical activity indoors, outdoors and within the local community?

## Influences on children's health and safety

There are many influences placed on children's health and safety throughout their childhood which can impact on their lives through to adulthood. Whilst practitioners have a responsibility to maintain children's health and well being when in their care, it is also important to recognise that some factors are beyond the control of those in the setting or the parents themselves.

**Table 8:** Influences on children's health and safety

| Influencing factor | Potential effects on children's health and safety |
|---|---|
| Environment | Where a child lives can have a huge impact on their health and safety. Access to clean water, sanitation and housing with adequate heating and ventilation is important for well being. Exposure to hazards such as a damp or unsafe home can have detrimental effects on the health and safety of young children |
| Language | When language is a barrier to effective communication between a child and others their health and safety can be compromised. Children may lack an understanding of the 'rules' placed on play for their own safety and not see the possible risks |
| Gender | Where stereotypical attitudes exist in families, health and safety can become an issue, e.g., if girls are not given the same opportunities in physical play as boys. Not being exposed to challenge and risk can result in a lack of resilience and confidence and a lack of ability to assess their own risk in play |
| Social background | Lifestyles have a significant influence on children's health and safety. Children brought up in a family where little or no emphasis is placed on hygiene practices, such as washing hands before eating or going to the toilet, could be exposed to health problems such as infections or gastro-enteritis |
| Ethnicity/culture | A family's cultural beliefs influence many aspects of their daily life, including attitudes towards diet. Viewpoints can differ regarding suitable diets for children. Different attitudes towards medical practices can also influence a child's health and safety, e.g., Jehovah's Witnesses, many of whom do not accept blood transfusions |
| Stage of development | A child's understanding of safety will depend on their age and stage of development. Young children will not understand that actions have consequences and need to be supervised to ensure their safety and well being. As children grow they can be exposed to risks in a safe environment that allows them to test their skills and abilities, such as the use of climbing frames to develop physical skills. These, however, pose a severe risk to a child's health and safety if not adequately supervised or provided in accordance with their developmental needs |
| Disability | A child who has a disability can be put at risk if their individual needs are not fully understood and provided for. A child who suffers from epilepsy will need the support of practitioners who know how to respond appropriately to the occurrence of seizures, so that these can be managed confidently and medical intervention can be sought as and when appropriate |

# Policies, procedures and practice

It is important for all settings to know, understand and implement robust procedures relating to the safety and well being of children, practitioners and visitors. It is everyone's responsibility within a setting to ensure that practices meet health and safety requirements. There are many regulations that detail the responsibilities of employers and employees in all workplaces. As Early Years practitioners it is important to consider the specific laws that relate to your everyday working practices, and indeed those which relate to the requirements of your regulatory and/or inspectorate body.

Regardless of the authority in which you work, clear guidelines will have been given relating to the requirements for providing a healthy and safe environment. The following Acts and Regulations look at the responsibilities and requirements relating to early years practice. Whilst this list is not exhaustive, it gives you a working insight to the requirements of law in relation to everyday practices.

The Health and Safety at Work Act 1974 places responsibilities on the employer and the employees in the setting. Employers must do the following.

- Provide a safe place of employment.
- Provide a safe working environment.
- Provide a written safety policy/risk assessment.
- Provide and maintain safety equipment and safe systems of work.
- Provide information, training, instruction and supervision.
- Ensure staff are aware of instructions provided by manufacturers and suppliers of equipment.
- Look after health and safety of others.
- Talk to safety representatives.

Employees must do the following.

- Cooperate with their employers.
- Take care of their own health and safety and that of other persons.
- Not interfere with anything provided in the interest of health and safety.

## Keys to Good Practice

Displaying a poster in your setting detailing what the law requires you to do as an employer or an employee is an effective way of reminding everybody of their personal responsibility to healthy and safe working practices. It is also a requirement to do so as stated in The Health and Safety Information for Employees Regulations 1989. In addition, it is important to identify on the poster who the designated health and safety officer is within the setting, so others know who they can talk to or report their concerns to.

## The Control of Substances Hazardous to Health Regulations 2002

Under The Control of Substances Hazardous to Health Regulations 2002, or COSHH as it is commonly known, settings need to consider how they store and control substances that could be hazardous to health. While most settings try to limit the amount of dangerous or toxic substances kept on the premises, some cleaning fluids are used for the effective sanitisation of the environment, for example anti-bacterial spray, toilet cleaner, sterilising fluids.

The regulations require settings to consider the risk these pose and require them to conduct risk assessments to determine measures that need to be taken to control the usage and storage of such substances.

## Keys to Good Practice

Identify an opportunity to remind your colleagues of the COSHH regulations. Make sure everyone is aware of how substances are controlled in your setting. Consider what you have in writing regarding the control of hazardous substances. In addition to a written risk assessment, a written policy can also provide practitioners with clear guidelines for good practice.

## Find it out

To find out more about Health and Safety requirements, visit www.hse.gov.uk.

## Reporting of Injuries, Diseases and Dangerous Occurrences Regulations 1995

This is commonly known as RIDDOR. It places a legal duty on employers, self employed people and people in control of premises to report:

- work-related deaths
- major injuries
- **over-three-day injuries**
- work-related diseases
- dangerous occurrences (near miss accidents).

### Key Term

Over-three-day injury – not a major injury, but where an injury has occurred that means an employee is away over three days from work or unable to do their full duties for more than three days of work.

### Did you know?

You have a legal duty to report any injuries, diseases or dangerous occurrences so that the HSE and your local authority can work with you to identify how such risks and incidents arose and provide your setting with information and advice to reduce risks of injury and ill-health.

To report any of the above you can call The Incident Contact Centre (ICC) on 0845 300 99 23.

## Manual Handling Operations Regulations 1992

This regulation sets out clear procedures for workplaces with regard to the following.

- Avoiding hazardous manual handling operations so far as reasonably practicable.
- Assessing any hazardous manual handling operations that cannot be avoided; and reducing the risk of injury so far as reasonably practicable.

Working with young children inevitably requires you to lift and carry in your everyday practice, for example when lifting a baby or child to offer comfort or reassurances or lifting a baby to change their nappy or laying them in a cot to sleep. In these instances it is essential to explore how the risk of injury can be reduced as the hazard of manual handling may not be avoidable.

For those of you involved in the induction processes for new team members of staff, or the training and development of staff, you need to ensure that they are following safe working practices with regard to lifting and carrying young children.

Other regulations to which settings must give due regard and attention are as follows.

- ***Health and Safety (First Aid) Regulations 1981:*** identifies requirements for first aid which includes the need for employers to provide their employees within the setting with adequate equipment (first aid kits) and human resources (appointed first aiders) to enable first aid to be administered to anyone who becomes ill or injured in the workplace.

- ***Personal Protective Equipment at Work Regulations 1992:*** requires employees to provide practitioners with appropriate protective clothing and equipment for duties that require it, which includes the use of gloves when dealing with bodily fluids and appropriate clothing for those preparing food for children. Employers also have a duty to ensure that such equipment is used and maintained correctly and used in accordance with manufacturer's instructions.

- ***Provision and use of Work Equipment Regulations 1998:*** identifies the need to assess and manage the risk posed by any equipment in the workplace and provide adequate training on its use. Whilst those working in the Early Years sector may have limited exposure to machinery, it is important to consider the management of risk of equipment such as televisions, computers and photocopiers. In addition, equipment used within the kitchen will need due regard and attention.

- ***Fire Precautions (Workplace) Regulations 1997:*** identifies the need for settings to have adequate equipment e.g. fire alarms and fire extinguishers which must be checked regularly. Settings must also display evacuation signs in every room of the setting and put in place measures and procedures for the evacuation of the building and provide evidence of such 'drills' or simulations taking place.

- ***Electricity at Work Regulations 1989:*** settings are required to use electrical equipment safely, for the purpose they are intended and keep it in good working order. For Early Years practitioners this will mean ensuring equipment such as CD players, light boxes and ICT equipment is suitably maintained and that they are alert to signs of damage or wear and tear.

- **Employers Liability (Compulsory Insurance) Act 1969:** employers have a legal responsibility to hold valid insurance against ill health and accidents to all those employed within the setting. This should be clearly displayed in the place of work where it can be easily read by employees e.g. the staff room, office or reception area.

- **Management of Health and Safety at Work Regulations 1999:** a practice that all settings should be familiar with is carrying out risk assessments of the environment, equipment and work practices. The regulations ask that employers carry out a risk assessment and that 'Employers with five or more employees need to record the significant findings of the risk assessment'. (Taken from www.hse.gov.uk/pubns/hscl3.pdf.)

- **Workplace (Health, Safety and welfare) Regulations 1992:** requires basic health, safety and issues regarding the well being of individuals to be addressed; facilities such as toilets, somewhere to eat and rest, adequate ventilation, heating and lighting and readily available access to drinking water are just a few of the requirements needed.

K4P778

## Find it out

Visit the HSE website at www.hse.gov.uk and find out what procedures are recommended for safe handling and lifting.

- What are the possible implications for Early Years practitioners who do not follow these guidelines?
- What should you do to ensure colleagues follow guidelines and do not put themselves at unnecessary risk?

## Points for Reflective Practice

Consider the health and safety regulations in relation to the activities you carry out day-to-day. Look at documentation and policies you have that are related to the management of health and safety in your environment. Ask yourself:

- Are they compliant with Health and Safety law?
- Do they take into consideration legislation related to specific elements of practice?
- Is there a robust system for the dissemination of requirements to colleagues?
- Is there an adequate system in place for regular review and improvements to health and safety practices?

## Did you know?

Even if you are self employed you need to make sure you have adequate provision, e.g. a first aid kit to provide first aid to yourself at work.

## Case Study: Health and safety in practice

Casey is in her first week of employment at Cavendish House day nursery. As yet she has received no formal induction. She is asked to change the nappy of a toddler in her care under the supervision of another member of staff. Casey fails to use gloves whilst changing and disposes of the nappy in the waste paper bin in the bathroom. The practitioner with her says nothing but reports the matter to the nursery

manager later in the day. The nursery manager thanks the practitioner for her communication and asks Casey to meet with her.

- Which specific health and safety regulations have been breached?
- Why did Casey fail to follow health and safety procedures when nappy changing?
- What should the nursery manager have done to prevent this from happening?
- How can the manager ensure good practice in accordance with regulations in the future?

## Risk assessments

K4H788

The term 'risk assessment' has already been evident in this section, but what is a risk assessment? Of what benefit are they? And how can you make sure those conducted in your setting are adequate?

Risk assessment is a means of identifying and assessing potential risks and hazards within your setting or service. Effective risk assessments go further to establish the methods of eliminating or reducing the risks that are posed to individuals including children, staff and visitors. Risk assessments should be recorded so that all those involved in the provision can be fully informed of measures in place to reduce and/ or eliminate hazards. It also gives them guidelines for practice and reminds them of their responsibility to follow health and safety practices in the setting when and where identified. Risk assessments should be regularly reviewed to ensure that any further hazards being presented can be identified and managed, reviews also help to ascertain whether existing control measures are sufficient or whether additional measures need to be considered or put in place.

Table 9 gives you a guide as to the information your documentation should contain. It is up to the individual, if self employed, or the setting to decide the layout and format of the document. However, presenting the data in a table is an easy way to present clear and legible information.

### Find it out

The HSE (Health and Safety Executive) has a free leaflet 'five steps to risk assessment' to download from their website which gives your more information. Take a look at www.hse.gov.uk.

**Table 9:** Example of completed risk assessment

| Name of setting: Little Scholars Nursery <br> Area, resource or room: Creative zone | | | | Date of assessment: 18/05/2009 <br> Completed by: Jamie Smith | | |
|---|---|---|---|---|---|---|
| | Identified hazard | Risk groups | Existing control measures | Additional control measures required | To be actioned by whom | To be actioned when | Review dates and comments |
| 1 | Water tray spillages, wet floor | Children and adults | Close supervision <br><br> Mopping of floor during water play | Display wet floor sign | Nursery Manager: Jamie Smith | Immediately: disseminate use of wet floor sign to all practitioners | Written memo sent to all team members 20/05/2009 |
| 2 | Sand play <br> Slipping on spilt sand <br> Sand in eyes <br> Eating sand | Children and adults | Supervision of play <br><br> Dust pan and brush located near sand tray | Poster to be displayed near sand tray to inform practitioners how to respond to sand in children's eyes | Admin Assistant: Jessica May | 18/06/2009 | Completed 12/06/2009 |
| 3 | | | | | | | |
| 4 | | | | | | | |
| Signature of Risk Assessor: <br><br> Date: | | | | | | Risk assessment review date: 18/11/2009 | |

# Working with families

## Information gathering

All settings providing services for children and families should have adequate systems for gathering and monitoring information about their needs, wishes and preferences.

For settings providing care for children, registration forms are required to document information relevant to the care and well being of each individual child

The information needed will include:

- child's name
- date of birth
- gender
- address of child and who they reside with
- name and address of parents and carers
- emergency contact details
- ethnicity
- SEN status
- sessions attended (funded and unfunded).

All the above information is required to be collated by the setting for the local authority in England as part of the Early Years Census.

In addition, the following information is essential in ensuring a child's needs are met whilst in your care.

- Personal care plan: including sleep routines and feeding patterns, which are particularly relevant for younger children and babies.
- Likes and dislikes: relating to foods, the environment, other people, toys and comfort objects
- Dietary needs: which can include their own personal preferences, the wishes of the parents, intolerances, food allergies, cultural customs relating to food restrictions and food preparation.
- Medical needs: including both long and short term illnesses and how these are managed including the use of prescribed long term medication and/or medical support.

Practitioners should ensure that the information gathered is shared with the appropriate people in the setting so that a child's needs can be met and routines provided for them.

The consequences of failing to gather sufficient evidence of needs, and indeed sharing such information

with others, can be far reaching when the health and well being of a child is compromised or put at risk. This is particularly important when caring for children with specific medical needs and/or dietary requirements.

Children whose health relies on medication should have specifically devised care plans that detail their condition, specific considerations and details of long-term medications needed. The setting will need to ensure that the information is accurate and, as well as asking parents to complete forms, time should be taken to discuss their child's needs in person and ensure clarification has been sought on all aspects of their care needs. Regular reviews of the care plan with parents will ensure the child's needs are met in accordance with their wishes and will take into account any changes to their medical needs, such as doses of medication. Managers and senior practitioners should ensure that all practitioners involved in the care and well being of a particular child with a specifically devised care plan are fully informed of the child's needs and kept up-to-date with any changes. In some circumstances it may be helpful to involve them in the review meetings with parents. The key to success in meeting care needs is effective and robust methods of communication between team members, having information written down and clearly presented is crucial in ensuring there is no room for error. Ensure that your team members don't assume the care plan is 'as it was.' You should always provide opportunities for practitioners to check and clarify the requirements: it is much better to ask than presume.

For children with dietary needs, which include allergies, intolerances and food restrictions, these need to be clearly documented and available to all colleagues who serve, handle, cook and manage the children's food and diets.

Many daycare settings have clearly displayed charts in food preparation and service areas detailing any specific dietary requirements children may have. In addition to displaying such information, practitioners should be fully versed on specific dietary requirements and strategies employed within the setting to ensure these are adhered to. For children who have food allergies and/or food intolerances it should be clear what types and range of foods can lead to a reaction. Information should also be available about the signs and symptoms of reactions and the course of action to be taken.

You can find out more about data protection in Unit 401.

## Keys to Good Practice

Although information sharing is important to enable the children's care, learning and development needs to be met, it is also important to consider that this information is adequately stored and is only shared with the relevant people.

## Points for Reflective Practice

Consider your own practices and procedures for managing long term medications and emergency medication (such as epi-pens).

■ Is your documentation for recording medication requirements clear and concise?

■ Do you have adequately assigned personnel for the administration of medications?

■ Do you address any additional training needs for personnel in the administration of specific medication, including injections?

■ What systems are in place to ensure regular review of medication needs?

## Monitoring the effectiveness of data collection methods

Whatever setting you work in, it is important to consider if the methods for data collection and monitoring are effective and continue to be over a period of time. One of the most effective ways of finding this out is to communicate regularly with those who use your service or setting. There are several ways in which you can ascertain whether your data collection methods are effective and serve the required purpose. They are as follows.

■ ***Talking to parents and service users:*** make time to talk to parents on a one-to-one basis, the most common time for this is when they arrive and depart from the setting. Ensure you are open in your communications and show that you have the time to listen to what they have to say. Ask

them openly if they have any requests, concerns or needs regarding any aspect of their child's well being. Inform them that you have an open door approach so they feel able to discuss their needs at any given time with you.

■ ***Talking to team members:*** talk to your colleagues regularly about the families who use the setting, they may have information that has not been shared with you. Highlight the need for effective communication with colleagues and foster an environment in which this can occur regularly so they can keep you well informed of any changes to a family's requirements. It is also important to remember that colleagues should be well informed and supported in the processes adopted in the setting for the sharing of sensitive information and the 'need to know' aspect of this.

■ ***Regular reviews of data:*** when parents fill in data forms, don't just put them on a shelf in a pretty folder. Make sure they are accessible, active and working at all times. Ensure you not only have regular verbal communications with families about their changing needs, but also provide them with written opportunities to collate and update data. Regular newsletters and emails to families will provide them with prompts for sharing and updating information held.

# Check Your Understanding

1.  Detail three pieces of legislation designed to protect children and ensure they are treated fairly.

2.  List five forms of discrimination and the effects of this discrimination on the child.

3.  What are 'barriers to participation'?

4.  Why are policies and procedure important to Early Years settings?

5.  What procedure would you follow if a child made a disclosure of abuse to you?

6.  Why is it important to update and review policies?

7.  How should children's data be stored, and which Act relates to this data?

8.  What strategies might you use to empower children to keep themselves safe?

9.  How would you ensure safe working practices for you and your colleagues?

10. Why is a healthy balanced diet and exercise important to a child's health?

# Further references

www.food.gov.uk

www.healthyschools.gov.uk

www.hse.gov.uk

*Early Years Foundation Stage Statutory Framework,*
DCSF, 2007

# Unit 403

## Support programmes for the promotion of children's development

Unit 403 deals with the observation, assessment and recording of children's development and behaviour, and discusses ways in which you can promote children's development and encourage positive behaviour. It also covers the norms of child development from 0 to 16 years.

This is an important Unit because it deals with the development of children from 0–16. It is essential you know and understand the norms of child development as this will affect your day-to-day work with the children, and the guidance and support you are able to give colleagues and staff members.

It is equally important that you understand the process of observation, assessment and recording, as it is through this process that you are able to promote the children's development, encourage their learning and achievements, and respond accurately to their needs.

The elements for Unit 403 are:

403.1    Support procedures for the regular monitoring and assessment of children's development.

403.2    Ensure provision meets children's developmental needs.

403.3    Ensure provision supports children's positive behaviour.

403.4    Monitor and evaluate records and recording procedures for the assessment of children's development.

## Learning Outcomes:

After reading this Unit you will be able to:

- Understand the processes and procedures for observation, assessment and recording.
- Identify the techniques of observation.
- Understand the stages of child development from 0–16.
- Realise the effect that outside influences have on children's development.
- Reflect on the different theories surrounding child development.
- Identify good practice when dealing with children's behaviour.
- Understand how to support children through transitions.
- Identify record keeping procedures.

This Unit includes the following themes and covers the knowledge statements listed below:

- Observation and assessment of children's development
  **K4D804, K4D805, K4D374, K4D375, K4D383**
- Meeting children's developmental needs
  **K4D376, K4D384, K4D385, K4D806, K4D807, K4D808, K4D809, K4D810, K4D811**
- Supporting positive behaviour
  **K4D380, K4T1113, K4D1114**
- Records and recording procedures
  **K4M802, K4M797, K4M378, K4M379, K4M381, K4M382, K4P377**

# 403.1 Support procedures for the regular monitoring and assessment of children's development

**K4D374**

## Observation and assessment of children's development

This element deals with the organisation and implementation of observation and assessment.

## Processes and procedures for observation, assessment and recording

Observations and assessments can be viewed as tools that allow us to know the children far better than we would otherwise do. This has many advantages.

- We are able to respond quickly to their interests, strengths and weaknesses.
- We are able to see what progress the children are making, and build on it.
- We are able to plan appropriately, basing our planning around the individual child.
- We can focus on a particular area where there may be a concern.
- We can gain an overall picture of the child and where they are in terms of normative development.
- We can share the information we gain with the child's parents.
- We can use the information gained to report back to other professionals who may be involved with the child.

Most settings operate a key person system that allows one practitioner to be responsible for a small group of children. The Early Years Foundation Stage places the emphasis on observation by a named and constant key person, who then plans for that child's interests. It is normally the key person who will carry out the observations for their group of children, and it will be the key person who carries out the assessments and any associated planning for their group. This allows for an excellent in-depth understanding of each child and leads to quality provision for the children. However, it is likely that observations will also come from other practitioners within the setting and from parents or other carers. These observations have equal value and can allow for a deeper understanding and give a new perspective.

It is important that observations and assessments are carried out on a regular basis to allow you to build up an overall picture of the child. The regularity will depend on the size of your setting and the number of children allocated to each key person. Some observations will be made as and when the practitioner sees events occurring, and will be very spontaneous. However it is important to allocate time to allow practitioners to carry out observations where they are able to step back from the children that they work with, as this will allow them to be objective, and to observe more fully. This can be achieved by scheduling time into the day, and possibly arranging cover, so that staff can work on the observations out of ratio.

## Parental involvement

It is essential to have written parental permission before carrying out any observations on the children. Many settings will ask parents to sign a permission form when the children first start at the setting. However, parents can and should be involved more fully than just giving their signature. They have valuable knowledge of their child which, when shared, can help you to build up a full picture of the child and their development. This will prevent practitioners from drawing the wrong conclusion based on observations and assessments taken from just one situation. If there are concerns about a child, it is expected that staff will first speak to their manager, and possibly other colleagues, about the child. If these concerns are upheld then the manager will discuss them with the parents, and this is a requirement of the Special Educational Needs Code of Practice in England and Wales.

## Points for Reflective Practice

- What is the procedure for observation, assessment and recording in your setting?
- Who carries out the observations and assessments?
- Do you operate the key person system or is there another process in place?
- How often are observations and assessments carried out in your setting?
- Do you feel it is sufficient?
- How is time allocated for practitioners?
- How do you ensure this time is used effectively?
- Do you have parental permission?
- How else are parents involved?

## Key Term

Formative assessment – ongoing assessment.

## Did you know?

The Early Years Foundation Stage became mandatory for all settings from September 2008. For more information see www.standards.dfes.gov.uk/eyfs or www.teachernet.gov.uk.

## Requirements of the Early Years Foundation Stage

The Early Years Foundation Stage requires practitioners to carry out ongoing observation, but this does not mean that the observations and assessments that you make need to be detailed. It requires practitioners to look at each child and note what their particular interests and needs are and where their particular skills lie. Record only what you feel to be necessary and relevant and remember that you know far more about a child than you can ever write down.

## Keys to Good Practice

A good method to record and collate these observations is through learning diaries. These are a method of **formative assessment** and will inform or guide your everyday planning. These can be kept for the entire period of time that the child is with you. They can be arranged into the six areas of learning and development and should include items such as anecdotal observations, photos and learning stories. This information will help you to plan challenging and exciting experiences.

**Figure I:** Learning diaries are a great way to record and collate your observations

## Techniques of observation

It is important that most observations are planned carefully in order to get the maximum benefit in a minimum amount of time. First you must consider the aim of your observation. What is it that you want to see or find out? You may decide to carry out a broad observation that will give you a general overview of the child, or you may have something more specific in mind. Knowing your aim will help you to decide the method of observation that is most suitable.

## Keys to Good Practice

It is important to remember that some observations will not be planned but will occur spontaneously as practitioners see interesting or important events occur. This is just as useful as planned observations.

You will need to consider if you will be a **participant** or **non-participant observer**. A participant observer will join in with the planned observation and will be able to ask questions and to carry out certain tasks that are key to the aim of the observation. However, being a participant observer also has its disadvantages, as the child may behave differently when an adult is present, and may also feel uncomfortable or under pressure.

The alternative is to be a non-participant observer. This means that the adult will sit back from the situation and be unobtrusive throughout. The advantages of this are that the children are more likely to be themselves throughout the observation, and it is easier to record what is happening. Disadvantages include the likelihood of the child not performing the task that you wanted to see!

## Key Terms

**Participant observer** – an observer who joins in with the planned observation.

**Non-participant observer** – an observer who sits back from the observation and remains unobtrusive.

## Carrying out an observation

Once you have decided on the aim of the observation and if you will be a participant or non-participant observer, you can then go on to choose a method of observation. There are several recognised formats of observation that can be used and these include: a checklist, a written record or free description, a time sample and an event sample.

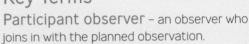

**Table I:** Checklist

| What is a checklist? | A checklist is a structured assessment showing children's development. It provides you with closed data. |
|---|---|
| Why is it used? | Checklists are used to assess children in particular areas. They are a good way of recording the developmental milestones of more than one child and can show you how they vary. They can also help you to focus on particular aspects of development. |
| What are the advantages? | <ul><li>Simple</li><li>Quick</li><li>Easy to use</li></ul> <ul><li>Can be repeated to check progress</li><li>Can be used with several children</li><li>Can design your own.</li></ul> |
| What are the disadvantages? | <ul><li>**Closed data**</li><li>Does not give a rounded picture</li><li>Only the skills assessed are recorded</li><li>Children might feel they have failed if they cannot do a task</li><li>Cannot record any other behaviour.</li></ul> |
| How is it used? | It can be used with children involved in free choice or structured activities, and you tick any skills as they are shown. There should be space for comments and the checklist used must be appropriate for the child's age and stage of development. |

## Points for Reflective Practice

- Have you used a checklist?
- Did you find it useful?
- Was it suitable for the aim of the observation?
- Did you need to be a participant or non-participant observer?
- Would you use it again?

## Key Terms

**Closed data** – refers to information that has just one meaning, and can be interpreted in just one way.

**Open data** – refers to information that could have more than one meaning, and can be interpreted in many ways.

**Table 2:** Written record

| What is a written record? (also known as free description) | A written record or a free description is a way of collecting **open data**. It is used for recording children's development and provides a snapshot of what a child was doing at a particular time. It is written in the present tense. |
|---|---|
| Why is it used? | It provides a record of events as they happen. |
| What are the advantages? | ■ Only need a pen and paper<br>■ Allows for spontaneous observations<br>■ Provides open data<br>■ Easy to do<br>■ You can record anything of interest. |
| What are the disadvantages? | ■ Can only be used for a short time<br>■ Can be difficult to record everything<br>■ Need to write up afterwards<br>■ Must write down key points. |
| How is it used? | It is used to write down as much as you can see and hear in the allocated period of time. It is usually only a few minutes long. You should always include the start and finish times. |

**Table 3:** Time sample

| What is a time sample? | A time sample assesses what a child does over a period of time. It helps you to gain a more complete picture of the child. You assess the child at regular intervals. |
|---|---|
| Why is it used? | Time samples are a useful way of doing assessments over a period of time. A child's activity is recorded over regular periods of time. It may look at specific behaviour or general activity. |
| What are the advantages? | ■ Can record activity over long periods<br>■ Open data<br>■ Simple<br>■ Specific behaviour and general activities can be observed<br>■ You can look at more than one child. |
| What are the disadvantages? | ■ Need good timekeeping<br>■ May miss important information or significant behaviour<br>■ May need to involve other adults. |
| How is it used? | You need to decide what behaviour you want to sample, the length of time in between samples and the number of samples. At the times decided, the observer watches what the child is doing and records it. |

## Points for Reflective Practice

- Have you used a written record or free description?
- Did you find it useful?
- Was it suitable for the aim of the observation?
- Did you need to be a participant or non-participant observer?
- Would you use it again?

## Points for Reflective Practice

- Have you used a time sample?
- Did you find it useful?
- Was it suitable for the aim of the observation?
- Did you need to be a participant or non-participant observer?
- Would you use it again?

**Table 4:** Event sample

| What is an event sample? | When using an event sample you record the behaviour you have decided to focus on every time it happens. |
|---|---|
| Why is it used? | An event sample is used to record the pattern or frequency of a particular behaviour. It is often used when there are concerns about a child. It is useful because it provides you with not only information on how often the behaviour happens but also why. |
| What are the advantages? | ■ Provides open data<br>■ Is quick and easy to use<br>■ Builds up a picture of specific behaviour. |
| What are the disadvantages? | ■ Needs to be carefully prepared<br>■ May need help from others. |
| How is it used? | Recording takes place when the behaviour happens. You will need to design a chart to meet your needs. |

## Points for Reflective Practice

- Have you used an event sample?
- Did you find it useful?
- Was it suitable for the aim of the observation?
- Did you need to be a participant or non-participant observer?
- Would you use it again?

## Ways of recording observations

As well as different methods, there are many different formats in which you can record observations. These are shown in Figure 2 on page 97.

## Using your observations in practice

The information that has been recorded will inform future planning and the parent/carers of the children's progress. Some information will be needed in the short term, while some will need to be kept for the longer term. It is important that any form of recording is not burdensome on staff and that the amount of paperwork is kept to a minimum.

**Figure 2:** There are many methods of recording information

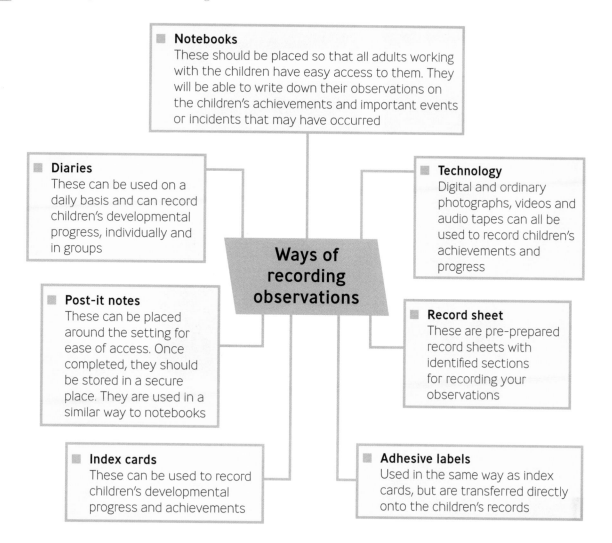

While observing children, adults can ask themselves questions which will help to lead to an evaluation of the setting and also help to identify the future training needs of staff. Key questions could include the following.

- Are the activities too easy or too difficult?
- How are the children using the resources?
- Is there anything missing that the children need?
- Are sufficient time/space provided for the experience?
- Are the children fully involved in the activity – if not why not?
- How independent are the children in their learning?
- Are the children able to work/play alongside/in cooperation with other children?
- Do the children need adult intervention?
- What needs to be done to encourage further learning?

Figure 3: Observations can be used to inform future planning

# Formative and summative assessments

Whilst you have a child in your care, you will probably complete many observations on them. At regular intervals, and when they leave your care, it is likely you will complete a report or summary of their development and achievements. These two things are known as **formative** and **summative assessment**.

Formative assessment means the ongoing observation and assessment you are making on the child. You have not reached a final conclusion, but instead are forming an opinion about the child, their strengths and weakness, and planning for the next steps.

Summative assessment means putting together a report or a summary about the child, based on your observations so far. This may be for a parents' evening, or because the child is changing settings or another professional has requested information on the child.

The Early Years Foundation Stage Profile is an example of this and it summarises children's progress towards the Early Learning Goals. It is important to recognise that the Early Learning Goals were not devised as assessment criteria. The eight profile statements are descriptions of children's achievements in the Early Years Foundation Stage, and are found in the EYFS Profile. The first three statements describe a child who is still progressing towards the Early Learning Goals. The next five statements are drawn from the Early Learning Goals themselves and the final statement in each scale describes a child who has achieved all the statements from one to eight on that scale, and is working consistently beyond the level of Early Learning Goals.

## Key Terms

**Formative assessment** – the ongoing observation and assessment you are making on the child.

**Summative assessment** – when you put together a report or a summary about the child, based on your observations so far.

# Validity and reliability

K4D804

It is important that all observations are **valid** and **reliable**, and all practitioners should make sure that they stay objective whilst observing. This means that they need to record exactly what is happening without interpreting it from their own point of view. It is important to record only what you see rather than what you think you know. This includes situations where you know a child can nearly do something, or that they have done it before.

There may be occasions where the child's behaviour is affected. These can include the child being excited, tired or unsettled. In these situations the observation is unlikely to give a true picture of the child's normal behaviour, and factors such as these should be recorded in the observation to make sure that others reading it are not misled.

It is also a good idea to carry out more than one observation of the child at different times and in different situations using different methods. This will give you a more rounded picture. Figure 4 on page 100 gives you different situations when a child could be observed.

## Key Terms

**Valid** – relevant and appropriate to the circumstances.

**Reliable** – can be trusted to be accurate.

There are many situations where children can be observed

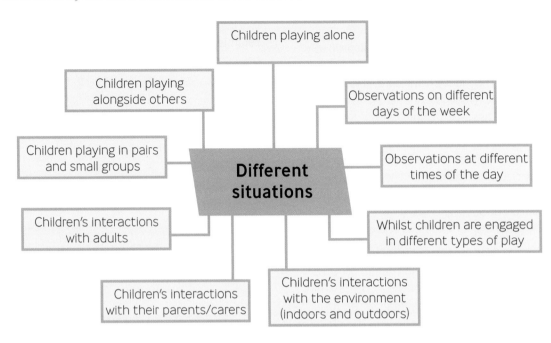

## 403.2 Ensure provision meets children's developmental needs

### Meeting children's developmental needs

This element deals with the norms of children development and the associated theories of development.

**K4D383**
**K4D384**
**K4D385** ### Understanding child development

There are five aspects of child development:

- social
- communication
- emotional.
- physical
- intellectual

Although children's **growth** and **development** is divided into five aspects, it is important to understand that development is holistic, or integrated. This means that while children are growing and developing, all of the five aspects of development are involved, rather than just one at a time. For example, while babies are developing fine and gross motor skills such as grasping and sitting, they are also developing language and communication skills by making sounds, and by interacting with others. This inter-relation occurs throughout a child's life.

It is also important to remember that children's skills will generally develop in the same sequence, for example, a child will learn to walk before they can run. All children will develop at different rates and this is because they have different experiences at different times. Because of this, it is important that adult expectations are realistic and that we do not expect too much from the children in our care.

### Key Terms

**Growth** – refers to the increase in physical size. This increase is measured by height, weight and by head circumference.

**Development** – refers to learning skills. These skills are normally learnt in a certain order, with the more simple skills learnt before the more difficult ones.

### Influences on child development

We have previously mentioned the holistic nature of child development, and this also applies to the many influences on children's development. Influences that affect one aspect of development are likely to affect other aspects too.

**Figure 5:** The main influences on child development

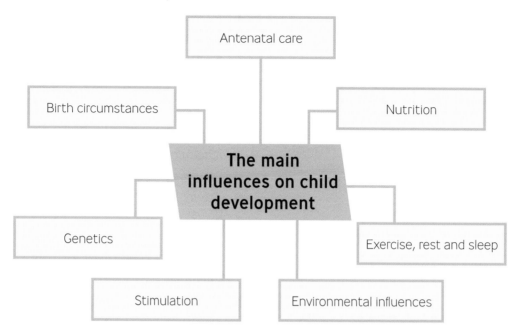

Antenatal care means the care of the health of the mother and of the unborn child during pregnancy. Specific tests are carried out during antenatal care, such as blood tests, urine tests, measurement of weight gain, palpitation of the abdomen and listening to the baby's heartbeat. If any warning signs of difficulties are detected during pregnancy, measures can be taken early on to deal with them and prevent long term effects. Lack of antenatal care may mean that developmental abnormalities and restricted growth in the unborn baby go undetected.

Birth circumstances can have an effect on the growth and physical development of children. Premature babies may have a low birth weight and may have difficulty in feeding and gaining weight. This may lead to their physical development becoming delayed. If they receive appropriate care they will gain weight and go on to make developmental progress. Low birth weight babies may have difficulty gaining weight and therefore could be more susceptible to illness. It is common for twins and multiple birth babies to have low birth weight.

Genes determine our sex and many other characteristics. In each cell of the human body there is a set of 46 chromosomes, arranged in 23 pairs. Chromosomes include all our genetic information. At conception 23 chromosomes come from the father and 23 come from the mother. Some genetic abnormalities

can result in inherited conditions such as Down syndrome and sickle cell anaemia.

Health and/or illness include short-term illness such as chickenpox and long-term illness such as cystic fibrosis and their impact on children's growth and physical development. Good health encourages children's growth and development, as they sleep and eat well and have more energy for exercise. This also means they are more able to fight infection, and will recover quickly from short-term illness.

Nutrition relates to children's diet and whether they are receiving balanced nutrition in relation to their age and stage of development. Exercise, rest and sleep relates to children's basic needs to maintain growth and physical developmental progress. Exercise helps to strengthen muscles and encourage sleep. Rest and sleep are important for growth and to allow children to relax.

Environmental influences include the effects of the mother's antenatal alcohol intake or use of prescribed or illegal drugs. It also includes the effect of one or both parents smoking tobacco. These factors can affect growth and physical development.

Stimulation can have a positive impact on children's growth and development. A stimulating environment will allow children the opportunity to explore, investigate and experiment. The adult role is equally important as adults can provide input and further stimulation. There is evidence to show that children deprived of stimulation may not develop all their cognitive abilities.

## Stages of child development

K4D807

The stages of child development shown below are examples of the norms that children can be expected to reach by a certain age. All children are different and one child may seem further ahead or behind than another.

## What is physical development?

Physical development is the increase in the size of the body and of muscle strength as children grow. It also includes the development of the control of the body.

Gross motor skills are those developed by the large muscles that control the spine and neck, arms, hands, feet and legs. They include walking, running and jumping.

Fine motor skills relate to the development of the manipulative skills of the fingers and/or toes. They include pointing, picking up objects and turning the pages of a book.

### 0–3 months

- At birth, the head will fall loosely if not supported
- By three months, can hold head erect and steady for several seconds
- Able to kick vigorously
- Able to open hands and fist
- By three months able to lift head up to 45 degrees when lying on their tummy
- Gazes attentively at faces
- Able to hold rattle briefly

### 3–6 months

- By six months may be able to lift head when lying on back
- Will try to grasp one or both feet
- Holds arms out to be lifted
- Rolls over from front to back and maybe visa versa
- If held in standing position may be able to bear some of own weight

### 6–9 months

- By nine months will be able to sit alone for up to fifteen minutes
- In sitting position, will lean forward to pick up toy without tumbling forward
- Tend to be very active and nappy changing can be difficult!
- May attempt to pull up to standing
- If held standing, will attempt to take steps
- Will get up on all fours and rock
- Attempts to crawl – sometimes succeeds, will often go backwards first
- Will attempt to drink from a beaker
- Plays with feet and may take them to the mouth

### 9–12 months

- Masters crawling or bottom shuffling
- May be able to crawl up stairs
- Can stand while supported
- Can raise self to sitting from lying
- May walk with help
- Can climb on low pieces of furniture
- May move around the room holding onto furniture
- Pokes at objects of interest with the index finger

### 12–18 months

- Begins to take steps independently
- May attempt to run
- Will go from bouncing to music to dancing, trotting and prancing
- Will begin to walk backwards
- Tries to kick a ball
- Will scribble with thick crayons
- Can hold spoon and cup
- Favours one hand
- Will walk up stairs
- Can build towers of blocks
- Can use door handles

### 18–24 months

- Walks well – stopping and starting safely
- Can hold a pencil and scribble with it
- Can turn pages – several at a time
- Feeds self with a spoon and can manage a cup without too much spilling

- Will try to help undressing by attempting to, and sometimes succeeding in, removing some items of clothing
- Can push and pull large toys or boxes on floor
- Runs confidently
- Rides large wheeled toys
- Draws circles, lines and dots
- Puts on shoes

### 2–3 years

- Eats skilfully, often managing to use a fork
- Helps with dressing
- Walks up and down stairs well
- Draws vertical line
- Can wash and dry hands
- Can jump and throw
- Walks and runs on tiptoes
- Enjoys climbing and sliding

### 3–7 years

- Can jump, hop and skip
- Able to ride a tricycle, progressing to a bike with stabilisers
- Throws and catches a ball
- Begins drawing circles and crossing, developing into recognisable figures leading to detailed drawings by 7 years
- Buttons front of clothes and uses large zips
- Beginning to use scissors competently
- Prints sentences
- Walks and runs on tiptoe
- Can kick a moving ball
- Learning to sew
- Beginning to tie shoelaces

### 7–12 years

- From about 10 years girls may begin to develop breasts and broader hips and may also grow body hair
- From about 10 years in girls and 12 years in boys there is usually a considerable growth spurt
- Develops coordination and balance in sport and other physical activities
- Controls speed when running
- Develops strength for games like tennis

- Plays sport with increased skill
- Increased manipulative skills
- Manually dexterous, and writes well
- Good computer skills with keyboard and mouse

### 12–16 years

- The feet and hands of most adolescents will reach their adult size before they gain their ultimate height
- Bodies change as children enter puberty
- May become good at a particular sport

## What is communication development?

Communication development involves the development of language and other communication skills and includes verbal and non-verbal communication. Children will gain a huge amount of complex language during their early years. It involves learning to use communication and understanding the communications of others. There are strong links to intellectual development.

### 0–3 months

- Startled by sudden loud noises
- Cries when hungry, uncomfortable or annoyed
- After about six weeks begins to coo in response to carers
- Can imitate low and high sounds
- By three months will show excitement at the sound of approaching voices or footsteps
- Will begin to laugh out loud and squeal in delight

### 3–6 months

- Will turn in the direction of a parent's voice
- Vocalises tunefully to self and others in a sing-song fashion
- Laughs, chuckles and squeals aloud when playing.
- Will scream with annoyance
- Tries to mimic sounds, watches speaker's mouth closely
- Enjoys rhymes

### 6–9 months

- Very attentive to everyday sounds, particularly others' voices
- Babbles loudly
- Will shout for attention, wait for response and shout again

- Beginning to understand turn-taking in conversations
- Understands 'no' and knows own name
- Enjoys holding 'conversations'

### 9–12 months

- Beginning to say simple words
- Understanding of language developing daily
- Babbles – sounds like conversation

### 12–18 months

- Likes to sing
- Says several words
- Can say 'no' and shake head
- Listens to sound-making toys and will repeat actions to make the sounds again
- May make first sentence.
- Communicates needs by vocalising and pointing
- Understands what is being said

### 18–24 months

- Jabbers loudly and continually to self
- Listens to others when they speak to him/her.
- Vocabulary increasing
- Often echoes last word of speaker's sentences (echolalia)
- Can point to and name some familiar pictures and objects
- May join two words together

### 2–3 years

- Vocabulary increasing but still many mistakes in grammar
- Continually asking questions
- Enjoys simple familiar stories
- Continually asks questions: 'why' and 'what'?
- Remembers and repeats songs and rhymes
- Talks to self while playing
- Longer sentences are used

### 3–7 years

- Large vocabulary
- Still asking many questions
- Can recite simple nursery rhymes
- Can carry out a good conversation
- Can learn more than one language

- Applies grammatical rules to all words unaware that some words have irregular forms e.g. 'I goed'
- Speech is clear and understandable
- Verbal negotiation with peers
- May 'answer back' to adults
- Enjoys jokes
- Tells stories from memory
- Holds long conversations
- Listening skills improve

### 7–12 years

- Expresses self clearly and fluently
- Participates in family discussions
- Reasons
- Reads a range of books by themselves
- Enjoys discussion and debate
- Discusses a variety of topics with knowledge and understanding

### 12–16 years

- Communication skills are excellent, although young people prefer to talk to their friends rather than adults
- May be reluctant to ask adults for advice or help

## What is intellectual and learning development?

Intellectual and learning development is about the way our thought processes develop. It also concerns our ability to think, reason, understand and learn and includes memory and recall. Cognitive development also includes understanding concepts such as time, size, shape and colour.

### 0–3 months

- Will recognise parents and respond to their approaches
- Will play with hands and feet
- At birth will look at high contrast pictures
- By three months will like detailed high contrast pictures
- Initiates social interaction within their first six weeks
- Their five senses are well developed from birth
- They can recognise the smell of their own mother and her voice within their first week of life
- Babies are also sensitive to touch and respond to comforting, cosy materials

### 3–6 months

- Objects if you try to take a toy away
- Will try to reach an object just out of grasp
- Will look for dropped toy
- Becomes aware that people and objects have names, labels, etc.
- Explores things by tasting
- Their sight is developed enough to respond to changes in shapes and patterns
- Babies show an awareness of object permanence

### 6–9 months

- May be able to wave bye-bye
- Can concentrate on chosen toys or activities for minutes at a time
- Will find partially hidden toys
- Their sense of taste is also developed as they are fed breast or formula milk and then progress to weaning to solid foods.

### 9–12 months

- Starts to understand phrases, e.g. 'come to Daddy'
- Will explore by touching everything
- May hand over an object on request
- Enjoys and anticipates daily routine

### 12–18 months

- Understands cause and effect
- Starts to pretend
- Beginning to remember separation, but anxiety eases as they start to remember that the parent returns
- Can match shapes
- Can point to familiar objects in simple pictures
- They recognise routines such as mealtimes, bath time and bedtime
- Toddlers can find hidden objects and remember where the biscuit tin is kept
- Their favourite question is 'What's that?'

### 18–24 months

- Enjoys nursery rhythms and tries to join in
- Remembers where objects belong
- Briefly imitates everyday activities e.g. feeding doll, reading book
- Understands and obeys simple instructions

- Will point to own or doll's hair, shoes, nose etc.
- Points to objects named by adult
- Obeys simple requests
- Wants to explore and investigate everything in reach
- Solves simple puzzles
- Uses trial and error when exploring

### 2–3 years

- Can follow two-step instructions
- Can identify familiar people by naming them
- Intensely curious about own world
- Matches colours
- Sorts objects into simple categories
- Solves more complex puzzles

### 3–7 years

- Knows names of many colours
- Knows full name and sometimes age
- Counts by rote but little concept of quantities beyond two or three
- Some appreciation of difference between past, present and future
- At 5 years old most children are in primary school and begin formal learning. This is the time when literacy and numeracy skills develop
- Remembers past events
- Concentrates on activities and completes them
- Shows interest in reading and writing
- Begins to develop concepts of quantity
- Begins to understand basic scientific principles
- Learns to tell the time
- Plays board games with understanding and skill
- Attention span increases

### 7–12 years

- More complex cognitive skills are developed
- Reading and writing becomes fluent and skilled
- Begin to use logical reasoning
- Understand concepts of weight and size
- Understand the value of coins
- Interested in reading books for research for project work
- Develops interests or hobbies.
- Considers all aspects of situations

- May understand abstract concepts

**12–16 years**

- Exam curriculum is followed and academic knowledge increases
- Young people are beginning to think about further education

## What is social, emotional and behavioural development?

Social, emotional and behavioural is about how children develop an awareness of themselves, how they feel about themselves and others, and how they interact in society. It includes understanding acceptable behaviour and understanding and controlling your emotions and feelings.

**0–3 months**

- The newborn will sleep for the majority of the time
- Feelings expressed by crying, vocalising and smiling
- Baby will begin to stop crying when picked up and soothed
- Babies will observe their carers' faces closely while being fed, changed, bathed and talked to
- Within their first two weeks babies are imitating facial expressions they see
- Babies as young as four to six weeks old are initiating social activity by smiling and vocalising
- Will recognise familiar adults and smile in response to their approaches
- At three months will begin to react to familiar situations and routines

**3–6 months**

- Will regard and play with feet as well as hands
- Will pat bottle or breast when being fed
- Will reach for and shake a rattle
- Passes objects from hand to hand
- Loves social interactions
- Sometimes at end of this period becomes shy of strangers
- Greets parent
- Beginning to discover what they can do thus creating a sense of self
- Shows feelings such as excitement

**6–9 months**

- May show distress at separation

- Will play 'give-and-take' with toys and household objects
- Will enjoy the company of other children and will play alongside them
- At around nine months old babies will clearly express emotions such as pleasure with laughs and squeals and may have words to express annoyance
- They will hold out their arms to be lifted and cuddled when distressed
- Clearly distinguishes strangers from familiars.
- Will imitate hand clapping and try to play peek-a-boo
- May copy others' facial expressions
- When being carried, will sit upright and look around

**9–12 months**

- Enjoys mimicking others
- Will watch other children at play but will not join in
- Loves being praised
- Will play same game over and over e.g. peek-a-boo Loves playing games and laughs often

**12–18 months**

- Children regularly return to their parent or carer for reassurance
- May express their frustration in 'toddler tantrums'
- May show jealousy if their mother/carer holds or pays attention to another child or baby
- Will attempt to comfort a sibling or another child who is crying
- Likes to look at books
- Waves bye-bye
- Laughs at funny things
- Starts to show temper when angry
- Very emotional, laughing and crying within short space of time
- Likes to be constantly within sight or hearing of familiar adult
- Demonstrates affection
- Will begin to indicate wet or soiled nappy

**18–24 months**

- Solitary play
- No concept of sharing
- May attend mother and toddler group
- Requires reassuring presence of familiar adult

- Plays contentedly alone but likes to be near familiar adults or children
- Enjoys putting small objects in and out of small containers
- Enjoys shows of affection.
- Demonstrates wide range of emotions
- Temper tantrums may be frequent

**2–3 years**

- Becomes more independent
- Begins simple cooperative play
- Likes routine
- Possessive of personal belongings
- Sits with family for meals
- May have tantrums when frustrated
- Develops self-feeding skills
- Beginning to engage in pretend play
- Able to pull pants down at toilet but may need help pulling them up
- Very active, restless and resistant to any form of restraint
- Frequent tantrums
- Can be very clingy
- Likes to play near others but does not tend to join in
- No concept of sharing

**3–7 years**

- Becomes interested in playing with other children
- A lot of make believe play
- Usually potty trained
- Likes to help adults
- Understands sharing but sometimes needs help to put it into practice!
- Shows affection towards younger siblings and children
- Temper tantrums not as frequent
- Complex cooperative play
- Has sense of 'mine' and 'yours'
- Has increased self-confidence
- May attend playgroup/nursery
- May have imaginary friend
- Chooses own friends
- Willing to share

- May defy parents as they assert independence
- Is able to negotiate verbally
- Makes efforts to control temper
- Cooperative and sympathetic
- Increased confidence
- Aware of different emotions
- Strong awareness of 'right' and 'wrong'
- May be frightened of the dark and/or imagined monsters
- May join after-school activities

**7–12 years**

- Peer group increasingly important
- Chooses best friend
- Joins clubs/organisations
- Plays in single-sex groups
- Finds it difficult to cope with being teased
- Strongly desires independence
- May join sports team
- Likes privacy to be respected
- May defy adult authority
- Awareness of the opposite sex

**12–16 years**

- Desire to be independent
- Strong desire to fit in with peers
- Concerns about physical appearance
- Pressure from school and exams is felt
- Morals, beliefs and values are formed
- May swing between maturity and childish behaviour
- Mood swings are experienced
- May not agree with parents

## Theoretical perspectives

K4D806

There are many theories that look into the way children develop and why they behave as they do. The main theories are discussed below. Most are based on observation and studies of children over time. Being aware of these theories helps us to understand why children act as they do and improves our knowledge and practice.

Figure 6: The main theories of social, emotional and behavioural development

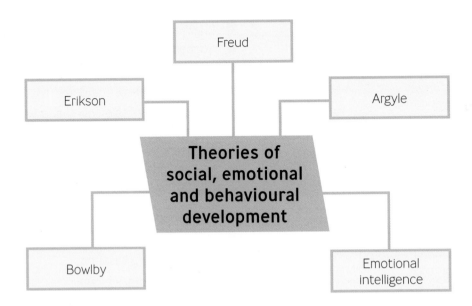

Figure 6: The main theories of social, emotional and behavioural development

## Theories of social, emotional and behavioural development

Theorists have been looking at the question 'What makes me the way I am?' for many years. It has not yet been fully answered but we do know that we are all different and our childhood has a huge effect on our personality.

There are many theories surrounding social, emotional and behavioural development.

### S. Freud (1856–1939)

Freud was the first theorist to believe that we have an unconscious mind. He was interested in the way people say and do things without always realising that they are doing them, for example, sucking the top of a pen or fiddling with hair.

Freud suggested our unconscious mind is split into three parts: the id, the ego and the super-ego. These three parts are not all present at birth, but develop gradually as the child develops.

The id is the instinctive part of our personality and represents our needs and wants. It is unable to consider the needs of other people. All babies will have only the id when they are born, and they will cry until their needs are met. When these needs have been met then this is known as gratification. Freud believed that the id works on the pleasure principle – everything happens in order to achieve pleasure.

The ego emerges a little later in development, usually within the first few months. It has a planning role and it considers how to meet the id's needs in the best way. For example, a baby may learn that by smiling, or by crying they are more likely to have their needs met. The ego may also make the id wait to have its needs met. This is known as deferred gratification, or common sense! Freud believed that the ego works on the reality principle – we will get as much satisfaction from the world as is possible.

The super-ego develops later in childhood, normally around four to six years. It is part of our moral development. The super-ego tries to control the ego. There are two parts to the super-ego: the conscience and the ego-ideal.

The conscience punishes the ego if it misbehaves. The ego-ideal rewards the ego if it shows good behaviour. Freud thought that our subconscious minds struggle with the id and the super-ego – what we really want, against what is the right thing to do

### E. Erikson (1902–1994)

Erikson was a student of Freud and was influenced by his work. He agreed personality was divided into three parts (id, ego, and super-ego). He also believed that the social environment a child grew up in affected their personality. He extended this to show that our personalities were not fixed were continually changing throughout our lives.

**Table 5:** Erikson's life stages

| Age | Dilemma | Effect on Personality |
|---|---|---|
| 0–1 | Trust vs. Mistrust | If babies' needs are not met, they may decide the world is hostile and this makes it harder for them to form relationships |
| 1–3 | Autonomy vs. Shame and Doubt | Children who successfully complete this stage feel secure and confident, while those who do not are left with a sense of inadequacy and self-doubt |
| 3–6 | Initiative vs. Guilt | Children who are successful at this stage feel capable and able to lead others. Those who fail to gain these skills are left with a sense of guilt, self-doubt, and lack of initiative |
| 6–12 | Industry vs. Inferiority | Children in this stage are capable of learning new skills and gaining new knowledge and if they are sucessful at this, develop a sense of industry. If children feel inadequate then this can lead to problems with self-esteem and inferiority |
| 12–18 | Identity vs. Role Confusion | From this stage onwards we begin to affect our development by our own actions. Adolescents are attempting to find their identity and place in the world and if they are unsuccessful in doing so this could lead to role confusion |
| 19–40 | Intimacy vs. Isolation | Those who are successful at this stage will develop relationships that are committed and secure. Those who are not will have a poor sense of self |
| 40–65 | Generativity vs. Stagnation | Those who are successful during this stage will feel that they are contributing to the world by being active in their home and community. Those who fail to attain this stage will feel unproductive and uninvolved in the world |
| 65–death | Ego Integrity vs. Despair | Those who are unsuccessful during this stage will feel that their life has been wasted and will experience many regrets. Those who feel proud of their accomplishments will feel a sense of integrity |

Erikson called his stages of personality development 'life stages' (there are eight of these, with two possible outcomes) and believed that they were linked to social stages. He saw each stage as a dilemma and considered that how we cope with this dilemma affects our personalities and how they develop. In order for children to successfully work through each of the dilemmas, they must have enough confidence. Failure to work through a stage may lead to difficulty in completing the other stages and thus lead to an unhealthy personality.

## J. Bowlby (1907–1990)

Bowlby was one of the first theorists to recognise that babies and young children need strong and stable relationships. He conducted a series of studies of children living in orphanages in the 1950s, looking at the effect that this had on them. He found that if children are deprived of a relationship with a primary carer, they are more likely to have behavioural problems in later life. This research changed childcare practice

at the time and is the reason why there are such high adult to child ratios for the under twos (1:3), and also why parents/carers are now enabled to stay with their children in hospital. The key points of his theory are as follows.

- Children who have been separated from their parents at an early stage, are more likely to suffer behavioural problems later on in life.
- Attachment is instinctive in babies and an attachment must be formed by the time they are 12 months old.
- Fear of strangers is also instinctive, and begins from around 8 months old.
- The first five years in life are the most important in a person's development.
- A child's relationships have an enormous effect on the child's overall development.

Bowlby also believed there were three stages of separation anxiety.

1. Protest – children cry, struggle, kick and are angry when their primary carer leaves.

2. Despair – calmer behaviour is shown, children may be withdrawn and show comfort behaviour such as thumb sucking.

3. Detachment – the child may seem to be over the separation and start to join in with the activities on offer. The child is coping with the separation by trying to forget the relationship.

## Keys to Good Practice

The next time a child starts at your setting, think carefully about your practice and about how the child is forming attachments. Observe how the child reacts upon leaving its parent or carer and compare your observations to Bowlby's Theory of Attachment. What stage of separation anxiety are you seeing?

You could extend this activity by researching further into John Bowlby and reflecting upon how your findings may affect the policies and procedures of your setting.

## Emotional intelligence

Emotional Intelligence is a relatively new theory. It considers the idea that there is a type of intelligence that is related to social and emotional development, in addition to intelligence related to intellectual development. The first theorist to look at this idea was Howard Gardner, although others have looked further into the subject.

It is believed having a good level of Emotional Intelligence Quotient (EQ) is just as important as having a good level of Intelligence Quotient (IQ). Emotional Intelligence is essential for effective learning. If a child has good EQ they will be happier, with higher self esteem. They will also perform better at school and grow up to become well-rounded adults.

Emotional Intelligence is made up of five characteristics and abilities as shown in Figure 7.

It is important that we teach children the following skills, to assist with their EQ and to make sure they understand how to learn:

- confidence
- curiosity
- cooperation.
- self-control
- communication

**Figure 7:** The five characteristics and abilities of emotional intelligence

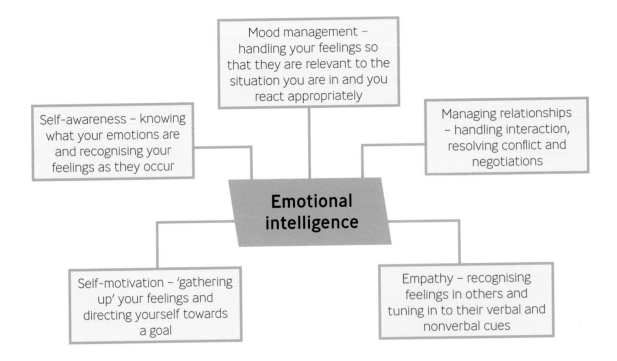

These are skills that can be taught in childcare settings, through day-to-day activities and through adults who are supportive. We can give children confidence by allowing them to take safe risks and try new things, and then praising them for their efforts as well as their achievements. We can encourage curiosity by providing new activities and experiences and giving them time to explore them. We can encourage self-control by making sure children are aware of their feelings, what they are and how to deal with them. Communication can be encouraged through constant conversation, about everyday things as well as asking and answering questions. Cooperation can be encouraged by allowing children to resolve conflict for themselves and by helping them to negotiate and compromise.

### Argyle (1925–2002)

Argyle looked at identity issues in children. He believed that there are four influences on the development of self-concept in young people.

- The reaction of others – young people are conscious and concerned about the way that others reaction to them, for example, what will their friends say and think if they get a new haircut or new clothes?
- Comparison with others – am I as good as my peers? Young people will often model themselves on someone they view as a role model.
- Social roles – where do young people see themselves as fitting in society? Do they have strong family ties, or are they closer to their peers?
- Identification – young people like to fit in. They have a need to have something in common or the need to identify with each other.

It is important that practitioners who work with older children are aware of these four influences. Supporting them through these will lead to children having a good self-concept and high self-esteem and confidence.

## Theories of communication development

There are several theories that consider how we learn to communicate. Some are based on the idea that language is instinctive, and some theories are based on the idea that children learn to communicate because they have been exposed to language. All agree that there is a strong link between language and cognitive development.

Two of the main theories have been proposed by Skinner and Chomsky.

It is generally accepted that babies are born with some inbuilt sense of language. Adults help children to learn the rules of communication, so adult interaction and support is therefore vital for good communication development. Adults should try to use shorter, repetitive sentences, use clear facial expressions, talk to babies frequently and be responsive to their communications.

### B. F. Skinner (1904–1990)

Skinner was a behaviourist theorist. Behaviourists believe that all behaviour is learned and can be shaped. Skinner carried out a wide range of experiments, most of which were on animals. His work is also applied to child development. Skinner believed that children learn language by reinforcement and that sounds which are not recognised are not reinforced. This explains why by the time a baby is nine months old their babbling consists of the sounds they are listening to.

The theory that language is learnt by imitation does not explain why children make sentences and words that they have not heard, such as 'daddy gone'.

### N. A. Chomsky (1928– )

Chomsky is an American professor of linguistics. He is opposed to Skinner's view and instead believes that language development is instinctive. His argument has stimulated experiment and thinking about language. Chomsky believes we are born with a cognitive ability to learn language and this includes learning the structure and grammar. He calls this ability a Language Acquisition Device.

He believes that this explains how children can work out the rules of grammar without being taught. For example, they quickly learn that 'the dog bit the duck' is very different from 'the duck bit the dog'.

It also explains why children make mistakes they would not have heard from adults around them such as 'I drinked it all'. He thinks that this shows children understand grammar and are trying to use it.

## Theories of physical development

There are few theories on physical development. We know that it happens and we know why it happens. The main theorist to look at physical development is Arnold Gessell.

## Arnold Gessell (1880–1961)

Arnold Gessell suggested there were three key principles to physical development.

- Development follows a definite sequence. Certain movements have to be in place before others can follow. For example a baby has to learn to sit before it can walk and children have to walk before they can skip and run.
- Development begins with the control of the head and continues downwards and outwards. This is a survival mechanism to allow babies to feed. They will initially learn how to lift the head and control the neck muscles.
- Development is uncontrolled and then becomes refined. The movements that babies make are uncontrolled to begin with and then they gradually gain control of the arms, wrists and hands.

We are all born with a central nervous system. Babies are born with survival reflexes. As babies mature, the body learns how to read and control these reflexes and they become less involuntary and evolve into voluntary movements. Physical development is underpinned by the brain and spinal cord. They collect information from the senses, respond to it, and send information back to the muscles. This happens very quickly, think of a time you have touched something hot!

Gessell also suggested that the maturation of the central nervous system underpinned development and that stimulation did not have a significant role. However, we now understand that stimulation is very important.

## Theories of learning and cognitive development

There are many theories about how children learn and these can be classed as either behaviourist or constructivist.

### Behaviourist theory

Behaviourists believe that learning is influenced by rewards, and by punishments. They often use the term 'conditioning'. This means you learn your behaviour because your past experiences have taught you to do or not to do something. Behaviourist theorists include Ivan Pavlov and B. F. Skinner.

### Constructivist theory

Constructivists believe that the child is an active learner, and learns through exploration and trial and error. They construct or build up their thoughts according to their experiences. Constructivist theorists include Jean Piaget, Lev Vygotsky and Jerome Bruner.

## Classical and operant conditioning

There are two main types of conditioning: classical conditioning and operant conditioning.

### I. Pavlov (1849–1936) and classical conditioning

Ivan Pavlov was conducting a study on dogs' digestive systems. He noticed they salivated before food was put down for them and concluded the dogs were anticipating the food. He also concluded the dogs associated the arrival of food with footsteps and buckets. He carried out an experiment where he fed the dogs while a bell was sounded. In the case of Pavlov's dogs, they began to associate the bell with food and salivated when hearing it. This is an example of classical conditioning.

### Skinner (1904–1990) and operant conditioning

Operant conditioning is based on the idea that learning is based on reinforcements or consequences that follow the initial behaviour. Skinner proposed that we also learn through making our own conclusions about the consequences of our behaviour. This means we are active and involved in our learning – unlike the theory of classical conditioning.

Skinner divided the consequences of actions into three groups, as shown in Table 6.

**Table 6:** Skinner's consequences of actions

| I. | Positive reinforcers (pleasant experiences) | If we get something we want then we are more likely to repeat the behaviour. In this way, positive reinforcement is a good way of encouraging new learning |
|---|---|---|
| 2. | Negative reinforcers (bad experiences) | Negative reinforcers will also make us repeat the behaviour, but the difference is that we repeat the behaviour to stop something from happening again |
| 3. | Punishers | These should act as a deterrent to repeating the behaviour |

Operant conditioning highlights that most behaviours are a response to a stimulus. To try and understand the processes involved in how behaviour is influenced or shaped, the ABC continuum was developed. 'A' stands for 'antecedent' – an event happens and as a result the person engages in certain behaviour, 'B', which is a response to 'A' immediately, or soon after the behaviour, and 'C' the consequences of the behaviour. ABC charts have been used in social care services. Many services have developed ABC charts so that they can try to understand the broader environment a person lives in.

Operant conditioning is often used to encourage children to show wanted behaviour and it is a powerful form of learning. Skinner also found that unpredictable reinforcement works better than continual reinforcement. This teaches us not to expect a reward every time and it follows that we will continue to show the behaviour in case a reward is given. Children need frequent positive reinforcement as this helps them learn wanted behaviour, which eventually will become automatic behaviour.

If reinforcement is delayed then this weakens the effect of the reinforcement. This applies to positive and negative reinforcers and to punishers. Immediate positive reinforcement is most effective as the behaviour is then linked strongly to the reinforcement. Positive reinforcement should not be given for unwanted behaviour, as this will further encourage it.

Examples of positive reinforcement include:

- giving adult attention
- giving praise
- giving a sticker
- using a 'star chart' where the child is given a star or similar for displaying wanted behaviour
- emphasising the positive behaviour 'Well done for sitting so well!'
- giving the child some responsibility 'You can help me get the outside toys out'.

## Did you know?

Skinner developed the idea of operant conditioning, but the first theorist to identify it was Edward Thorndike (1874–1949). Thorndike developed the law of effect, which says that: 'If a response is followed by a satisfying state of affairs it tends to be repeated. Other responses fade away'.

## J. Piaget (1896–1980) and schemas

Piaget had a great interest in the intellectual development of children. His work has influenced the way children are taught. His overall conclusion was that children were not less intelligent than adults, they simply think in different ways. He also felt that there should be little intervention from adults.

He suggested children constructed or built up their thoughts according to their experiences. He called this conclusion or thought a 'schema' (a pattern of repeatable behaviour). Piaget felt that learning was an ongoing process and he believed that children adapt their schemas when they have new experiences. He used specific vocabulary to describe this learning.

- Assimilation – the child constructs a theory, or takes in information.
- Equilibrium – the experiences that the child has seem to fit their schema.
- Disequilibrium – something happens to cause the child to doubt their schema.
- Accommodation – the child adapts the original schema so their new ideas fit.

## J. Piaget and conceptual development

Piaget felt that as well as learning about their world by developing and adapting schemas, children also passed through four stages of conceptual development: object permanence; egocentrism; animism; and conservation.

1. Object permanence
   - Babies do not have a mental picture of the world.
   - They learn through their senses.
   - If they cannot see an object, they believe it no longer exists.
   - At about 8 months, if they are shown an object and it is hidden, they look for it, or cry.

2. Egocentrism
   - Children under 6 or 7 tend to be 'self-centred' in the way they view the world.
   - This does not mean they are selfish.
   - It does mean they do not yet understand the views of others.
   - For example, they do not understand that what you can see depends on where you are sitting.

3. Animism

- Children under 6 or 7 tend to imagine that objects and animals have the same thoughts and feelings as they have.

- For example, if a child bumped into a table, that child may say 'naughty table!'.

- Children's drawings often show animism, for example, a cat with a smile.

4. Conservation

- Piaget had several tests to see if children could understand that even if a material changed shape or form, its other properties would remain the same.

- This included showing children two identical glasses of water, then pouring one glass into a taller and thinner glass. A child who could conserve knew the amounts were still the same.

- He suggested that children under 6 could not conserve.

## J. Piaget and stages of learning

Piaget felt there were four stages of learning. These are: sensory motor, pre-operational, concrete operations and formal operations.

Piaget called the concept of being able to see things from someone else's view 'de-centring'.

## L. Vygotsky (1896–1934) and the zone of proximal development

Vygotsky was a Russian theorist whose ideas had a lot of influence in the 1990s. He was one of the first academics to disagree with Jean Piaget. Vygotsky believed that the social environment that children lived in and the experiences that children had were very important. He saw children as 'apprentices' who learnt through being with others. He also thought that play enabled children to understand and accommodate what they have learnt and he believed this was because children are free from any constraints during play and can explore their ideas fully.

Vygotsky believed play enabled children to move from their present thinking to a higher level and he also believed that the role of the adult was important. He believed that adults could stretch children so they developed ideas and thinking in their play. Vygotsky believed that play experiences should be focused on what children could do in the next stage. This stage was called the 'zone of proximal development' (we might call it 'potential'). When translated from Russian, proximal means next or nearby.

Vygotsky also talked of 'scaffolding', which he saw as a way of enabling children to find their way to the top of a problem. Adults create a scaffold by maintaining interest, giving support and pointing out information. This is the main difference from Piaget's theory.

Table 7: Piaget's stages of learning

| Stage | Title | Age | Stage of learning | Links to Piaget's other theories |
|---|---|---|---|---|
| **Stage one** | Sensory motor | 0–2 | Babies learn about the environment from their senses and from trial and error | They are egocentric<br>They develop object permanence |
| **Stage two** | Pre-operational | 2–7 | Children are starting to use language to express their thoughts and are starting to use symbols in play | They are egocentric<br>They think animals and non living objects have feelings – animism |
| **Stage three** | Concrete operations | 7–11 | Children can use abstract symbols such as writing and numbers. They are developing reasoning skills | Children can see things from another's point of view – decentring<br>Children are less fooled by appearances – they are able to conserve |
| **Stage four** | Formal operations | 11–18 | He felt children would be logical and methodical and can think in the abstract (in their heads) | He suggested that not everyone would move onto this stage |

## J. Bruner (1915– ) and the modes of thinking

Bruner agreed with many areas of Piaget's work, but built on the ideas of Vygotsky. Bruner proposed the idea that they developed different ways of thinking and he called these 'modes of thinking'.

There are three modes; children start with one and develop the other two. The modes of thinking are: enactive, iconic and symbolic.

### Enactive

- Children develop this way of thinking at 0 to 1 years.
- Information is stored according to physical movements.
- When something has to be remembered, the movement is recreated.
- Adults use this when making movements such as plastering a wall, sewing or typing.
- It is important that children have real first-hand experiences to help their thought processes to develop.

### Iconic

- Children develop this way of thinking between 1 and 7 years.
- Information is stored using images which may be based on smell, hearing or touch. A smell can trigger a memory.
- Books and interest tables are useful aids to help children recall prior experiences.
- He felt the development of children's language was the key to children moving from the iconic to symbolic mode.

### Symbolic

- Children develop this way of thinking from 7 years old onwards
- As not everything can be pictured, we use symbols such as language, music and numbers to store information.

Bruner's aim was not to teach children, but to allow them to reach their own solutions. He also felt that older children could guide other children and that adults have a very important role by working alongside children and asking questions. Bruner believed that cognitive development could be sped up if children were stimulated. He also promoted the idea of a 'spiral curriculum' – this is where children learn through exploration and investigation with the help of adults, who are able to provide opportunities for them to return to the same activities but at a higher level of complexity. This extends and deepens learning.

## Promote the development of children

K4D808
K4D809
K4D810
K4D811

### The Early Years Foundation Stage

The Early Years Foundation Stage is part of the 10-year childcare strategy and the Children Act 2006. It provides a single quality framework that covers babies from birth until the end of their first year in reception class (from 0 to 5 years). It then becomes the foundation for learning and development when children progress into Key Stage 1. It replaces Birth to Three Matters and the Foundation Stage but at the same time strengthens the links between these two frameworks. Some information from these aforementioned packs has been taken over into the Early Years Foundation Stage. It also incorporates the National Standards for Under 8s Day Care and Childminding.

The Early Years Foundation Stage has an integrated approach to care and education and also has a principled play-based approach. This helps practitioners and settings to deliver a consistent approach to the care, learning and development of the children in their settings right from birth to the end of the Foundation Stage. It also helps practitioners to ensure that this approach is right for each child at their individual stage of development.

The main aim of the Early Years Foundation Stage is to help babies and young children achieve the five Every Child Matters outcomes, which are as follows:

- Stay Safe
- Be Healthy
- Achieve Economic Well being
- Make a Positive Contribution
- Enjoy and Achieve.

The Early Years Foundation Stage will achieve this aim by being based on the following principles:

- Setting Standards
- Promoting Equality of Opportunity
- Creating a Framework for Partnership Working
- Improving Quality and Consistency
- Laying a Secure Foundation for Future Learning and Development.

The Early Years Foundation Stage will help childcare settings to improve on quality and thus to improve the service and experiences they offer to children and their families. This will be a continuous process and will be achieved by building on existing practice and through using reflective practice.

## Themes, principles and commitments

There are four guiding themes to the Early Years Foundation Stage and each theme is backed up by a principle that underpins effective practice. Each theme is also broken down into four commitments that describe how the principle can be put into practice. These principles underpin the Early Years Foundation Stage and the rest of the framework relates back to these. Everything you offer children needs to show these principles in action. The wall poster shows the commitments in compact format, and the associated 'principles into practice' cards go into further detail. The themes are arranged to show the needs of the child come first, and that learning follows on.

**Table 8:** EYFS themes, principles and commitments

| Theme | A Unique Child |
|---|---|
| Principle | Every child is a competent learner from birth who can be resilient, capable, confident and self-assured. |
| Commitment | 1.1 Child Development<br>1.2 Inclusive Practice<br>1.3 Keeping Safe<br>1.4 Health and Well being |

| Theme | Positive Relationships |
|---|---|
| Principle | Children learn to be strong and independent from a base of loving and secure relationships with parents and/or a key person |
| Commitment | 3.1 Observation, Assessment and Planning<br>3.2 Supporting Every Child<br>3.3 The Learning Environment<br>3.4 The Wider Context |

| Theme | Enabling Environments |
|---|---|
| Principle | The environment plays a key role in supporting and extending children's development and learning |
| Commitment | 3.1 Observation, Assessment and Planning<br>3.2 Supporting Every Child<br>3.3 The Learning Environment<br>3.4 The Wider Context |

| Theme | Learning and Development |
|---|---|
| Principle | Children develop and learn in different ways and at different rates and all areas of learning and development are equally important and interconnected |
| Commitment | 4.1 Play and Exploration<br>4.2 Active Learning<br>4.3 Creativity and Critical Thinking<br>4.4 Areas of Learning and Development |

## The Early Years Foundation Stage Pack

The Early Years Foundation Stage pack is made up of five parts:

1. Statutory framework
2. Practice guidance
3. Principles into practice cards
4. Wall poster
5. CD-ROM.

### 1. Statutory framework

This document sets out all the legal requirements of the Early Years Foundation Stage relating to Learning, Development and Welfare. All providers must meet these requirements. It also includes detailed guidance and information about childcare provider's obligations under the framework. This guidance must be taken into account and providers must have clear reasons if they chose not to follow it. Ofsted will base their inspection judgements on whether the general and specific legal guidelines have been met and if providers have followed the guidance given.

### 2. Practice guidance

This document contains essential advice and guidance for all practitioners working with children from birth to five.

The practice guidance booklet contains Learning and Development guidance. This supports the continuous assessment of children and can be used as a reference for planning. It is also designed to assist with assessment, but should NOT be used as a checklist and should not be developed into one. It can, however, be seen as a learning map. There are six areas of Learning and Development:

- Personal, Social and Emotional Development
- Problem Solving, Reasoning and Numeracy
- Communication, Language and Literacy
- Creative Development
- Physical Development
- Knowledge and Understanding of the World.

The sections are split into four columns:

- Development Matters: this column identifies the knowledge, skills and understanding that children will need in order for them to achieve the Early Learning Goals. (The Early Learning Goals are highlighted in bold within this column.)
- Look listen and note: this column contains guidance on what you should look out for when you are carrying out observations and assessments on the children.
- Effective practice: this column offers guidance on how practitioners can support the children towards achieving the knowledge, skills and understanding outlined in the development matters column.
- Planning and resourcing: this column offers ideas that will support the children in achieving. It is important to remember that planning should be flexible.

The Early Learning Goals establish what most children should be able to do by the end of the Early Years Foundation Stage. They are no longer organised as stepping stones. They can be found within the Statutory Framework for the Early Years Foundation Stage.

The age ranges shown within the Learning and Development guidance overlap to allow for individuality. They are a guide to what the child might be doing. The child development overview card explains the age ranges and summarises what children will be learning.

The age ranges are:

- Birth to 11 months
- 8–20 months
- 16–26 months
- 22–36 months
- 30–50 months
- 40–60+ months.

### 3. Principles into practice cards

These 24 cards demonstrate how the Early Years Foundation Stage can help children to reach their full potential and contain examples of best practice within each individual area.

Table 9: Principles into practice cards

| x 1 | **Principles into practice card** | This card details the themes, principles and commitments of the Early Years Foundation Stage |
|---|---|---|
| x 1 | **Child development overview** | This card summarises the broad phases of development that children go through and that are used within the Early Years Foundation Stage |
| x 6 | **Learning and development cards** | There is one card for each area of Learning and Development. Each card explains the requirements of the specified area of Learning and Development, the aspects it is made up of and what it means for children. Each card also gives guidance on how settings can implement the area of Learning and Development through Positive Relationships, Enabling Environments and Learning and Development focus boxes |
| x 16 | **Commitment cards** | There is one numbered card for each of the Commitments and they expand on what the Commitments mean and how they can be implemented in practice. They contain information, hints and tips, further questions to prompt reflection and useful pointers for day-to-day work with children |

## 4. Wall poster

The wall poster sets out the four principles of the Early Years Foundation Stage, together with the themes and commitments which each principle covers. This poster can be used as a daily reminder of children's needs and a reminder of how to give each child a fulfilling and challenging experience within the Early Years Foundation Stage.

## 5. CD-ROM

The CD-ROM incorporates all of the above, as well as further examples of practice and links to other resources, reading and information.

## How can the Early Years Foundation Stage work day to day?

The Early Years Foundation Stage puts the individual needs of children first. It ends the distinction between care and learning and integrates them, requiring practitioners to offer each child a rich and personalised learning experience and individual care to meet each child's needs. Practitioners must support each child individually to allow them to progress at their own pace with support if needed. This includes ensuring equality of opportunity for each child, making sure that every child is included and that all children grow up to value diversity and difference. This gives children the best possible start in life.

Children's early experiences build foundations for their learning and for their later life. Children must be viewed as individuals and should be stretched in their learning while still making it an enjoyable experience.

This can be achieved through the following.

- Ongoing observation and assessment that leads to individual planning for each child through play-based activities.
- Flexibility when responding to each child to meet their learning and development needs.
- Relating learning to the child's experiences at home.

### Planning

Planning should be focused on well-planned play-based activities and experiences. Play is at the heart of the Early Years Foundation Stage and this includes both indoors and outdoors play. It underpins learning and development for all children. All activities and experiences must meet children's individual needs and the practitioner will be able to extend or simplify activities as needed. Themes and topics are not relevant and should not be used.

Long-term planning has already been completed for you – the principles, themes and commitments form your long-term plan. From this you can go on to broadly plan for the six areas of Learning and Development, and then lead on to individual planning using your observations of the children. Again consider how much detail you need to record your planning in – simplicity is key.

Planning and the associated paperwork (proving what you do) are far down the line. Practitioners should first look at providing enabling environments and stimulation so that the child cannot fail to learn.

Activities

All of the six areas of Learning and Development must be delivered through planned, purposeful play activities and experiences, with a balance of adult-led and child-initiated activities. The focus is on play activities, not worksheets or workbooks. There should be no emphasis on an end product. The question we should ask as practitioners is not what should the children be making, but what do we want them to learn and experience?

## Putting the Early Years Foundation Stage into practice

The majority of your time should be spent being with the children and playing and interacting with them. Your time should not be spent doing long observations – these are no longer relevant and they tell you little other than that you have good eyesight. Any observation should be short and snappy and focused on the child's interests. Try using sticky notes!

Set the play activities and experiences out and see what the children do with them. Allow them to make mistakes and be supportive of them as they do so. You can then observe this to find out how the children respond, and plan to support these interests. Remember children's interests change daily and weekly – one child may want to put things in a bucket and carry it around for a week – and may then show no further interest. He has learnt all he needs to know for now. Be ready to respond to these changes.

Everything that you do with the children is a learning experience for them and therefore can be included as planning. It is useful to record all the day-to-day activities that you carry out and keep a long term list that can be added to, rather than recording it on a planning sheet every time. This can be organised under the six areas of Leaning and Development, or using the commitment headings. It can include activities such as hand washing, snack time, rest time and so on.

The Early Years Foundation Stage is a change for the better. For some practitioners it will require a major shift in thinking, away from the highly organised days of worksheets and specific activities where the children were required to make a particular product. For some, it is a welcome return to the days of learning through play and flexible planning with less paperwork and more hands-on time. Either way, it requires a change of attitude and a commitment to improve the services we offer for children.

The key messages of the Early Years Foundation Stage (EYFS) are:

- The EYFS is for all children from birth to 5 years
- The EYFS principles are the starting point for effective practice
- The EYFS builds on what practitioners already do well
- The EYFS brings learning and welfare requirements together
- The EYFS supports continuity and coherence for all children.

## Guidance in other UK countries

Different frameworks apply in different UK countries. The relevant curriculum and web links are shown below.

- Scotland – Curriculum for Excellence
  www.ltscotland.org.uk/curriculumforexcellence
- Wales – Foundation Phase
  http://wales.gov.uk/topics/educationandskills/
  policy_strategy_and_planning/early-wales/
  foundation_phase/?lang=en
- Northern Ireland – Foundation Stage
  www.nicurriculum.org.uk/foundation_stage/
  index.asp

# 403.3 Ensure provision supports children's positive behaviour

## Supporting positive behaviour

This element deals with the methods and techniques for supporting children's positive behaviour, and for supporting those who deal with behaviour.

## Defining appropriate and inappropriate behaviour

Deciding what appropriate behaviour is for a child can be dependent on your own attitudes and beliefs, and as a term it is quite vague. In general, our society values people who show themselves to be independent, individualistic and assertive. However, there are other cultural groups who are more likely to deem cooperation and **interdependence** as appropriate behaviour. This means that it is important to consider the social and cultural background of the families of the children in our care and not to impose any behavioural expectations and values which may be inappropriate. There are many positive aspects of behaviour that are accepted throughout the world and these should be encouraged; they include sharing, turn-taking,

considering others and showing caring and kind behaviour. It is also important that children are taught to negotiate and to see other points of view.

### Key Term

Interdependence – when two or more things depend on each other.

Inappropriate behaviour is behaviour that affects others in a negative way. Children who withdraw or seek attention, self-harm or display anti-social traits are exhibiting inappropriate behaviour. This also includes verbal and physical aggression, tantrums, breath holding and ignoring instructions.

## Factors affecting children's behaviour

Children's behaviour can be influenced by any of the factors shown in Figure 9 on page 121, and may be influenced by more than one at the same time.

### Did you know?

The *Concise Oxford Dictionary* defines behaviour as 'manners, moral conduct, and treatment shown to or towards others'.

Kitty, there's enough LEGO® for both of you. Wouldn't it be nice to share it with Devan?

Figure 8: Sharing should be encouraged in all children

There are many influences on children's behaviour

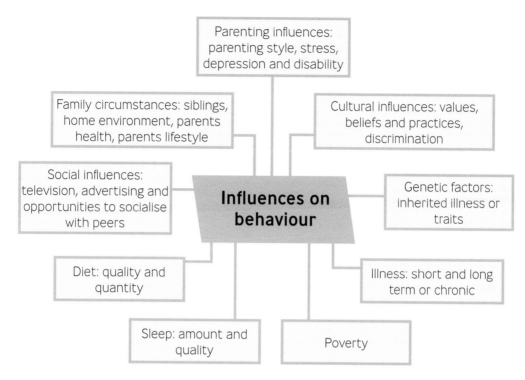

## Adult expectations

Your expectations of a child's behaviour should be realistic and take into account the child's age and stage of development and the circumstances at the time of the behaviour. We all have days where we are tired or unwell and this is the same for children! It is also important to communicate your expectations clearly to the children, and to remind them when they need it.

It is very important for adults to have the same expectations of children, in other words to be consistent. Consistency is essential to the behaviour learning process because if the child receives a different reaction to the same behaviour they become confused and may feel insecure and uncertain how to behave.

## Goals and boundaries

Adults need to set **behavioural goals** and **boundaries** for children and these provide a framework within which children learn acceptable behaviour. These goals and boundaries must be appropriate for their particular age and stage of development and it is often a good idea to include the children when setting them. If children have involvement in setting the goals and boundaries, they are much more likely to understand them and keep to them.

Goals and boundaries for the under 5s should be kept to a minimum so that they remain achievable. This age group will need frequent reminders so that they can learn what they are. It can take many months for them to do so!

All age groups need goals and boundaries explained to them, along with the reasons for needing them. It is important to phrase the goals and boundaries *positively*. There is a big difference between 'Don't run inside' and 'We walk when we are inside'. The first statement tells children what they should not be doing, but doesn't tell them what is right. The second statement teaches them appropriate behaviour.

## Key Terms

**Behavioural goals** – a goal is an aim or a target. Setting a behavioural goal for children means having a positive aim for their behaviour.

**Behavioural boundaries** – a boundary is a limit or a margin. It is important to make children aware of the behavioural limits.

## Points for Reflective Practice

How do you communicate your expectations to the children, families and other adults in the setting?

## Avoiding inappropriate behaviour

If children are aware of the goals and boundaries and they are consistently applied, then this goes a long way to encouraging positive behaviour. There are times when you will be able to 'head off' inappropriate behaviour before it begins. Some strategies for avoiding inappropriate behaviour may include the following.

- Provide plenty of varied and interesting equipment.
- Give sympathy and reassurance to anyone who is hurt or crying.
- Explain calmly what has happened to help the children to understand the situation.
- Help them to solve the problem – for example to find another buggy.
- Teach 'please' and 'thank you'.
- Teach the goals and boundaries.
- Act as a good role model – talk calmly and kindly to all the children.
- Keep noise levels reasonable.

By the time children reach 5, they are beginning to understand goals and boundaries, and their behaviour is usually guided by these. However, they are not ready to control their behaviour in all situations. They may be aware that the book corner is not the place for zooming around in cars, but their enthusiasm helps them to forget this!

## Self-esteem

It is important for children of all ages to have high levels of self-esteem, as their behaviour will often reflect how they are feeling about themselves.

A child with high self-esteem will be able to:

- act independently
- tolerate frustration
- attempt new tasks and challenges
- be helpful to others.

A child with low self-esteem may:

- avoid trying new things
- be unable to tolerate frustration
- be unwilling to try new tasks and challenges
- need constant adult support.

High self-esteem can be encouraged by:

- avoiding criticising the child
- providing positive feedback
- praising and encouraging
- helping children to realise their strengths
- teaching decision making
- encouraging hobbies and interests
- teaching children to resolve minor conflicts.

## Strategies for encouraging positive behaviour

You should always focus first on children's positive behaviour, rather than their inappropriate behaviour, and there are several ways you can do this:

- positive attention
- role modelling
- reward.

### Positive attention

Children love to be given positive attention, as it helps them to feel loved and appreciated. It is important to give children regular positive attention, as generally children will try harder to please if their behaviour results in this outcome. Some ways of giving positive attention are listed below.

- That was very good!
- Well done!
- I really liked the way you helped each other with that activity.
- That's it – you've got the hang of it.
- That's a beautiful picture – shall we put it on the wall?
- You've been so helpful today – thank you.
- You sat very still to listen to that story – well done.

**Figure 10:** Positive attention is very important to children

## Role modelling

Children will copy the behaviour of adults around them. Because of this, it is important that adults model appropriate behaviour and act in the way they would like the children to act, for example saying please and thank you. It is also important not to contradict yourself. There is no point in shouting to a group of children 'There's far too much noise in here' as by shouting you only model an inappropriate behaviour to the children.

Later on in this Unit you will read about social learning theory, which looks in more detail at role modelling and how it affects children.

## Rewards

Children also love being given rewards and they are likely to repeat the behaviour that earned them the reward. Eventually this behaviour will become the norm. Rewards for young children must be instant, but older children can be told about rewards in advance so they can look forward to them. Rewards can either be something that a child can have, such as stickers, certificates or a toy, or they can be something such as praise, or a round of applause.

Later on in this Unit you will read about behaviourism which looks in more detail at how rewards affect children.

## Other strategies for dealing with behaviour

When responding to children's behaviour it is important to make your response appropriate to the level of challenge. If a baby is banging a brick on the radiator to make a noise then the best method for dealing with this is probably distraction. On the other hand, if a child is running around hitting and shouting your response will need to be more direct.

- Ignore – if the behaviour is not causing any harm to others or to equipment, and is possible attention seeking, then it can be ignored. Often if a child realises their behaviour is not getting them the attention they want, then they will stop.

- Negotiate – this works well with older children, as they are able to wait to have their needs met and may be able to understand the consequences of their actions.

- Distract – this works wells with younger children, who can easily be distracted from something they should not be doing.

- Allow child to learn from natural consequences – if the behaviour is not causing harm, allow them to continue to see what happens. Often children will learn from this experience.

- Time out – during time out a child is taken away from the activity and supervised until the time out is over. The length of time is generally the child's age in minutes. During time out the child gets no or little response from the supervising adult. There should not be a specific chair or specific area for time out.

- Say no – a firm no is useful for younger children so they understand the boundaries. It can quickly stop inappropriate behaviour.

- Eye contact and facial expression – sometimes a 'look' will help remind children that they are nearing the boundaries. Once the child shows appropriate behaviour it is important to praise them for doing so.

It is important to remember that it is the child's *behaviour* that is inappropriate, and that the child is not 'being naughty'.

As children begin to get older, their behaviour can be supported in other ways.

These strategies will help children to understand their behaviour and think of ways of putting right what they have done wrong.

When a child has behaved inappropriately, this information must be shared with parents. This should happen calmly and at an appropriate time and place, preferably in a separate room. It should not be shared loudly in front of other parents, with the intention of humiliating or shaming the child.

## Keys to Good Practice

Physical punishment is *never* an acceptable method of dealing with child behaviour. It is illegal. You must *never* deal with behaviour in a way that frightens, physically hurts, threatens or humiliates a child.

In extreme circumstances it may be necessary to physically restrain a child to prevent them from hurting themselves or someone else. If this occurs you must use the minimum force possible, record the incident and report it to a superior and parents as soon as possible.

**Figure 11:** The behaviour of 6–12 year olds can be supported in many ways

**Figure 12:** The behaviour of 12–16 year olds should be supported in different ways

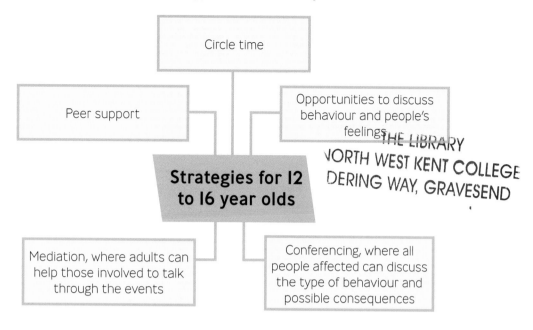

**Figure 12:** The behaviour of 12–16 year olds should be supported in different ways

# Behaviour policies

Behaviour policies are essential. They help to staff to decide what behaviour is acceptable and when action needs to be taken. They also help to protect the children and staff in the setting as it should clearly state not only when action will be taken but also the type of action. It will exclude the use of physical punishment, and make it clear that frightening, embarrassing or humiliating children is not acceptable. It should emphasise the promotion of appropriate behaviour.

The behaviour policy will normally explain:

- the aims of the policy
- the goals and boundaries of the setting
- positive behaviour management strategies to be used by staff
- inappropriate behaviour strategies to be used by staff
- parental involvement
- record keeping guidance.

It is important that policies are regularly reviewed to make sure they are still suitable and useful. It is important that all staff are fully updated when any changes are made and that the policy is applied consistently.

## Points for Reflective Practice

How is your behaviour policy reviewed, updated and disseminated?

# Theories of how children learn behaviour

K4D380

There are many theories about how children learn behaviour. In this section we will look at:

- social learning theory
- socialisation
- nature versus nurture
- Piaget's stages of moral judgement
- Kohlberg's six stages of moral development.

## Social learning theory

Social learning theorists believe that children learn by 'observational learning', i.e. by watching others. Observational learning is spontaneous and children learn naturally by imitating rather than by being shown or taught. Often children may copy behaviour without being aware of it. There are two terms used in observational learning: **model** and **modelling**.

Albert Bandura conducted a well-known experiment in 1965 using inflatable dolls called Bobo dolls. This experiment looked at the effects on children of seeing aggressive adults and showed that children learned behaviour by watching adults.

Bandura showed individual children a film when an adult 'attacked' the Bobo doll. The adult kicks it, throws it around the room, sits on and hits it with a toy hammer, bombards it with balls, etc.

The children are then led to a different playroom for free-play. It is stocked with a variety of interesting toys – including a Bobo doll, toy hammer, etc. – and 88 per cent of children imitated the model's aggressive behaviour. Bandura believed this showed children naturally imitate behaviour.

## Socialisation

Socialisation is the process through which children learn the behaviour that is acceptable and appropriate to the society in which they live. The process of socialisation involves children learning from the experiences and relationships they form during childhood.

The socialisation theory believes that children learn expected behaviour in different ways.

■ Rewards – adults encourage acceptable behaviour by rewarding it. A reward can be a smile, saying thank you or giving praise; it also includes giving children toys or a treat. Children also feel rewarded by the good feeling they get when they please an adult. Children want rewards to be repeated and this encourages them to repeat the behaviour that gave them the reward.

**Figure 13:** In Bandura's classic experiment, 88 per cent of children imitated an adult's aggressive behaviour towards the Bobo doll

- Punishment – adults discourage behaviour by ignoring it or punishing it. Punishments can take a variety of forms: they include telling children that their behaviour is inappropriate, depriving them of something they want or ignoring their behaviour.

## Did you know?
### Nature vs. nurture debate

One side of this argument, the 'nature' view, believes that our intelligence, personality and behaviour are genetically inherited in the same way as our gender or the colour of our eyes.

However, others disagree. They argue that we are the product of all the experiences that we have had as we have grown. This is the nurture view.

The nature side of the 'nature vs nurture' debate says that our skills are innate; the nurture side says that they are socially learned.

Do you think that our behaviour is the result of:

- nature
- nurture
- or both?

## Piaget's stages of moral judgement

Piaget studied moral judgement, and formed a two-stage theory.

- Children younger than 10 or 11 years think about moral dilemmas in one way, but older children (11 and 12 years) think about them in a different way.

- Younger children regard rules as fixed.
- The older child understands that rules can be changed if everyone agrees.
- Younger children base their moral judgements on the expected consequences, whereas older children base their judgements on intentions.

## Kohlberg's six stages of moral development

The work of Kohlberg led on from that of Piaget. Kohlberg saw moral development as a series of levels, each having two stages. These are outlined in Table 10.

## Supporting children through transitions

K4TIII3

All children of all ages experience transitions. A transition occurs when a child moves from one care setting to another. Typical transitions include:

- starting a setting for the first time i.e. nursery, childminder, school
- moving within settings i.e. from baby to toddler room or from one class to another
- new living arrangements i.e. leaving home, going into hospital
- leaving school and going into work or further education.

**Table 10:** Kohlberg's six stages of moral development

| Level 1 Pre-conventional morality (7–13 years approx) | Stage 1 | Children are only concerned with their own actions – they have no real empathy and are only interested in escaping punishment |
| --- | --- | --- |
| | Stage 2 | Children make judgements based on what pleases themselves or those close to them |
| Level 2 Conventional morality (13–16 years) | Stage 3 | The emphasis is on winning approval and praise from others |
| | Stage 4 | The insistence is on not breaking rules or punishment will inevitably follow – guilt kicks in around now and children will blatantly lie rather than admit to wrongdoing |
| Level 3 Post-conventional morality (16–20 years) | Stage 5 | The wider society becomes a factor, and the needs of other individuals are seen as not always of prime importance |
| | Stage 6 | Moral principles and conscience now govern the reasoning of those individuals who reach this height of moral development |

During a transition a child may experience a wide range of feelings, as they will be losing familiar people and may be feeling unsettled by this. It is important to prepare children for transitions where possible and support them during the transitional phase.

Making a smooth transition:

- prepare the child before the event
- listen to children's concerns
- be honest when answering questions
- be positive
- keep explanations simple and reassuring
- allow children to discuss the transition as much as they would like to
- teach children strategies to deal with their concerns
- arrange to visit the new setting
- read books or watch DVDs on the subject.

## 403.4 Monitor and evaluate records and recording procedures for the assessment of children's development

### Records and recording procedures

This section looks at the records that you keep, the safety of that information and how it is shared with others.

### Confidentiality

K4M802
K4M382

When working with children and families it is safest to consider all information as being confidential. This includes paper-based or computer records. As you are likely to be working as a manager you will have access to a full range of information about the children and families who attend your setting and it will be your decision who else should have access to this information. Giving out information when you should not do so can have serious repercussions, as it can cause the parents to lose trust in you and the setting, which could affect your reputation and that of the setting. In extreme circumstances disciplinary action may be taken against the person who breached confidentiality.

It is important that you understand the confidentiality policy and that you are able to explain it clearly to other staff. It is your responsibility to makes sure the staff that are under your direction understand and follow the policy.

Information should be made available to others only on a need-to-know basis. Not everyone in the setting needs to have all the information about every child. There may be information that you need to pass on, such as details of an allergy or medication. In this case it is good practice to discuss with the parents how this information will be shared amongst the other staff members. Parents may ask to see the information stored on their child at any time.

You may only pass on confidential information without permission to the relevant person in authority if you believe a child's welfare to be at stake, or if there is a medical emergency.

## Points for Reflective Practice

The information that you have on the children and families in your care must be stored securely in a place where only the relevant staff can access it.

- How do you achieve this?
- Why is this important?
- How do you ensure security is maintained?

### Data protection

All the personal records you keep, both handwritten and on the computer, are protected under the Data Protection Act 1998. This Act was put in place to prevent personal information from being used inappropriately or unnecessarily.

The Act gives the public the right to know what information is stored by your setting about them. It means that employees must make sure that they handle personal information responsibly and that they protect the privacy of individuals.

See Unit 401 for more information on the Data Protection Act.

You and other people have the right to:

- ask if the setting holds personal information about them
- ask what it uses the information for
- be provided with a copy of the information
- be given details of the purposes for which the setting uses the information
- ask for incorrect data to be corrected.

There are a number of important exceptions to the right of people to see personal information held about them.

- Where dealing with the request would involve excessive time/expense.
- Where the information includes sensitive personal information and disclosing this may harm the individual.
- Where information includes details about another individual.

It is good practice when collecting information to explain why, where and for how long it will be stored, what the information will be used for and the rights of access to this information. You should only store personal information for as long as you need to. This information should be kept in a secure place and should be organised so that it is easy to retrieve information about individuals. It is also good practice to regularly review records to ensure that these are accurate and up-to-date. Records need to be kept for varying amounts of time and will need to be destroyed from time to time. Any information which can identify an individual must be shredded, incinerated or otherwise destroyed.

## Evidence-based practice

K4P377

Evidence-based practice is an approach that is more commonly applied in health and social care, as well as in other fields. It has its roots in medicine (where it was originally known as 'evidence-based medicine'), where it is the guiding principle of patient care. It emerged from a realisation that doctors were not always applying the latest evidence of what works when reaching decisions about what was best for their patients.

It is best described as the systematic use of the best available evidence of what works when reaching decisions about how best to care for or support the children in our care.

This means basing your practice with the child on the following.

- The evidence you have about them (i.e. your knowledge of them, the observations you have made on them).
- The research you can access about current theories of childcare and child development.
- Understanding the child's and the parent/carer's wishes.

## Multi-agency, multi-professional approach

K4M378
K4M379

A multi-agency, multi-professional approach is the best way to help a child if you have concerns about their development. Other agencies and professionals are able to provide extra support and expertise to assist you in planning for extra support and learning opportunities for these children. You must always gain parental permission before contacting outside agencies.

## Points for Reflective Practice

- Think about the information that you keep.
- Is it kept in a particular format?
- Why do you use this format?
- Is it suitable for the purpose?
- How do you update the information that you keep?
- How do you make sure that staff understand the purpose of the format?
- How do you make sure staff are aware of how to correctly complete it?

**Figure 14:** There are many agencies that may be able to help you if you have concerns over a child's development

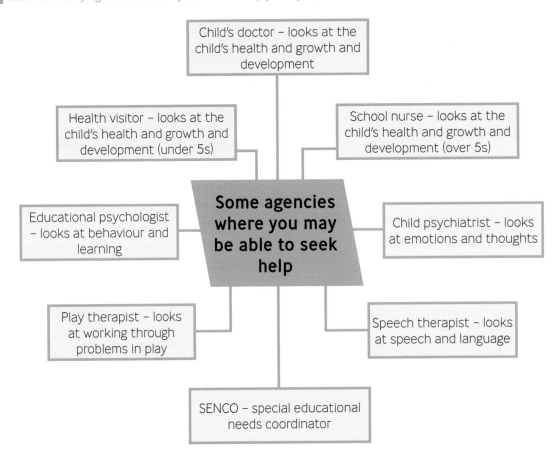

# Check Your Understanding

1. What are the advantages of observation?
2. Why is parental involvement and permission important when carrying out observations?
3. What is the difference between formative and summative?
4. What does the term 'holistic development' mean?
5. Give three examples of influences of child development.
6. What is meant by the term 'positive reinforcement'?
7. Give four factors that may influence children's behaviour.
8. Why should goals and boundaries be positive?
9. What is socialisation?
10. What records are protected under the Data Protection Act?

# Further references

www.allkids.co.uk

www.babyworld.co.uk

www.cwdcouncil.gov.uk

www.family.go.com

www.ncb.org.uk

www.parentsplace.com

www.playeducation.co.uk

www.raisingkids.co.uk

www.smallfolk.com

www.standards.dcsf.gov.uk/eyfs

www.surestart.gov.uk

www.teachernet.gov.uk

www.zerotothree.org

Meggitt, C. (2006) *Child Development: An illustrated Guide*, Heinemann

Pound, L. (2005) *How Children Learn Book 1*, Step Forward Publishing

Pound, L. (2008) *How Children Learn Book 2*, Step Forward Publishing

Sheridan, M. D. (1997) *From Birth to Five*, Routledge

Tassoni, P. (2008) *Penny Tassoni's Practical EYFS Handbook*, Heinemann

# Unit 404

## Reflect on, review and develop own practice

In this Unit you will look at the ways in which you can become a reflective practitioner and use these skills to review and develop your own practice.

The key to personal and professional development is identification of your own skills including any strengths and weaknesses you may possess.

This Unit will help you explore all of these and provide you with evaluative information on which to build your personal development and professional practice.

This Unit will also show you how to develop effective training and development plans and assess their uses in supporting you to apply new found knowledge and skills in your daily practice.

The elements for Unit 404 are:

404.1    Investigate ways of reflecting on, reviewing and evaluating own practice.
404.2    Reflect on and develop practice.
404.3    Take part in continuing professional development.

## Learning Outcomes

After reading this Unit you will be able to:

- Define reflective practice and understand how reflection benefits practice.
- Identify methods of reflection and their purpose.
- Understand the importance of examining your own beliefs and attitudes.
- Identify ways in which you can continue your own professional development and the rationale for this.
- Structure your training and development plan based on your own skills and knowledge requirements.

This Unit includes the following themes and covers the knowledge statements listed below:

- The reflective practitioner
  **K4P812, K4D815, K4P818**
- Reflection as a tool for learning
  **K4P813, K4P814, K4P816, K4P817, K4M823**
- Continuing your professional development
  **K4P819, K4D820, K4P821, K4P822**

# 404.1   Investigate ways of reflecting on, reviewing and evaluating own practice

## The reflective practitioner

### What is reflection?

Reflection is a tool which we use in all aspects of our life to analyse our actions and responses. **Reflective practice** enables us to make sense of what we have done, said or thought and in return makes us think about possible future actions and consequences. Reflection gives us a greater understanding of ourselves as individuals as when analysing why we have done or said something we are in actual fact analysing ourselves.

Reflection can be seen as an essential tool in furthering your own development and your knowledge and understanding of your own practice. In the Early Years sector, reflection is highly valuable as it enables you to provide best practice in service delivery to children and

families by analysing the provision and practice you offer and seeking to improve on this.

As a senior practitioner or manager your ability to use reflective practice can have a direct impact on those colleagues you support, work with and manage. Modelling effective reflective skills will help them to do the same. Often practitioners find it difficult to externalise their thoughts and ideas, but with your support and guidance these become skills they can tune in to in their everyday practice.

### Key Term

Reflective practice – the process of thinking about and critically analysing your actions with the goal of changing and improving occupational practice.

## Theories of reflective practice

Reflective practice is not a modern-day phenomenon, and the works of Dewey, Schön and Kolb have all contributed to the development of the reflective process.

Dewey (1859–1952) believed that reflection exists to help practitioners look back at situations and events that have occurred and turn them into learning experiences. He thought we should: Look at an event – Understand it – Learn from it.

As early years practitioners many opportunities present themselves on a daily basis to look at what we did, why we did it and what we would do next time. This process allows us to learn from our experiences and solve problems we may have encountered in the workplace or in our own thoughts, words and actions.

Donald Schön (1930–1997) is well known in the field of reflective practice and is recognised for his model 'reflection in action' and 'reflection on action'. This is one of the three themes which were the focus of his studies on self-reflecting practice. Much of what he has written on and around the reflective practitioner can be easily interpreted for the early years practitioner.

**Reflection in action** requires practitioners to reflect whilst acting or carrying out duties, or, to put it in the words of Schön, 'to think on their feet': to connect feelings with the current situation and act upon them.

**Reflection on action** requires more of a 'step back and think' approach from practitioners after the event. Many strategies that you will have come across in this approach include questioning why, what and how, talking things through with colleagues or even writing down what happened and what you are going to do as a result. Schön saw these processes as essential to reflective thought.

There are critics who would challenge Schön's theory of reflection in action, since there is often little time for reflection to take place and snap decisions may need to be made. However, it is fair to say that although every situation is unique, there is value in applying previous experience to new situations.

David Kolb's (1939–) model of experiential learning is widely recognised as an effective model for reflective practice. Figure 1 shows how reflection works in this cycle. This is a snapshot understanding of how you could use reflection to evaluate and develop practice. The following descriptions give you more detail of how this is done.

**Figure 1:** Kolb's experiential learning cycle

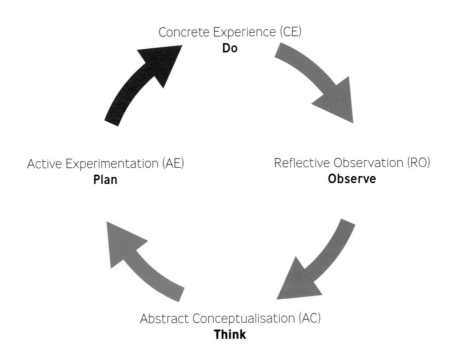

Concrete Experience (CE)
**Do**

Reflective Observation (RO)
**Observe**

Abstract Conceptualisation (AC)
**Think**

Active Experimentation (AE)
**Plan**

## Concrete Experience (doing or having the experience)

'Concrete Experience' is the 'doing' component which evolves from your everyday practice in the setting to include your work with the children, your relationships with colleagues, your communications with families and your partnerships with professionals from other agencies.

## Reflective Observation (reviewing or reflecting on the experience)

The 'Reflective Observation' element brings forward your thinking, analysis and perception of the events that have occurred in your working day and your reflections on your own input and the value of this.

Looking again at the techniques for reflective analysis in Figure 1, you may adopt several approaches to help you reflect, including questioning of your practice. The skills and knowledge you already possess will be valuable in helping you to ascertain your own personal effectiveness in practice too.

It is important that reflection is used as a tool to promote development and learning and increase knowledge and skills. Reflection alone will not enable you to do this, but with more thought given to 'what happens next' and identifying how you can increase skills and knowledge, then development can benefit as a result of reflection.

## Abstract Conceptualisation (concluding or learning from the experience)

To establish how you may approach work issues or practice differently you need to identify your own personal development needs. By reflecting you may have already discovered gaps in knowledge and skills or areas of practice that would benefit from further learning and understanding. This comes in many formats, from reading up-to-date public policies affecting your working, to attending more formal training days and events. Reflection helps you to understand what you know and what you need to know and helps you to reach conclusions about your own practice.

## Active Experimentation (planning or trying out what you have learned)

Reaching conclusions about your own practice and seeking ways forward in developing this through further learning and training opportunities can then set in motion the process for change. You will be keen to return to your setting and apply these new found skills to benefit practice. This approach to change is termed 'active experimentation'. Active experimentation then starts the cycle where you implement those changes in your practice to generate another concrete experience, taking us back to the start of the process of experiential learning.

You should now be able to see the process of reflection and can identify how you use this in your everyday practice.

In addition to the experiential learning cycle, Kolb (1976) developed a learning style inventory which allows students to identify their preferred learning styles.

Kolb identifies four learning styles.

1. Divergers: view a situation from many perspectives and rely heavily on brainstorming and generation of ideas.
2. Assimilators: use inductive reasoning and have the ability to create theoretical models.
3. Convergers: rely heavily on hypothetical-deductive reasoning.
4. Accomodators: carry out plans and experiments and adapt to immediate circumstances.

It is important to recognise that this is only one model presented for reflective practice and does not necessarily reflect the learning needs or reflective practice styles of every individual in society. More recently, other researchers have developed Kolb's theories of learning and produced their own inventories.

The learning styles listed in Table 1 on page 136 may be more familiar to you, particularly if you have undertaken further education in recent years as many colleges, training providers and tutors use this style of inventory to gauge the preferred learning style of each individual student, so that these can be accommodated through the presentation of appropriate learning materials best suited to each learner's way of thinking.

## Points for Reflective Practice

What type of learner do you think you are?

■ Look at the learning styles in Table 1 and identify which learning style best describes you.

**Table 1:** Honey and Mumford's learning styles inventory

| Learning style | Type of learner |
|---|---|
| Activists | 'Hands-on' learners who prefer to have a go and learn through trial and error |
| Reflectors | 'Tell me' learners who prefer to be thoroughly briefed before proceeding |
| Theorists | 'Convince me' learners who want reassurance that a project makes sense |
| Pragmatists | 'Show me' learners who want a demonstration from an acknowledged expert |

# 404.2 Reflect on and develop practice

## Reflection as a tool for learning

K4P8I2

### The benefits of reflecting on practice

There are many benefits to you and your team as a result of being an effective reflector, as shown in Figure 2. These benefits include the following.

**Meeting the individual needs of children:** by identifying the needs of individual children and reflecting on how you have provided for their individual learning needs and evaluating how successful these have been.

**Identifying how the environment meets the care, learning and development needs of children:** by reflecting on the way in which the environment is equipped and resourced to meet the children's needs and considering if this is 'working' in meeting the needs of children.

**Evaluating observations and assessments carried out on children:** by analysing your findings from such opportunities you can reflect on your own practice and how it has met the learning and development needs of children in your care.

**Analysing your own effectiveness in practice:** reflection will help you to identify how your input can benefit children and why aspects of your practice may need adapting or changing. You will also be able to consider differing approaches to differing circumstances.

**Figure 2:** The benefits of reflective practice

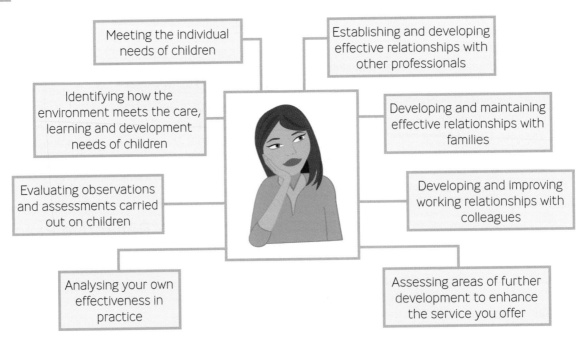

- Meeting the individual needs of children
- Establishing and developing effective relationships with other professionals
- Identifying how the environment meets the care, learning and development needs of children
- Developing and maintaining effective relationships with families
- Evaluating observations and assessments carried out on children
- Developing and improving working relationships with colleagues
- Analysing your own effectiveness in practice
- Assessing areas of further development to enhance the service you offer

**Assessing areas of further development to enhance the service you offer:** reflecting on your own input you may be able to identify weaknesses or skills and knowledge gaps in your own practice that need further development.

**Developing and improving working relationships with colleagues:** reflecting on your effectiveness as a manger or team leader and encouraging others to give you feedback on your performance will help to identify strategies for improving the way in which you communicate and work with others.

**Developing and maintaining effective relationships with families:** reflecting on the ways in which you seek to communicate and work in partnership with parents to meet their children's needs, you can strive for continual improvement and consistent communications.

**Establishing and developing effective relationships with other professionals:** reflecting on your communications with other professionals and the roles and responsibilities you uphold, you can identify best working practices and use reflection to analyse your own personal effectiveness and contributions to multi-agency working objectives.

## Find it out

Look again at Kolb's experiential learning cycle in Figure I (page I34). Can you see any patterns emerging from these in the way you evaluate your own practice?

## Points for Reflective Practice

Look at the reasons why reflecting on practice is beneficial and think about the importance of analysing your own personal effectiveness.

- How can reflecting on your own practice benefit how effective you are in the setting?

Early Years practitioners reflect as part of their everyday working life, yet many would not necessarily consider themselves to be reflective practitioners.

## Points for Reflective Practice

Have you ever said the following?

- 'That activity was great fun, the children really enjoyed themselves. Did you see the looks on their faces?'
- 'Well changing their routine around was the worst thing we could have done today, the babies were really unsettled this afternoon. I don't think we should try that again.'
- 'I've been thinking about the layout of this room since this morning, the children didn't access the book corner at all. Perhaps we should relocate over there.'
  If the answer is yes then you are a reflective practitioner, you've just never considered it like that before!

**Figure 3:** Opportunities to reflect

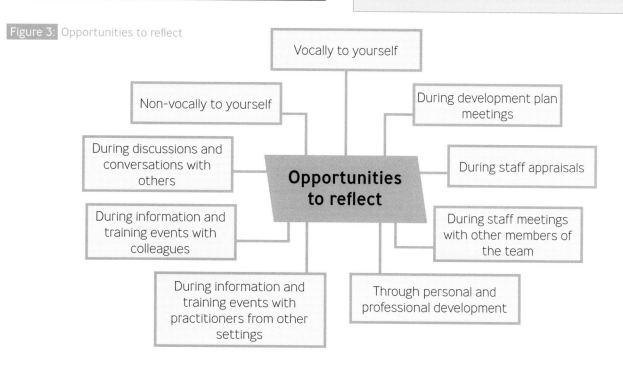

**Vocally to yourself:** you will often 'think out loud' and find you are talking to yourself. That is absolutely fine if you are using this technique to work through what you have done and why you have done it. People often find it easier to evaluate their thoughts if they can vocalise them and put them in some sense of order.

**Non-vocally to yourself:** you may be a quiet reflective individual who takes time to become absorbed in their own thoughts and ideas. Often this will include visualising your practice and working through possible approaches and reflections in your head.

**During discussions and conversations with others:** throughout your working day, if you work in an environment alongside others, you will be presented with the opportunity to reflect on practice on many occasions as children indulge in play and learning experiences and as you work through the day ahead of you. It is important to share your reflections as they present themselves as they can be a valuable tool in looking at practice in the 'here and now' context.

**During information and training events with colleagues:** these events enable you to take time to reflect in a controlled environment where your thoughts and focus may be channelled to specific areas or practice in learning. This is a great opportunity for you to consider 'the whys and hows' of particular areas of practice or personal input.

**During information and training events with practitioners from other settings:** networking with practitioners from other settings is a valuable way of sharing good practice, and helping others to seek solutions to challenges in practice by looking at how problems were identified and remedied.

**Through personal and professional development:** by attending personal and professional development opportunities you will be able to look at your own role and your effectiveness in practice. Many training courses make time during programme delivery to enable you to reflect on your learning and identify how these reflections will impact your work.

**During staff meetings with other members of the team:** staff meetings are essential to effective communications in a team working environment, but they also provide practitioners with the opportunity to reflect on practice in the setting. Staff meetings also provide the opportunity for teams to discuss best practice benchmarks and establish how these

can be achieved by reviewing and reflecting on current practice.

**During staff appraisals:** well-organised appraisal systems will allow time for the individual being appraised to reflect on their practice and identify their strengths and weaknesses in relation to their job role and question how they can develop their skills both personally and professionally.

**During development plan meetings:** reflecting on practice may present you with the opportunity to identify skills and gaps in knowledge and skills. You may feel you could have been more effective in the learning environment if you had more understanding about certain elements of practice. Development plan meetings, and indeed appraisals, will prove useful in enabling you to reflect and seek training and developments that can bridge such skills gaps.

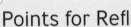

## Points for Reflective Practice

Think about instances when you have reflected on practice, and look at some of the examples just discussed. Can you think of any situations in which you have increased your own knowledge and understanding as a result of reflecting on events?

## When to use reflection

These examples give you a broad scope of when and how you use reflection. You might think that you just use reflection to evaluate curriculum activities and experiences on offer to the children you care for. In actual fact you use reflection in all aspects of your work and beyond.

**To analyse the care we offer children:** part of your everyday practice is to think about the standard of care that you give the children and the level of support that you give to fellow practitioners. You will often measure this by stepping back and looking at how things are 'running' in the setting and it is this process that will help you identify whether you are effective in your work role or whether you need to think about adjusting or changing what you do to meet the needs of those you support in the setting. Not only do you use reflection to analyse your effectiveness in meeting the needs of children but also to identify whether your personal input meets best practice benchmarks. Later on in this Unit you will discover more about what these benchmarks are and how they affect you.

**To make sure the environment meets the needs of children and families:** as well as ensuring the care and learning needs of children are met you have a duty of care to provide an adequate environment in which this can all take place. Regulatory guidance detailed in the Five Welfare Requirements of the Early Years Foundation Stage Framework help you ascertain what is considered as an adequate environment for children and goes further to detail aspects of the environment with which you should give due regard. In Scotland 'Getting It Right For Every Child' sets out its agenda for ensuring provision is adequate to meet the needs of children and families. By ensuring you understand what these requirements are, and reflecting on your own provision, you can hopefully identify areas for improvement or review so that both you and the setting as a whole are compliant with regulatory requirements.

**To ensure colleagues and fellow practitioners can fulfil their job roles effectively:** reflection here can be seen as a three-way observation: looking at the practitioner, the setting and yourself. By reflecting on their performance, which can be measured by the impact it has on the daily occurrences within the setting, and your performance in terms of the support that is offered to practitioners e.g. job mentoring and job descriptions, you can be provided with evidence that will help you to conclude if the practitioner is fulfilling their job role sufficiently. Reflection can be used further to ascertain how processes can be moved on where there is an obvious need for practitioners to have further support and development opportunities.

**To ensure best practice is being implemented at all times:** reflecting on how things are done and why they are done that way is only beneficial if you seek to find better methods of working where there is a need. There are many public policies that affect your working practices and it is to these you must give due regard when trying to establish what best practice is. When reflecting on how things are done it is important to consider if your ways of working complement the goals and desired outcomes set by national and local government agencies. By measuring and contrasting the two you will be able to identify any issues for development and improvement and support the setting in progressing to the next stage in the process, which is to put in place strategies to enable achievement in meeting best practice benchmarks.

**To look at your own effectiveness in the setting:** reflection can be used to look at your own personal effectiveness in a setting and identify how you model good practice in service delivery and how this impacts others. You may use reflection and observation to consider how others work under your direction and the dynamics of the team. If working alone you may consider how you manage your time effectively and how effective you are in getting things done in an orderly manner.

## Understanding reflective analysis

There are many ways in which you reflect on your own practice throughout your working day. You will find you regularly use a number of these techniques, including the following.

- Questioning what, why and how: questioning yourself will help identify if you are employing the best possible strategies in your work.

---

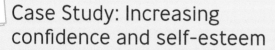

# Case Study: Increasing confidence and self-esteem

Sarah has been working in a nursery for five years. She enjoys working with the toddlers but is soon to take up a position in the pre-school room. Although Sarah is looking forward to the challenge she is a little nervous about embarking on the Early Years Foundation Stage Framework. She has asked her manager if she can attend some forthcoming training events on the implementation of the framework.

- Why has Sarah approached her manager for further training?
- How can this training opportunity enhance Sarah's confidence?
- How has Sarah already demonstrated she is a reflective practitioner?
- How will the setting benefit from Sarah's new found knowledge and confidence?

■ Seeking alternatives: identifying different ways of working when methods currently used are not beneficial.

■ Keeping an open mind: trying not to be set in your ways or negative towards change. Be open to change and alternative ways of doing things.

■ Viewing from different perspectives: taking on board the views and opinions of others and understanding their perceptions including those of colleagues, other professionals, children and families.

■ Thinking about consequences: taking time to ask yourself how outcomes from actions can impact the setting and those who have an interest in it.

■ Testing ideas through comparing and contrasting: using knowledge of others to try varying approaches to a task to seek the best outcome.

■ Asking 'what if?': considering different options and trialling these in practice to seek best option.

■ Synthesising ideas: bringing together ideas from a variety of sources and forming a common objective for your practice.

■ Seeking, identifying and resolving problems: identifying difficulties at the earliest opportunity and being strategic in sourcing solutions to problems.

Look at Table 2, where you will see these techniques for reflective analysis and the scenarios they link to.

**K4P8I5** **Table 2:** Examples of reflective analysis

| Techniques for reflective analysis | Possible scenario |
|---|---|
| Questioning what, why and how | Using the outcomes of observations on children in your care to see if the environment and practitioners are meeting their care, learning and development needs |
| Seeking alternatives | The paperwork currently used to record children's learning journeys is arduous and time-consuming. Research and develop your own formats that suit the needs of the setting and practitioners whilst gathering the relevant information |
| Keeping an open mind | The Early Years Advisory teacher has been in to talk to you about the indoor/outdoors environment, you are not convinced her proposals will work in your setting but are willing to adopt this approach and see how it works |
| Viewing from different perspectives | Ask parents for feedback on the setting or service, you can do this as a regular written activity. By having their feedback you will be able to view the setting from their perspective |
| Thinking about consequences | Re-deployment of staff in the setting can be beneficial to the logistics of the service but consequences such as the impact on children and team dynamics must be considered very carefully |
| Testing ideas through comparing and contrasting | Visiting another setting to see how they provide continuous provision for the children in their care |
| Asking 'what if?' | Trial new ideas with colleagues for instance 'How about we change the health and safety checklist for one week, if you feel this works then we can look at adopting this method long term?' |
| Synthesising ideas | Utilising the environment effectively. Ask colleagues to draw up a plan of the provision that they think suits the needs of children, spend time discussing each other's plans and draw together a more effective working environment |
| Seeking, identifying and resolving problems | Reflecting on practice can help find the root cause of a problem, such as children may lack exposure to outdoor play opportunities on a regular basis. Once this is identified you can then establish how this need can be accommodated and how practitioners can be supported in providing outdoor play with its associated benefits |

## Points for Reflective Practice

Using the techniques identified in Table 2 (page 140) consider examples that have occurred in your practice. Make notes of these and link them to the techniques.

- Does your reflection incorporate a range of reflective techniques?
- Are there some techniques that you use more than others?
- Do certain techniques lend themselves to particular situations and events?

## Points for Reflective Practice

Look at your policies and procedures for practice. Consider how you ensure that yourself and colleagues adhere to these on a daily basis.

- Can you think of any aspects where you do not fully adhere to the setting's guidelines?
- How can you review practice and procedure to ensure that you do?

## Contrasting what we say and what we do

Reflection is a form of evaluation; by looking back at how 'something was done' or 'how a situation went' you can often then identify the best way forward. Equally you may already have a pre-conceived idea as to the outcomes of a particular situation. By having pre-determined objectives and evaluation of outcome you can then make comparisons between the two which often leads to asking yourself numerous questions about what you set out to achieve and what in reality you did achieve.

When providing opportunities for children's learning and development you often have an idea of what you think the children will gain from the experiences and activities on offer. Many practitioners will link these in with the Development Matters aspects of the Early Years Foundation stage Framework.

Observation of children at play then becomes a valuable tool in assessing the value of the activities and experiences children are given. When evaluating activities and observations you will also reflect on practice as a matter of course and often question yourself to see if you achieved what you set out to do.

When looking at the policies and procedures of the setting your written policies inform all those involved in the setting or service of the guidelines for practice or how things are done. But how do you ensure that practice relates to policy and that you do what you say you are going to do?

## Challenging existing practice

By becoming an effective reflective practitioner and by attending regular training and development events you will have the opportunity to look at your practice and analyse its effectiveness in meeting the needs of the children and the setting you work in. By reflecting on what you do and how you do it you will have evidence that can suggest why things do or don't work in practice.

This evidence can then form the basis of challenging what you currently do and the way you do it. If something isn't working then change it!

It is easy for any practitioner to say 'we shouldn't be doing it like this, it isn't working' but it is certainly of more benefit to identify why it isn't working and think about how things can be changed to achieve better outcomes.

## Points for Reflective Practice

Consider any elements of practice that have been challenged or changed in any way recently. Did you:

- Share your thoughts and ideas with members of your team or other professionals around you?
- Give them the opportunity to share their thoughts and voice their concerns?
- Identify why changes to practice would be beneficial?
- Provide opportunities to receive and give feedback on changes to practice?

K4P817

## Case Study: A better way

Teresa is the manager at Little Tots Day Nursery. She has observed practice in the pre-school room which caters for 12 children aged 3–4 years at any one time. The three practitioners who work in the room have attended an information evening about providing continuous provision in the setting which Teresa took them along to.

Teresa has been observing practice to see if their new-found knowledge has helped them to develop their continuous provision. From her observations she has concluded that little has changed in the room and that children are still having set time for access to certain play and learning opportunities such as water play and painting. Teresa has decided to have a meeting with the team to discuss what she has observed.

- How can Teresa prepare for the meeting with her team?
- How can Teresa encourage the team to reflect on the training they attended?
- What should Teresa do to encourage the team to embrace the changes needed in the environment?

## Examining beliefs, values and feelings

Your personal **beliefs**, **values** and **feelings** affect your perceptions of issues in all aspects of your life. As the key terms tell you, these form the basis of your expectations in society. The way in which you develop your values and beliefs will be dependent on your own experiences through childhood and into adulthood, your upbringing and those who have been influential to you during your life may also play a part in the development of your own belief system.

It is perfectly acceptable for you to have you own opinions and principles; it is these that make you who you are, an individual. But of equal importance is the need to acknowledge and understand the values and beliefs of others because they too are entitled to their own opinions and principles. Difficulties will occur when you do not respect the opinions of others.

You can find out more about showing respect for others and their individuality in Unit 401.

Opinions are personal to the individual and may not be those of society as a whole. Considering this in Early Years practice is crucial as your own opinions may not be beneficial to practice; that is not to say they are worthless, but much consideration must also be given to the opinions of others so that best practice can be at the forefront in service delivery.

## Key Terms

**Beliefs** – opinions firmly held.

**Values** – moral principles or standards of behaviour.

**Feelings** – an emotional state or reaction.

K4P818

## Case Study: Examining your own feelings

Handa is the deputy manager of the pre-school; she has overall responsibility for the implementation of the Early Years Foundation Stage (EYFS) Framework. Handa has been very negative towards the new framework and feels that she shouldn't have to change what she does. Handa notices that her colleagues have become de-motivated and that they also speak of the EYFS in a negative way. On reflection Handa realises that it is down to her to shift the negative attitudes of the team to positive outcomes for the setting.

- How have Handa's perceptions affected those of others in the setting?
- Why should Handa examine her own beliefs and feelings?
- How can Handa change her attitude to the EYFS to benefit the setting?

**Figure 4:** It is important to keep up to date with legislation

## Keeping up to date with public policy

As a senior practitioner or manager of a setting, it is of extreme importance that you know and understand legal requirements that govern the way in which the setting and provision is developed and administered.

Legislation is constantly changing, as The Childcare Act 2006 demonstrates. It is extremely important that public policies change to keep up-to-date with ever increasing changes in society and our ever increasing knowledge of the needs of children.

You can find more information on The Childcare Act 2006 in Unit 402.

There are many policies that you need to be aware of and it is vital that all practitioners have a sound understanding of such policies both nationally and locally. Managers of settings need to be aware of their responsibilities in ensuring provision is compliant or acting in accordance with requirements. It is also the overall responsibility of the lead person in the setting to ensure all team members are well informed and understand any such policy requirements relating to their job role. Of equal importance is the practitioner's individual responsibility to ensure they know and understand such policies that affect their practice.

### Keys to Good Practice

Spend some time familiarising yourself with the legislation outlined below:

- The Childcare Act 2006
- Protection of Children (Scotland) Act 2003
- Every Child Matters
- Getting It Right For Every Child (Scotland)
- The Early Years Foundation Stage Framework
- The UN Conventions on the Rights of the Child
- Race Relations (Amendment) Act 2000
- Special Educational Needs and Disability Act 2001 (SENDA)
- Disability Discrimination Act 1995 (DDA)
- The Human Rights Act 1998
- The Rehabilitation of Offenders Act (1974)
- The Police Act (1997)
- Criminal Justice and Court Services Act (2000).

### Did you know?

K4P8I9

The Regulatory body Ofsted currently has overall responsibility to ensure all settings in England comply with government legislation regarding the provision and care offered to young children.

Central government disseminates the responsibility of compliance with national policies down to local government offices, and it will be your local authority with whom you should liaise with regard to implementation to any such policies and procedures. As Early Years practitioners you will be aware of the need for all daycare settings in England to be registered with and regulated by Ofsted.

The new Ofsted – the Office for Standards in Education, Children's Services and Skills – came into being on 1 April 2007. It brings together the wide experience of four formerly separate inspectorates. It will inspect and regulate care for children and young people, and inspect education and training for learners of all ages.

'We want to raise aspirations and contribute to the long term achievement of ambitious standards and better life chances for service users. Their educational, economic and social well being will in turn promote England's national success

To achieve this we will report fairly and truthfully; we will listen to service users and providers; and we will communicate our findings with all who share our vision, from service providers to policy-makers. We do not report to government ministers but directly to Parliament (and to the Lord Chancellor about children and family courts administration). This independence means you can rely on us for impartial information.

The Education and Inspections Act, which established the new Ofsted, specifically requires that in everything we do we should:

- promote service improvement
- ensure services focus on the interests of their users
- see that services are efficient, effective and promote value for money.'

The Childcare Act has four parts:

- Part 1: duties on local authorities in England.
- Part 2: duties on local authorities in Wales.
- Part 3: regulation and inspection arrangements for childcare providers in England.
- Part 4: general provisions.

Key provisions are as follows.

**K4P8I9**

- **Sections 1–5** require local authorities and their NHS and Jobcentre Plus partners to work together to improve the outcomes of all children up to 5 and reduce inequalities between them, by ensuring early childhood services are integrated to maximise access and benefits to families - underpinning a Sure Start Children's Centre for every community.

- **Sections 6, 8–11 and 13** require local authorities to assess the local childcare market and to secure sufficient childcare for working parents. Childcare will only be deemed sufficient if meets the needs of the community in general and in particular those families on lower incomes and those with disabled children. Local authorities take the strategic lead in their local childcare market, planning, supporting and commissioning childcare. Local authorities will not be expected to provide childcare direct but will be expected to work with local private, voluntary and independent sector providers to meet local need.

- **Section 7** re-enacts the duty for local authorities to secure a free minimum amount of early learning and care for all 3 and 4 year olds whose parents want it.

- **Section 12** extends the existing duty to provide information to parents, to ensure parents and prospective parents can access the full range of information they may need for their children right through to their 20th birthday. Local authorities will be required to ensure that this service is available to all parents and that it is pro-active in reaching those parents who might otherwise have difficulty accessing the information service.

- **Sections 39–48** introduce the Early Years Foundation Stage (EYFS) which will build on and bring together the existing Birth to Three Matters, Foundation Stage and national standards for under 8s daycare and child minding. The EYFS will support providers in delivering high quality integrated early education and care for children from birth to age 5.

- **Sections 31–98** reform and simplify the framework for the regulation of childcare and early education to reduce bureaucracy and focus on raising quality and standards. All providers caring for children from birth to the 31 August following their 5th birthday will be required to register on the Early Years register and deliver the Early Years Foundation Stage (unless exceptionally exempted). Childcare settings providing for children from the 1 September following their fourth birthday up to the age of 8 must register on the compulsory part of the Ofsted Childcare Register (unless they are exempt.) The Act introduced certain requirements that all providers

**Figure 5:** The Early Years Foundation Stage supports providers in delivering high-quality early education and care for children from birth to age 5

who are registering on the Ofsted Childcare Register will need to meet, some of which are provided for in the Act but most of which are laid down in associated Regulations made under the Act. Those childcare providers who are not obliged to register on the compulsory part of the Ofsted Childcare Register can choose to join the voluntary part of the Register. These providers will also need to meet certain requirements, which are laid down in Regulations made under the Act.

- **Sections 99–101** allow for the collection of information about young children to inform funding and support the local authority duties under the Act.

(The above was taken from www.surestart.gov.uk.)

## Protection of Children (Scotland) Act 2003

For practitioners working in Scotland the following applies.

- The Act plugs a gap in existing safeguards which allows unsuitable people to move from one childcare post to another without detection if they have not been convicted of an offence.

- The Act provides for Scottish Ministers to keep the Disqualified from Working with Children List (DWCL).

- An individual working in a childcare position, whether paid or unpaid, is to be referred to Scottish Ministers for inclusion on the DWCL, when they have harmed a child or put a child at risk of harm and have been dismissed or moved away from contact with children as a consequence.

- Organisations have a duty to refer such individuals to Scottish Ministers for possible inclusion on the DWCL.

- Failure to make a referral is an offence under the Act.

- The DWCL will also include those convicted of an offence against a child, when the court has referred them because it considers them to be unsuitable to work with children.

- Those on the DWCL (other than provisionally) are disqualified from working with children and will commit a criminal offence if they apply to or work with children.

- The Act extends disqualifications which already exist in England and Wales to Scotland too, except for those listed provisionally on the list kept for England and Wales under the Protection of Children Act 1999.

- It will be an offence for an organisation to knowingly employ a person to work with children if that person is disqualified from working with children.

- The Act provides safeguards for an individual including the right to appeal to a sheriff against inclusion on the DWCL.

- The fact that someone is disqualified from working with children will be released as part of a Disclosure for a childcare position available from Disclosure Scotland.

(Taken from www.scotland.gov.uk/Topics/People/ Young-People/children-families/17834/12088.)

## Every Child Matters

K4P8I9

The Change for Children programme aims to support parents from pregnancy onwards. The vision is to create a joined-up system of health, family support, childcare and education services so that all children get the best start possible in the vital Early Years.

- Ten Year Strategy for Childcare
  The strategy focuses on choice, availability, quality and affordability in childcare.

- Childcare Act 2006
  The act takes forward key commitments from the Ten Year Strategy to help transform childcare and Early Years services in England.

- Sure Start
  The programme aims to increase the availability of childcare for all, improve children's health and emotional development and provide a range of support to parents.

- Assessing and securing sufficient childcare
  From April 2008 local authorities have a new duty to secure sufficient childcare, which follows on from the childcare sufficiency assessments they are carrying out in their local areas.

- Childcare Implementation Project
  This is a collaborative project working with a group of local authorities to determine effective and innovative approaches to delivering the Ten Year Strategy.

- Early Support – services for disabled children in Early Years
  This is the central government programme for achieving better coordinated, family-focused

services for very young disabled children and their families.

- Affordable childcare campaign (DCSF Local Authority website)
  This is a communications campaign to help local authorities promote formal childcare settings to parents.

(Taken from www.everychildmatters.gov.uk/earlyyears.)

## Getting It Right For Every Child (Scotland)

Getting It Right For Every Child is a programme that aims to improve outcomes for all children and young people.

It promotes a shared approach that:

- builds solutions with and around children and families

- enables children to get the help they need when they need it

- supports a positive shift in culture, systems and practice

- involves working together to make things better.

Getting It Right For Every Child is the foundation for work with all children and young people, including adult services where parents are involved. It builds on universal health and education services, and is embedded in the developing Early Years and Youth frameworks. Developments in the universal services of health and education, such as Better Health Better Care and Curriculum for Excellence, are identifying what needs to be done in those particular areas to improve outcomes for children. Figure 6 on page 147 shows a practical model for this programme.

(Taken from: www.scotland.gov.uk.)

## Public policy affecting practice

These are the statutory guidelines to which you must give due regard in your everyday practice.

- Race Relations (Amendment) Act 2000. This act amends the 1976 Act, which outlawed racial discrimination.

- Special Educational Needs and Disability Act 2001 (SENDA). This Act ensures the right for disabled children and young people to access education and training without being discriminated against.

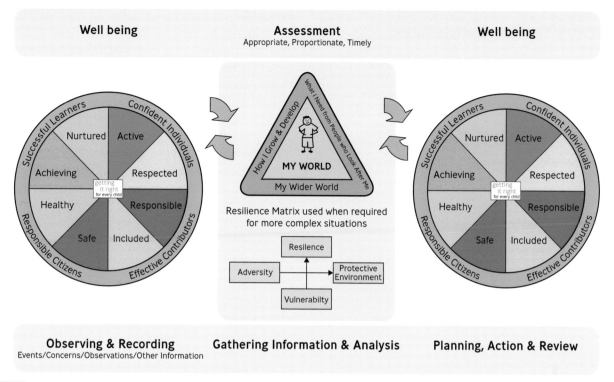

**Figure 6:** The Getting It Right For Every Child practical model

- Disability Discrimination Act 1995 (DDA). This Act is intended to prevent the discrimination that many disabled children and young people face.

- The Human Rights Act 1998. This Act outlines the basic rights of everyone in our society. These include: the right to life, protection from slavery, the right to education, the right to marriage.

- The Rehabilitation of Offenders Act (1974). All applicants for positions which give them 'substantial, unsupervised access on a sustained or regular basis' to children, must declare all previous convictions whether spent or unspent, and all pending cases against them.

- The Police Act (1997). This Act facilitated the set up of the Criminal Records Bureau for England and Wales.

- Criminal Justice and Court Services Act (2000) This Act covers disclosures and safeguarding children issues. It contains the list of convictions that bar offenders from working with children in 'regulated positions', such as employment in schools, children's homes and daycare premises where children are present.

- The UN Conventions on the Rights of the Child. This treaty aims to ensure that all children are treated fairly, and given equal access to care and education. A major part of this legislation is the United Nations Convention on the Rights of the Child. This is an international treaty that determines the human rights of the child, and to which the United Kingdom is a signatory.

> **Find it out**
>
> How do you ensure your setting meets regulatory requirements?
>
> Self-assessment forms are one way of establishing how you meet these.
>
> How pro-active are you and your setting in using self-assessment as a tool for reflection?

More information about this legislation can be found in Unit 402.

## Keys to Good Practice

When using reflection as a tool for learning, consider how your practice meets the needs of children, families, colleagues and other professionals you work with. Also consider how your practice meets the needs of regulatory and statutory requirements. How can this be achieved?

# 404.3 Take part in continuing professional development

## Continuing your professional development

### Training and development plans

Training and development plans provide an ideal opportunity to link the needs of the individual with the needs of children, families and the setting. A 'plan' for training and development can help you identify, source and achieve specific courses, workshops or training opportunities that will extend your current level of skill, understanding and knowledge.

You may have supported team members in building training and development plans to develop their skills, understanding and knowledge that may have been identified through your setting's appraisal system. In addition to supporting their learning and development it is also important to identify the gaps in skills and knowledge regarding your own practice and adopt strategies to fill these gaps and shortfalls. As discussed previously, this is where your ability to be a reflective practitioner will be important to enable you to think about further learning needs.

### How to develop a personal development plan

A personal development plan needs to be a clear and concise written document that navigates you on the appropriate path of learning and development. The personal development plan should focus on your needs and identify how meeting your needs can have a positive impact on the setting.

Personal development plans do not only need to consider any training needs you may have, but also any opportunities that can enrich your personal development and skills. It is important to consider that in addition to attending a child protection course to fulfil your training needs you may also benefit from development events such as assertiveness courses. This type of development is usually not associated with the general needs of the setting but would certainly increase your effectiveness in practice if you need support to adjust to a management or leadership role. Training and development that can enhance your personal attributes are just as important as those that increase your knowledge and skills.

As a senior practitioner or manager in a setting you may have little support in developing your training and development plan and will need to be proactive in identifying what your personal development needs are. These need to be shared with the person you are accountable too, which in some cases may be an absent proprietor. It is important that you engage their input and demonstrate to them your commitment to achieving goals. This demonstrates your continuing commitment to good practice and to the setting.

If you are a childminder you may find it difficult to engage the input of another, so you will play a dual role in seeking to enhance your professional development and support it. Accredited childminders may seek the support of their network coordinator to support them and encourage them to seek further training and development opportunities.

In any setting it is important that you are fully involved in building a professional development plan, and this should not be the responsibility of the setting's proprietor or a network childminding coordinator. The reason for this is that the plan needs to meet your needs and not theirs. Being fully involved in this will ensure you are committed to training and development as you have set these targets for yourself.

### Short-term and long-term objectives

Professional development plans generally account for a 12-month period in which you are aiming to identify and achieve training needs. This enables objectives to remain on track and not lose focus.

Your long-term objectives should form the basis of your plan, from there you can identify short-term objectives that will enable you to reach your final goal.

K4D820
K4P82I

Once you have identified your short-term and long-term goals you can decide how these will be achieved and the support you may need in achieving them.

Although personal development plans can be developed on an annual basis, this does not mean they only need looking at once a year. Once you have set your objectives you need to visit your personal development plan on a regular basis to see how you are progressing and identifying if you are on track, or if you need additional support to reach your goals or if you need more time to obtain your objectives.

## Reviewing your plan

How and when you review your plan will be entirely dependent on the environment you are working in and the time constraints of your job. As a childminder it will be easy to review your plan on a regular basis. For those seeking the support of a setting's manager or proprietor, time will need to be allocated so this can be discussed.

Appraisals are an ideal opportunity to review your personal development plan and identify if you are on target to meet your specified objectives. During appraisals you can also discuss any issues you have in achieving your goal and identify interim measures to support you, so that you don't lose the motivation to continue. Following appraisal, one-to-one sessions with your line manager will help in keeping the review process going.

## Setting objectives

When developing your training and professional development plan you need to consider whether your personal development plan is:

S = Specific

M = Measurable

A = Achievable

R = Relevant

T = Time-limited

- Specific: be clear about what it is you want to achieve, that way you are more likely to source the appropriate courses for your professional development.
- Measurable: you should be able to identify your progress and the benefits of accessing and attending any training and development opportunities.

- Achievable: consider your chosen outcomes very carefully and think about your time constraints and your ability to commit to the required time frames and requirements of training and development opportunities.
- Relevant: consider if the training and development you are thinking of attending meets not only your needs but those of your working practices. Consider the ways in which they can benefit you, your practice and your setting.
- Time-limited: set yourself time frames for achieving your desired goals. You will need to consider many aspects of the training and development before you set in place time frames for achievement. As well as considering the amount of study and attendance required for your development you will also need to consider the time scales of such undertakings.

An example of using SMART objectives in a professional development plan is shown in Table 3.

**Table 3:** Targets for completing NVQ CCLD Level 4

K4P82I

| Specific | I will undertake my NVQ CCLD Level 4 |
|---|---|
| Measurable | I will receive regular feedback from my assessor of my progress and overall achievement |
| Achievable | My role in the setting is appropriate for the requirements of the NVQ 4 framework |
| Relevant | The NVQ 4 will help develop my management skills and knowledge |
| Time-limited | I will complete my training in 12–15 months |

To help you identify your objectives for your personal development plan you can ask yourself a series of questions.

- What skills and abilities do I want to develop?
- What weaknesses in my practice could be strengthened?
- What training would benefit my practice?
- What type of learner am I?
- What time do I have to commit to training and development?
- What financial support can I access for training and development?

By seeking to find answers to these questions you will have identified opportunities to enhance your skills and knowledge.

**Figure 7:** What time do you have to devote to training and development?

K4D820

## Points for Reflective Practice

Write down your own responses to the questions on page 149.

■ Can you identify any training and development opportunities?
■ Are these opportunities you have already considered?
■ Are these opportunities you can incorporate in your personal development plan?

For more information on study skills and research techniques relating to K4D820, see Part One: The NVQ/SVQ – A Survival Guide.

How you set out your personal development plan will be dependent on your own preferences and those already adopted by the setting you work in if you are not working alone. Figure 8 on page 151 gives an example of a personal development plan. If you do not already have a working template you may find this useful to develop your own.

An example of a personal development plan

| Little Gems Day Nursery – Professional Development Plan | | | | | |
|---|---|---|---|---|---|
| Name: | | Setting: | | Job Role: | |
| Identified training or development need | Objectives | Learning activities | Progress review | Outcomes | Date achieved |
| EYFS support | To understand requirements of Early Years Foundation Stage framework | Attendance at information workshops | Course attendance on 12th November and 10th December | Successfully implement requirements of framework | Review December 2008 |
| First aid training | To gain qualification in Paediatric First Aid | Attendance on 12-hour programme | Course booked for 18th January | Early Years Paediatric First Aid | Projected for 20th January |

## Keys to Good Practice

Look at Figure 8.

- Are their any similarities to the ones used in your setting?
- Has your training and development plan identified SMART targets?
- How often is your training and development plan reviewed?

## Training and development opportunities

Once you have established your objectives for your personal development plan you will need to find out how you can achieve these, and much research may be needed in sourcing the most appropriate training. When doing this you will need to consider the following points.

- Is the training in house or at a designated training centre?
- Is the outside training within my locality or reasonably accessible?
- Will the training programme meet my objectives?
- Is the training cost effective?
- Can I or the setting afford to fund the training?

- Will I be required to take time out of work to attend training?
- Will I be required to attend training in my own personal time?
- Is the time scale of the training realistic and achievable?
- Are there any additional costs I will need to consider before committing to training?

## Training venues

There are many diverse training venues today, including traditional colleges, private training centres, in-house training providers and web-based training providers. The type of provider you use will depend on the training or development you are undertaking and the accessibility of the training provider.

If you live in a rural community you may find it difficult to travel to a college or training centre in a town location, and so may prefer to use a company that provides your training within your setting in the working day, or web-based learning if you have access to a computer and the Internet. Colleges are certainly a beneficial learning environment if you are the type of learner who needs support to stay on track and remain focused.

Look at Table 4 on page 152, which may show the most suitable option for you for a particular course or venue.

K4P822 | **Table 4:** Advantages and disadvantages of training venues

| Training venue | Advantages | Disadvantages |
|---|---|---|
| **Local FE college** | Regular classes or workshops to keep you motivated<br><br>Access to learning resources<br><br>Weekday contact with tutors or assessors<br><br>Extensive choice of programmes of study | Out of reach to rural communities<br><br>Programme timings not fitting with work and family commitments<br><br>Fear of traditional learning environments due to prior experiences |
| **Private training venue** | Access to small classes or drop in sessions<br><br>Access to learning materials | May not run sessions to suit individual needs<br><br>Out of reach to rural communities |
| **In-house training providers** | Brings the learning environment to your place of work<br><br>Bespoke training tailored to your individual needs<br><br>Training at a time suitable to you | Out of hours access to training provider may be limited.<br><br>May have to access own resources through public libraries |
| **Web-based learning** | Accessible any time of day or night<br><br>Regular email contact with tutors and learning mentors<br><br>Easy transfer of documentation and learning materials | Not suitable for those who do not have access to a computer<br><br>May seem daunting to those with little computer skills<br><br>Not appropriate for all aspects of all courses particularly where assessment of practice is required |

## Suitability of training or development

You will need to research the courses and events available to you and identify whether they will meet your learning requirements. The best way to do this will be to contact training providers and find out about the range of courses available and the learning outcomes of these. You can do this in a number of ways:

- request prospectus and course details
- attend open days
- speak to tutors.

All training providers should be able to provide you with comprehensive information about the courses you are interested in and the qualifications or awards you can gain.

## Cost

The cost of training will be a key consideration for you and your setting, particularly in an environment where many of your colleagues will be seeking to have their training and development needs met. Settings will need to consider if the training is value for money and beneficial to both the learner and the setting. It is important to make comparisons between training providers and ascertain what you are getting for your money.

It may be necessary for you to fund your own training, particularly if it is not seen to enhance your work performance or benefit the setting. However many managers and proprietors of settings will endeavour to help fund training to keep you motivated and show an interest in your development. Their commitment can in turn help you remain in employment there because you will feel well supported.

It is always worthwhile finding out if there is any additional funding available to support you or your setting. Local authorities are often a very good starting point for this as many of them have access to funds to support learners in the Early Years sector. Whilst they may not be able to fund the entire cost of your training they may certainly be able to help if there is an allocation of funds to the sector.

You may also be entitled to funding through other government initiatives and directives.

## Find it out

Contact your local authority to find out about funding available for training in the Early Years sector.

Visit the Learning and Skills Council website for other government initiatives and directives. You can find them at www.lsc.gov.uk.

## Time commitment

Time is a valuable commodity and it is often this that puts people off undertaking further training and development. Fitting learning in with work and family commitments can prove to be very difficult for many practitioners.

Having already sourced information on training and development opportunities, you will hopefully have identified the time you need to commit to your chosen programme of study. Before proceeding further it is worth identifying how you will make time for your learning.

Time management will be a valuable tool in enabling you to achieve your learning objectives. Sometimes you just have to make time, particularly when you know that the training you are wishing to undertake will be beneficial. You may be able to find time for yourself by asking family members to help around the house more, taking yourself off to a public library for a couple of hours study or maybe saving time by doing your grocery shopping online.

Many training providers will help you with study skills and the allocation of time to your studies. If you are undertaking assessment-based learning your assessor will work closely with you to plan assessments and requirements to meet the course objectives. By utilising their skills and experience you will be able to manage your time more effectively as you progress through your training.

If you are attending short courses, you may look at the options for attendance: is the course run in the day or on an evening or weekend? Due to home life commitments you may find it difficult to attend courses that are run at a specific time so will need to seek alternative options. Equally you may think that due to the limited time of attendance you can juggle your home life commitments in the short term to enable you to benefit from a valuable learning opportunity.

As well as identifying time commitments on a weekly or monthly basis you will want to know the overall time scale of the course you are attending. Formal qualification and programmes of study can range from a term, to a year to three years. If you are looking at starting a degree course, for example, you will need to consider your time management and your commitment over at least a three-year period.

Don't be put off by time commitment but use it well. In Part One study skills are discussed in greater detail. Revisit this section and see how you can manage your time effectively.

## Additional costs

Whilst all training providers will endeavour to inform you of all the cost implications of courses, there will be a need for additional costs. You will need adequate stationery to present your evidence of learning for most formal qualifications. You may also wish to access your own learning resources, such as subscriptions to magazines, journals and course textbooks. This can be made more cost effective by sharing resources with other learners or accessing your public library for learning materials.

## Identifying your own learning style

Earlier, you looked at learning styles (pages 135–36) and hopefully you have been able to identify the learning style that best suits your needs. Being able to do this will inevitably help you in choosing the most appropriate training opportunities available.

For example, if you are an activist you may benefit from a hands-on learning environment, such as a practical workshop or a qualification that is mainly work-based assessment, such as a NVQ programme.

Theorists will benefit from a learning environment that looks at varying approaches to practice and will want theoretical evidence that these make sense. A foundation degree in Early Years may be the right learning choice for you.

## Points for Reflective Practice

What do you think?

- Are your training choices determined by the style of learner you are?
- Are they determined by skills or knowledge gaps?
- Do you think that your learning style plays a part in your ability to acquire new knowledge and skills?

## Find it out

When you review your training and development plan, find out about training opportunities available to you. You may research by using the Internet, Early Years publications and community resources, such as the library or local Early Years Support services.

Consider how these opportunities can enhance your personal and professional development.

## Taking the plunge

Once you have considered all of the implications for training and development, and are well-informed of the requirements, you can take the plunge and be proactive in getting started. Beginning a course can be a daunting prospect, but keep focused about your learning objectives and just think about the untold benefits further training will have on your personal and professional development.

Table 5 gives some examples of different types of training events.

## Integrating new information

For any practitioner it is important that new information and skills gained from attendance at any training and development event have a positive impact on personal skills and professional knowledge and ability. Time does not stand still in the Early Years sector, and all those working with children should seek to continually update knowledge and skills and furthermore use these to develop practice.

It is inevitable that on training events you will be required to reflect on your own practice and it is this process that enables us to set benchmarks for continuing improvement. The very fact that you have taken time to attend the training or development

**Table 5:** Training and development opportunities

| Training and development opportunity | Examples of courses available | Type of training |
|---|---|---|
| **Regulatory training** | Getting ready for Inspection<br>Paediatric First Aid<br>Basic Food Hygiene | Information<br>Training<br>Training |
| **Professional qualifications** | NVQ CCLD Level 4<br>Early Years Foundation Degree<br>Early Years Professional Status | Qualification<br>Qualification<br>Qualification |
| **Short courses** | Behaviour Management<br>Creative Play Ideas<br>Makaton | Training/Information<br>Information<br>Training/Qualification |

K4P822

opportunity shows that you are striving for the best possible professional outcomes for yourselves and those you work with.

Share your learning with colleagues so that they too can use this information to inform and develop practice. Regular attendance at events such as requirements for registration and operation will ensure that you are well informed of regulatory requirements and encourage best practice, as you will strive to ensure compliance on your return to the setting.

## Points for Reflective Practice

Think about a training or development opportunity you have attended recently. Then consider how beneficial this has been to your practice.

- Did you increase your knowledge and/or skills from attending?
- Has this made you think about any aspects of your practice?
- What has changed as a result of gaining new knowledge and/or skills?

## Check Your Understanding

1.  What is reflection?
2.  How can reflection increase skills and knowledge?
3.  How can reflection increase confidence and self-esteem?
4.  What types of reflective analysis help you to reflect?
5.  How can reflection encourage best practice?
6.  What is the purpose and benefit of a continuing professional development plan?
7.  Why is it important to identify your own learning style?
8.  Where can you go to access additional training and development needs?

## Further references

www.everychildmatters.gov.uk

www.lsc.gov.uk

www.ofsted.gov.uk

www.scotland.gov.uk

www.surestart.gov.uk

Daly, M., Byers, E. & Taylor, W. (2009) *Early Years Management in Practice*, 2nd edition, Heinemann

Dewey, J. (1933) *How We Think*, D. C. Heath

Edgington, M. (2005) *What Makes a Reflective Practitioner? Practical Pre-School*, Step Forward Publishing

Ghaye, A. & Ghaye, K. (1998) *Teaching and Learning through Critical Reflective Practice*, David Fulton

Honey, P. & Mumford, A. (1986) *Using Your Learning Styles*, Peter Honey

Jay, R. (2002), *How to Build a Great Team*, Prentice Hall

Kolb, D. A. (1984) *Experiential Learning: Experience as the Source of Learning and Development*, Prentice Hall

Macleod-Brudenell, I. & Kay, J. (2008), *Advanced Early Years*, 2nd edition, Heinemann

Mann, P. (2005) *Sharpening the Instrument: Challenges to Improving Practice from Interactive and Self-Reflective Growth*, Sage Online

Schön, D. (1983) *The Reflective Practitioner*, Basic Books

Smith, P. A. C. (2001) *Action Learning and Reflective Practice in Project Environments that are related to Leadership Development*, Sage Publications

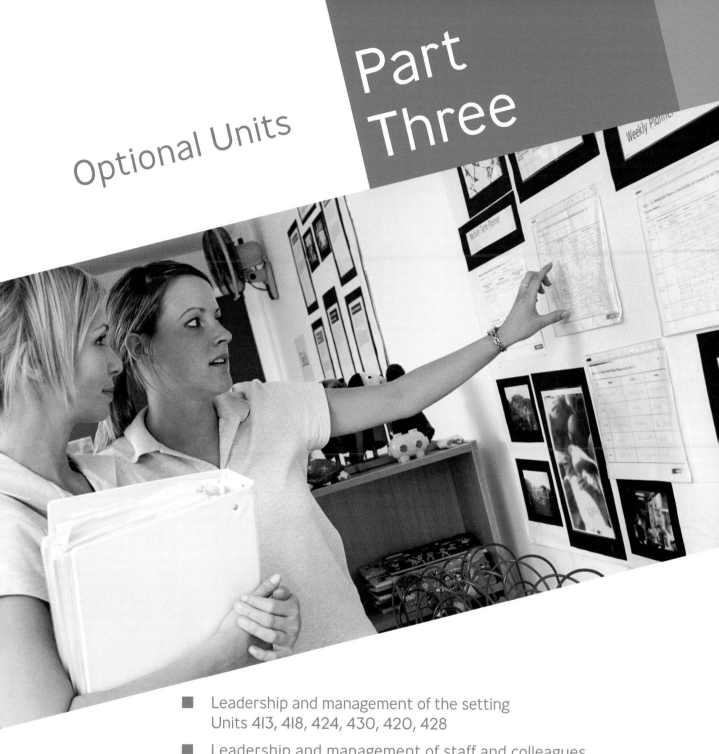

# Part Three

## Optional Units

- Leadership and management of the setting
  Units 413, 418, 424, 430, 420, 428

- Leadership and management of staff and colleagues
  Units 425, 426, 427, 429, 333

- Learning and curriculum development
  Units 405, 406, 407, 408, 409, 410, 411, 419

- Working in partnership
  Units 412, 416, 417, 421, 422, 423, 431

- Coordinating special educational needs and safeguarding children
  Units 414, 415, 326

# Leadership and management of the setting

The Units grouped here all relate to leading and managing the setting that you work in. They range from creating operational plans and reviewing policies and procedures to finance and health and safety.

These Units may be suitable if you are working in one of the following job roles:
- Manager of a nursery.
- Lead or senior practitioner.
- Manager of an aspect of a service within a group of nurseries.
- Working within Sure Start.
- Providing support to families and groups.

The Units covered by this section are:

| | |
|---|---|
| 413 | Develop and implement operational plans for your area of responsibility. |
| 418 | Coordinate and support the revision of policies, procedures and practice for registration and inspection. |
| 424 | Obtain additional finance for the organisation. |
| 430 | Manage finance for your area of responsibility. |
| 420 | Research and develop an area of practice. |
| 428 | Ensure health and safety requirements are met in your area of responsibility. |

# Unit 413   Develop and implement operational plans for your area of responsibility

This Unit is about developing an overall business plan for the setting and an operational plan for each area of responsibility showing how the business targets are to be met.

This Unit is not divided into individual elements, and so it has been divided into themes, with the Knowledge Statements detailed beside each section. The unit originates from the National Occupational Standards for Management and Leadership and is laid out in a different style than the other Units in this book. It is very important to have a realistic business plan when you are running a business. A business plan is a written document that describes a business, its objectives, its strategies, the market it is in and its financial forecasts. It also helps you to secure external funding and to measure success within your business. An operational plan will relate to the everyday operations in a setting.

## Your organisation

**413K015**
**413K016**
**413K018**
**413K019**

Your plan should begin by detailing the environment in which your organisation works. This is useful as it helps those who are considering attending the group. It will also help you if you decide to apply to outside funding.

You will need to include background information such as:

- the name of the setting
- history of the setting
- how the setting has developed
- the purpose of the setting
- the location of the setting
- who the setting caters for.

You should then go on to consider what the visions of your setting are, and the goals you wish to achieve.

This part of your plan should include the following:

- the aims and objectives of your setting
- the goals and future plans
- details of any changes planned

- any plans for expansion
- future training plans
- any plans for Quality Assurance
- how your setting follows the Early Years Foundation Stage, or the framework or curriculum relevant to your home country
- how you meet local needs, the groups who use the setting and who the potential users might be
- potential difficulties accessing the setting and how you plan to overcome this.

Having these items explained in your plan helps you to look at how you can improve performance and gives you a clearly defined vision of how you would like the future for your setting to look.

## Legislation

You will need to consider the legislation that your setting should be meeting and that affects your work with the children. You could list this in your business plan, or you could explain how you meet or plan to meet each legislative guideline. It is likely that these will have a huge effect on your work with children, as they form the foundation of the care and service that you are offering. In addition to Every Child Matters, some of the legislation that you will need to consider includes:

- The Childcare Act 2006
- The Early Years Foundation Stage (England)
- Curriculum for Excellence (Scotland)
- Foundation Phase (Wales)
- Foundation Stage (Northern Ireland)
- The Children Act 1989 and 2004
- Health and Safety at Work Act 1974 and 1992
- Health and Safety (First Aid) Regulations 1981
- Disability Discrimination Act 1995 (DDA)
- Special Educational Needs and Disability Act (SENDA) 2001
- The Disability Discrimination Act 2005
- Special Educational Needs Act (SEN)
- Race Relations (Amendment) Act 2000
- Fire Precautions (Workplace) Regulations 1997
- Food Safety Act 1990
- Control of Substances Hazardous to Health 1994
- Reporting of Injuries, Diseases and Dangerous Occurrences Regulations 1995 (RIDDOR).

You will also need to consider the specific local requirements, and the requirements of your home country.

Another area to consider is the scope of your policies and procedures. These must be accessible to parents, members of staff and Ofsted at all times and reviewed regularly (at least once a term). Staff should read and sign to show that they have read the policies and procedures. The suggested list of policies and procedures shown below is not exhaustive, and you may wish to include other policies and procedures.

- Operational plan.
- Procedures for lost or uncollected children.
- Staff/volunteer/committee member information.
- Registration system for children and staff .
- Planning of activities and opportunities for children to include how the needs of all ages and abilities will be met.
- Risk assessment.
- Record of visitors.
- Fire safety procedures/fire safety records and certificates.
- Operational procedures for outings.
- Vehicle records including insurance to include a list of named drivers.
- Child protection statement.
- Administration of medicines policy, to include prior parental consent to administer medicines and a record of medicines administered.
- Prior parental consent for emergency treatment.
- Accident record.
- Sick children policy.
- No smoking policy.
- Individual children's dietary needs records.
- Equal opportunities policy, to include an inclusion policy.
- Written statement about special needs.
- Behaviour management policy, to include an incident record.
- Admissions policy.
- Complaints procedure, to include a record of complaints.

## Planning

**Planning** itself is fairly simple. It is the process of working out how you will get from one point to another. This forms a large part of the manager's role.

Planning involves deciding what you wish to achieve (your goals) and making plans to ensure that these goals are met. This is a skill and one that will be learnt and improved with practice! Your plans should be a reflection of the service you offer and aim to offer within your setting. Try to remember that your operational plan is likely to be a working document and will reflect your individual setting. Information provided in the plan should be presented clearly, concisely, accurately and in a way that is clearly understandable. All plans should be flexible to allow for unforeseen circumstances.

Once you are sure that you are clear on what the objectives of the setting are and where you would like to see it develop, you can go on to create a plan that details how you will achieve your objectives. Any plan must be consistent with the objectives that you have identified.

Your plans should also include the arrangements for monitoring and evaluating the business plan itself, to ensure that it is working effectively.

### Key Term

Planning – the establishment of goals, policies and procedures for a business or economic unit.

## Short- and medium-term planning

413K001

There are many ways in which **short-** and **medium-term** plans can be created, two of which are detailed below.

- Task breakdown – this breaks the plan down into parts, i.e. the tasks that have to be accomplished if the objectives are to be achieved.
- Flow charts – these show a flow of the activities required to achieve the objectives, usually against a time scale.

**4I3K002**

## The importance of creativity and innovation

Planning is often seen as a dry process and not one where you would immediately think that creative thinking was needed. However, creative thinking and innovation are important, especially if problems have been encountered, or if an unforeseen change has happened. Creative thinking does not necessarily mean having a sudden piece of inspiration; it can also mean drawing on past experiences to reach a solution. Creative and innovative thinking often means that plans can be achieved more quickly and efficiently.

**4I3K003**

## SMART objectives

In order to make any objective achievable it should be SMART. This applies to all objectives including those that have been set for operational plans.

SMART means: Specific, Measurable, Achievable, Relevant and Time limited. (See page I49.)

When you are setting your objectives, it is important to be clear about what it is what you want to achieve, and also understand how you will know when you have achieved it.

**4I3K020**

## Building sustainability into your planning

A sustainable plan is one that will carry on working even when something goes wrong. Your plan should be flexible enough to cope with this. You should be aware of the levers in your plan, i.e. those things that make it work; the barriers in your plan, i.e. those things that might cause it to run into difficulties and also the constraints or limitations of the plan. Being aware of these will help your plan to be more sustainable.

### Funding streams

There is a large amount of funding available for the childcare sector. The A–Z Funding List, provided on the Sure Start website, lists all the available funding, with details about how to, and who can, apply for the various funding. This can be found on: www.surestart.gov.uk/surestartservices/support/funding/Funding & capital grants

### Consulting others

Managers who consult others are seen as more effective as they get better feedback. It is essential for managers to have a network of contacts. These contacts will probably include colleagues, other team members and managers and team members from other settings.

**Stakeholders** can be both internal and external and are those who have an interest in the performance of the setting. Colleagues are internal stakeholders. External stakeholders include families and shareholders, or those who pay for the service that you provide.

Any consultation should take place within this network. The wider the manager's network is then the more opportunities for consultation there will be.

**Figure 1:** A manager's consulting network may include colleagues, a manager, families or local community members

Consultation involves seeking the views of others and listening to what they say. This does not mean that the manager has to take account of it, but it is likely that they will review the way things are done because of it. By hearing what others have to say, a manager will be more likely to be able to make operational plans which will work.

## Methods of consultation

- Verbal, including face-to-face discussions, using a telephone or video conferencing.
- E-mails or letters.
- Meetings.
- Appraisals: a good opportunity to discuss issues one-to-one.
- Notice boards.
- In-house magazines.
- Surveys, either paper-based or telephone.
- Questionnaires.

Not all these methods are equally suitable for consultation. A notice board is a good way of informing people but is not much help if you wish to find out what people think. The method of communication will also depend on what managers want to consult about.

### Using resources effectively

413K007

Using resources effectively is a key part of the work of any manager. It is important that you understand how you can use the resources available to achieve the objectives set in your plan. The most obvious resources at your disposal are human, materials and equipment.

When planning to use human resources, managers may find that it is possible to use staff more flexibly than was originally thought possible. You may find that fewer staff are needed, or that they can work in other areas of the setting. The desired result will be that costs are reduced and quality is increased.

## Points for Reflective Practice

- What resources do you make use of in your job as a manager?
- How do you plan to use them?
- How do you know if you have used them effectively?

**Figure 2:** Think carefully about the method of consultation that you wish to use

**4I3K005** Planning for contingencies

It is likely you will face **contingencies** on a regular basis. One contingency that is likely to happen is a member of staff being ill and unable to work. This could cause major problems in your setting if you did not have a plan in place to deal with it. Your operational plan should try to predict situations that might occur and plan to deal with them. It is likely you will need a variety of ways to deal with each possible situation, and the option chosen will depend on the circumstance of the problem.

> ## Key Term
> Contingency – a possibility, something which may or may not happen.

## Delegation
**4I3K006**

Delegation does not mean giving someone the work they are employed to do, but giving them some work that you were expected to do. When you choose to delegate a task, it is still up to you to ensure that

it is carried out correctly. If it is not, you remain accountable for it because it still remains your work.

Delegating work to others frees up some of your time to do other tasks. It helps to develop other members of your team as they learn new skills though carrying out the set task. It can also help staff to feel valued.

Analysing and managing risk

Risk means the chance that something might go wrong. Your operational plan will need to identify where this might happen, predict what effect it might have and decide how you will manage it.

One way to deal with risk is 'risk assessment' where you identify a hazard and put a procedure in place to make it safer. Other risks may be more implicit and could include staff not doing their jobs correctly. You should include all of these in your operational plan.

Another form of risk is that associated with decision making. All decisions involve taking a risk, as the wrong option could be chosen. This is why contingency planning is important.

## Monitoring and evaluating

Monitoring and control are necessary if the operational plan is to be a success. If you check what is happening then you can respond quickly if things go wrong. This means that problems can be dealt with before they have any serious effect.

In order to monitor and control the plan you will need to have information to help monitor its progress. This may include budgetary information, quality assurance data, market research and time management. Depending on your role, this may either be provided for you, or you will need to source it yourself.

If things do go wrong then there are three paths open to you.

1.  Make changes in the work still to be done. This allows your plan to be maintained.

2.  Revise the objectives. This needs to be carried out in consultation with others.

3.  Do nothing. This may be appropriate, depending on the circumstances. You should exercise great caution if you decide to choose this path.

## Evaluation frameworks

413K010
413K026
413K022

Evaluation is not the same thing as monitoring. Whereas monitoring and controlling involve gathering information and taking corrective action to ensure that the objectives of operational plans are being met, evaluation means reflecting on how well the planning process has gone, and if the plan is working or not.

The evaluation framework is a cycle and there are four steps, as shown in Figure 3.

Once you have this information you may be required to report back and make recommendations. This will depend on your role and you should always follow the procedure of the setting.

**Figure 3:** The four steps in the evaluation framework

4. Make the required changes

1. Review the effectiveness of the operational plan

3. Consider what needs to be changed

2. Gather information on how well the plan is working

# Unit 418    Coordinate and support the revision of policies, procedures and practice for registration and inspection

This Unit is about preparing for registration and inspection by evaluating and updating the policies, procedures and practice of your setting.

The elements in this Unit are:

**418.1**    Evaluate policies, procedures and documentation in the light of requirements for registration and inspection.

**418.2**    Evaluate practice in the light of requirements for registration and inspection

**418.3**    Coordinate and support changes and development to meet registration and inspection requirements.

## 418.1 Evaluate policies, procedures and documentation in the light of requirements for registration and inspection

### The requirements of registration and inspection

K4P1038
K4P1040
K4M1041

Ofsted Early Years Directorate is the government department that deals with the **registration** and **inspection** of childcare. From April 2007 the organisation's full title changed to the Office for Standards in Education, Children's Services and Skills, but it continues to be known as Ofsted.

There are two childcare registers:

1.    Compulsory Childcare Register
Any person looking after children under 8 for more than two hours a day and receiving payment for doing so must by law register with Ofsted. This includes those looking after children in their own homes and those working on non-domestic premises.

2.    Voluntary Childcare Register
This register is mainly for those who look after children aged 8 and over, and those who provide care in the child's own home, including **home childcarers**.

### Key Terms

**Registration** – the process of checking that an applicant is suitable to care for children in a safe and stimulating environment.

**Inspection** – the system that provides a regular check to ensure that providers of childcare meet regulatory requirements.

**Home childcarers** – those who care for the children of no more than two families, wholly or mainly at the home of one of the children. This includes nannies.

The aim of registration is to:

- protect children
- ensure the welfare requirements of the Early Years Foundation Stage are met
- ensure that children are safe and well cared for
- promote high quality provision
- reassure parents.

Ofsted also carries out inspections of a **registered person** to ensure that the requirements and conditions of registration are being met and that the childcare provision provided not only meets the required standards but is of good or high quality. When an inspection is carried out, the inspector is trying to find out several things: what it is like for a child in your setting, how well the EYFS or relevant framework is delivered, and how children are helped to achieve the five Every Child Matters outcomes. It does this by making four judgements.

- How effective is the provision in meeting the needs of the children?
- How effectively are children helped to learn and develop?
- How effectively is the welfare of the children promoted?
- How effectively is provision led and managed or, in the case of childminders, organised?

## Find it out

Look at the following website to find out more about how these four judgements will be made http://ofsted.gov.uk/ofsted-home/forms-and-guidance

## Key Term

Registered person – an individual or organisation who is registered to provide childcare and/or Early Years provision.

Ofsted does not expect providers to make special preparations for inspection and this is one of the reasons why inspections occur unannounced. They do expect all providers to be continually working to improve their provision, and this can happen by self-evaluation and by continually searching out best practice.

You are required to keep the following records.

- A record of complaints from parents and detail of how they were resolved. These must be shown to the inspector if they contain complaints that relate to the EYFS, or the relevant framework in your home country.
- A record of medicine administered to children.
- An accident record, including treatment given.
- A record of Criminal Record Bureau checks.
- Records for each of the children in your care, to include: full name, date of birth, names and addresses of parents and carers and emergency contact details.
- Name, address and telephone number of the registered person, employees and anyone who lives on the premises.
- A daily record of the names of the children, and the times they attend.
- A list of the key persons and the children they are responsible for.
- Records of risk assessments.

You are also required to have and implement the following policies and procedures:

- safeguarding children
- equal opportunities
- supporting children with additional needs
- short- and long-term medicine
- behaviour management
- concerns and complaints
- missing children
- emergency evacuation
- uncollected children.

## Consultation with others

It is useful to check these policies, procedures and documentation to see if they meet current requirements and to carefully check if there are any gaps or inaccuracies. This will help you to meet the inspection requirements. It is also helpful to involve other stakeholders when you are carrying out this task. This can include colleagues, management committees, trustees and parents and families.

**Figure 4:** You are legally required to keep records, whatever type of setting you are in

There are many ways you could do this and they could include staff meetings, asking for feedback and questionnaires. The method you choose will depend on the type of setting that you work in.

### Previous inspections

K4PI044

It is important that any actions from previous inspections are dealt with quickly and in line with the inspectors' recommendations. You should also look at putting right any weaknesses that were identified. You can then begin to consider how to ensure that your policies, procedures and documentation are ready for the next inspection. If you have already carried out the consultation process then you will have made a good start. Other areas you can consider in order to prepare for the next inspection include the following.

- Check your last report and consider if the changes you have made have had a positive effect on the setting.

- Make sure you and your staff know, understand and implement the EYFS.
- Ensure you continue to meet the requirements of registration.

## 418.2 Evaluate practice in the light of requirements for registration and inspection

### How the requirements of registration and inspection affect practice

As well as considering your policies, procedures and documentation you will also need to consider how the inspection requirements will affect your practice and that of your staff. There may be areas that show good practice and need supporting and there may also be areas where improvement is required.

## Consultation with others

A useful part of evaluating your practice and that of staff is to consult with others. This can include colleagues, children and families.

Colleagues could be involved by carrying out peer observations on each other, and by providing peer support. This process must be carried out in a sensitive manner.

Children and families can be involved by inviting them to attend some staff meetings, having a suggestion box and by encouraging good communication at all times. You could also send out questionnaires and keep copies of these to show Ofsted.

When the inspection happens, remember to introduce the Ofsted inspector to the children. You should also encourage the parents to talk to the inspector. Following the inspection you need to make copies of the report available to the parents.

## Inspection

Newly registered providers are inspected within the first year of their registration. All settings will be inspected at least once within the first three or four years of the implementation of the EYFS. Inspections will be a priority for those settings that received an 'inadequate' grading, or those settings that have experienced a high number of changes. If Ofsted receive a complaint they will always follow it up with an inspection. All other settings are randomly inspected and you will receive little or no notice.

Normally inspections take a few hours. They will usually be carried out by one inspector. You should carry on with the normal routines during an inspection.

During an inspection, the inspector will check your provision and that the conditions of registration are understood and are being met. It is likely the inspector will talk to the staff, children and parents and observe their practice to see if the policies and procedures are being followed. They will assess the safety of the premises and check your risk assessments. They will also want to see how you ensure that persons without a CRB check do not have unsupervised access to the children.

You will be given feedback at the end of the visit, and this normally takes about an hour. If the requirements have not been met, the inspector will explain to you what you need to do and what will happen next. If you have any concerns or complaints then these should be raised with Ofsted as soon as possible. You also have the right of appeal against any decisions made.

## 4\8.3 Coordinate and support changes and development to meet registration and inspection requirements

### The role of self-assessment

K4P\043

Evaluation and self-assessment helps you to identify and build on effective practice, and to recognise areas where practice is not as good. Carrying out self-assessment helps you to ensure that the provision you offer is of a high standard and meets the children's learning, development and welfare needs.

Ofsted provide you with a self-evaluation form to help you to complete this process. This form is not compulsory, but if it is not completed Ofsted will still want to see how you carry out self-evaluation.

Self-assessment should be carried out on a regular basis, at a minimum once a year. The period of time between evaluations is likely to depend on the type of setting you work in.

### Implementing change

K4P\046

Once you have completed your self-assessment you will then be able to clearly see where you need to make improvements. You should consider how best to make these changes and improvements and present your ideas to your colleagues and other stakeholders in the setting. You will need to explain exactly what you would like to see happen and set in place an action plan to ensure that any change happens in an organised and managed way.

These changes need to be seen in a positive light, and you may need to be sensitive to colleagues' feelings when implementing them. You should emphasise that the outcome of these changes will be beneficial for the children and will improve the provision overall.

As part of this process you may identify training and qualification needs, and should encourage your colleagues to take these up, both to improve their skills and to improve the provision of the setting.

K4PI039
K4PI047

## After the inspection

After the inspection you will receive a letter from Ofsted that will either confirm the requirements for registration were met, or outline what you need to be doing in order to meet the requirements. You will also receive a short report which will include your grading, a summary about the effectiveness and quality of your provision, a summary of improvements made and detail about what you need to do before the next inspection.

If your provision did not meet the requirements of registration then you will need to take action to put this right. Ofsted will explain to you what you need to do.

Registration may be suspended if Ofsted has reason to believe that the children in your care are or could be at risk of harm. Registration may be cancelled if Ofsted have reason to believe that you are failing to meet the requirements and conditions of registration. In some cases, Ofsted will decide to prosecute if an offence under the Childcare Act 2006 has been committed.

There are four grades that your provision can be given, as outlined in Table I.

**Table I:** Ofsted gradings

| Grade | Description | Why this grade has been given | What happens next |
|---|---|---|---|
| I | Outstanding | Provision that is of an exceptional standard. Children receive excellent care and make very good progress in their learning and development | Re-inspection in 3 years, unless a complaint is received. Practice may be disseminated to other settings |
| 2 | Good | Children are well cared for and make good progress in their learning and development | Re-inspection in 3 years, unless a complaint is received |
| 3 | Satisfactory | Provision is adequate but could be better. Children make steady progress, but there is scope for improvement | Re-inspection in 3 years, unless a complaint is received |
| 4-I | Inadequate Category I | Provision is weak and the standard of care that the children receive is not good enough. Little progress is made by the children and there has been little improvement since the last inspection | A notice to improve will be send, detailing what needs to be done to improve. An unannounced inspection will happen to check that actions have been taken. A full inspection will take place within the next year |
| 4-2 | Inadequate Category 2 | Provision is poor and needs urgent attention. Standards of care and progress are unacceptable. Provision gives cause for concern | If children are at risk, registration will be suspended. If not, immediate improvements must be made. The setting will be visited every 3 months to check if the improvements are being made |

## Can't find what you were looking for?

| Level 4 KS Number | Knowledge Statement | Can be found in... |
|---|---|---|
| K4M797 | Data protection | Unit 403 |

## Did you know?

The Childcare Act 2006 is the law that explains the duties that local authorities have to improve outcomes for children and to ensure access to information about provision in their area. It also details the legal frameworks for the regulation and inspection of the childcare provision for children from birth to age 17 and legislates the Early Years Foundation Stage (EYFS).

## Keys to Good Practice

- Spend some time thinking about what your organisation's vision, objectives and plans for the future are. Write these down.
- Make a note of which of these activities will require additional finance, i.e. that which will not come from the revenue of the setting.
- Next to each one, write an estimated cost.

# Unit 424   Obtain additional finance for the organisation

This Unit is about identifying the need for and obtaining additional finance.

This Unit is not divided into individual elements, and so this section has been divided into themes, with the Knowledge Statements detailed beside each section. The Unit originates from the National Occupational Standards for Management and Leadership and is laid out in a different style from the Units you are familiar with.

## Why additional finance is needed

Your organisation is likely to have a vision and plans for its future, i.e. how and where it sees the provision developing, and what resources and steps it needs to take to get there. It may already be generating some surplus income, but this may be insufficient to fund activities such as investment in new equipment or proposed changes. If this is the case, you may need to seek out additional finance. Childcare and Early Years education are high on the government's agenda so there is a lot of money available. However, it can be difficult to get funding and it is useful to seek out expert advice.

## Sources of financial expertise

424K28
424K03

Financial expertise can help you when you are trying to seek out additional funding. Your setting may have experts that it already uses, or you may be looking into additional funding for the first time. In this case, Table 2 on page 172 may help you to find the correct expert.

## Types of finance available

424K22
424K04
424K05
424KI7
424K07

There is a large amount of finance available, some of which is listed below. These are the main sources as recommended by Sure Start.

- Awards for All is a national grant programme to help small groups enjoy community activities.
- Charitable trusts will fund the voluntary sector, including voluntary childcare.
- Children's Centre Funding will fund the development of integrated care and education for young children.
- Children's Fund will help children who are in poverty or at risk by providing local solutions aimed at involving childcare in the community.
- Community Fund has two programmes, a main programme and a programme for projects up to £60,000. Both of these aim to help disadvantaged groups and improve the well being of the community.
- Countryside Agency helps to develop childcare in the countryside.

**Table 2:** Sources of financial expertise

| Source | Brief description |
|---|---|
| Business Link www.businesslink.gov.uk | Business Link provides independent and unbiased business advice, information and services to help small firms. Advisors can help by offering practical guidance, such as helping you to draw up a business plan or cash-flow forecast |
| Councils for Voluntary Action (CVS) | There are over 300 CVS in England. They help to promote local voluntary and community action, and develop initiatives among other areas. They offer support to voluntary groups |
| Department for Children, Schools and Families www.dcsf.gov.uk | The Sure Start Unit is a government unit. It works with local authorities, local communities, and voluntary, independent and private-sector organisations. It has regional advisors who can give advice about developing a funding strategy |
| Early Years Development and Childcare Partnerships (EYDCPs) | EYDCPs work with their local authority to plan and develop high-quality, affordable early years education and childcare for all families and children who need it |
| Sure Start local programmes | There is a network of regional officers who are based in Government Offices for the Regions. They provide support and advice on all Sure Start local programmes |
| Government Offices for the Regions www.gos.gov.uk | Government Offices for the Regions are responsible for managing various funds including European funding and Community Chests. They are also responsible for administering funds for regional initiatives. Government Offices can give guidance and information about what funding is available and how to apply |
| Local authorities | Local authorities are responsible for accessing and coordinating funds to develop Early Years education. Local authority business support officers can give advice and information about expressions of interest, funding bids and proposals that are in progress |
| National Early Years Education and Childcare Organisations | National childcare organisations can give information and support through websites, publications, conferences and seminars, and help lines. These organisations include: Daycare Trust Kids' Clubs Network National Childminding Association National Day Nurseries Association Pre-school Learning Alliance |
| New Opportunities Fund www.nof.org.uk | The website provides lots of information including frequently-asked questions; case studies and copies of letters sent to local childcare partnerships. You can also call the information team |
| Regional Development Agencies www.englandsrdas.com | Regional Development Agencies are responsible for coordinating regional economic development and regeneration, and work closely with Government Offices for the Regions. Officers can answer questions about local strategies for your region |

■ Department for Children, Schools and Families provides the Early Years and Childcare Grant which is the main grant for local authorities to develop the National Childcare Strategy. They also make funding available for disadvantaged areas, children's centres special educational needs, training and quality, and childcare development.

■ Early Excellence Centres provide funding that aims to support one-stop services for children and their parents.

■ European Social Funding aims to improve training and education and show adaptability and enterprise.

■ Housing associations can contribute to new childcare places as a part of maintaining communities.

■ Local authority funding may be available from your local EYDCP, including childcare services, sport, health improvement, Healthstart and Bookstart.

- Neighbourhood Renewal Fund helps local partnerships to improve childcare in disadvantaged areas.
- Community Chests aim to help local people get involved in local communities.
- New Opportunities Fund supports creating play opportunities for children and young people.
- Small Firms Loan Guarantee Scheme guarantees loans from banks for small firms such as childcare businesses.

## Find it out

Look at www.surestart.gov.uk/surestartservices/support/funding for more detailed information.

## Guidelines and codes of practice for funding

It is likely that individual funding bodies will have their own guidelines and codes of practice to operate within and it is worthwhile checking the requirements of these and ensuring that you are happy with them when you begin the funding application process(for example, many people choose to use the Co-operative Bank because it has strong ethics). Be aware that these will vary between providers.

You also need to ensure that you are aware of the terms and conditions of the funding, and be clear about any conditions that are attached to it. You should ensure that you can meet these conditions and will not be in danger of defaulting.

The Financial Services Authority is the independent government body that regulates the behaviour of the financial services industry. It ensures that rules and regulations are being followed and that businesses understand what they can and cannot do. It also ensures that all customers are treated fairly.

## Find it out

You can find out more about the Financial Services Authority and their role from the following website. www.fsa.gov.uk

## Costs, benefits and risks

424K23
424K06
424K08

Each organisation had its own particular needs for additional finance, and a different attitude to the risks that they are prepared to take to secure it. All types and providers of finance have their different costs, benefits and risks, which may include some of the following:

- interest rates on loans
- grants have to be used for stated purpose
- time cost when applying for finance
- most lenders require some type of security on a loan
- some types of funding may take longer to secure than others.

It is important to consider the potential risk when applying for finance, to ensure that the business does not take any risks that might put it in an unsecure position. This includes the risk of raising finance to fund something that may or may not work out (for example doubling the capacity of the nursery but then being unable to fill the spaces).

When working out the cost of obtaining finance from providers, you should include any hidden costs, fees or charges, as well as interest rates and the way in which interest is charged (daily, monthly or yearly).

## Consultation with others

424K10
424K21
424K24

It is important to consult with other relevant people in the organisation prior to seeking additional finance. You may find that they have previous experience of doing so, or a better of knowledge of where and how to seek funding. You may also find that they have specialist skills that you will be able to utilise when going through the application process. It is important to be sensitive to the needs of the stakeholders, and also to ensure that you stay within the limits of your authority.

## Applying for finance

424K02
424KII
424K25
424KI2
424K26
424KI5
424K29

It is important to make a business or funding plan prior to applying for funding so you understand and are able to clearly explain what your requirements are. All plans should be SMART.

> You can find out more about SMART objectives in Unit 413.

You should also ensure that the aims of your plan are clear and provide the reader with evidence about why you need more funding. Ensure that the fund you are applying for is suitable for your requirements and that you or your setting is eligible. You can do this by checking that the aims of your plan match the conditions for securing funding.

You will need to allow time for your plan to be considered, and ensure you spend time checking on the progress of your application.

Once finance has been agreed it is likely that a formal agreement will be put in place. This will probably cover the term of repayments, the amount of payments, when you will receive the finance, and if any exceptions can be made, for example if you run into difficulties making repayments. They may also cover the conditions for you to receive the grant. When monitoring the effectiveness of agreements you are looking to make sure that payments come in on time and that paperwork is accurate and up to date.

## Dealing with contingencies

One of the contingencies that you may need to deal with is a shortfall in additional funding. If this happens you should have a strategy in your plan to deal with it. This is likely to include applying for funds from elsewhere, or cutting back on the costs of the project. Other contingencies may include the funding coming through later than expected or deadlines being missed and having to reapply. You may also need to consider what will happen if you are unable to repay the loan. Again, it is important that you have plans in place to deal with these in order to prevent your project being severely affected.

# Unit 430   Manage finance for your area of responsibility

This Unit is about managing finance, including budgets and using this to control performance and deal with variances.

This Unit is not divided into individual elements, and so this section has been divided into themes, with the Knowledge Statements detailed beside each section. The Unit originates from the National Occupational Standards for Management and Leadership and is laid out in a different style than the Units you are familiar with.

## Budgets within your setting

A budget is a financial plan that shows the income (money coming in) and expenditure (money going out) in your setting for the year ahead. It helps to identify what money you need to cover the costs in the setting and helps control the expenditure. It also monitors your income. It is unlikely that your budget will be 100% accurate, as most budgets are usually a guess at what you think you will need when you prepare plans for the year ahead. Things are likely to change in the coming year, some costs may increase and some may decrease. The main objective of a budget is to make your total income for a given period greater than or equal to your outgoings.

In your setting you may be responsible for the whole budget, or just part of it. It is important that you understand your financial responsibilities, and that they are agreed with your manager early on. This will ensure that there are no misunderstandings, and no unplanned or unauthorised spending. You must act within the limits of your authority at all times.

## Points for Reflective Practice

Reflect on the responsibility that you have for budgets within your setting, in particular the following items.

- What is your area of responsibility?
- What is the vision of your setting?
- What are the objectives of your setting?
- Are these reflected in the operational plans?
- What are your financial responsibilities?
- What are the limits of your authority regarding financial responsibilities?
- What is the budgeting period used in your organisation?
- What are the procedures in your setting for preparing and approving budgets?
- What are the procedures in your setting for monitoring and reporting on performance against budgets?
- What are the procedures in your setting for revising budgets?
  Are you clear about your responsibility and what it means for you? Why not make a note of your thoughts and arrange to have a professional discussion about them with your NVQ assessor?

## Legal, regulatory and ethical requirements in the sector

You need to ensure that you comply with any legal, regulatory and ethical requirements of your setting and of the sector. These may include the following.

- Ensuring that your bookkeeping is accurate.
- Declaring all income.
- Complying with codes of practice relating to any grants (e.g. Nursery Education Grant for 3 and 4 year olds).
- Completing and filing tax returns on time.
- Ensuring data protection requirements are met.

- Handling cash correctly.
- Complying with Minimum Wage legislation.
- Being aware of the PAYE requirements.

## Find it out

For more information look at the following website: www.financehub.org.uk/managing_money_and_resources/default.aspa.

## Points for Reflective Practice

Think about any codes of practice to which you are required to adhere in your setting. For example, do you receive any grants which have terms and conditions attached to them? Have you read the 'small print'? Make sure you have read any codes of practice and that you fully understand the procedures for reporting information back to the funding source.

## Setting a budget

430K03
430K04
430KI5
430K22
430K26

A budget is drawn up in order to help you to achieve your objectives. Because of this, the first thing you need to do when budgeting is decide what your objectives are. You can then set the budget to help meet them.

Next you will decide how long you are budgeting for. Normally this is one year, but this can be broken down into more manageable chunks.

You then need to gather together information to help you compile the budget. This may include:

- past and current performance figures from **profit and loss accounts**
- **balance sheets**
- **cash flow forecasts**
- costs
- predicted income.

## Key Terms

**Profit and loss accounts** – the financial records you need to keep in order to report your profit or loss.

**Balance sheet** – a financial statement at a given point in time. It provides a summary of what a business owns and what it owes at a particular date.

**Cash flow forecast** – this enables you to predict highs and lows in your cash balance.

It is important to make sure that your figures are as accurate as possible. You may need to do some research if you are unsure. To make it easier, it can often be useful to break down the budget into groups, like the example below:

- staff – salaries, national insurance, training etc.
- premises – rent, rates, heat, light, insurance, maintenance, repairs etc.
- resources – books, subscriptions, equipment, materials etc.
- admin/stationery – stamps, phone, paper etc.

You may also find it useful to consult with colleagues as you go through this process, as they may be able to help you to identify any priorities and potential problems. You can also use this as an opportunity to encourage your colleagues to think about ways of reducing expenditure and increasing income, and reinforcing the importance of this.

Once you have created your budget you will need to submit it to the relevant person in your organisation.

## Delegating responsibility

It is a large task to undertake a budget and if you are confident in the team around you then you may be able to delegate part of it to other colleagues. You may also be able to split the budget down into different areas and delegate a specific part, such as the art and craft materials for the term or year. If you choose to do this then it is important that you explain clearly to them what is required and that they will be held responsible for it. You should also explain that you are happy to give them support as they undertake this task, and discuss the proposed budget with them once it is completed.

## Variances in a budget

When budgets are actually put into practice, it is likely that the budgeting figures will differ from the actual figures. This could be for several reasons; because of a calculation error that has occurred, because of a change in plan, or due to external factors such as changes in interest rate and fluctuations in demand for the services you offer. All these differences are known as variances, and they can be favourable or unfavourable. Variances can also happen to income and expenditure figures.

**Figure 5:** It can be helpful to break down your budget into segments

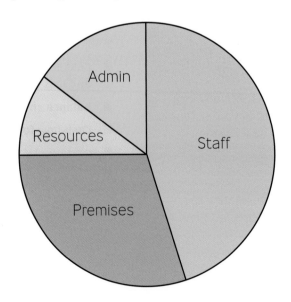

If you do identify a variance, it is important to act on it quickly in order to keep your budget up-to-date and remain in control. You should calculate the difference between the actual figure and the budgeted figure.

If the variance is small then it can be overlooked, as there is likely to be a small degree of variance in most figures. If it is a larger variance and has a negative effect then you will need to look into it as a matter of urgency. This will help to identify the reason why it happened and hopefully enable you to prevent it from happening again in the future. It is possible that the budget will need to be rewritten to reflect this change.

## Dealing with contingencies

It is important to have a contingency plan so that you are prepared for any unforeseen circumstances that may occur and have a detrimental effect on the budget. You may consider putting money aside for this, or being able to access extra funds. For example, you may experience loss or damage to property and the solution to this would be having the correct insurance, or alternative premises. Another example would be a loss of staff or long-term staff illness, and the solution for this would be to have the funds in place to employ extra staff.

## Consultation with others

When you are communicating with others you need to ensure that you use an appropriate style of communication depending on the person and the situation. You may be able to consult with colleagues who already have financial responsibility, and ask them to provide you with an estimated figure to go into your budget. This should mean that the budget is more realistic. They will also be more involved with the budget, which means they will be more committed to trying to meet it. You should also communicate any changes in the budget that have been made in response to variances or unforeseen development. This will help to keep everyone fully informed.

You can find out more about communication styles in Unit 401.

**Points for Reflective Practice**

Think about the people who you need to consult with in your setting. Who do you need to report to regarding budgets? Who needs information on the financial performance of your area? What information do they need? When do they need it and in what format is it presented?

## Fraud

430KI4
430K29

Your budget may help you to identify suspected **fraud**. Types of fraudulent activities may include ordering equipment that is for personal use through company accounts, inaccurate record keeping or failure to keep accounts up to date in order to disguise the movement of money.

If you suspect fraud you should make an immediate note of your concerns and all the relevant details. You should then pass this on to someone with appropriate authority, which is normally your line manager.

You can also contact the following places if you suspect fraud:

- Audit Commission Fraud Hotline 0845 0533646
  www.audit-commission.gov.uk
- Public Concern at Work 020 7404 6609
  www.pcaw.co.uk

### Key Term
Fraud – a deception made for personal gain or the illegal acquisition of money or goods.

## Reviewing a budget

430KI6
430KI7
430K08
430K27

Part of budgeting is to carry out regular reviews. This helps you to identify any problems and allows you to manage your cash flow. When you are carrying out reviews you will need to compare your actual income with your projected income and identify any shortfalls or reasons for increased income. This helps you to be more accurate when planning future budgets. You also need to look at your expenditure and look at how any costs differed from those detailed in your budget and analyse these. There may be trends that will affect your finances and budget. These could include changes in the market, such as new competitors in the market, price changes and cost increases.

Your budget can help you to measure performance, because you can compare your projected figures with those from previous years. Falling profits are an indicator that performance is not up to standard and you should be able to deal with this quickly.

> ## Did you know?
> The Public Interest Disclosure Act 1998 provides you with protection from any reprisals as long as you meet the rules set out in the Act:
> - you must disclose the information in good faith
> - you must believe it to be substantially true
> - you must not act maliciously or make false allegations
> - you must not seek any personal gain.

# Unit 420  Research and develop an area of practice

This Unit is about researching an area of practice through data collection, analysis and evaluation. It leads on to how to identify potential changes to practice and the impact of these changes.

> ## Key Term
> Literature search – looking up existing relevant information on your topic, using textbooks, journals, published work and the Internet.

> ## Find it out
> Alliance for Childhood publishes many good papers which may be useful for your literature search. www.allianceforchildhood.org.uk.

> The elements in this Unit are:
> **420.1**   Identify research opportunities.
> **420.2**   Collect and analyse data.
> **420.3**   Identify changes to practice resulting from research.

## 420.1 Identify research opportunities

### Literature search

All research requires you to carry out reading, and to provide evidence of that reading. Once you have decided on your broad topic (in this case, best practice developments in childcare) your next step is to read about what other people have written on this topic, known as a **literature search**. You could research this on the Internet or use the library to read research papers. You need to keep evidence of this and a good way to do so is to use the Harvard referencing system. Reading further into a topic not only helps you to find out more, but you will be able to see what other methods of research have been used.

## Areas of best practice

You then need to narrow this down and decide exactly what area of practice you want to focus on. This can be quite daunting, so a good place to start is to think about where your interests lie and what areas you think could be improved either in your own practice or in your provision. Make a list of all these and then try to narrow it down and choose one that you feel would be of real benefit to you. Some ideas are as follows:

- early language development
- learning theories
- learning through play
- the value of outdoor play
- Early Years Foundation Stage
- government studies: Researching Effective Pedagogy in the Early Years (REPEY), Study of Pedagogical Effectiveness in Early Learning (SPEEL) and Effective Provision of Pre-School Education (EPPE)
- alternative curriculums: Reggio Emilia, Steiner and Te Whariki.

## Find it out

Why not read more into some of these topics? Have a look at the following web links.

REPEY: www.dcsf.gov.uk/research/data/uploadfiles/RR356.pdf

SPEEL: www.dfes.gov.uk/research/data/uploadfiles/RB363.doc

EPPE: www.surestart.gov.uk/research/keyresearch/eppe

## Research methods

Once you have decided on the area you wish to research, and carried out a literature review into this area, you will then need to decide what methods of research you will use in your own project.

Some research methods you may like to consider are described in the table below.

**Table 3:** Research methods

| Research method | Description |
| --- | --- |
| **Surveys** | Surveys can include interviews or questionnaires and the aim is to obtain information from a representative part of the group chosen |
| **Interviews** | Interviews are normally carried out one-to-one and allow you to find out people's ideas and opinions |
| **Experiments** | Normally scientific and carried out with control groups. An example of an experiment was Albert Bandura's Bobo doll experiment (see Further references on page 184 for more information) |
| **Observations** | Observations allow you to carry out in-depth studies |

You can find out more about Bandura's Bobo doll experiment in Unit 403.

It is likely that you will be collecting both **primary** and **secondary** data. Primary data is the information that is collected by you, for example questionnaires, interviews and observations. Secondary data is the information that comes from other sources such as books or magazines.

You will also need to consider the difference between qualitative and quantitative information sources. Quantitative data is in the form of numbers. For example, you may want to find out how many parents agree or disagree with giving their child fizzy drinks. Quantitative research methods include experiments and structured questionnaires. Qualitative data is about finding out ideas and opinions. For example, you may want to find out if parents think that outside play is important. Qualitative research methods include open interviews and observations.

Questionnaires are a common way to conduct research. In their simplest form they are a list of questions and can either be given out to be collected later or completed with you in person. They allow you to collect information quickly and easily. They will probably be a mix of open questions, where you ask the respondent to fill in their own answers, and closed questions where the respondent chooses from several set answers.

## Key Terms

**Primary data** – information that you collect yourself.

**Secondary data** – information that you use from other sources.

## Ethics

K4PI068

Ethics must be considered when carrying out research, especially if children are involved. Some guidelines to follow include the following.

- Treat all participants with respect, regardless of personal differences.
- Ensure all participants understand the research process and their part in it.
- Ensure all participants understand how their participation will be used and who will see it.
- Ensure you have consent to use the information you gather.
- Give participants the right to withdraw at any time.

- If children are involved, remember that the best interests of the child must come first.

- Children should also give their consent to participate, after first seeking permission from their parents.

- Research should not cause distress or harm.

- All participants are entitled to privacy.

- You must comply with the Data Protection Act 1998.

> ### Find it out
> Find out more about these guidelines at www.bera.ac.uk/publications/guides.php.

## 420.2  Collect and analyse data

### Collecting data

K4P1069

The steps you have taken so far are as follows:

- deciding the area you are going to research
- carrying out a literature review
- deciding on your method/s of research
- considering ethics issues.

Your next step is to go ahead and collect the data, using primary and secondary sources as appropriate. You need to make sure that you are using a statistically significant sample, and to ensure this you will need to think about who you are going to ask to participate in your research. You need to ensure that you cover all the different possible groups and sources in your sample, for example mothers, fathers, carers, parents, colleagues and so on. The sample will probably depend on the topic you have decided to research.

### Validity and reliability

K4P1067

All results should be valid and reliable. When considering validity you will need to decide if the research method used was correct for the topic of research. For example, if you wanted to find out how often children played outside, an observation may not have been the most valid method to find this out. When thinking about reliability you will need to consider: if the research was repeated, would someone else get the same data? The overall idea is to ensure that your choice of research methods can

be justified and that you can have confidence in the results that they give you.

### Data analysis

Data on its own is not information. It needs to be analysed in order to give you information. This is carried out with statistical methods. There are two main methods you can use:

1. Descriptive: charts, tables, averages etc. These provide you with a picture of the group.

2. Inferential: descriptions of what the data tells you.

### Present results

You now need to draw conclusions and present your research. Most projects will use the headings shown in Table 4:

Table 4:  Presenting your research

| Heading | Description |
| --- | --- |
| Title page | The title of the project and the date |
| Contents | A list of the contents |
| Abstract | A summary of the project |
| Aim | What your aims and objectives were |
| Literature | Where you researched and what review you found out |
| Method | Who the participants were and how you collected the data |
| Results | Present your data |
| Analysis | What have you found out? |
| Conclusions | A conclusion of what you have found out |
| Bibliography | List all the references and reading that you have referred to |
| Appendices | Copies of research methods |

Here is a step-by-step guide to research.

1. Decide on your topic
2. Literature search
3. Decide on methods of research
4. Consider ethics
5. Collect data
6. Analyse data
7. Conclusions
8. Present results

## 420.3 Identify changes to practice resulting from research

### Discuss results with others

The aim of your research was to develop an area of your practice or provision. Hopefully you have identified ways of doing this and also been able to identify improvements that you want to make. You now need to discuss this information with your colleagues and identify the changes that you think need to be made. You need to be clear about the benefits of the changes and how they will improve the quality of your practice and the childcare provision in your setting. You also need to identify the resources that are needed to implement these changes.

Once these things have been decided you will be able to create a plan in order to implement these changes. This may be an individual action plan for you, or one that applies to the setting.

### Barriers to change

You may experience some barriers or difficulties when implementing changes to practice. Some of these may come from colleagues who find change hard to come to terms with, but equally you may also find changing your own practice difficult. It is important to keep the positive benefits in mind and to understand the positive effect these changes are having. You can also use the support of your manager and colleagues to help work through any difficulties.

## Unit 428   Ensure health and safety requirements are met in your area of responsibility

This Unit is about managing overall health and safety in your setting, or in the area of responsibility that you have.

This Unit is not divided into individual elements, and so this section has been divided into themes, with the Knowledge Statements detailed beside each section. The Unit originates from the National Occupational Standards for Management and Leadership and is laid out in a different style from the Units you are familiar with.

## Health and safety in the workplace

428K0I
428K02
428K09
428K22

Health and safety in the workplace is very important. Not only will it keep safe the staff and children in your care, but it will go some way to prevent accidents and emergencies and will help to make your organisation more efficient.

As a manager, you are likely to have responsibilities under health and safety legislation. Your job role, and the size and type of your setting, will affect how far reaching these responsibilities are. It will include making sure that you know the relevant rules, regulations and procedures and also ensuring that they are being followed. You will need to check your job description and contract to find out what your exact responsibilities are.

As a manager, it is also important that you develop a culture where health and safety comes first. You need to act as a good role model and demonstrate that you take this seriously. You should explain to colleagues the positive benefits of good health and safety.

### Points for Reflective Practice

- What are your responsibilities regarding health and safety?
- What actions are you expected to take regarding these responsibilities?

If you are unsure, check with your manager.

### Health and safety legislation

428K03
428KI5

As a manager it is your responsibility to keep up to date about health and safety developments and make any necessary changes. You also need to keep up to date with any changes in policies and procedures.

As a manager, you will have responsibilities under some of the major areas of legislation. As a minimum, these will include the following.

**For employers**

- Take reasonable care of employees.
- Safeguard employees against avoidable hazards.

**For employees**

- Cooperate with employers regarding health and safety.
- Follow health and safety polices and procedures.

The Health and Safety at Work Act 1974 is the main piece of legislation you need to abide by. It sets out the following responsibilities.

**For employers**

- Maintain a safe and healthy workplace.
- Provide a health and safety policy if five or more people are employed.
- Provide and maintain equipment that is safe and healthy.
- Provide information and training.
- Deal with hazardous materials safely.
- Carry out risk assessments.
- Monitor and review health and safety policies.
- Provide emergency procedures.
- Ensure that the workplace does not put visitors or the public at risk.

**For employees**

- Take care of their own health and safety at work.
- Take care of the health and safety of others.
- Cooperate with their employer.

Other regulations that you may have to consider include:

- Control of Substances Hazardous to Health Regulations 2002 (COSHH)
- Management of Health and Safety at Work Regulations 1999
- Manual Handling Operations 1992 (Amended 2002)
- Personal Protective Equipment (PPE) Work Regulations 1992
- Working Time Regulations 1998
- Reporting of Injuries, Diseases and Dangerous Occurrences Legislation 1995 (RIDDOR)
- Electricity at Work Regulations 1998.

## Find it out

Visit www.hse.gov.uk to find out about any recent changes to health and safety legislation.

## Health and safety policies

If your setting employs five or more staff then you are required to have a written health and safety policy. This will set out how your setting will manage health and safety. If your setting is large, there may be different policies for different areas.

It is important that all staff are aware of the health and safety policy and their responsibility to follow it. It is also a good idea to ensure that staff regularly refresh their memories. This can be achieved by either ensuring that they read the policy on a regular basis, discussing it at staff meetings, giving out leaflets, and by ensuring staff understand their job descriptions.

## Points for Reflective Practice

- What is your organisation's health and safety policy?
- Where is it stored?
- How often is it reviewed?
- How do you ensure staff are aware of it?
- How often do staff read it?
- How do you keep a record of this?

## Find it out

For a sample health and safety policy see www.hse.gov.uk/business/policy-statement.pdf.

It is important to regularly review your policy. This may be because of changes in the workplace that make this necessary or because new guidance or regulations become available. You also need to keep a record of these changes. You could review the policy through one or more of the following activities:

- discuss changes with other specialists
- review risk assessments
- health and safety training
- accident and incident record analysis.

The best way to encourage staff to follow the health and safety policy is to set a good example yourself and act as a role model. If you can demonstrate that you take health and safety seriously then it is likely that others will as well. This will help to reduce risks, accidents and ultimately stress.

## Resources for health and safety

Resources to deal with health and safety are either practical or knowledge-based.

Practical resources are those which must be provided to comply with legislation. They include personal protective equipment, safe storage areas and regular checks for equipment.

Knowledge-based resources are about communicating the relevant information and advice. They include being aware of relevant legislation, providing training and advice, and understanding the reporting procedures for risks and hazards.

### Points for Reflective Practice

- What resources do you have for health and safety?
- Are they knowledge-based or practical?
- How do you ensure you have sufficient resources?

## Consulting with others

There may be times when you need to consult with others about health and safety in your setting. It can be useful to find out the views of others and take them into account when updating your policies and procedures. You may have members of senior management who you can consult with, or specialist safety representatives. You may also be able to carry out consultations through a quick discussion with staff, and as you carry out any regular health and safety checks. It is a good idea to try to carry these out regularly, in order to avoid having to consult as a 'knee jerk' reaction to an accident or incident.

The best place to seek specialist advice is from the Health and Safety Executive. This government body gives advice on the obligations and duties of small and large settings, provides you with information and forms to assist as you carry out your health and safety responsibilities and also has local offices that provide further support.

You may choose to employ a consultant to assist with health and safety matters, especially if there are specific issues that need resolving swiftly.

Another place where you can seek specialist advice is within the setting itself. There may be staff members who have attended further training and have updated knowledge that will be useful to you as a manager. Your setting may have also appointed a safety representative.

### Points for Reflective Practice

- Where do you access specialist advice from?
- Have you used the Health and Safety Executive?
- Have you ever employed an outside consultant?
- Have you used specialist knowledge from within your setting?
- What did you achieve by doing so?

## Risk assessment

A hazard is something that could cause harm. A risk is the chance of harm being done by the hazard. A risk assessment aims to identify the hazards and the risks attached to them. Risk assessments are the best way to control or eliminate hazards and risks. It is likely that your setting has its own procedure for carrying out risk assessments.

Some hazards in childcare settings could include:

- use of chemicals
- infection and illness
- stairs
- slips, trips and falls
- electricity
- outings.

This list is not exhaustive and there are likely to be many more that will be individual to each setting.

It is always best to eliminate the risk, but where this is not possible then it should be reduced to a manageable level. You could do this by providing personal protective clothing, using warning signs and by having procedures for specific activities.

## Monitoring, measuring and reporting on health and safety

Health and safety performance should be monitored to ensure that policies and procedures are effective. You could do this through carrying out an audit, a safety inspection or through accident prevention. An audit checks that the policies and procedures are being carried out correctly. Safety inspections should be carried out on a regular basis to ensure equipment is safe, and is being used safely. Accident prevention is generally carried out by reviewing the accident records and looking at the reasons for recurring accidents.

All planning and decision making should be underpinned by knowledge of health and safety. Information gained from reviewing, monitoring and measuring should be fed back and taken into account when carrying out business planning and decision making. This means that you can plan and make decisions to avoid possible risks. You may be able to show this in your operational plans.

## Further references

www.allianceforchildhood.org.uk

www.audit-commission.gov.uk

www.bera.ac.uk/publications/guides.php

www.bized.co.uk

www.businesballs.com

www.dcsf.gov.uk

www.englandsrdas.com

www.fundinginformation.org

www.hse.gov.uk

www.pcaw.co.uk

www.surestart.gov.uk/surestartservices/support/funding

www.tutor2u.net

Bell, J. (1999) *Doing Your Research Project,* 3rd edition, Open University Press

Brech, E. F. L. (1965) *Principles of Management*, Longman

Goodman, M. (1995) *Creative Management*, Prentice Hall

West, M. A. (1997) *Developing Creativity in Organisations*, BPS

# Leadership and management of staff and colleagues

The following Units form part of the optional framework for NVQ CCLD Level 4. You may choose one or a number of the Units in this section if you are responsible for managing people in your setting.

These Units may be suitable if you are working in one of the following job roles:

- Manager of a nursery.
- Lead or senior practitioner.
- Manager of an aspect of a service within a group of nurseries.
- Working within Sure Start.
- Providing support to families and groups.
- Operations manager for a setting or group of settings.
- Training and development coordinator within a service.

The Units covered in this section are:

| | |
|---|---|
| 425 | Provide leadership in your area of responsibility. |
| 426 | Encourage innovation in your area of responsibility. |
| 427 | Allocate and monitor the progress and quality of work in your area of responsibility. |
| 429 | Provide learning opportunities for colleagues. |
| 333 | Recruit, select and keep colleagues. |

Unlike many of the units presented in the NVQ framework this group of Units follows a slightly different pattern. Traditionally you will have looked at performance criteria for elements and knowledge specifications that follow these.

Within this section you will find that all units are set in the following format.

- Outcomes of effective performance.
- Behaviours which underpin effective performance.
- General knowledge and understanding, known as 'knowledge specification'.

Part One of this handbook will have given you more information about the structure of these Units.

# Unit 425   Provide leadership in your area of responsibility

425K0I

This Unit requires you to provide support and direction to others in a given area of the service or setting and to help them achieve the objectives for this area. The area can relate to a number of wide-ranging aspects of the service.

Areas of leadership could include:

- regulatory frameworks for service provision
- implementation of policies and procedures for practices
- the well being and safe-guarding of children
- managing services for children and families in the community.

## Creating a compelling vision

425K02
425KI3
425KI4
425KI6
425KI7
425KI8

A **vision** should be compelling and those within the organisation need to have a good understanding of what that vision is and their role in making the vision a reality. Your vision is your focus for your given area of responsibility and should act as the basis on which to build both yours and your team's objectives to make it happen.

To create a compelling vision, consider your responses to the following questions.

- What impact do you want your setting and/or organisation to have in the industry?
- How do you want others you work with to feel about the organisation and/or setting in the future?
- How do you want service users to benefit from the setting and/or organisation?

As well as considering your own vision for your area of responsibility, seek to understand the visions of those you work with. Their input can provide additional support in the creation and achievement of your vision and that of the setting as a whole.

> **Key Term**
>
> Vision – the ability to think about the future with imagination or wisdom.

## Leadership and management

To understand how to provide leadership in your area of responsibility, you first need to be able to identify the fundamental differences between leadership and management.

Leadership requires you to set an agenda for the directions and visions of the people you work with in any given environment. The role of the leader is to be the point of contact, or the person having overall responsibility for making the direction or vision happen.

Management requires you to ensure that directions set in leadership are followed and essentially controlled in accordance with the overall vision of the setting, following principles of good practice already well established.

As the manager of a setting or service it may not necessarily be your role to provide leadership in any given aspect of service delivery. An effective manager is one who can recognise their own role in controlling the organisation and support those with specific areas of responsibility to lead their team in ensuring the vision and direction are fulfilled.

## The role of the leader

Leadership should not be seen as a role in isolation from the rest of the team, and recognising when a leader should step up to the task of supporting and motivating the team is important in making this effective. As a leader you will need to give a great deal of thought to your own attitudes, behaviour and limits of responsibility.

The role of the leader includes the following:

■ Supporting others and getting the best from the team: as a leader you will need to identify ways in which you can support team members to fulfil their job role requirements and remain motivated in practice.

> You can find out more about supporting colleagues in Unit 401.

■ Handling problems and overcoming workplace issues: problems will occur without a doubt in your area of responsibility, as a leader it is important to recognise how these problems have arisen and what strategies you can employ to prevent re-occurrences of problems.

■ Being an effective communicator: keeping a team well-informed is vital for any leader wanting their team to work well together. Share your visions for the setting with the team; tell them where you want to go and how you expect you will all get there. Don't forget the value of their own visions in all of this. A collaborative approach to achieving your objectives is far more productive and of greater value to the organisation than a one-person race.

■ Having good interpersonal skills with others: as discussed throughout this book, be respectful of others, be polite and courteous in all of your communications, value the thoughts, feelings and opinions of others. Being respectful of your team and approachable will benefit the working dynamics of the team, as individuals will feel able to consult you on any issues arising in their job role.

Finally a good team leader knows and accepts the limits of their own responsibilities. Consider your roles and responsibilities carefully when making any decisions regarding your area of responsibility. You may also want to look at the roles and responsibilities of the person you report to so you have a greater understanding of where your responsibilities cease and theirs commence. Be honest with members of your team when decisions that need to be made are beyond your level of authority. Acting beyond the limits of your authority may not be seen as an act

of initiative but a lack of judgement that can have negative consequences for you and the organisation.

## Points for Reflective Practice

425KI4
425KI6

Do you know your job role and responsibilities? Look back at your job description and person specification and ask yourself:

■ What areas of responsibility are you required to fulfil?
■ What attributes and skills are required for this role?
■ How do you ensure you meet these work role requirements?

## Leadership styles

425K04

There are many styles of leadership that you use in different situations with different people in the setting or organisation. To be able to lead a team successfully, it is important to be able to identify your own style of leadership, and how this is currently used in practice, and reflect on the advantages and disadvantages of this. You can then adapt your leadership style for any given circumstance so your practice and personal effectiveness can be improved.

Table 1 on page 188 details some of the most commonly understood leadership styles, some of which you will have implemented in your role as a leader.

**Table I:** Leadership styles

| Leadership style | Interpretation |
|---|---|
| **Autocratic** | Leaders who exercise overall control of their team with little or no consideration for their thoughts and opinions |
| **Bureaucratic** | Leaders who lack the creativity to think beyond the policy and procedure of the setting and ensure staff work to the 'rule of thumb' allowing little or no room for flexibility in practice |
| **Servant leadership** | Leaders who feel it is their task to meet the needs of their team who themselves are often the driving force behind leadership |
| **Democratic** | Leaders who consider the thoughts, opinions and input of others. Participation of the team in the decision making process is a key feature of this style of leadership |
| **Charismatic** | A leader who brings a lot of charisma to the team and whose motivation inspires others, but whose absence may mean objectives are not accomplished as the driving force is missing |
| **People orientated** | Leaders whose primary focus is to develop a culture of team work through supporting the people in their team, perhaps forgetting the logistics of the tasks involved |
| **Task orientated** | Leaders whose primary focus is the task in hand and ensuring that processes are in place for task to be accomplished, with little emphasis on the human resources (people) involved |
| **Transactional** | Leadership whereby the team are seen as a 'transaction' and are duty bound to perform to the requirements of the leader |
| **Laissez-faire** | The 'leave it be' leader who lets the team get on with the task in hand, often with little or no leadership. This can create a culture where people work in different directions |
| **Transformational** | A leader who is pro-active within an organisation and leads people through effective communication and delegation of tasks to appropriate personnel equipped to manage them |

## Points for Reflective Practice

425K04
425KII
425K20
425K08
425K09
425KI5

Consider the leadership styles mentioned above.

- Can you identify any particular styles you have employed in your own leadership within your organisation?
- Can you identify leadership styles that lend themselves to specific aspects of your practice?
- Does your role as a leader require you to apply more than one of these styles in your everyday practice?
- Reflect on a situation in which you have applied your leadership skills successfully and identify the style used to do this. Why did this style have positive outcomes for reaching your objective?

# Empowering your team

Empowering individuals enables them to have more control and confidence in their abilities and more importantly encourages them to play a fundamental role in the decision making and planning processes of the organisation. Involving your team in these processes will inevitably develop a working culture where they feel valued, happy and motivated. An effective leader is one that recognises the importance of empowerment and takes active steps in the organisation to achieve this.

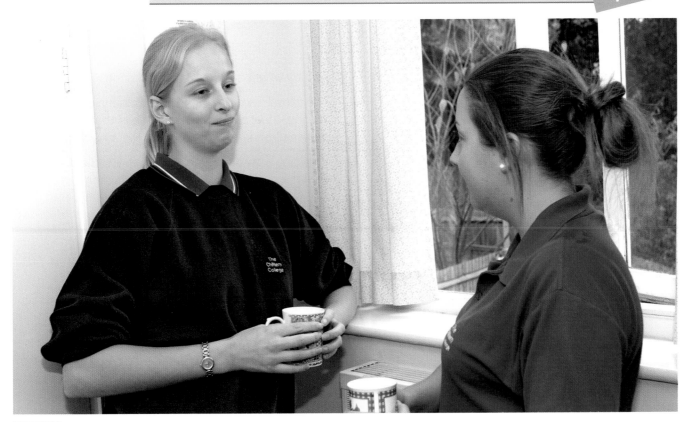

**Figure 1:** You need to talk to your team to develop their motivation

# Effective steps in empowering your team

**Show your appreciation of others:** demonstrating that you value the people you work with is vital for motivating others to perform to the best of their ability and to be enthusiastic about their role within the organisation. Not only is it important to value people for their commitment and their ability to fulfil their role successfully but it is also crucial to recognise people as individuals and as human beings for successful people management. Your own actions towards others need careful consideration as people will learn how you value them from the interpersonal skills you display.

**Trust your team:** as a leader it is important to develop a culture of trust within your team and have faith in their abilities and intentions. Your perceptions may differ slightly, and you may even tackle tasks and situations in a different way from others, but trust them in making the right decisions.

**Communicate effectively with your team:** communicating effectively with others is important to achieve objectives. If you don't tell others what is happening or share the expectations of their role within this you cannot expect them to contribute fully. Share your visions and goals with them and provide relevant information about how you anticipate the achievement of this; that way individuals will be well informed of desired outcomes.

**Recognise the opportunities presented by others:** a crucial element of your work as a leader is to recognise the skills and strengths of others and use these to benefit delivery of provision. A good leader is one who can delegate tasks and responsibilities to individuals who have the capacity to drive visions and objectives forward. Many individuals make a team and an effective team is one that works together to get things done. An inability to delegate tasks to others can result in an overload of work for you, making you far less efficient in your leadership role, and can also make staff feel de-motivated or even resentful when their ability to contribute is not recognised.

**Involve others in decision making:** every individual involved within the organisation is committed to achieving the best possible outcomes for service users so involve them in doing this. A good leader recognises when others have valid contributions to make and can also encourage others to become involved in the decision making process by asking questions and encouraging reflection to form evaluations and decisions.

425KIO

## Motivating your team

As a leader, motivating your team is essential in enabling them to work to the best of their ability. To do this you need to consider what motivates individuals and what motivates the team as whole. Successful identification of answers to this will enable you to put in place both a physically and emotionally enabling environment where colleagues and members of your team feel enthusiastic and motivated about their job role.

> You can find out more about supporting team members in Unit 401.

Colleagues who know what is expected of them and what their targets and objectives are will have an increased level of motivation as they have a challenge they can rise to. A good team leader can identify what motivates individuals and perhaps set them challenges in practice that can benefit the organisation. For example, you could have a member of the team who is neat and methodical – liking everything in order. This person would relish the opportunity of sorting out all the toys and resources ensuring they are clearly labelled, attractively presented and located where they are supposed to be. The reward for the individual in this instance is the satisfaction that the task has been accomplished and that the environment has been

organised. Additional motivation will come from the feedback received from others. For example, 'Wow Hardeep, it looks really tidy in here and I can find exactly what I am looking for, well done'.

The verbal reward is a great motivational tool; it gives the individual a real sense of pride in their work and makes them feel their contributions are valued.

Providing a physically motivating environment is equally important. Colleagues working with broken, old and scruffy resources will feel that the manager and/or leaders within the organisation have no pride in it. This in turn can have a knock-on effect to people themselves, who may end up feeling a bit like a broken old toy!

It is amazing how motivated staff become when new resources arrive or when the setting has received a new lick of paint over the weekend. Never underestimate the power that material resources have in helping staff to become motivated. Involve the team in making decisions about their physical environment and the contents within it. This will inevitably give them a sense of purpose and belonging within the organisation, which is crucial if they are to remain motivated.

## Points for Reflective Practice

What methods do you employ in your organisation to:

■ motivate staff?
■ encourage staff?
■ reward staff?

## Can't find what you were looking for?

| Level 4 KS Number | Knowledge Statement | Can be found in... |
|---|---|---|
| 425K03 | How to select and successfully apply different methods for communicating with people across an area of responsibility | Unit 401 |
| 425K05 | How to get and make use of feedback from people on your leadership performance | Unit 401 |
| 425K06 | Types of difficulties and challenges that may arise, including conflict within the area, and ways of identifying and overcoming this | Unit 401 |
| 425K07 | The benefits of and how to create and maintain a culture which encourages and recognises creativity and innovation | Unit 426 |
| 425KI2 | Legal, regulatory and ethical requirements in the industry/sector | Unit 402 |

# Unit 426 Encourage innovation in your area of responsibility

This Unit is suitable for those in senior positions whose job role requires them to identify and implement innovative ways of working in the setting, whether that be in a small organisation or as a department in a significantly larger setting or service relating to Early Years.

Innovation may present itself in the form of new products and services, improvements to existing products or services or improvements to existing practices, procedures and systems.

## What is innovation?

As the definition suggests, **innovation** is the process of identifying new ideas and ways of working in the sector and ensuring the idea is put into practice. By being innovative in your work you can seek to improve the services and provision offered to children and families and add considerable value to the setting itself.

There are two ways in which you can be innovative in practice which are:

1. Incremental innovation: the process whereby practice, service or attitudes are adapted or improved to suit the ever-changing needs of the sector.
2. Radical innovation: the process which involves embedding new ideas and ways of thinking in the setting.

Innovation in the Early Years sector will require the involvement of all practitioners within the setting, as successful implementation of innovative ideas requires the skills and knowledge of everyone who plays a key part in service delivery. To be innovative you will need to draw on the strengths and perceptions of others so you can ensure the best possible outcomes for new ideas and initiatives.

Innovation is crucial to settings if they are seeking to offer the best services to clients, namely children and families. By improving products and services you can improve the efficiency and professional standing of the setting, which can increase the setting's ability to lead its competitors in the marketplace. It can increase the client base, income and overall sustainability of the setting.

> ### Key Term
> Innovation – the successful exploitation of new ideas.

## Where innovative ideas come from

426K01
426K02
426K29

Innovative ideas are generated by all those who have an interest in the setting, whether that is you, colleagues, children and families or external stakeholders. This is commonly known as the creative process; creativity is the ability to generate new ideas whilst innovation is about making these ideas happen.

People that have the creativity to think of new ideas are not necessarily the ones equipped with the skills to take ideas forward. This demonstrates to you that the process of innovation is very much a team effort.

## Encouraging innovation in the workplace

426K09
426K10

To encourage colleagues to be innovative you need to have them 'on board' when considering new ideas or adapting existing ideas and practices. Colleagues who are kept fully informed and involved in potential changes will be more enthusiastic and motivated by ideas as they feel that their thoughts and opinions are valued. For many, being involved will provide them with a renewed enthusiasm and motivation in the workplace.

426K04
426K06
426K08
426KII
426KI2
426KI7

## Keys To Good Practice

How can you promote innovation in the workplace? Consider the following steps when encouraging colleagues to be involved in innovation.

- Provide appropriate communication opportunities for colleagues to share their thoughts and ideas. This could include team meetings or suggestion boxes in the setting.
- Be supportive and take time to listen to what others have to say so they feel they can express their ideas.
- Encourage openness in your team and the sharing of ideas.
- Encourage practitioners to share even the most radical ideas. Innovation requires some element of risk and experimentation which should be explored without the possibility of blame for ideas that do not come to fruition.
- Encourage colleagues to reflect on their own strengths and abilities as these may prove to be an essential asset in the innovation process.
- Encourage a team culture where everyone takes some form of responsibility and ownership of ideas.
- Acknowledge the input of others, their enthusiasm and their constructive use of imagination.

## Identifying opportunities for innovation

Areas for innovation could include the following.

- New products and/or services: a day nursery expanding to include after-school provision where this has not been provided before; a children's centre offering new services such as adult learning for parents.
- Improvements to existing products or services: a childminder developing outdoor provision; resourcing an area of practice, such as sensory play for children with special needs.
- Improvements to existing practices, procedures, systems or ways of working within the team or those of the wider organisation or customers or suppliers: changes in layout of nursery

environments, improved documentation and record keeping, including installation of electronic databases.

## How to select ideas for innovation

Through discussions with colleagues, families and other stakeholders there may be many ideas that are presented to you for innovation. It would be impossible to put all the ideas into practice at once so you will need to consider how you prioritise these.

A useful method of doing this is asking all those involved to compile a 'wish list' in which they can detail the ideas brought forward in an order of importance or priority from their perspective. This will certainly give you a better idea of everybody else's thoughts and opinions and from this you may be able to reach some common ground as to which project or projects to drive forward.

Having made a decision about the innovation that will be taken forward it is important that this is fed back to all those involved and that the reasons for going with the chosen project have been clearly explained. Time and cost may have a huge bearing on your chosen idea, and this will need to be clearly communicated to people so they do not feel that their ideas have been dismissed.

## Putting ideas into practice

Once you have identified ideas and innovations, you will need to consider how these are going to be moved forward. It is essential in order for ideas to work that you plan the processes you want to follow and identify the desired outcomes from these. Having plans for your innovations in place will also help you to look at other issues that may be presented in bringing your ideas to fruition.

### Find it out

What support mechanisms are available in your community to help you take innovative ideas forward? (Your ideas could include enriching the outdoor environment, developing ICT resources or even considering a new service for children and families, such as a stay and play morning.)

## Keys to Good Practice

When building a plan to take your idea forward it is important to consider the following points.

- Time: how long will it take to achieve your objectives? What time will have to be dedicated to your innovative idea? Change does not happen overnight; it can often be quite lengthy as you gather the resources – both human and material – to bring about changes.
- Cost: what cost implications does it have for the setting? Sometimes innovations can be funded by allocated budgets for such activities in the setting. More often than not you will have to source additional funding mechanisms, which can involve risk and time.
- Expertise: what additional support or advice does the project need? You may need advice from other experts in relation to the product or service that you are seeking to innovate.
- Objectives: how will the innovation benefit the service and/or provision that is currently offered? You will need to consider how beneficial this will be and how service users and colleagues can see the way it has enhanced the setting.

## Points for Reflective Practice

426K03
426K26
426K27
426K28

Think about the human resources involved in innovation.

- Consider the roles and responsibilities of yourself and others.
- Does your setting have procedures for building a business plan and developing innovative ideas?

426K05
426KI3
426KI5
426KI8
426K24
426K25
426K29

Involving others in the development of your plan can help in seeking solutions to problems that may come to light. One particular area for consideration is the cost implications. As previously discussed, costs for new projects and ideas can be funded with allocated budgets of the setting but where the innovation is a costly project you may need to consider alternative sources of funding.

One way of doing this is to have fundraising events in your setting, such as raffles, fun days and sponsorships. These are a great way of involving colleagues, children and families in the project. It is important that you inform them about why you are raising funds and how it will impact the setting. People

**Figure 2:** Fun days are a great way to involve colleagues, children and families in your project

will more readily come on board and support your cause if they can see where their money is being spent. To engage the support of families you can ask them for their suggestions for fundraising events and get them involved with activities such as fun days. These also provide the ideal opportunity for you to market your services with some free press coverage of events taking place at your setting.

Sending out a weekly or monthly newsletter to individuals and parents and families about how your fundraising efforts are going and how near you are to your target for fundraising can be a great way of keeping everyone enthused and motivated in raising funds.

Another funding avenue that is worth exploring is whether grants for the Early Years sector in your locality may be available for enhancing existing provision. The ideal way of finding out if such grants are available is by talking to your local council, Early Years support team or other settings who have accessed financial support for their own projects. Before applying for any grants that may be available to your setting you must consider the restrictions and compliance issues related to these. For example, one restriction on grant applications could be if the setting ceases trading during a specified period of grant allocation, money received may have to be repaid.

## Risks and mistakes

**426KI4**
**426KI9**
**426K20**

Not all innovative ideas will become a product that everyone will be proud of. Just think of inventors; they can have many failures before hitting on the one big idea!

There are many risks associated with innovation but sometimes it is necessary to take risks for outcomes to be reached. For example, when applying for funding for a particular project you may ask yourself: 'what if we don't get the money?' But that is a risk you will have to take; if you don't try you'll never find out. Other risks can be easily avoided, such as getting good value for money for equipment and labour costs of projects. By ensuring you have done your research into such costs and getting several quotes you can avoid the pitfalls of spending money needlessly.

Mistakes can happen; for whatever reason your project or idea may come crashing to the ground. If this

happens it is important to identify why so that it can be avoided the next time you embark on a creative journey!

It is easy to go around blaming everyone else for the failing, but that won't solve the problem. Be accountable and ask those who may have been involved to be accountable too. You can only learn from a mistake after you admit you have made it. The process of understanding why you might have come to this point can then begin. Reflect on the process of the innovation that has failed and ask yourself questions about this.

- Was the idea well thought through?
- Did I give enough time commitment to the idea?
- Did I have adequate support, guidance and advice?
- Were there earlier errors that could have been recognised?
- Did I have the right objectives?

By asking yourself and others these sorts of questions you will be able to see why mistakes were made and put in place strategies to ensure it doesn't happen again. This may also involve you reviewing your business plan and making sure it is detailed in content and that every avenue of possibility is explored. Robust business plans help in dissolving many mistakes that are easily avoided.

## Celebrating success

Once the hard work is done and you can see the fruits of your labour it is important to recognise these and indeed highlight the achievement to all involved. Whatever the innovation, it will have been one incredible journey where you have learnt much about yourself, those around you and the setting you work within, and that certainly gives cause for celebration.

A personal thank you to all those involved is important to show that you recognise and value their input. In addition you can celebrate the success with the wider community, involve the press or have an open day to show off your new product or services to others. But remember there will be nothing more rewarding than the positive impact this has on your service or setting and knowing that you were someone who could make it happen!

## Can't find what you were looking for?

| Level 4 KS Number | Knowledge Statement | Can be found in... |
|---|---|---|
| 426K07 | The importance of communication in innovation and how to encourage communication across your area of responsibility | Unit 401 |
| 426KI6 | How to unlock creativity in yourself and others | Units 401 and 404 |
| 426K2I | The sector and market in which your organisation works, links to government policy objectives for children's services | Units 402 and 403 |
| 426K23 | Current and emerging political, economic, social, technological, environmental and legal developments in the sector and in related sectors | Units 402 and 403 |

# Unit 427 Allocate and monitor the progress and quality of work in your area of responsibility

Focusing on leadership skills, this Unit is appropriate for those whose responsibility is to allocate workloads and agreements to others within the organisation, to ensure that those agreements are fulfilled to the required standard and that support is given for the ongoing review of work allocation and job performance.

## Your health and safety obligations

An essential part of the process in planning, allocating and monitoring the work in your area of responsibility is health and safety. You have a duty to ensure that those who have input in your area are following safe working practices and that they possess the competencies and knowledge to do so. You must also ensure that resources and equipment are readily available for safe working practices to be successfully implemented.

Settings and employers give careful consideration to health and safety policies and clear procedures for practice which demonstrates their commitment in keeping their employees safe. Employees, and certainly those within your team, need to act in a safe working manner and have an individual responsibility to comply with any health and safety policies of the organisation and legislation detailed in The Heath and Safety at Work Act 1974.

> You can find out more about the Health and Safety at Work Act in Unit 428.

Risk assessments further affirm your commitment to working in a healthy and safe manner. It is good practice to look at the risk assessments already in place within your organisation and make any necessary adaptations or additions that are specific to the planning, monitoring and allocation of work in your area of responsibility. Involving those to whom work loads are to be allocated is equally important as they may identify additional considerations relating to their own needs and abilities.

## Planning and allocating work

427K03
427K27
427K29

Before you can allocate work and/or responsibilities to members of your team you first need to identify what those work requirements are. Often individuals will have an understanding of the work requirements as these are detailed within their job description. Further detail and clarification is always good practice as it enables you to think about those everyday tasks that you take for granted get done, such as sterilising the feeding equipment in the baby room of a setting, fresh water being put in the water tray for pre-school children before the beginning of the session or even putting the washing on! People will often think it is not their job unless you tell them otherwise.

Making written records of your plan helps you to visualise what the requirements are and are a great way of communicating these to the team. Bring the team together to form your plan for your allocated area of responsibility. You may already have a template to share with your team for work requirements that can then be developed through discussion and reflection in team meetings.

## Keys to Good Practice

Use the following points to help you produce a plan of work.

- Your plan should be developed in order of priority of tasks and which areas or specific tasks need immediate attention.
- Meet with your team to discuss the plan.
- Ask your team to share their thoughts about work requirements.
- Make additions to your plan based on your team's input.
- Identify specific requirements of tasks and roles needed for your plan to be implemented successfully.
- Ask your team if they have any particular preferences regarding the allocation of tasks to them.
- Identify on your plan when and how it will be reviewed.
- Include the resources that will need to be provided or purchased to make your plan operational.
- Consider health and safety implications for the implementation of your plan.

427K04
427K10
427K11
427K18
427K21
427K24
427K25
427K26

427K02
427K05
427K06
427K07
427K08
427K09

Once your plan is developed, look at what you have produced and summarise this with your team so they are fully informed of its requirements. This is also a good opportunity to check that they are happy with tasks that have been allocated to them. Having it down on paper will also help to identify if anybody has been overloaded with tasks or not been included in the plan at all.

Your skills as a team leader will come into play here as it will be your responsibility to ensure colleagues do not feel burdened by their workload or feel they are being asked to do something they feel ill equipped for. Overloading individuals will result in the work potentially not getting done as they will not have the time to do

it; this can then result in them feeling inadequate in their role and lead to a decline in their own confidence and self-esteem. This is certainly something you want to and can avoid. Knowing your workforce and the strengths and weaknesses of their practice will be crucial in ensuring they can do what has been asked of them.

During meetings and discussions some of your colleagues may be forthcoming with the tasks they are happy to take on board, but others may sit back and not volunteer their support. Utilise this opportunity to discuss with them how they can help and how their knowledge and skills can enable the plan to come to fruition. Help them to identify what they are good at and reflect on their practice; when they feel you have faith in them to take on board specifics of the plan they will then feel empowered and useful and will inevitably be more motivated in their work. Make sure the allocation of work is fair to the whole team; those who have more tasks than others to achieve can become resentful of this which can cause discord in the team. Keep the lines of communication open so that colleagues can ascertain the requirements of their work and related tasks and so that you can check they are happy to do what has been asked of them.

## Review and feedback

It is never enough to draw up a plan and put it in the drawer! This is a working document for practice and should be available and evident to all those involved, so they can continuously review their own input and check that they are doing what is required of them.

Opportunities for reviewing your work plan will be presented daily through discussions with your colleagues and observations of their work performance. This will provide you with information to decide whether things are getting done. In addition to this you need to provide your team with more formal opportunities to review their work allocation and give feedback on their performance. Both team meetings and one-to-ones with members of your team will be beneficial in analysing the progress in your area of responsibility.

When progress is slower than anticipated the review process will help in identifying the reasons why. This may result in the need to adapt the plan or re-allocate roles and tasks to individuals based on what they feel they can or cannot achieve. Once again, keep the lines of communication with colleagues wide open, inform them of any changes made to your plan and check that they are happy with any alterations that have been made.

Regular meetings with your team are an effective way of reviewing how successful the plan is in meeting the work allocation requirements. It is important to recognise that this may not be an appropriate time to discuss and review the performance of individuals.

You can find out more about the processes involved in performance review in Unit 429.

## Keys to Good Practice

When giving feedback to individuals on their work performance consider the following.

- Ensure feedback is given privately and face-to-face.
- Inform colleagues that you wish to discuss their progress with them so they have time to prepare.
- Explain to them why feedback and review of personal effectiveness is important to colleagues.
- Discuss specific aspects of their roles and related tasks and how these are being met or not being met.
- Give time to colleagues to respond to your feedback and listen carefully to what they have to say.
- Provide support and strategies for the colleague to progress with their given roles and tasks.

## Causes for concern

Through effective monitoring of your team's performance and review of their allocated roles and tasks, issues regarding practice may come to light. You may have cause for concern about a colleague's ability to fulfil their role effectively or their lack of understanding relating to practice and expectations. Do not let these go unnoticed; try to identify them at the earliest opportunity so that you can seek a plan of action and way forward.

There are many reasons why a member of your team may not be performing to the best of their ability or

pulling their weight, so you need to ensure you have valid and reliable evidence regarding your concerns to present to the individual so that the process of support and guidance can begin.

## Keys to Good Practice

427KI3

Consider the points below when dealing with poor performance issues of colleagues.

- Provide a confidential opportunity to discuss the concerns you have.
- Keep your communications factual.
- Ensure you have the necessary facts and evidence first.
- Avoid emotional responses and inflammatory remarks.
- Make sure you listen as well as speak so your colleague can explain their position.
- Do not be judgemental or presumptuous in your communications with them.
- Be clear and concise so that your colleague knows exactly what your concerns are.

## Points for Reflective Practice

427KII
427K29

Consider how the setting deals with poor performance of team members.

- Does the setting have systems in place for recording concerns about poor performance?
- Do you have a defined structure within the management team for reporting concerns about performance issues?
- Does your setting have a policy detailing how poor performance issues will be responded to?

Once you have gone through the process of identifying concerns relating to work performance, and discussed this thoroughly with the individual in question, you can then identify a way forward which involves input from you, your colleague and often others in the team. Knowing what these issues are will help in identifying who could be involved in resolving them.

Performance-related issues could include:

- inability to manage workload
- lacking a team player approach

**Figure 3:** Avoid emotional responses and inflammatory language when discussing concerns!

- refusing to undertake roles and responsibilities
- personal issues
- lack of understanding of practice issues
- lack of confidence in own abilities.

Issues related to performance vary greatly and the tactics employed to respond to one issue may be wholly inappropriate for responding to another issue. Issues of a personal nature may require your colleague to take time off work so they can deal with these in the privacy of their own home; equally they may need your guidance in being signposted to appropriate agencies who can give them the support they need. Issues relating to their lack of understanding and knowledge regarding practice may require you to source additional training opportunities for them; this can include formal training such as an NVQ or a more information-based course such as one on time management strategies. When the issue relates to their ability to contribute to a team or refusal to take roles and tasks on board you may need to adopt a more formal approach, including devising an action plan for your colleague that can be used to identify with them what is expected of them, how this can be done and when this is going to be reviewed.

This is an important process not only for the colleague involved but for the team as a whole. An individual's poor performance will have an impact on the whole team. When someone is not pulling their weight or not working as a team player other members of the team can become upset, angry and frustrated. This will inevitably lead to conflict in the team which can sometimes escalate to the point where people refuse to work together.

Ensuring you are pro-active in dealing with these types of poor performance issues demonstrates to the involved individual and the wider team that it is unacceptable practice and will not be tolerated.

If an initial feedback session with the individual and an agreed plan of action is not fruitful you need to think about your next course of action, ensuring it is in line with the policies and procedures of the setting and/or organisation.

In extreme circumstances you may need to explore the disciplinary route with colleagues, but this should only be considered when all other avenues of support and guidance have been exhausted.

## Find it out

When considering disciplinary and grievance procedures with colleagues you need to ensure that not only are you adhering to the policies and procedures of the setting and/or organisation but that you have also given due regard to the principles and policies of current legislation.

Go to www.acas.org.uk and read its code of practice on disciplinary and grievance procedures to ensure you are acting within the law.

# Can't find what you were looking for?

| Level 3 KS Number | Knowledge Statement | Can be found in... |
|---|---|---|
| 427KOI | How to select and successfully apply different methods of communicating with people across an area of responsibility | Unit 40I |
| 427KI5 | The additional support and/or resources which individuals and/or teams might require to help them complete their work and how to assist in providing this | Unit 429 |
| 427KI6 | How to select and successfully apply different methods for encouraging, motivating and supporting individuals and/or teams to complete the work they have been allocated, improve their performance and for recognising their achievements | Units 426 and 429 |
| 427KI7 | How to log information on the ongoing performance of individuals and/or teams and use this information for formal appraisal purposes | Unit 429 |
| 427KI9 | Sector requirements for the development or maintenance of knowledge, understanding and skills through continuing professional development | Units 404 and 429 |
| 427K22 | The vision and objectives for your area of responsibility | Unit 425 |
| 427K23 | The vision and aims of the overall organisation | Unit 425 |
| 427K28 | Your organisation's policy and procedures in terms of personal development | Unit 429 |
| 427K32 | Organisational performance appraisal systems | Unit 429 |

# Unit 429   Provide learning opportunities for colleagues

This Unit is applicable to those in senior positions who are responsible for supporting colleagues' training and development within the setting. In addition, the role includes addressing individuals' development needs within the setting and supporting them to access appropriate opportunities to build their skills and knowledge. Support should also be given to help colleagues identify how new knowledge and skills can benefit practice.

## Promoting learning to colleagues

429KOI
429K05
429K22
429K23

It doesn't matter how long a colleague or team member has been working in the setting, or indeed the sector, it is still imperative that training and development opportunities are explored. In this ever-changing world government initiatives and directives impact the delivery of service and the need to continually review and develop the way in which you work to meet children's and families' needs. To ensure that you remain up to date in your way of thinking and working, you and your team should ensure that training and information opportunities are taken up.

As an advanced practitioner or team leader it may be your responsibility to ensure that others in the setting are encouraged to seek opportunities to gain new knowledge and skills.

Figure 4: There are many benefits of staff training

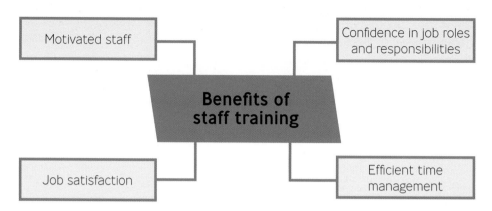

Having a skilled workforce can have a significant impact on work performance and on service delivery, which has positive benefits for children and families. Not only is training and development important to ensure compliance with regulatory policies and issues of compliance, but also to put the setting at the forefront of its competitors. Parents have the ultimate choice when it comes to choosing the best care for their children. Having a highly skilled workforce whose objective is a first class service will capture their attention and their business.

When training meets the needs of parents and of the staff it can lead to an improvement in the quality of the service available which is demonstrated through effective working practices, an efficient child-centred working environment and a customer care-based approach to service delivery.

## Identifying learning needs of colleagues

The process of identifying and providing for colleagues' learning needs will be ongoing throughout their period of employment with the organisation. Opportunities to establish what these are will present themselves in both formal and informal situations.

Thorough interview processes and appraisal systems provide an ideal time for discussions to take place between management and colleagues to decide what training and development opportunities would be beneficial to the individual and the setting. Later in this Unit you will gather more information about the role of appraisals.

You can find out more about the role of interviews in Unit 401.

429K01
429K02
429K03

## Case Study: Promoting learning to colleagues

Serena has recently started work at the children's centre where her roles and responsibilities include organising and running stay and play sessions for children under 5 and their families. In her interview she discussed her desire to learn more about the role of play in providing for children's learning and development needs. The manager agreed this would be beneficial to enable her to fulfil her role fully at the centre. During the first month of her employment, Serena has the opportunity to chat with her manager about an information day she would like to attend

that would give her valuable knowledge about the role of play in early years. The manager rings the training provider immediately to book Serena a place on the course and ensures that adequate cover is in place at the setting for Serena to attend.

■ How does the manager's approach to this situation demonstrate support for Serena and her willingness to explore and undertake development opportunities?

■ Why is it important that Serena is able to identify her own training and development needs?

■ How can the manager help Serena to identify if the training offered has met her needs?

Some settings use an alternative formal process by observing practice and giving colleagues feedback on their performance. Although being 'watched' can seem quite a daunting prospect, it can also provide you with first-hand evidence of colleagues' performance in practice. You could make the experience less daunting by making yourself available to 'cover' shifts of others so that you can work alongside your colleagues and observe their daily practice.

It is important that you involve colleagues in this process, particularly when you are going to make formal accounts or recordings of their performance, just as you would when observing children.

Preparing colleagues prior to formal observations of practice taking place is also important in enabling them to prepare themselves emotionally and understand the objectives of the exercise. Making time to discuss this process with colleagues will also present them with the opportunity to ask questions about the observation of practice. In some instances it may be necessary to adapt the way in which you assess colleagues' abilities; for really nervous practitioners it may be more beneficial to discuss their abilities with their team leader and ask them to conduct unobtrusive observations of practice.

Regular discussions are a valuable way of collating information regarding colleagues' skills and abilities. Discussions in informal environments, such as when on a lunch break, can provide the ideal opportunity for colleagues to 'open up' and share their thoughts and feelings with you. Formal discussions occur in the form of staff meetings where colleagues can discuss practice and practice issues with the support of other members of the team. Staff meetings may also be the time at which you share information with colleagues about training and development events happening in your locality that they may express a wish to attend.

Whatever method of evaluating colleagues' performance you use, it is important you use the information collated to identify gaps in their current knowledge, understanding and skills.

## Prioritising learning needs of colleagues

For many reasons, not all training and development needs of colleagues can be met at the first opportunity, including time spent away from the setting, adequate provision for covering colleagues and costs relating to training and development. It is therefore essential that you prioritise these needs from both the perspective of the individual and the perspective of the organisation itself.

It is not unreasonable for you to say 'no' to specific requests as long as you can justify the reasons why these have been declined. Situations when you may have to say 'no' could include the following.

- When the same practitioner attends all training events without opening the opportunity to others.
- Where costs cannot be covered by the setting, the individual or other funding sources.
- When training is more suited to the roles and responsibilities of others.

Looking at the training and development plans of colleagues will help you to prioritise these opportunities by identifying from individual plans who will benefit most greatly from attendance. Practitioners will invariably have very different learning needs, and as an effective manager it is your role to organise these needs into some form of agenda of priority. High on your agenda will be training and learning opportunities for colleagues who have a distinct lack of knowledge and understanding of issues that affect their daily practice. Of equal importance is prioritising training needs that have a direct impact on compliance issues and best practice benchmarks to benefit the setting itself.

## Training and development plans

429KI4
429KI5
429K24

Creating your own personal development plan can help you in providing appropriate support with the training and development plans of colleagues. Having identified with individuals their needs and how these are going to be met, you need to consider the processes for continual review to ensure they have been met. Again, this can take the form of formal and informal opportunities to discuss whether the objectives have been achieved. During discussions you will also be able to ascertain how the learning experience has been of benefit to the individuals' knowledge and practice. Discussions can also help people reflect on learning activities and draw conclusions about the impact they have had on their knowledge and skills.

429K06

You can find out more about creating a training and development plan in Unit 404.

**429K27**
**429K28**

# In-house training

Many settings utilise the opportunity to conduct staff development sessions in staff meetings as it can be one of the only times when all practitioners are gathered together.

Leaning activities that could occur in-house include:

- policy review and development
- basic food hygiene
- first aid training
- behaviour management
- understanding of children's play and learning needs.

It may not be appropriate for you to conduct all in-house training opportunities, but instead to utilise the support of specialists in developing the skills and knowledge of colleagues to enhance their practice and range of understanding of practice issues.

**429KI8**
**429KI7**

# Gaining qualifications in the sector

In addition to in-house training opportunities, colleagues should be supported in gaining formal qualifications in the Early Years Sector. In England, the Early Years Foundation Stage Framework recognises the need for skilled practitioners in the Early Years workforce to ensure quality in the delivery of services to children and families. For managers of settings this means there is a need to ensure colleagues' skills meet the requirements set out in the statutory framework.

It states: 'In registered settings other than child minding settings, all supervisors and managers must hold a full and relevant level 3 qualification (as defined by the Children's Workforce Development Council (CWDC)) and half of all other staff must hold a full and relevant level 2 qualification (as defined by CWDC).'

In Scotland the National Care Standards for early education and childcare up to the age of 16 identifies within its regulations the need to have confidence in the service (standards 4 to II) and confidence in management (standards I2 to I4).

It states: 'You can expect staff to have a good understanding of the stages and young people's development and learning (taken from standard 4). You can be confident that the service applies procedures to select staff with a range of qualifications, skills and experience relevant to the aims of the service. (taken from standard I2).'

Annexe A, Input standards, recognises the need 'to move to a position where all staff in centres providing childcare or pre-school education either hold an appropriate qualification, are seeking accreditation of skills or are pursuing on-the-job training with a view to registering with the Scottish Social Services Council in due course.'

The National Minimum Standards for Full Day Care in Wales state under Standard I3: Suitable Person: 'Prior to their appointment, a manager has at least 2 years experience of working in a day care setting (I3.4). The registered person ensures the person in charge has at least a level 3 qualification appropriate to the post (I3.5). At least 80% of the non-supervisory staff hold a qualification at least at level 2; and at least half of these have a qualification at level 3. Where this cannot be achieved immediately, the registered person will set out an action plan detailing how they intend to meet this criterion and agree a timescale by which it will be achieved.'

The Day Care Setting Regulations (Northern Ireland) 2007 states that it is the responsibility of the registered person to ensure 'the registered manager shall undertake from time to time such training as is appropriate to ensure that he has the experience and skills necessary for managing the day care setting (II.3).' In addition registered persons need to 'ensure that at all times suitably qualified, competent and experienced persons who are working in the day care setting in such numbers as are appropriate for the care of the service users (20.Ia).'

You can find out more about the regulations and requirements specific to the country in which you work by visiting the following websites:

- www.standards.dfes.gov.uk
- www.opsi.gov.uk
- www.new.wales.gov.uk
- www.scotland.gov.uk

## Find it out

Visit the Qualifications Curriculum Authority (QCA) website to find out more about the standardised programme for vocational qualifications at www.qca.org.uk. You can find additional information by visiting www.cwdc.org.uk.

## Did you know?

It is good practice for settings to have a training policy in place so that all practitioners know what is expected of them in terms of continuing their professional development whilst with the organisation.

when looking at performance-related issues that require further training and development on the team member's part; a regular review of progress may be considered as part of the overall appraisal system.

Revisit Unit 402 to recap on specifics of legislation.

## Appraisal systems

Many settings have appraisals systems in place, and whilst employers are not required by law to implement such systems it is important to bear in mind specific laws that relate to this if you do. They include:

- The Data Protection Act 1998
- Race Relations Act
- Sex Discrimination Act
- Employment Equality Regulations
- The Disability Discrimination Act 1995.

The main objectives of your setting's appraisal systems should be to review the performance and potential of the members of your team and to give them constructive feedback on this. In addition it can be a valuable tool in identifying real issues that impact on the performance and practices of the setting. By identifying issues in the workplace of the individual or by looking at the weaknesses of practice demonstrated at appraisal you can then move forward in seeking ways to resolve such issues to the benefit of all concerned.

How often staff members are appraised is for you to decide, knowing why you are using an appraisal system might help you in determining how often the process takes place. This is particularly important to consider

**429K3I**

## Keys to Good Practice

Consider the objectives of your appraisal process.

- Identify how performance is measured and prioritised.
- Identify how areas for staff development are recognised and addressed.
- Identify how staff development and progress is reviewed.
- Identify how the appraisal system takes place.

In addition to or in place of formal appraisal systems there will be other opportunities presented within the daily practice of the setting for more informal discussions about performance and progress of team members.

**429K04**
**429K3I**

## Points for Reflective Practice

Consider the structure of your setting and the systems currently in place. Do you think that formal appraisals are of more benefit than informal opportunities? What are the advantages and disadvantages of these?

## Can't find what you were looking for?

| Level 4 KS Number | Knowledge Statement | Can be found in... |
|---|---|---|
| 429K07 | The range of different learning styles and how to support colleagues in identifying the particular learning style(s) or combination of learning styles which works best for them | Unit 404 |
| 429KO8 | Different types of learning activities, their advantages and disadvantages and the required resources | Unit 404 |

| Level 4 KS Number | Knowledge Statement | Can be found in... |
|---|---|---|
| 429K09 | How/where to identify and obtain information on different learning activities | Unit 404 |
| 429KIO | Why it is important for colleagues to have a written development plan and what it should contain | Unit 404 |
| 429KII | How to set learning objectives which are SMART | Unit 404 |
| 429KI2 | Sources of specialist expertise in relation to identifying and providing learning for colleagues | Unit 404 |
| 429KI3 | What type of support colleagues might need to undertake learning activities, the resources needed and the types of obstacles they may face and how these can be resolved | Unit 404 |
| 429KI9 | Working culture and practices of the organisation/sector | Unit 333 |
| 429K20 | Relevant information on the purpose, objectives and plans of your team or area of responsibility or the wider organisation | Unit 333 |
| 429K2I | The work roles of colleagues, including the limits of their responsibilities and their personal work objectives | Unit 333 |
| 429K25 | Learning style(s) or combinations of styles preferred by colleagues | Unit 404 |
| 429K26 | The written development plans of colleagues | Unit 404 |
| 429K29 | Your organisation's policies in relation to equality and diversity | Unit 402 |

# Unit 333   Recruit, select and keep colleagues

If you have responsibility for recruiting and selecting colleagues in your setting or service then this Unit may be appropriate for you. The Unit involves the processes followed through from initial identification of personnel shortage, advertising, interviewing, recruiting and supporting in the job role. Identification of why practitioners leave the setting or service is a crucial element also covered to enable strategies for keeping employees to be implemented.

## Supporting colleagues wanting to leave the setting and/or sector

333K0I
333K02
333KI7

In a managerial role you will sometimes be presented with situations where team members want to move

on. In many cases this is to develop their skills and career further, and seeking employment within other organisations that may give them the opportunity to do so should be celebrated and valued. Opportunities may not exist within your setting or service for them to progress further and so looking for challenges elsewhere would seem an obvious way forward.

Where it is important for you to pay due regard and attention is when a colleague is leaving the setting because they feel unmotivated or undervalued. As a manager it is imperative that you identify colleague's feelings towards their job and the people they work with. Address such issues at the earliest opportunity to prevent colleagues leaving the setting, in worst case scenarios where you do not know how someone is feeling until they hand in their notice, make sure you take time to find the root cause of any issues that present themselves so that you can then address them effectively.

Colleagues may cite a number of reasons for handing in their notice including those given in Figure 5.

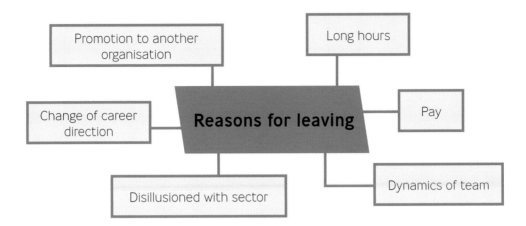

**Figure 5:** There are many reasons why staff may give for handing in their notice

You can see that there are both positive and negative reasons why colleagues may leave and it is not uncommon for there to be peaks and troughs in turnover of staff in the Early Years sector.

## Exit interviews

Exit interviews are a valuable management tool that can be used to ascertain why colleagues might be leaving the setting. When a colleague is leaving to pursue career progression the exit interview can be used as an opportunity to reflect on their learning and development within the setting and the skills they are taking forward to their new post. This is also a great opportunity to thank individuals who have had a significant impact on the setting and whose input will be greatly missed.

When a colleague is leaving for negative reasons the exit interview can be an opportunity to explore their feelings and emotions, hopefully you will have already explored strategies to enable colleagues to stay in post. Being able to speak openly is crucial for the individual, and also for the setting, as once the pressure is off in terms of continuing to come to work, they can have the opportunity to 'tell it how it is' – as long as this is done in a constructive and professional manner.

Practitioners often forget that managers are not psychic and therefore cannot read other people's minds; they rely heavily on the communications of others to tell them when they are not happy.

> **Find it out**  333K03 333K04 333K22
>
> Do you have any systems in place in your setting to measure staff turnover rates?
>
> What are the most common reasons for colleagues handing their notice in?
>
> Do you have any team members who have a long service history?
>
> What might be the reasons for this?

## Seeking to recruit  333K06 333KI9

Before you start placing an ad in the local paper for new practitioners, you should find out if shortfalls in staffing can be addressed within your current team. It may be that some part-time members of the team are looking for more hours of work or that skills can be redeployed in the setting. Perhaps you work for an organisation that has other settings that can supply you with staff. Other options include the use of agency staff where the shortfall is short term.

> **Points for Reflective Practice**  333K07
>
> What do you think are the advantages and disadvantages of using these methods of addressing staff shortfalls?

333K08
333KI5
333KI7
333K20
333K2I
333K23

# Job descriptions and person specifications

At the start of the recruiting process it is important to analyse what it is you are looking for in potential applicants. Ensuring this is clear and detailed in content helps you to focus on the qualities and skills you require for the post.

Clear job descriptions and person specifications give potential candidates accurate information about the post they are applying for and ensure that the skills and knowledge they have match the setting's requirements prior to applying for posts. Presenting these in a detailed format to those involved in the recruitment process will help to identify appropriate candidates for interview and subsequently for the post. Looking at job descriptions and person specifications can help you in evaluating the requirements of practitioners and can be a useful tool in reviewing job roles and responsibilities within the setting, particularly where there is an identified gap of skills or knowledge within the team that needs filling.

- Job descriptions: should give details of the roles and responsibilities of practitioners in their daily practice.
- Person specifications: should state the skills, knowledge, experience and personal attributes that potential applicants should be able to bring to the post.
- Essential and desirable: it is useful to identify if the skills you are looking for are essential or desirable, that way individuals can indicate their ability and experience and their ability to take on new learning and development in post.

So what should a job description include?

- Job title, hours and salary.
- Specific responsibilities.
- Aims and objectives of job role.
- Line of reporting: who they are responsible to?
- Day-to-day duties.

And what should a person specification include?

- Qualifications possessed.
- Level of experience in sector.

- Previous experience at level required.
- Abilities of candidate e.g. communication, organisation or management skills.
- Personal qualities e.g. enthusiasm, motivation, people skills.
- Qualities required by post holder e.g. ability to use initiative, seeking to resolve practice issues.

By identifying the skills and abilities required in job descriptions and person specifications you will be able to avoid unnecessary disputes between the expectations of both the practitioner and the setting. If these documents are communicated effectively to prospective candidates, job roles can be fulfilled to the maximum benefit of all involved. It can also help in the retention process as candidates who become employees will have the ability to meet the requirements of the post and understand fully what is expected of them, making for a happy and harmonious working environment.

## Points for Reflective Practice

How do you go about attracting the right applicant for a post? Look at the job description and person specification for a recently advertised post in your setting.

- Did you examine the requirements of these and adapt any aspects to suit the post being advertised?
- Did you ensure all potential applicants had access to these prior to application?
- Did these help in attracting appropriate candidates to the post?
- How do you use these in the ongoing process of retaining staff?

In addition to providing potential applicants with job descriptions and person specifications it is also useful to provide them with some general information about the setting, including its structure, values and culture. This can give them a clearer vision of the organisation they are seeking employment with.

## Points for Reflective Practice

Does your organisation have a prospectus outlining the organisation's structure, values and culture?

- Is this regularly reviewed and amended to accommodate the changing needs of the setting?
- Do you ensure prospective employees have a copy of your organisation's prospectus?

## Recruitment methods

There are many avenues which you can explore to recruit practitioners to the setting, some of which you will have used on previous occasions.

These could include:

- advertising in local press
- placing ads in local shops
- running recruitment days
- registering with the local job centre
- website advertising: on own or other web pages
- using recruitment agencies.

Whatever method of advertising you choose, and remember this could include a range of opportunities, you will need to consider the associated advantages and disadvantages of these in relation to your organisation.

## Local press

This can be useful as practitioners already living within your locality may be looking for employment; they may also already know a bit about your organisation and its practice. In some circumstances potential candidates are already waiting for an opportunity to apply for a job in your setting as they feel this is suited to their needs. Press advertising can be costly and newspapers will often have submission deadlines that you will need to think about if you want a post to go to press at a particular time. Using the local press can be advantageous as you can call in to discuss your recruitment requirements with them, look at the way in which advertisements will be displayed in the paper and adjust these to suit your needs. Local newspapers will often offer you a package for your advertising, including incentives to run adverts on a repetitive basis.

## Local shops

Using the local post office or corner shop can be useful as little is charged for their services. You will need to consider how long you want them to place the advert in their window and will need to draw up your own advertisement to display. The main disadvantage to using this method is the availability of potential candidates in such a small locality and sometimes adverts will generate little or no interest.

## National press

There may be occasions when advertising with the national press or national publications specific to the early year's sector will be appropriate for the recruitment needs of the setting. This is more commonly seen in bigger companies and corporations that offer services and settings countrywide. Companies seeking to recruit regional and national managers often find this type of recruitment useful as the advertisements can reach a large number of people who are able and willing to relocate for such challenges in their career.

## Running recruitment days

This is often common practice in larger organisations and settings where days or evenings are allocated to opening up the building to allow visitors and potential candidates to come and see the working environment. This is a service often used by new settings opening their doors and having recruitment drives for both staff and clients. The downfall to this method is the amount of work you will need to put in to the organisation of the event and the support needed by others to ensure that potential candidates have the opportunity to look around the setting, ask any questions about jobs being advertised and get the information to enable them to apply for the post.

## Registering with the local job centre

Registration with your local job centre can prove to be valuable in sourcing practitioners in your locality, and with the help of modern day technology this search can be widespread via their Internet-based job search sites. Support and advice is free with the added bonus of telephone support from individuals specialising in recruitment and employment.

**Figure 6:** Your local job centre can be valuable in identifying local employment market conditions

333K24

> ## Did you know?
>
> Your local job centre can be a valuable tool in identifying local employment market conditions. It can also help with job grants, work trials, business starts and much more. Visit www.jobcentreplus.gov.uk to find out how it can help you.

## Advertising on your own website

Many settings, from childminders to day nurseries, have their own websites to inform the general public about the services available. In addition to being useful in enticing potential clients, they can be useful for practitioners who are trawling the Internet in their own time to seek new job opportunities. By using your own website for advertising you not only keep the cost of advertising down but also give valuable information to the potential candidate about the setting in which they are seeking employment. The only major downside to this is the site's ability to pull in appropriate candidates, as the search base may be limited to those who can find your website.

## Advertising with other web-based companies

A really effective way of advertising your company's vacancies is to use the services of specialist advertising websites. These can come in two forms: first are websites that are in some way related to government or county council websites and support the business of early years and, second, is the private sector where a subscription or search fee may be applicable for using the service. Websites of this nature are far-reaching across the country and can potentially reach candidates from other localities who would consider relocating for the right job.

## Recruitment agencies

Whether you are registered with a recruitment agency or not your setting will inevitably get a call from at least one offering their services in staff recruitment. They have access to a database of potential candidates looking for work in the Early Years sector and can quickly identify and match the needs of vacancies to candidates on their books. Recruitment agents often have a lot of knowledge about the associated problems of recruiting in early years, particularly where knowledge and skills are required, which can make the search process a lot less arduous. You will, however, need to consider the costs of such services and should identify the financial implications with recruitment agencies from the outset.

### Find it out

Can you think of any additional methods of recruiting staff?

Find out how these can meet you recruitment needs.

### Find it out

Does your local authority have a website where potential vacancies can be advertised? Find out by visiting the early years sector of their website.

## Writing job advertisements

When advertising for practitioners, you must consider the type of practitioner you are seeking in order to ensure the right candidates are attracted to the post.

When drawing up your advertisement you should ask yourself a number of questions.

- What experience should they have?
- What level of qualification should they have?
- What attributes are we looking for?
- What additional skills do we want the post holder to possess?

**Figure 7:** Job advertisement I

> **Little Tots Pre-school, Main Street, Little Watling**
>
> Is seeking to recruit
>
> NVQ Level 3 Practitioner (part-time)
>
> The post holder will ideally have experience of planning and providing learning experiences for children aged 3–5 years.
>
> For an application form, job description, salary details and prospectus please contact Lesley on 01746 786 786
>
> Applications should be received no later than 18th March
>
> Interviews to be held week commencing 28th March

**Figure 8:** Job advertisement 2

> **Pre-school assistant needed**
>
> Part-time hours – term time only.
>
> Contact 01746 786 786
>
> For more information

## Points for Reflective Practice

Look at the two job adverts in Figures 7 and 8.

- Which one would you consider to be the most informative?
- Why do you think advertisements should be detailed and clear?
- What information do you think should be included?
- How does this help in the recruitment process?

## Find it out

Can you find out about the services offered by private HR/personnel companies?

Visit the ACAS website at www.acas.org.uk to find out how this organisation can help you.

## Specialist advice

Although you are a specialist in the Early Years sector, you may not necessarily be an expert in personnel issues which involve the recruitment and selection processes of staff. Larger organisations often have departments dedicated to such operations. You may be familiar with the term HR or Human Resources, this is generally a specific team of professionals whose main purpose is to support the people within an organisation and to ensure that business and services can benefit from maximum employee competence, commitment and engagement.

For smaller organisations, where the job of HR is left to the nursery manager, there are many sources of support in the community including private/independent personnel companies and government funded organisations.

## Private/independent personnel companies

Many companies advertise their services on the Internet and their websites give a host of valuable information regarding the services they offer, which can range from helping draw up interview techniques through to disciplinary policies and procedures. Companies often charge a service or subscription fee for their information services and the use of their document templates.

## Government-funded organisations

With easy access via websites and telephone help lines you can source free and impartial advice about all types of employment issues. Locally, there may be services available specifically to the Early Years sector which can be accessed via your borough or county council website.

## Employment policies and practices

It is essential for any organisation that employs staff to have in place both policies and procedures relating to all aspects of employment. It is also the organisation's responsibility to act fairly and lawfully in relation to any employment issues.

Employment matters you will need to consider include:

- the national minimum wage
- pregnancy and maternity rights
- paternity and adoption rights in the workplace
- parental leave and flexible working
- employment contracts and conditions
- training and development opportunities
- grievance procedures
- disciplinary procedures
- mediation, conciliation and arbitration
- unfair dismissal
- discrimination and bullying in the workplace
- employers' and employees' health and safety responsibilities.

Many organisations will ensure that their policies for practice encompass these elements in order to keep within the law. Having such policies in place demonstrates to employees your commitment not only to the setting but also to them as an individual.

## Find it out

Find out your legal obligations to your staff by researching employment law in the UK. Take the opportunity to review your policies and procedures in relation to selection, recruitment and retention to ensure you are acting lawfully and fairly.

## Keeping colleagues

For any setting it is crucial to consider how practitioners are going to be encouraged to stay within the organisation once they have been appointed. The role of the manager and colleagues within the setting is to ensure effective working relationships and robust induction processes.

You can find out more about working relationships and induction processes in Unit 401.

It is also essential to identify both the personal and professional development needs of individuals and provide for these. This means staff feel valued in the setting and can continually contribute effectively to the working environment and practices and furthermore develop their own knowledge and skills which can be very fulfilling and motivating.

You can find more on providing for professional development needs in Unit 429.

## Can't find what you were looking for?

| Level 3 KS Number | Knowledge Statement | Can be found in... |
|---|---|---|
| 333KO5 | Measures which can be undertaken to address staff turnover problems | Unit 401 |
| 333KO9 | Different stages in the recruitment and selection process and why it is important to consult with others on the stages, recruitment and selection methods to be used, associated timings and who is going to be involved | Unit 401 |
| 333KI2 | How to judge whether the applicant meets the stated requirements of the vacancy | Unit 401 |
| 333KI8 | Working culture and practices of the sector/industry | Units 402 and 403 |

# Further references

www.acas.org.uk

www.cwdc.org.uk

www.dcsf.gov.uk

www.jobcentreplus.gov.uk

www.new.wales.gov.uk

www.opsi.gov.uk

www.qca.org.uk

www.scotland.gov.uk

www.standards.dfes.gov.uk

Daly, M., Byers, E. & Taylor, W. (2009) *Early Years Management in Practice*, 2nd edition, Heinemann

Jay, R. (2002) *How to Build a Great Team*, Prentice Hall

Macleod-Brudenell, I. & Kay, J. (2008) *Advanced Early Years*, 2nd edition, Heinemann

# Learning and curriculum development

The Units grouped here all relate to children's learning and development. They begin by looking in particular at babies and children under 3 years old, as this age group have specific needs. This then leads on to a discussion on early education, focusing on each area of development in turn.

These Units may be suitable if you are working in one of the following job roles:

- In support of settings offering early education.
- Working within an advisory service.
- Working within a specialist service.
- Manager of a setting.
- Lead or senior practitioner in a setting.
- Supporting other professionals with children's development.
- Supporting children or their families.
- Responsible for babies and children under 3.
- Responsible for supporting a teacher.

The Units covered by this section are:

| 405 | Coordinate provision for babies and children under 3 years in partnership with their families. |
| 406 | Develop and support children's early learning in partnership with teachers. |
| 407 | Support and evaluate the curriculum for children's early learning. |
| 408 | Evaluate, assess and support the physical, intellectual, emotional and social development of children. |
| 409 | Evaluate, assess and support children's communication. |
| 410 | Evaluate, assess and support children's creativity. |
| 411 | Evaluate, assess and support children's mathematical learning, exploration and problem solving. |
| 419 | Contribute to the enhancement of early education for children. |

# Unit 405   Coordinate provision for babies and children under 3 years in partnership with their families

This Unit is about the provision of services for babies and children under 3. It includes working in partnership with parents and families and providing information for them. It also includes developing provision and encouraging best practice.

The elements in this Unit are:

**405.1**   Provide information on services and provision for parents.

**405.2**   Coordinate and develop provision.

**405.3**   Encourage best practice in work with babies and children under 3 years.

## 405.1  Provide information on services and provision for parents

### Providing information for parents and families

When providing services for babies and children under three, it is important to communicate with the parents and find out what their needs are from your setting. Ideally, you will discuss their needs with them when their child starts attending your setting. It is also a good idea to check that these needs are being met by taking the time to speak to them on a regular basis. This may be when they collect their child or it may be on a more formal occasion, such as parents' evening or in an arranged meeting.

It is also important that you provide the parents with detailed information about your setting, making sure that parents and families are able to access it without difficulty. This may be in the form of a brochure or a welcome pack, and you may display updated information on a notice board or distribute a regular newsletter.

Seeking and distributing information in this way has many benefits. You will be more aware of the child's and the parent's needs, and better placed to meet them. It may help you to identify any gaps in your provision and find out the best ways to fill them. It is also useful to look at this as a way of gaining feedback and being able to identify any improvements that need to be made or any good practice that needs to be supported.

It is important to make sure that any information distributed is accessible to all parents. Not all parents are able to read English, and there may be some who are not able to read. You will need to consider ways of making sure that information is distributed in a way that allows all parents to receive it.

### Involving parents

K4D832

The main way that parents will be involved in your setting is through the daily sharing of information, both when they drop their child off and when they collect. You may also be able to involve parents by making them aware that they are welcome to stay and play with their child, or by running specific sessions to allow them to do so. You could also ask them to contribute their knowledge and skills to the activities you have planned, or ask them to come in and help with outings and trips. All these ways of involving parents are likely to make them feel more valued, and more confident in you as their provider.

## Additional services

**K4M830**
**K4D834**

It can be helpful to parents to provide them with information about additional services for babies and children under 3 in the local area. As a childcare provider you are likely to have more knowledge and information about this than the parents, and are likely to be called upon for your expertise! Additional services may include local toddler's groups, playgroups, organised groups and activities, play centres and antenatal clinics. It can also be helpful to parents if you are able to provide them with the costs of these services. This type of information can be displayed on a notice board in the setting, or could be in the form of a booklet or information binder. If parents need further advice or guidance, then consider directing them to their local Sure Start centre or to their health visitor for this.

## 405.2 Coordinate and develop provision

**K4D837**
**K4M835**

It is important that your provision is continually developing and improving, both to keep up with the requirements and needs of parents, and to keep up with current legislation and advice on best practice. Requirements for current best practice can be found within the Early Years Foundation Stage Guidance documents, or the documents that are relevant to your home country, and practitioners should be aiming to meet these. There are many ways in which you can evaluate your provision, and these include talking to staff and parents, carrying out observations, reflecting on your practice, looking at use of resources and reviewing policies and procedures to see if they are up-to-date and if your provision is actually following them. Once you have this information you can then act on the information that you have and look to see where improvements can be made, implement any changes and then review your provision again to see if the improvements have worked. You may be able to access funding from your Early Years team in your local area to contribute towards the costs of making any improvements, or you may be able to approach your local stakeholders to see if they would be prepared to offer any funding.

## 405.3 Encourage best practice in work with babies and children under 3 years

### Best practice

Your practice with the children directly affects their development and it is for this reason that you must ensure you strive to meet best practice at all times. In simple terms, best practice means 'a way or method that is superior to all other methods'. Current best practice is detailed in the Early Years Foundation Stage, both in the Practice Guidance and Statutory Framework, or the guidance relevant to your home country. You can also find information on the Every Child Matters website, and from your local Early Years advisors. You may find it worthwhile to undertake a quality assurance scheme that will help you to improve on your previous best and will show parents and families who use your setting that you have a commitment to improvement.

> You can find out more on using the Early Years Foundation Stage in planning in Unit 403.

### Find it out
More information about Every Child Matters can be found on the following website:
www.everychildmatters.gov.uk.

### Key elements in best practice

Two of the key elements in best practice are the key person system and the provision of stable and consistent environments.

A key person has responsibility for a small group of children and will form an attachment with those children and relationships with their parents. It will be this person who settles the child in and meets the care needs of that child. It is a good idea to have a second key person for each group, so that the children always have someone who is familiar and trusted to turn to.

A stable and consistent environment supports the children's learning and development and gives them confidence to explore in a safe space. It includes the indoor environment, the outdoor environment and the emotional environment.

**Figure I:** A stable and consistent indoor environment

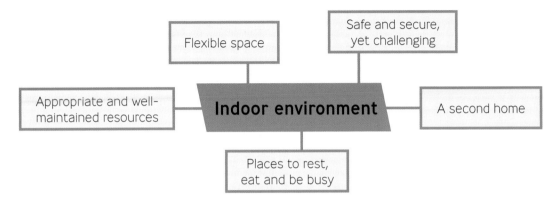

**Figure 2:** A stable and consistent outdoor environment

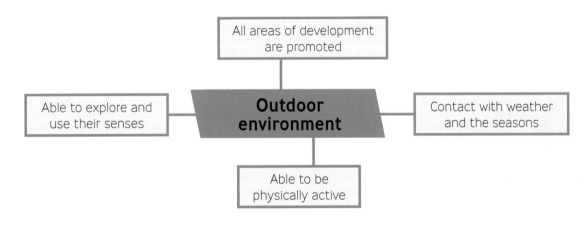

**Figure 3:** A stable and consistent emotional environment

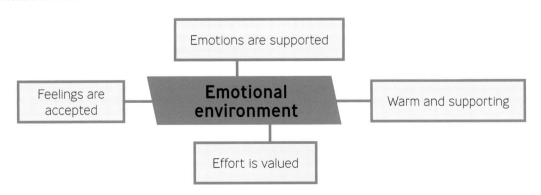

## K4D836 Multilingual and bilingual settings

It is important to value diversity in language, both in the children and their parents. Our language is part of our identity, and by showing you value it you are showing the child that you value them.

Children who are learning two or more languages may have difficulties with pronunciation and may start to talk later than other children. This is because they have twice as much language to absorb! You may also find that children mix languages – this often happens when the people around them are not consistent with the language they use around the child. Generally, overall language development is not affected.

### Key Terms

Bilingual – someone who speaks two languages.

Multilingual – someone who speaks three or more languages.

## K4D838 K4DIII5 Reflective, responsive and knowledgeable practitioners

Babies and young children under 3 need the practitioners who look after them to be reflective, responsive and knowledgeable.

Practitioners can be reflective by looking back on their practice and considering what went well and what did not go so well. It can also help you to identify children's needs and how to meet them. Another good reason for reflective practice is to identify your own strengths and weaknesses and recognise where further training is needed. It will also improve the quality of care for the children, as it will enable you to become a better practitioner.

Being responsive includes responding to the children when they communicate with you, whether this is just with a smile or a noise, or whether the child makes a comment or initiates a conversation. It also includes knowing when a child needs physical contact such as a cuddle or a hand to hold. These things are important because they help the child to feel cared for and to feel secure.

## Professional development

There are many ways in which professional development can be encouraged. It can be useful to arrange times when staff can get together to share their ideas about good practice and plan improvements. It can also work well if you are able to work with the children and model good practice for the staff. This can help to show them what good practice looks like in action, and also motivate them to realise that they are able to do it. Regular one-to-ones or appraisals are important as they give you and your staff the time to discuss what their strengths and weaknesses are, and what development needs they have. This can then lead onto opportunities being identified for continuous professional development (CPD).

There are many places where further training can be accessed. These include colleges, training providers, courses run by the local council and courses run by Sure Start. Your local Early Years advisor, or the Early Years team in your local authority, will be able to provide you with a list of what is on offer.

Other ways of keeping up to date include reading magazines specific to childcare, regular checking on websites such as Every Child Matters for new developments, visiting the library or accessing the Internet to do some further reading on a subject.

### Did you know?

One of the areas in which research is constantly being carried out is Sudden Infant Death Syndrome (SIDS). This is the sudden and unexplained death of an infant. You can find out more at www.fsid.org.uk.

## Can't find what you were looking for?

| Level 4 KS Number | Knowledge Statement | Can be found in... |
|---|---|---|
| K4D826 | Theoretical perspectives | Unit 403 |
| K4D827 | Expected patterns of development | Unit 403 |
| K4D828 | Referral systems | Unit 403 |

# Unit 406   Develop and support children's early learning in partnership with teachers

This Unit is about working with teachers and supporting and developing children's early education. It provides information for those who work alongside teachers and includes working with individuals, small groups and large groups. There is also information about planning, monitoring and recording.

THE LIBRARY
NORTH WEST KENT COLLEGE
DERING WAY, GRAVESEND

The elements in this Unit are:

**406.1**    Contribute to planning and preparing for children's learning.

**406.2**    Implement teaching and learning activities to deliver the curriculum.

**406.3**    Contribute to the monitoring and assessment of children's progress.

## 406.1 Contribute to planning and preparing for children's learning

### The role of the teacher

Teachers within nurseries have an important role to play. The Effective Provision of Pre-School Education (EPPE) study showed that children did better when the nursery was led by a qualified teacher.

They have specialist knowledge not only of the curriculum requirements, but also a thorough understanding of how children learn, and the methods that can be used to help them do so. Understanding exactly how the curriculum needs to be used in practice means that the children are able to gain from it fully, as the teacher is able to implement all parts of it. The teacher will also be able to understand that any curriculum used with young children is based on play and will be able to help the children make sense of the world using play-based learning. They are also able to ensure that their work with the children prepares them for Key Stage 1 and the Primary Framework. The teacher may be able to work with the other staff and show them how the planned curriculum works and help them to understand their role within it.

Because the role of the teacher is a highly skilled one, it is important that you, as their manager, are able to support them fully. You may be able to offer assistance with the planning and preparation of lessons, and also with the implementation of learning opportunities. You should also encourage collaborative working between the teacher and other staff. This could happen through regular meetings to discuss the children in the setting and the activities that are being planned for them. The more involved all staff are, the more likely it is that the children will benefit from what is on offer to them.

## Find it out

Find out more about the EPPE project at: www.surestart.gov.uk/research/keyresearch.

## Curriculum frameworks

The EYFS framework provides guidance to help settings develop a curriculum to meet children's needs from birth to the end of their reception year. Links are made to Key Stage I and the **Primary Framework** in the EYFS booklet. At the beginning of Year I children in maintained schools enter the National Curriculum, and will remain under this framework until they are 16. The aim of the National Curriculum is to make sure that teaching and learning is balanced and consistent. It details the subjects to be taught, what knowledge, skills and understanding are required in each subject and the targets by which children are measured.

The National Curriculum is organised into key stages, which are detailed in Table I:

You can find more on the Early Years Foundation Stage (EYFS) in Unit 403.

## Key Term

**Primary Framework** – the Primary Framework has been designed to support teachers and schools to deliver high quality learning and teaching for all children. It contains detailed guidance and materials to support literacy and maths in primary schools and settings.

## Planning and preparing

The environment that children are in directly affects their learning. It is important that environments are welcoming and stimulating and celebrate the children's efforts. They should also support children's efforts to become independent. This could be achieved by displaying the children's artwork at a level where they

**Table I:** Key Stages in the National Curriculum

| Age | Stage | Year | Assessment |
|---|---|---|---|
| 4–5 | EYFS | Reception | EYFS Profile |
| 5–6 | Key Stage I | Year I | |
| 6–7 | Key Stage I | Year 2 | Teacher assessments in English, Maths and Science |
| 7–8 | Key Stage 2 | Year 3 | |
| 8–9 | Key Stage 2 | Year 4 | |
| 9–10 | Key Stage 2 | Year 5 | |
| 10–11 | Key Stage 2 | Year 6 | National tests and teacher assessments in English, Maths and Science |
| 11–12 | Key Stage 3 | Year 7 | |
| 12–13 | Key Stage 3 | Year 8 | |
| 13–14 | Key Stage 3 | Year 9 | Optional teacher assessments in English, Maths, Science and other foundation subjects |
| 14–15 | Key Stage 4 | Year 10 | Some children take GCSEs |
| 15–16 | Key Stage 4 | Year 11 | Most children take GCSEs or other national qualifications |

can see it, providing activities such as self-registration boards and making sure children know where their toys belong, so they are able to put them away at tidy up time. Changing the environment round occasionally will also help to keep children stimulated, as will changing resources frequently and laying out activities in an attractive manner.

# 406.2 Implement teaching and learning activities to deliver the curriculum

## Implementing activities

Children all learn in different ways. When implementing a planned teaching or learning activity it is important that the method of teaching that you use is suitable for both the planned session and the children involved. You should make sure that both the method and the activity are interesting to the children and that they will enthuse and motivate them to join in fully and learn from it.

> You can find out more about some of the main theories about learning in Unit 403.

It is also important to consider how the curriculum used in your setting is differentiated. Differentiation means the adjustment of the teaching process according to the learning needs of the children. You may need to differentiate for a whole group, for a small group or just for individual children.

As all children are at different levels in their development and therefore will gain different learning and understanding from an activity, you need to consider how you will support those children who need extra help, and how you will take the learning further for those who are ready. This is important in order for children's learning to move forward.

## Keeping the children's interest

When implementing any teaching and learning activity, communication with the children is very important. If your method of communication is effective, children will be more likely to listen and to join in. It is also

important to listen carefully to their questions and respond to them, as this will help the children to feel part of the activity and to keep their interest. Try to use words which the children will understand easily, and if new words are introduced explain them clearly and let them children repeat them and try to use them. Illustrations and examples are also excellent ways of making a subject interesting.

Children will respond quickly to praise and encouragement, and if they feel that they are doing well they are more likely to want to continue. This will help them to gain confidence with the activity, and is likely to encourage them to persevere and to continue to want to take part. This in turn, will further encourage their learning.

## Equality of access

K4D849

All teaching and learning activities within the setting should be open for all children to take part in and all children should be treated fairly regardless of their backgrounds. All children should be encouraged and, if necessary, assisted to join in, and this is where differentiation may have a role to play. It is equally important that practitioners have an up-to-date knowledge of the needs of the children in their care, and of any special educational needs they may have. Practitioners should also ensure their knowledge of different cultural backgrounds is up-to-date. It is also the practitioner's responsibility to ensure the children in their care develop positive attitudes to diversity and difference and learn to value these.

If a child requires extra support it is important that this is identified and accessed as early as possible, so that children get the help that they need. The child's family will also need to be involved to help practitioners gain a full picture of the child and to make sure that any support is given consistently.

## Inclusion

K4D851

Inclusion means that children with learning difficulties or special educational needs are included in mainstream society. In order to ensure that your setting is inclusive you will need to treat all children as individuals and ensure that you are aware of and able to support their individual needs. There is specific legislation that covers this, and the basic information can be found below.

You can find out more about legislation covering inclusive practices in Unit 402.

## Find it out

Look at www.direct.gov.uk to find out more about the legislation that covers inclusion.

## Disability Discrimination Act 1995 (DDA)

The Disability Discrimination Act (DDA) 1995 was introduced with the aim of ending the discrimination that many disabled people face. This Act has been significantly extended, including by the Disability Discrimination Act 2005. It makes it illegal to treat disabled people less favourably due to their impairment, and reasonable adjustments must be made so that disabled people can access the services on offer.

## Special Educational Needs and Disability Act (SENDA) 2001

The Special Educational Needs and Disability Act 2001 amended the Disability Discrimination Act 1995 and made it unlawful for education providers to allow unjustified discrimination. It strengthened the rights of disabled people to attend mainstream education.

## The Disability Discrimination Act 2005

This Act took things a step further and introduced new duties and required public bodies to promote equality, to take steps to eliminate discrimination and harassment and to publish a Disability Equality Scheme, which will set out how they plan to do so. The aim of this act is to influence the decision making and policy writing of public bodies and to encourage them to consider the needs of disabled people further.

## Special Educational Needs (SEN)

The Education Act 1996 included the publication of a Special Educational Needs (SEN) Code of Practice. This code of practice gives settings practical guidance on how to identify and assess children with special educational needs.

## Points for Reflective Practice

Look back at the four Acts that have just been covered. How do you meet these Acts in your setting?

## 406.3 Contribute to the monitoring and assessment of children's progress

It is important to monitor and assess children's progress to ensure that the planned activities are suitable and are encouraging their learning. It is likely that the teacher will carry out various assessment activities using the format required by your setting in order to do this, and may need your support and the support of other staff members while doing so. The process of compiling assessments and profiles is likely to require time and as a manager you will need to provide opportunities for this to happen out of ratio. You may also need to arrange opportunities for the teacher and other staff to liaise regarding the children's progress.

Teachers may need your feedback about the children, and you may have important observations to contribute. For example, you will have been able to observe the children whilst the teacher has been carrying out planned teaching and learning activities with them, and you will be able to feedback the way the children responded to the activity, how they participated and if progress was shown. This is an important step when evaluating any planned activity, as it will inform the way the activity is carried out in the future.

This type of information can also help to you to identify any learning needs, whether your own, that of the teachers or that of other staff. If there is a weakness in a particular area shown by staff then it is likely that the provision of the setting will be weaker in that area and further training could remedy this.

## Can't find what you are looking for?

| Level 4 KS Number | Knowledge Statement | Can be found in... |
|---|---|---|
| K4D843 | Children's learning | Unit 403 |
| K4D850 | Supporting positive behaviour | Unit 403 |
| K4D797 | Data protection | Unit 403 |
| K4D836 | Multi- or bilingual children | Unit 405 |

# Unit 407   Support and evaluate the curriculum for children's early learning

This Unit is about supporting the curriculum for children's early learning. It includes planning and delivering the curriculum, supporting colleagues, providing resources and the evaluation of the curriculum.

The elements in this Unit are:

**407.1** Identify and support activities, resources and programmes for children's early learning.

**407.2** Support the implementation of the curriculum for children's early learning.

**407.3** Work with colleagues to monitor and evaluate the curriculum for children's early learning.

## 407.1 Identify and support activities, resources and programmes for children's early learning

### Supporting planning

It is important to remember that the curriculum your setting uses with the children must be accessible by all. All planned activities, experiences and resources must be capable of being adapted to suit the needs of all the children in the setting. They must also present the children with a well-rounded view of the world, and show them positive images such as people with disabilities and people from other cultures and religions. You will need to think carefully when planning to ensure that your curriculum plans allow all children to participate.

You may use the Early Years Foundation Stage Framework to plan the curriculum for your setting, or you may use the guidance relevant to your home country. Alternatively, if you care for children who are not participating in early education then you may use another framework to help plan a less formal curriculum.

You can find out more about the EYFS in Unit 403.

## Involving others

K4D859
K4C860
K4D861

Planning should not be something that is undertaken by just one person without reference to others. Colleagues, parents and carers and also children have experiences and ideas that can be taken into account and used when planning activities.

All settings should be working in partnership with parents and families. Parents have an in-depth knowledge of their children that is extremely useful when planning activities to support the children's strengths and weaknesses.

Parents can also provide you with information about their child's culture and religion, to ensure that these needs are being met and that you can celebrate any festivals that may be appropriate.

It is also important to listen to the child's wishes when planning activities. You may find that a group of children in your setting are particularly interested in bugs at the moments, and you will be able to support this interest through planning activities to take it further. It is a good idea to sit down regularly with the children and talk to them about their interests, to ensure that their voice is heard. You will also be able to find out about their interests through regular observations.

Working with colleagues when planning will allow you to ensure that they are confident in their role and that they understand it fully. They will also understand the aims of the planned activities and will be able to identify if they need extra resources to support them.

## 407.2 Support the implementation of the curriculum for children's early learning

### Implementing the curriculum

There is no set format that must be used when planning the curriculum for your setting. Any format must ensure that is shows it is based on play activities, and that the six areas of learning and development from the EYFS Statutory Framework, or the requirements of your home country, are covered, where appropriate. It is worth forming links with other settings and sharing their experiences and ideas on planning. All plans must also be capable of being flexible and adapted to suit the circumstances and the children's needs. Spontaneous learning should be allowed for and you should also allow children's reactions to activities to guide you.

When implementing your curriculum plans, you should aim for high-quality learning experiences that are based on play. This can be achieved in a variety of ways.

### The role of play

Planning should be focused on well-planned play-based activities and experiences. Play is at the heart of the Early Years Foundation Stage and this includes both indoors and outdoors play. There is no longer a place for worksheets or rigid planned activities within Early Years settings.

## Case Study: Working in partnership with parents

Natia is 4 years old and has been attending the local nursery for several years. She was happy at the setting and confident to talk to the staff about her experiences. One day, in circle time, Natia said that she was going to visit her aunt in hospital. Staff at the nursery mentioned this to Natia's parents at the end of the day and they expressed concern that Natia

may be upset by the visit. As a result of this the staff at the setting decided to set up a hospital role play setting, to help Natia deal with her feelings about the visit and work though her experience.

■ Why was it important that staff discussed this with Natia's parents?
■ How will this role play help Natia?
■ How can this role play help the other children in the setting?

**Figure 4:** How to achieve high-quality learning

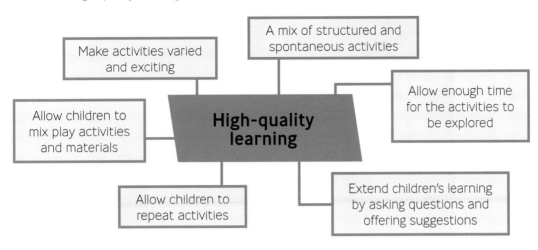

The best way that children can learn is through play. Children enjoy playing and want to play, and there are many benefits to children when this happens. Play helps them to become confident, as they are able to experiment and try without fear of failure. It helps them to develop their imagination and language and allows them to reason and think for themselves. Play can either be **spontaneous** or it can be **planned**. Often planned play will lead into something spontaneous and vice versa.

> ## Key Terms
>
> Spontaneous activities – an activity of the child's own free choice.
>
> Planned activities – an activity planned by the practitioner in the setting.

## Adapting your practice

You should have high expectations of children, but it is important to base these on what the children's current capabilities are, and what they might be able to achieve. It is also important that you and your staff are able to identify quickly if children need extra support, as the quicker this is given the better it is for the children.

There are likely to be occasions when you need to adapt your practice with the children. This includes when the children are of different genders, different ethnicities or if they have different needs and abilities.

When adapting your practice because of gender, you must ensure that the children are not discriminated against in any way because of their gender, and that they have equal access to all activities and experiences. When adapting your practice because of ethnicity you need to ensure that you communicate in an appropriate manner, that the activities reflect and respect the child's culture and cultural needs and that you work alongside the parents. When adapting your practice to meet the child's different needs and abilities, you must make sure you adapt experiences accordingly and that the equipment and resources are appropriate. You should also be aware of the child's capabilities.

## Resources

K4D864
K4D865

Activities and experiences often depend on the availability of resources. If these are not available it can be frustrating for staff and affect the children's learning. Many items such as glue and paint need ordering on a regular basis, and it is worthwhile having a stock control system that ensures you do not run out and have to wait weeks for the next delivery. It is likely that one person will be responsible for stock, but all staff should take responsibility to inform this person if stocks are running low, or if they are likely to need more of a particular resource. You will also need to ensure resources are cost effective and good value for money. Some catalogues offer a bulk discount, and you may be able to source resources from your local library or scrap store.

**Figure 5:** Children enjoy playing with positive resources such as multicultural dolls

Resources must support equality of opportunity. They should also be age and stage appropriate for the children in your setting. They should reflect the diversity of cultures, and promote respect for other cultures. They should also promote a positive view of genders and of those with disabilities.

> **Find it out**
>
> Check your local listing to see if you have a local scrap store in your area www.childrensscrapstore.co.uk.

## 407.3 Work with colleagues to monitor and evaluate the curriculum for children's early learning

### Systems for monitoring and evaluating

K4D866

All plans need to be evaluated so that their strengths and weaknesses can be identified and the plan updated and improved upon ready for the next time. The findings should be recorded in line with organisational procedures and policies. There are several ways you can do this.

■ Check the assessments of children's progress. If the children have made good progress then you can assume the planning and implementation has been good.

■ Ask staff and colleagues for their comments on the plan. It is likely they have worked closely with the plans they so will have an in-depth understanding and ideas for improvement.

■ Reflect back on how the plans went. You may have noted the things that went well and not so well the last time you carried it out.

- Consult with parents and children. Ask the children if they enjoyed the activities. Check your records to see if they participated in the planned activities. Ask the parents what they thought and if they have noticed any progression in their children.

- Check inspection reports or findings from Quality Assurance schemes. These may contain written feedback that may be useful.

## Find it out

Look at www.surestart.gov.uk/improvingquality/guidance/nqin to find out more about Quality Assurance schemes.

## Reflective practice

Reflection is important as it helps you to see what you did well and what didn't go as well. You can then consider how you can improve.

When reflecting on the planning you can ask questions such as the following.

- Was the plan effective?
- Were the activities well organised?
- Was the plan well implemented?
- Was the plan flexible?

You should also ask colleagues for their reflections and together decide on any improvements. These improvements may be made by making changes in the plans, or you may be able to work directly with the children and model good practice, to enable your staff and colleagues to understand the improvements that you wish to be made.

In some cases, you may decide that further information or training is needed. You may be able to access this from your local authority, or you may decide to run an in-house workshop. If you are a member of the National Day Nurseries Association or the Preschool Learning Alliance you may also be able to access support from them.

## Find it out

Look at www.ndna.org.uk and www.pre-school.org.uk for more information about the National Day Nurseries Association or the Preschool Learning Alliance.

## Can't find what you were looking for?

| Level 4 KS Number | Knowledge Statement | Can be found in... |
|---|---|---|
| K4D855 | Pattern of learning and intellectual development | Unit 403 |
| K4D862 | Multi- and bilingual children | Unit 405 |
| K4D853 | Requirements of legislation, regulation and guidance | Unit 403 |

# Unit 408   Evaluate, assess and support the physical, intellectual, emotional and social development of children

This Unit is about evaluating, assessing and supporting the physical, intellectual, emotional and social development of children. It looks at the relevant curricula and activities that are suitable for children in early education.

The elements in this Unit are:

**408.1**   Facilitate the assessment and support of children's physical development.

**408.2**   Facilitate the assessment and support of children's intellectual development.

**408.3**   Facilitate the assessment and support of children's personal, social and emotional development.

**408.4**   Support the collection of data and the monitoring and evaluation of provision to support children's development.

## 408.1 Facilitate the assessment and support of children's physical development

K4D873

### Curriculum

When planning a curriculum for your setting, the relevant guidance to be used in England is the Early Years Foundation Stage. Other UK countries have their own guidance and you should make sure you use the correct one. This applies to all children in state funded education until the end of their reception year.

You can find out more about guidance in UK countries in Unit 403.

### Assessment

It is important that you support and encourage opportunities for staff and practitioners to assess the children's physical development, and there are many ways that observation and assessment can be carried out.

You can find out more about observation and assessment of children in Unit 403.

### Facilitating physical development

Physical skills are essential for children. Children need to be able to carry out and control a variety of movements in order to carry out activities and day-to-day life. Experiences and activities planned in Early Years education have to be suitable for the child's age, needs and ability, and they must also promote confidence, so that the child feels able to try again. All children develop at different rates and activities must be easily adaptable to suit individual children's needs.

Physical activities can be encouraged indoors or outdoors. Outdoors provides more opportunities for large scale and noisy games, whereas indoors allows for physical activity during bad weather or for dancing, drama and singing games.

> You can find out more about the physical development of children in Unit 403.

## Gross and fine manipulative skills

Fine manipulative skills are those movements where the fingers and thumbs work together to complete small tasks, such as drawing or writing. Fine motor skills are those movements where the hand and the wrist work together, for example opening a door handle. These skills link closely to hand–eye coordination.

Activities to develop fine motor skills include:

- using pens and pencils
- using a variety of different sized brushes
- using scissors
- weaving
- using Playdoh
- sewing or threading
- dressing, both themselves and dressing up
- making a collage
- junk modelling
- completing puzzles.

Gross motor skills are whole limb movements. They are closely linked to locomotion skills. Learning these skills helps children to learn to control their bodies.

Activities to help children develop gross motor skills include:

- throwing a ball
- large scale painting
- lifting
- pedalling
- swimming
- climbing
- hopping
- jumping
- running races
- parachute play.

**Figure 6:** Parachute play is a great activity to help children develop gross motor skills

K4D888

# Locomotion, balance, strength, and coordination

Locomotion means the movements that children use in order to be mobile. It links to gross motor skills. Activities to develop locomotion skills are very similar to those that develop gross motor skills (see above).

Balance is an important part of learning to control the body. It is a skill acquired with age. Activities to develop balance include:

- riding bicycles
- riding tricycles
- riding scooters
- using swings
- playing on a seesaw
- walking on beams
- using stilts
- walking along a chalk line.

It is important for children to develop strength and stamina. Activities to develop this should be enjoyable and should allow time for children to continue with it until they are tired.

Coordination includes hand–eye coordination and foot–eye coordination and it should be structured to suit the children's needs. These skills are gradually learnt as children learn to use their hands, eyes and feet together.

Activities to develop coordination include:

- catching balls
- kicking balls
- using small hand tools
- pouring a drink
- climbing stairs
- running safely.

## Body awareness and spatial awareness

This includes learning control over the body and also learning to move safely. These are skills that are learnt very gradually and that are learnt through experience.

K4H889

## Risk and physical activities

As with all activities, it is important to think about the risk involved to the children when they are involved in physical play. If it is judged to be too risky for a certain age group then it may not be suitable or it may need some modification or safety rules brought in.

## Keys to Good Practice

Children have to be allowed to take some element of risk in their activities, as this is how they will grow in confidence, and develop and learn. You can support this by:

- providing good supervision
- setting rules and boundaries so children know what they are allowed to do
- discussing the risk involved with the children
- allowing them to consider what the risks might be and how to deal with them
- trying not to overprotect the children as this may lead to them becoming afraid to try new things, for fear of danger or failure.

# 408.2 Facilitate the assessment and support of children's intellectual development

## Assessment

Children's intellectual development should be assessed on a regular basis and opportunities to do so should be encouraged.

## Facilitating intellectual development

Intellectual development is also known as cognitive development. It is a massive area and is about the way that our brains process the information that they receive. Experiences and activities planned in Early Years education must be suitable for the child's age, needs and ability, and they should also promote confidence, so that the child feels able to try again.

You can find out more about children's intellectual development in Unit 403.

# Attention

Children's attention span can vary and can be influenced by many things. For example, if the activity is not interesting, or is not what the child wants to do, or even if there is something interesting happening out of the window, the child is not likely to be able to give their attention to the task that you are asking them to do! When trying to support and increase children's attention it is important that the activity is appealing and interesting. You also need to consider factors such as temperature and noise in the room. You can help to keep children's attention by talking to them about what they are doing, and by asking questions and suggesting ideas.

# Concentration and motivation

Concentration is an important skill and it will affect children's ability to learn. It includes learning to finish a task, but also knowing what to do if they come across a problem. Learning to concentrate does not necessarily mean sitting at a table, but can mean playing with water or building a long train track. If children are very interested, they are more likely to concentrate for a longer period of time. You can encourage concentration by allowing children to choose their own activities and by making sure the equipment they are using is attractive and suitable for their age and stage of development.

# Persistence

It is easy for children to become frustrated and give up while doing an activity. You need to teach them how to persevere and not be put off by difficulties. It is important to praise the children's efforts, and offer help if they need it to get to the next stage, or to finish the activity. Activities should be at the right level for the child's abilities.

# Exposure to different and varied concepts and ideas

A concept is a difficult thing to understand. How do we know that something is blue, or that something is square? Children are able to practise their understanding of concepts as they are playing; this may be through using wet and dry sand, or by using the building blocks. You need to make sure that you are on hand to explain and to discuss the children's ideas with them.

# Challenging and stimulating learning and a love of learning

All activities should be challenging to allow the children to learn from them. It is important not to make them too hard; otherwise the children may lose interest and move on to something else. Activities should also be stimulating and interesting. Children should not be forced to do an activity they are not interested in or do not want to do, and they should not be made to do an activity just so they have something to take home! If children genuinely enjoy the activities and experiences laid out for them then they are likely to begin to develop a love of learning, which will continue as they start school.

# 408.3 Facilitate the assessment and support of children's personal, social and emotional development

## Curriculum

K4D873

Each UK country has guidance for settings to develop curricula. In England, the relevant guidance is the Early Years Foundation Stage.

## Assessment

Practitioners should make the most of opportunities to assess the children's personal, social and emotional development, in the most appropriate way for your setting.

> You can find out more about children's personal, social and emotional development in Unit 403.

## Facilitating personal, social and emotional development

K4D893

Personal, social and emotional development forms the base for children's learning and interaction with others. Good skills in these areas are essential for later life. Experiences and activities planned in Early Years education need to be suitable for the children in your setting, remembering that all children develop at different rates.

## Confidence, self-esteem and resilience

Self-esteem refers to the way that children feel about themselves. It is important that you help children to feel good about themselves and give them confidence in their abilities. One of the best ways to do this is through praise and encouragement. If a child hears they have done well and know the adult appreciates their efforts they are likely to have high self-esteem. Other ways include displaying the children's work, giving stickers, giving a round of applause or letting them choose the story.

Resilience is the ability to 'bounce back' when things do not go your way, or being able to cope with a disappointment with little effect on your self-esteem. Having good self-esteem is therefore at the heart of developing resilience.

## Independence

As a child becomes more independent, then their self-esteem will increase. This leads to a positive spiral, where the child will want to try to do more and more for themselves. When a child is learning the skills needed for independence it is important to give them as much

responsibility as they are able to take on. Activities such as giving out the biscuits, wiping up spills, or helping to lay the table are useful. It is important that adults do not criticise children's efforts and are patient as they carry out these tasks.

## Social skills

Turn taking and self-care skills are two important skills that children need to learn. Turn taking is a skill developed with age and is often a difficult one! Practitioners should model turn taking, prompt the children to do it for themselves and praise them when they do.

Self-care skills include being able to dress themselves, and personal hygiene skills include washing hands and blowing noses. Children should be allowed to do these tasks for themselves as much as possible and you may need to leave extra time for them to do so! You should offer praise and support to the children.

## Positive relationships

Children need to learn several things in order to have positive relationships with others. They need to be able to work as part of a group, to be able to express their feelings, to understand the feelings of others, and to learn how to care and respect others and their environment. You can support this by offering them opportunities to practise these skills, through activities in the home corner and through reading stories.

**Figure 7:** Visitors to the setting can share cultural themes and new experiences with the children

It is also important to teach children not only to respect the cultural diversity of others, but also about the other culture itself. This can be done by asking visitors into the setting to talk to the children about their culture, implementing themes about a particular culture, cooking foods from other countries or providing books.

# 408.4 Support the collection of data and the monitoring and evaluation of provision to support children's development

## Curriculum

You should use the guidance that is relevant to your home country. If you are in England this will be the Early Years Foundation Stage.

## Assessment

Staff and practitioners should make the most of opportunities to assess the children's physical, intellectual and personal, social and emotional development. Once you have this information, you will be able to track and report on the children's development, and this will help you to plan the next steps in their progress.

## Consulting with others

K4D872

In order to gain an overall picture of the children you will need to consult with others rather than just using your own observations and assessments. This will make any assessment more reliable and give you more information about the children. It is a good idea to consult with the families and ask them for their observations on the child, and also the children themselves. Colleagues and other professionals may also have more information that you can use to build up a rounded picture. These consultations should be carried out in a manner where information is kept confidential and is only used in the children's best interests.

## The role of play

K4D885

Play is essential in helping children to learn. The Early Years Foundation Stage is based on play, and activities and experiences that are offered to the children should be play based. Some of the ways in which play encourages development are shown in Figure 8.

**Figure 8:** Some of the ways that play encourages a child's development

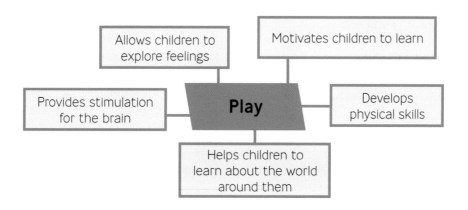

## Can't find what you are looking for?

| Level 4 KS Number | Knowledge Statement | Can be found in... |
|---|---|---|
| K4M802 | Confidentiality | Unit 403 |
| K4M797 | Data protection | Unit 403 |
| K4D804 | Valid and reliable data | Unit 403 |
| K4D374 | Processes for observing, assessing and recording | Unit 403 |
| K4D375 | Formative and summative assessments | Unit 403 |
| K4D376 | Influences on children's development | Unit 403 |
| K4M378 | Referral of concerns | Unit 403 |
| K4M379 | A multi-professional approach | Unit 403 |
| K4D1122 | Multi- and bilingual settings | Unit 405 |
| K4D380 | Supporting positive behaviour | Unit 403 |
| K4M381 | Formats for recording information | Unit 403 |
| K4M382 | Sharing information | Unit 403 |
| K4D383 | Holistic development | Unit 403 |
| K4D806 | Theories on development | Unit 403 |
| K4D385 | Adult expectations | Unit 403 |
| K4D887 | Pattern of physical development | Unit 403 |
| K4D890 | Pattern of intellectual development | Unit 403 |
| K4D892 | Pattern of personal, social and emotional development | Unit 403 |
| K4M894 | Referral of concerns | Unit 403 |

# Unit 409   Evaluate, assess and support children's communication

This Unit is about evaluating, assessing and supporting the communication, language and literacy development of children. It looks at the relevant curricula and activities that are suitable for children in early education.

The elements in this Unit are:

**409.1** Support the assessment of children's communication, language and literacy.

**409.2** Facilitate the provision of an environment that promotes and enhances children's communication, language and literacy.

**409.3** Support the monitoring, evaluation and planning of improvements to support children's communication, language and literacy.

# 409.1 Support the assessment of children's communication, language and literacy

## Curriculum

In England, the relevant guidance for developing a curriculum is the Early Years Foundation Stage. Other UK countries have difference guidance.

You can find out more about the EYFS in Unit 403.

## Assessment

It is important that you encourage opportunities for staff and practitioners to assess the children's communication, language and literacy development. It is also essential to get feedback from colleagues, parents and the children as they all have valuable information that will help towards assessment. You should remind staff that assessment of communication is not just about language, but all the different aspects of communication including verbal and non verbal, and also sign language.

## Communication, language and literacy and learning

There is a strong link between language skills and intellectual development. Children need to develop language in order to think. You have probably seen children talking out loud as they carry out a task or activity, and using language to give themselves directions and also to work through problems – it is almost a running commentary on what they are doing! As children learn more words and language so their thinking and learning is enabled to move on. Children are able to use the language when they have to work through complex problems in their thoughts.

## Involving families and communities in children learning

Families and the local community can bring a wealth of experiences to children's learning, especially their development of communication, language and literacy. Inviting families and members of the community into the setting means they will be able to share these experiences with the children, and introduce them to new ideas and new words in the context of the experience. It also gives the children the opportunity to listen carefully to what the visitors have to say, and to think about it and ask questions. You could implement this in your setting by asking the parents if they feel they have anything that they would like to contribute, or by asking members of the community, such as police officers, to come and visit.

# 409.2 Facilitate the provision of an environment that promotes and enhances children's communication, language and literacy

## Supporting communication, language and literacy

Communication has many different parts: listening, reading, writing, drawing, gestures, facial expressions, using language, and using sign language. A good curriculum plan will aim to develop all of these skills. Babies and children need to hear the people around them providing a running commentary on events, and to have them listen and respond to their attempts to communicate. Any activity provided must be suitable for the child's age, needs and abilities so that confidence and an enjoyment of learning are promoted.

## Strategies to support literacy

K4D913
K4D914
K4D924

Literacy should be integrated into children's learning, and all activities should aim to promote it. Some ideas to do this are as follows:

- encourage children to communicate with adults and each other
- provide opportunities to look at books
- sing songs and rhymes and play music
- tell stories and read poetry
- allow the children to see you writing
- allow children to experiment with writing and mark making

- encourage children to communicate through dance, drama or art
- encourage awareness of other languages, signing and Braille
- use labels of objects and name labels
- encourage use of ICT
- provide opportunities for literacy to be used in role play
- encourage listening in circle and news time
- provide a variety of pens and pencils for mark making.

## Learning environment

The learning environment can do a great deal to help promote children's communication, language and literacy. You should try to make the children's environment rich with signs and symbols on objects around the room, provide notices, numbers and words, areas for books and reading and areas for writing. The idea is that children will pick up on the language without even realising they are doing so! You should also consider the use of music – if this is on all the time it may affect children's concentration and their ability to listen carefully. Used carefully, music can enhance learning but you should use it selectively.

## Good practice

It is important to encourage staff to listen carefully to the children and to respond to them when they ask questions or offer ideas. You should also encourage staff to model correct language when speaking to children, rather than correcting the children's mistakes. Confidence should be encouraged at all times, and children should be allowed to try out new words without fear of being wrong. Try to encourage your staff to watch the children at first to see if their intervention will enrich their play; often children are happy to play in groups and sometimes lose interest when an adult becomes involved.

You must also ensure that all activities and experiences allow equality of access. If the children in your setting speak another language, then you

should reflect this in the resources and the learning environment that you provide. You should also provide the children with opportunities to explore other languages, including sign language and Braille, and allow them to experiment with it.

## Supporting children

Children of different ages will need adults to communicate with them in different ways.

Babies of 0–6 months will appreciate facial gestures and eye contact. They also need caring staff who will respond to their attempts to communicate, and praise them for it. A running commentary on events will help them to build up their language.

Babies of 6–12 months will need eye contact. Adults will need to be receptive to gestures such as pointing and encourage babies to enjoy books and rhymes. They still need a running commentary on events.

Children begin to use their first words at 1 to 2 years old. Often the words are only distinguishable to close family. Conversation between children and adults should be encouraged.

From this age to 4 years, children's language develops rapidly and children love to talk. Children need time to communicate and opportunities to practise their language.

As children become older their language becomes more fluent and adults should introduce new words and new ideas.

If your setting has children whose first language is not English, then they are likely to need extra support. Staff should not mix languages, and should be aware that children may need support in filling the gaps in their knowledge of language. Staff should be sensitive to their needs and should encourage them to feel comfortable in the setting.

If children require extra support in developing their communication, language and literacy, staff should be responsive to their needs and be flexible in the way that they communicate with the children. Calmness and patience are also needed.

# 409.3 Support the monitoring, evaluation and planning of improvements to support children's communication, language and literacy

## Monitoring and evaluation

Monitoring and evaluation of children's progress and the provision of the setting should be carried out using your setting's guidelines. These are likely to include using the Early Years Foundation Stage Profile, or the relevant guidance in your UK country, and internal procedures for checking on staff development and that the provision of the setting meets children's needs. It is useful to see if there are any trends in the children's progress that may be due to the activities and experiences provided. You can then use this information to plan for improvements in the setting and for the continuous development of the staff.

## Including families and children

Children and families may be able to help with the process of evaluating the setting and the activities and experiences that are on offer. Opportunities for discussion with parents may be available at parents' evenings and open days, and more informally at the start or the end of the day. Parents will be able to give feedback on their children's progress and will be able to give their opinions on the activities on offer. If children are involved in assessing their development, they should not be made to feel as if they are being tested, or that they are in some way not good enough. It is fine to ask the children questions about their knowledge but the focus must be on the positive side and children must be given praise. You can also discuss with the children their preferred activities, and thus look to promote communication, language and literacy further through these.

## Concerns about development

K4D904
K4D921

If you have concerns about a child's development it is important that these are looked into as soon as possible. If a child is having difficulties with communication, language and literacy then the sooner this is identified and a strategy put in place, the sooner the child can be helped. Not intervening can cause a child's development to be delayed. This is especially important for communication development, as it can have a huge effect on intellectual development and learning. It is likely that staff will speak to you if they have concerns about a child. You should take the time to discuss it with them, ask why they feel there is a concern and what evidence they have to back it up. It will most likely be your responsibility to speak to the parents and see if they have noticed anything that concerns them about their child's development.

## Continuous professional development

K4D922

There is likely to be support and training on communication, language and literacy available from the local authority and Early Years team. There are also many websites that can be accessed for ideas and support.

> ### Find it out
> If you are supporting children who have communication difficulties try researching further on www.ican.org.uk.

## Can't find what you are looking for?

| Level 4 KS Number | Knowledge Statement | Can be found in... |
| --- | --- | --- |
| K4M802 | Confidentiality | Unit 403 |
| K4M797 | Data protection | Unit 403 |
| K4M804 | Valid and reliable data | Unit 403 |
| K4D873 | Curriculum frameworks | Unit 403 |
| K4D374 | Observation and assessment | Unit 403 |
| K4D375 | Formative and summative observations | Unit 403 |
| K4D902 | Influences on development | Unit 403 |
| K4D903 | Pattern of communication development | Unit 403 |
| K4M905 | Multi-agency and multi-professional | Unit 403. |
| K4D1122 | Multi- and bilingual settings | Unit 405 |
| K4M381 | Recording information | Unit 403 |
| K4M382 | Sharing information | Unit 403 |
| K4D383 | Holistic development | Unit 403 |
| K4D910 | Theories on development | Unit 403 |

# Unit 410   Evaluate, assess and support children's creativity

This Unit is about evaluating, assessing and supporting the creative development of children. It looks at the relevant curriculums and activities that are suitable for children in early education.

The elements in this Unit are:

410.1    Support the assessment of children's creative development.

410.2    Facilitate the provision of an environment that promotes and enhances children's creativity.

410.3    Support the monitoring, evaluation and planning of improvements to support children's creative development.

# 410.1  Support the assessment of children's creative development

## Curriculum

The relevant curriculum to be used in England is the Early Years Foundation Stage. This applies to all children in state-funded education until the end of their reception year. Other UK countries have their own relevant guidance.

> You can find out more about the EYFS in Unit 403.

## Assessment

There are many ways that observation and assessment can be carried out on children's creative development. It is also essential to get feedback from colleagues, parents and the children as they all have valuable information that will help towards assessment. These assessments should recognise the scope of creative development; it includes many things such as drawing, painting, dance, drama, role play, modelling, singing, sewing and music. Staff should also be reminded that creative development includes the appreciation of the world around them.

> You can find out more about observation and assessment of children in Unit 403.

# 410.2  Facilitate the provision of an environment that promotes and enhances children's creativity

## Supporting creative development

There is a strong link between creativity and emotional development. Children need the opportunity to express themselves, to use their imagination and work through their feelings. Curriculum planning should give ample opportunities for creative play. It is important to remember with all creative activities that the emphasis should be on process not product. Children are often not concerned with the end product but more interested in the actual process of doing the activities and exploring the materials. They will also learn more from the making rather than the outcome. Adults should therefore consider their responses to children's work – comments such as 'what is it?' are often unhelpful as children do not always aim to create a 'something' and may feel as if they have failed. It is better to ask a child to tell you about their picture and how they made it, so they learn to enjoy the process rather than creating a picture to please an adult.

## Exploration of materials

K4D942
K4D943

Creative activities should give children the opportunity to explore different materials and textures. This will allow them to find out about the properties of the materials and the similarities and differences between them. It will also help them to learn about how they can be used. Children should have time to explore and should be encouraged to do so. Adults can support this by providing new and interesting materials, and by asking questions and suggesting ideas as the children are carrying out their exploration. It should be remembered that the outside environment is an excellent space to explore materials, as outdoors gives the opportunity for large-scale messy activities that may not always be possible indoors.

Letting children explore and discover also allows them to find new ways of using the materials available. Children should be able to mix materials when this is practical and all efforts should be met with lots of praise and encouragement.

## Development of the imagination

K4D945

Creativity also includes the development of the imagination. Children will most often use their imagination when they take on roles and act them out. This frequently happens in the home corner, or when children are playing with small world toys. This type of play allows children to express themselves freely, and take their play in any direction that they wish. Children are also able to use their imagination in art activities, and in music and dance activities.

Art activities such as painting and drawing can be hugely enjoyable for young children. They are often absorbed in what they are doing, and are in control of the outcome. This is another reason why process and not product is so important. The role of the adult here is to provide more paint and paper, and if you chose to join in, to show the children how enjoyable the process can be.

Children should be introduced to a range of different styles of music. From very early on babies have been shown to appreciate music, and for many people music is part of their cultural identity. A good activity for children is to allow themselves to express their imagination through dance. This also helps their coordination. Dancing in this way should be spontaneous, and there is no need to teach the children to dance in a particular way.

## Art therapy

K4D944

The concept of art therapy is relatively new. Sigmund Freud discovered that artwork done by traumatised patients could communicate their emotions and events where language could not. He also found that creating the images caused the patients less anxiety than having to communicate.

Art therapy is particularly suitable for children because children often have more difficulty than adults trying to put their feelings into words. Drawings often help as children can talk about their picture and this can lead on to a discussion about the child's thoughts, experiences and feelings.

## Resources

There is a huge range of activities and resources to choose from when planning creative play. It is important to try to follow the children's interests, as this will mean they find the activity more enjoyable. You should also try not to have the same activities, equipment, experiences and materials on offer too often. Children do learn from repetition, but there is a danger their play will become stilted or stifled if they are not offered variety.

## The learning environment

Children's creativity can be supported through the learning environment. Children should have access to creative materials and the confidence to ask if they need something else. The environment should also be supportive of their efforts and adults should be receptive and welcoming. Adults should also have high expectations of the children and confidence in their abilities. It is good practice to have a display area at the children's level so children can put up their own work for others to look at and know that it will be safe and not become damaged. Children will also need to learn to treat the work of others on the board with respect. Children love to see their work displayed, and work to go on the wall should be named and mounted. Any of the children's art work can go on the display board, and not just the 'perfect' pictures!

Figure 9: Art therapy is particularly suitable for children

**Table 2:** Support needed during creative play

| Factor | Type of support |
|---|---|
| Age | Children will be able to participate differently in creative activities according to their age. Younger children will need more support and a gentle introduction to new experiences. Older children will need new experiences and materials and opportunities to experiment |
| Gender | Not all boys will readily take part in art or mark-making activities, so you will need to consider how to encourage their participation. You could for example use cars and trains to push through the paint, or use shaving foam (just like daddy!) |
| Ethnicity | Children from different ethnicities may not have had the opportunity to experience creative play, or may not be encouraged to do so. You need to consider their past experiences and what is culturally appropriate for them to participate in |
| Disabilities and Special Educational Needs (SEN) | Children with varying needs will need extra support. A child who has sensory issues may not like the textures of some messy play, such as shaving foam and gloop. You need to try to encourage their participation in small stages until they are comfortable with the experience |

## Equality of access

Creative play should be available for all children. Some children may need more support than others to participate. Children should be encouraged and allowed to slowly build up to activities they are unsure of until they have the confidence to carry them out independently.

Children will need different support during creative abilities according to their age and abilities. Not all children will take part readily unless the activity is adapted in some way.

## 410.3 Support the monitoring, evaluation and planning of improvements to support children's creative development

## Monitoring and evaluation

Monitoring and evaluation of children's progress and the provision of the setting should be carried out using your setting's guidelines. You should use the correct guidance for your home country. It is useful to see if there are any trends in the children's progress that may be due to the activities and experiences provided. You can then use this information to plan for improvements in the setting and for the continuous development of the staff.

## Including families and children

K4D948

Children and families may be able to help with the process of evaluating the setting and the activities and experiences that are on offer.

### Points for Reflective Practice

Do you include children and families in the evaluation of the setting in any of these ways?

- Talk to parents at open days.
- Ask for opinions at parents' evening.
- Initiate discussions at the start and end of the day.
- Ask parents for feedback on their children's progress.
- Ask parents for their opinions on the activities on offer.
- Ask children to reflect on their experiences.

K4D926

## Continuous Professional Development (CPD)

Local training courses can be found through your local authority and Early Years team. There is much information to be found on the Internet as well. You could also consider whether you have any staff who are particularly experienced in delivering one area of creativity and if they would be willing to deliver a session on it for the other staff. Another CPD activity could be to invite local artists in to work alongside the staff and children.

## Can't find what you are looking for?

| Level 4 KS Number | Knowledge Statement | Can be found in... |
|---|---|---|
| K4M802 | Confidentiality | Unit 403 |
| K4M797 | Data protection | Unit 403 |
| K4M804 | Valid and reliable data | Unit 403 |
| K4D873 | Curriculum frameworks | Unit 403 |
| K4D374 | Observation and assessment | Unit 403 |
| K4D375 | Formative and summative observations | Unit 403 |
| K4D376 | Influences on development | Unit 403 |
| K4M378 | Referral of concerns | Unit 403 |
| K4M379 | Multi-professional approach | Unit 403 |
| K4D936 | Multi- or bilingual settings | Unit 405 |
| K4M381 | Recording information | Unit 403 |
| K4M938 | Sharing information | Unit 403 |
| K4D383 | Holistic development | Unit 403 |
| K4D385 | Adult expectations | Unit 403 |
| K4M949 | Referral systems | Unit 409 |

# Unit 411 Evaluate, assess and support children's mathematical learning, exploration and problem solving

This Unit is about evaluating, assessing and supporting children's mathematical learning, exploration and problem solving. It looks at the relevant curricula and activities that are suitable for children in early education.

The elements in this Unit are:

411.1 Facilitate the assessment and support of children's exploration and problem solving.

411.2 Facilitate the assessment and support of children's mathematical learning.

411.3 Support the monitoring, evaluation and planning of improvements to support children's mathematical learning, exploration and problem solving.

# 411.1 Facilitate the assessment and support of children's exploration and problem solving

## Curriculum

The Early Years Foundation Stage provides guidance to developing a curriculum in England. Other UK countries have their own guidance and you should use the appropriate documents. Children's skills in exploration are supported and listed under the Early Learning Goal 'Knowledge and Understanding of the World'. This explains that exploration is about the way children investigate materials and their properties and learn about them and how they work. Children's skills in problem solving are supported and listed under the Early Learning Goal 'Problem Solving, Reasoning and Numeracy'. This explains that problem solving includes using numbers as labels and for counting and calculating, and also the understanding of shape, space and measure.

## Assessment

You should support and encourage opportunities for staff and practitioners to assess the children's exploration and problem-solving skills. There are many ways that observation and assessment can be carried out, and more information can be found in Unit 403. It is also essential to get feedback from colleagues, parents and the children as they all have valuable information that will help towards assessment.

These assessments should recognise and include the different aspects of exploration and problem solving. Some of these include:

- sorting and classifying objects
- comparing objects
- working through problems
- finding out what materials can do

- using shape sorters and jigsaw puzzles
- using building blocks
- learning about cause and effect
- exploring and investigating the environment
- examining objects
- ask why things happen
- talking about their explorations
- learning how to care for living objects.

## Additional support

When carrying out assessment of children's skills you may sometimes recognise that they need extra support in the areas of exploration and problem solving. You should remind your staff that children all develop at a different pace and the need for additional support isn't necessarily a concern. It is, however, good to pick up on this need early so that extra activities and experiences can be planned to encourage the children's development. If there are still concerns then you will need to consult with the parents to decide on the appropriate course of action.

## Activities

K4D962
K4D964

All activities provided for children with the aim of developing their problem solving and exploration skills should be based on play and play activities. Children are naturally curious and eager to explore the world around them and this should be encouraged in a way that is safe and allows them to learn in real life situations. This should happen both indoors and outdoors. You should encourage your staff to allow children to discover for themselves, whilst being on hand to both answer and pose questions to the children. This will help to extend and develop children's skills. Staff can also provide materials that are new and interesting. Any intervention in children's play should be sensitive, and should aim to boost the children's confidence and learning without causing them to lose interest. Some children may have less confidence than others, and may need more support to take part.

**Table 3:** Support needed with exploration and problem-solving activities

| Factor | Type of support |
|---|---|
| **Age** | Children will be able to participate differently in exploration and problem-solving activities according to their age. Younger children will need more support and a gentle introduction to new experiences. They will also need materials that are safe and suitable for their age range, as there is a tendency to 'mouth' objects. They will also gain a great deal from exploring everyday objects. Older children will need new experiences and materials and opportunities to experiment |
| **Gender** | You may find that both genders need encouragement to join in, depending on their past experiences and likes and dislikes. Try to consider their individual interests and use activities that lead from these |
| **Ethnicity** | Children from different ethnicities may not have had the opportunity to experience exploration and investigation, or may not be encouraged to do so. You need to consider their past experiences and what is culturally appropriate for them to participate in. You also need to offer lots of praise and encouragement |
| **Disabilities and SEN** | Children with additional needs will need extra support. Some children may not enjoy or understand the process of exploring, and will need to have the activity broken down into small steps, that are repeated frequently to encourage learning through repetition |

## Resources

K4D965

There is a huge range of activities and resources to choose from when planning activities for exploration and problem solving. It is important to try to follow the children's interests, as this will mean they find the activity more enjoyable.

Some examples for use indoors and outdoors, as appropriate, may include:

- balls to throw
- magnifying glasses
- everyday materials
- plants and seeds
- junk box
- feathers
- stones and pebbles
- windmills
- bubbles
- pets
- messy play materials
- streamers
- computers
- programmable toys/roamers/remote control vehicles
- going for walks
- wind chimes.

## 4||.2 Facilitate the assessment and support of children's mathematical learning

### Curriculum

Children's skills in exploration are supported and listed under the Early Learning Goal 'Problem Solving, Reasoning and Numeracy'. This explains that mathematical learning is about the way children use numbers as labels and for counting and calculating, develop mathematical ideas, learn mathematical vocabulary and also the understanding of shape, space and measure.

### Assessment

When carrying out observations and assessments on children's mathematical development, staff and practitioners should recognise and include the different aspects mathematical development. Some of these include:

- learning about patterns
- naming numbers
- using numbers
- recognising numbers
- recognising shapes

- carrying out simple calculations
- counting
- sorting and matching
- using mathematical language.

## Additional support

When carrying out your assessment of children's skills you may recognise that they need extra support in their mathematical learning. All children develop at a different pace and the need for additional support is not necessarily a concern. It is important to pick up on this need early so that extra activities and experiences can be planned to encourage the children's development.

## Activities

All activities provided for children with the aim of developing their mathematical skills should be based on play and play activities. Mathematics is important in all of our lives and the skills it teaches us allow us to carry out everyday tasks such as shopping. If children are given an early confidence with numbers, they are more likely to feel confident with them in later life. Remember that practitioners should be careful to avoid putting children off 'doing maths'. You should encourage your staff to allow children to initiate

mathematics activities, whilst being available to model skills and discuss concepts. This will help to extend and develop children's skills. Any intervention in children's play should be sensitive, and should aim to boost the children's confidence and learning without causing them to lose interest. Some children may have less confidence than others, and may need more support to take part.

## Resources

There is a huge range of activities and resources to choose from when planning activities for mathematical development. It is important to try to follow the children's interests, as this will mean they find the activity more enjoyable.

Some examples for use indoors and outdoors, as appropriate, may include:

- objects to count and sort
- calculators
- rulers and tape measures
- treasure baskets for babies
- clock
- telephone
- number labels
- money

**Table 4:** Support needed with mathematical activities

| Factor | Type of support |
|--------|-----------------|
| **Age** | Children will be able to participate differently in mathematical activities according to their age. Younger children will need more support and simple activities. They need to develop an awareness of mathematics through activities such as number rhymes and clapping. Older children will need meaningful real-life experiences and opportunities to practise new skills |
| **Gender** | There is a long held belief that girls are 'no good' at maths. Practitioners should be careful to offer equal opportunities to participate in activities to both boys and girls. You may find that both genders need encouragement to join in, depending on their past experiences and likes and dislikes. Try to consider their individual interests and use activities that lead from these |
| **Ethnicity** | Children from different ethnicities may not have had the same opportunities to experience and practise mathematics, or may not be encouraged to do so. You can make mathematics interesting by using familiar topics from their own backgrounds. This will also be a good learning experience for the other children in your care |
| **Disabilities and SEN** | Children with additional needs will need extra support. Some children may find mathematics a hard concept to grasp and will need to have the activity broken down into small steps, which are repeated frequently to encourage learning through repetition |

- books about number
- number games
- sand and water play
- pictures to illustrate numbers
- number lines
- big and small objects
- malleable materials
- puzzles
- different sized containers.

# 411.3 Support the monitoring, evaluation and planning of improvements to support children's mathematical learning, exploration and problem solving

## Monitoring and evaluation

K4D970

Monitoring and evaluation of children's progress and the provision of the setting should be carried out using your setting's guidelines. You should have internal procedures for checking on staff development and for checking that the provision of the setting meets children's needs.

## Including families and children

Children and families can help with the process of evaluating the setting as has been discussed previously.

## Continuous Professional Development (CPD)

Mathematics is an area that often causes concern for staff. Training courses can be sourced from your local authority and Early Years team. You may find that by providing extra training to staff around the area of mathematics it gives them new confidence and skills to try activities with the children. You could consider, if you have any staff who are particularly experienced in delivering one area of mathematics, whether they would be willing to deliver a session on it for the other staff. You can also encourage CPD through using reflection, and by showing the staff how to reflect and model these skills. This may encourage new ideas and new ways of doing things. Guidance can also be found in the Early Years Foundation Stage Guidance.

## Can't find what you are looking for?

| Level 4 KS Number | Knowledge Statement | Can be found in... |
|---|---|---|
| K4M802 | Confidentiality | Unit 403 |
| K4M797 | Data protection | Unit 403 |
| K4M804 | Valid and reliable data | Unit 403 |
| K4D374 | Observation and assessment | Unit 403 |
| K4D375 | Formative and summative observations | Unit 403 |
| K4D957 | Influences on development | Unit 403 |
| K4M958 | Multi-professional approach | Unit 403 |
| K4M381 | Recording information | Unit 403 |
| K4M938 | Sharing information | Unit 403 and 410 |
| K4D890 | Pattern of intellectual development | Unit 403 |
| K4D1122 | Multi- or bilingual settings | Unit 405 |
| K4M949 | Referral systems | Unit 409 |

# Unit 419   Contribute to the enhancement of early education for children

This Unit is about supporting settings that offer formal or informal early education. It deals with evaluation and the provision of strategies for improvement.

The elements in this Unit are:

**419.1**    Evaluate current educational practices within the setting.

**419.2**    Provide advice to the provision on strategies for improvement.

**419.3**    Support curriculum planning and development.

**419.4**    Work alongside those within the setting to enhance educational provision.

## 419.1  Evaluate current educational practices within the setting

In order to ensure that the quality of your provision is constantly improving, it is useful to regularly review your practice. This can be done through monitoring meetings, and records kept in the minutes of the meeting, or some settings may use specific forms. These should be dated and reviewed. These records will help you to make any necessary changes and will give the rationale for doing so when feeding the information back to other staff members.

There are several areas that can be looked at when doing so, and these include:

■ delivery of the curriculum

■ resources

■ plans, programmes and routines

■ children's involvement

■ the childcare environment

■ use of ICT.

### Delivery of the curriculum

It is useful to spend some time observing the delivery of the curriculum to see if the plans are being carried out correctly and effectively. This will also help you to see if the staff implementing the curriculum understand their roles and responsibilities, and if they are organised and well prepared.

It is important to remember that all six areas of learning and development, as detailed in the EYFS, need to be delivered consistently and well in order to promote the children's learning. This is another area you can look at during your observation.

### Resources

K4DI059

Resources are essential if activities and experiences are going to be of value. There should be a good range of resources, covering all six areas of learning and development and promoting equality and diversity. They should also be of good quality and good condition and you should make sure they meet relevant safety standards.

You will need to check that your staff have time to check and prepare the resources ready for the day's activities. The children are more likely to participate if they see an activity set up attractively and ready to go, rather than one that is half ready. It will also be less frustrating for staff.

It is important to check that staff can access these resources when they are needed, and that there are systems in place to make sure they do not run out. You should also encourage staff to check stock at the end of the session as the activities are put away, and inform you or the person responsible if more are needed.

There is a wealth of resources to choose from if you decide to increase your stock.

## Plans, programmes and routines

K4DI050

In this area you should be looking to see if the plans are effective, if they promote a balanced curriculum that covers all of the areas of learning and development, and if they use the available resources. You will need to consider if it is clear and specific from the plans what the children should be learning and how it should be done. You also need to ensure that the children's needs are met through varied activities that can be adapted to suit each individual.

When evaluating the routine, consider if it allows times for quiet activity as well as active play, and look at where times for eating and drinking are allocated. Do you notice that the children become restless at a certain point in the day? You should also consider if the plans and routines are flexible enough to deal with an unplanned or spontaneous event.

## Children's involvement

Take some time to both observe and talk to the children about the activities they are doing. You will need to look to see if the children are engaged in purposeful play and if they are interested enough to stay at an activity. If the children seem motivated and keen to join in then this is a good sign that the planned activities are encouraging their learning.

Some settings keep a note of children's participation, either by writing initials or names on the plan. This helps you to see if an activity has been popular and you can track trends in the types of children who tend to join in, and look at encouraging those who don't seem to.

You can also use the formative and summative assessments of the children's progress; as a general rule if they are making good progress it probably means that the planning and implementation of the activities is successful.

Another important area is the involvement of the children's families. You can ask the parents if the children have talked about any particular activities at home, or if they have noticed any improvement in the children's skills. You should also evaluate the extent to which families are involved in the setting.

## The childcare environment

When evaluating the environment, both inside and out, try to consider it from a child's point of view. Get down to their level, or even lie on the floor, to see if the ceiling is attractive and stimulating!

When organising space there should be a good variety of toys out, but be aware that too much going on can be overwhelming to a child. It is sometimes better to put out less equipment, but change it frequently.

## Use of ICT

Consider how your setting uses ICT to support the children's learning. ICT should be integrated in the curriculum, and it may include computers, talking books, programmable toys, tape recorders, CD players, dictaphones, videos or DVDs and television. Is the use of ICT interesting to the children? Are they familiar with the equipment and how to use it? Is the use of ICT balanced with other activities?

## Evaluating

Once you have gathered this information you can then begin to interpret and evaluate it. It is likely you will find examples of good practice as well as areas that you would like to improve on. You should consider how you will recognise the good practice, and how to support it to continue, and also what improvements are needed and how these can be implemented.

# 419.2 Provide advice to the provision on strategies for improvement

## Providing feedback on the evaluation

It is likely you will need to discuss your findings with other senior colleagues. Be aware that sometimes this can cause tension, as change can be seen as threatening and is difficult for some people to cope with. You should try to feed back in a way that is positive and emphasises the good points rather than focusing solely on what needs to be improved. Listen carefully to others' ideas on your suggested improvements and try to agree a way forward that you can take to the other members of staff. It may also be worth setting a timescale, and considering if a budget is needed.

## Advise your colleagues

The evaluation process that you have undertaken should be fed back to other staff if it is to be effective in making changes. It should be seen as a chance to improve current plans and to enhance the practice that your setting offers. Take care to ensure that it is not seen as an opportunity to place blame or criticism. Make staff aware that sometimes new ideas will not work, but they need to be tried and that everyone's feedback will be welcomed. You also need to make yourself available to staff if they wish to discuss their ideas and concerns.

Staff will need to be consulted about development and improvement opportunities and offered additional training to enhance their skills.

## 419.3 Support curriculum planning and development

### Supporting curriculum planning

All settings must show that they are following the guidance from the Early Years Foundation Stage, or the relevant guidance of your home country. The way that curriculum plans are recorded will vary from setting to setting.

> You can find out more about curriculum planning in Unit 403.

All curriculum plans should be capable of differentiation in order to meet the needs of all children.

> You can find out more about differentiation in Unit 403.

## Involving others

The involvement of others in curriculum planning can be very useful. Children are normally very happy to talk about the activities that they enjoy, as well as those they don't enjoy. Children will also talk to their parents about the activities they have enjoyed, and the parents can give feedback to you. The parents will be able to inform you of their children's current interests and they may also be able to provide you with materials you can use in the setting to support these.

## The planning cycle

The planning cycle is often seen in its most simple form as 'plan, do, observe, and review'. Your evaluation of the provision is likely to have made it more complete with the addition of evaluation and continuous improvement. The cycle will most probably follow the process of 'plan, implement, observe, review, evaluate, and plan improvements'.

## 419.4 Work alongside those within the setting to enhance educational provision

### Modelling good practice

One of the best ways for staff and colleagues to understand what your expectations are is to see you modelling good practice through hands-on work with the families and children. In this way they understand exactly what your requirements are and are able to put it into practice themselves.

### Support colleagues

Once changes have been agreed and disseminated to all staff, it is reasonable to expect to see them happen. However, staff will still need your support and guidance to implement the changes, especially if they are unsure or wish to report back any particular success or difficulties they have had. They may also need your help persuading other colleagues to implement the changes that have been decided on. It is important that you are always available for advice and support, and that staff feel confident that they can speak to you.

## Can't find what you are looking for?

| Level 4 KS Number | Knowledge Statement | Can be found in... |
| --- | --- | --- |
| K4D853 | Requirements of legislation | Unit 407 |
| K4D856 | The role of play | Unit 407 |
| K4D857 | Equality of access | Unit 407 |
| K4D1053 | Stages of development | Unit 403 |
| K4D859 | Partnership with parents | Unit 407 |
| K4D860 | The voice of the child | Unit 407 |
| K4D861 | Involving others in the setting | Unit 407 |
| K4D863 | Curriculum planning | Unit 407 |
| K4D864 | Resources | Unit 407 |
| K4D865 | Sources of information | Unit 407 |
| K4D1122 | Multi- or bilingual settings | Unit 405 |
| K4P866 | Monitoring and evaluation | Unit 407 |
| K4P867 | Training and updating | Unit 407 |

# Further references

www.allkids.co.uk

www.babyworld.co.uk

www.cwdcouncil.gov.uk

www.everychildmatters.gov.uk

www.fsid.org.uk

www.parentsplace.com

www.playeducation.co.uk

www.raisingkids.co.uk

www.standards.dcsf.gov.uk/eyfs

www.surestart.gov.uk

www.teachernet.gov.uk

Duffy, A., et al (2006) *Working with Babies and Children Under Three,* Heinemann

Tassoni, P. (2009) *Penny Tassoni's Practical EYFS Handbook*, Heinemann

# Working in partnership

The Units grouped here all relate to working with and assisting improvements to different childcare settings. They look at self-evaluation, quality assurance, supporting settings and families and multi-agency working.

These Units may be suitable if you are working in one of the following job roles:

- Supporting the care, learning and development of children.
- Manager of a setting.
- Lead practitioner in a setting.
- working with other agencies.
- A practitioner with responsibility for the childcare environment.
- Responsible for coordinating work with families.
- A role within information services.
- National, regional or local support worker.
- National, regional or local development worker.
- Responsible for assessing quality assurance.

The Units covered by this section are:

| | |
|---|---|
| 412 | Evaluate and coordinate the environment for children and families. |
| 416 | Assess quality assurance schemes against agreed criteria. |
| 417 | Establish and sustain relationships with providers of services to children and families. |
| 421 | Provide information about children's and families' services. |
| 422 | Coordinate work with families. |
| 423 | Manage multi-agency working arrangements. |
| 431 | Contribute to the leadership and management of integrated childcare provision. |

# Unit 412   Evaluate and coordinate the environment for children and families

This Unit is about coordinating and evaluating the childcare environment, leading to making changes and improvements for the benefit of children and families.

The elements in this Unit are:

412.1   Evaluate and coordinate the environment for children and families.

412.2   Coordinate resources to meet the needs of children and families.

412.3   Lead a process of change and improvement for the environment for children and families.

## 412.1  Evaluate and coordinate the environment for children and families

### Developing a monitoring system

K4D972

It is important to regularly review the environment to ensure it is still meeting the needs of the children and families that attend your setting. You may already have systems in place to do so, but if not then you will need to develop a system. This could range from initiating discussions during staff meetings that are minuted, or developing a form that can be regularly completed and reviewed. The areas that you choose to evaluate will depend very much on the type of setting you are working in, but they may include some of the following.

- Does the environment meet the relevant legislation?
- Are the children able to make choices?
- Does the environment offer the children the chance to be independent?
- Does the environment help children to feel they belong?
- Are children able to tidy toys away?
- Does the layout allow for supervision?

- Do families feel welcome in the setting?
- Are the resources suitable?
- Are the activities on offer appealing?
- Are the children provided with personal care?
- Is the routine working?

Some of your monitoring and evaluation can be carried out through observation, but it is likely you will need to speak to staff, parents, children and other users of the setting to find out their views. This may need to be carried out through a questionnaire, or through general everyday discussion.

### Legislation affecting the environment

There is a large amount of legislation and regulation that affects the childcare environment. It is likely you will evaluate the way your setting meets this when carrying out your review of the environment. Some of the legislation you will need to consider is as follows.

- Welfare requirements of the Early Years Foundation Stage. This document sets out statutory and non-statutory obligations that all settings must meet. You will be inspected by Ofsted to ensure that you comply with them.

You can find out more about the EYFS welfare requirements in Unit 403.

**Find it out**

Find out more about the RIDDOR requirements by looking at www.hse.gov.uk/riddor.

- Requirements expected by your home country. These requirements may vary depending on which UK country you live in.
- The Children Act 1989 and 2004. This Act covers equality of access and opportunity for children up to the age of 18. It also deals with child protection.
- Health and Safety at Work Act 1974 and 1992. This Act relates to all places of work. Employers must ensure that the workplace and equipment within it are safe, and employees must ensure they act in a safe manner.
- Health and Safety (First Aid) Regulations 1981. These regulations explain the minimum requirements for first aid.
- Disability Discrimination Act 1995 (DDA), Special Educational Needs and Disability Act (SENDA) 2001, The Disability Discrimination Act 2005, Special Educational Needs (SEN).

You can find out more about laws relating to disability in Unit 402.

- Race Relations Act 1975. This Act deals with rights of access and makes racial discrimination illegal.
- Fire Precautions (Workplace) Regulations 1997. These Regulations mean workplaces must carry out a fire risk assessment.
- Food Safety Act 1990. This Act covers the way in which food is prepared and stored and how food areas are maintained. It also deals with staff training in food safety.
- Control of Substances Hazardous to Health 1994. This law means you must assess which substances and chemicals your setting uses that may be harmful to health, and carry out a risk assessment on them.
- Reporting of Injuries, Diseases and Dangerous Occurrences Regulations 1995 (RIDDOR). Under these Regulations, you must have an accident book. If a serious accident occurs, you may need to report it to the Health and Safety Executive.

## Equality of access

K4D973

Whilst carrying out your evaluation of the environment you will also want to ensure that it offers equality of access to all children and families who use it. This includes not only physical access to the setting, but also making visitors feel welcome and having the confidence to come in. You may be able to encourage this by making sure that all staff are friendly and greet each parent or carer as they enter. It may also be worthwhile spending some time yourself talking to the parents and carers as they collect and pick up their children, this may help them to feel more valued. You should ensure that people are addressed in the manner they prefer. Some parents prefer to be called by the first name, and some prefer to be called Mr or Mrs. You should never assume that a child's surname will be the same as their parents' surname. You can help parents and families feel valued by asking them for their opinions on the setting and on their child's progress, and showing that these comments are valuable to you by acting on them.

You may need to identify if there are any particular barriers that prevent families from visiting the setting. These can be numerous, and may include language, transport, fear of discrimination, lack of confidence and lack of time. Once these have been identified you will need to work on ways of overcoming these barriers. These could include providing information in the relevant home language, organising open days, promoting the cultures of the children and asking parents for assistance. The problems that you identify and the solutions that you decide upon are likely to be individual to your setting.

## Adapting your practice to meet children's needs

K4D975

You are likely to have a wide range of different children in your setting, all of whom will have different needs and abilities. You must make sure that the environment and your practice meets their care, learning and play

**Figure 1:** Make visitors feel welcome when they collect their children

needs at all times. Some of the varying needs and abilities to consider may include different genders, ethnicities, ages and abilities, disabilities and special educational needs.

When considering how to adapt your practice the first thing to do is to observe the children to determine exactly what their needs and abilities are. You will also need to liaise with the parents and any other professionals who are involved with the child/children.

You may be able to adapt your practice by using some of the following ideas:

- using specialist equipment
- having a flexible routine
- differentiating your activities and curriculum planning
- using indoor and outdoor space fully
- ensuring indoor and outdoor space is accessible to all groups of children.
- providing culturally diverse materials
- providing eye-catching displays of the children's work
- ensuring there are areas for rest and quiet
- ensuring children are able to have privacy when attending to their care needs

- ensuring easy access to materials
- planning to celebrate key festivals.

## Multilingual and bilingual environments

Your evaluation of the environment will also need to look at how children who have more than one language are supported. Children who are multilingual, bilingual or learning through an additional language tend to develop their language skills in a different way. Generally their language will develop more slowly, as they have to learn two languages at once, but they will catch up given the right support and encouragement. The environment can support this by having books with simple pictures of object and activities, to help the child learn key words. Good lighting is important, as is a low noise level. The child who is learning needs to be able to concentrate on what you say to them.

## The childcare environment

There are further issues which your evaluation should look at. You will want to ensure that the environment meets the health, care, learning and play needs of the children. You should also evaluate whether it is safe, stimulating and interesting.

# 412.2 Coordinate resources to meet the needs of children and families

## Resources

Resources in the environment include both material and human resources. When dealing with human resources the main points to consider are that staff ratios are maintained, that staff are checked by the Criminal Record Bureau (CRB), and have relevant qualifications. Material resources must meet the relevant safety standards, and should be used in line with manufacturer's instructions. You will also need to ensure they are used only for the correct age group. You should make sure that you have adequate resources to support all areas of children's play.

You should routinely check the materials to ensure they are safe and in good condition. If something is found to be broken then consider if it could be safely mended. If not, it is better to remove it, and replace it. Both small and large equipment, such as furniture, need to be checked.

You should have in place a system to monitor the use of resources and ensure that stock levels are adequate. This may be as simple as a list of resources that are required, or a member of staff may be responsible for doing regular stock checks, the systems used will depend on your setting and its needs. It is likely that this will be one of the areas considered in your evaluation.

## Physical care

You may also want to monitor the physical care offered to the children. This may include some of the following: toileting, washing, bathing, washing hair, cutting nails and applying lotions and sun cream. You will need

to consider in your evaluation if and how you carry out this type of personal care, if it is effective and if it is well organised. Children should be offered the opportunity to do these things for themselves, as it will promote their independence and self-esteem.

## Health and hygiene

K4H976
K4H977

Your evaluation should consider how your environment promotes positive health, and how it is hygienic. Some of the items you may want to consider in your evaluation may include the following.

- Do staff understand the principles of **cross-infection**, and how to prevent it? You will need to find out if they understand that cross-infection is a transferral of germs from one person to another, and if staff understand the written guidelines that should be already in place.
- Is there an understanding of how to dispose of different types of waste? Are staff aware that there are designated bins for different types of waste, and that these must be emptied daily?
- Is there an awareness of food safety? Do staff involved in food preparation need to undergo training?
- Are staff aware of how to handle bodily fluids safely? Is there an awareness of the need to wear gloves and are written guidelines in place and followed?
- Is there an awareness of how to deal with potential viruses such as HIV/Aids? If the affected person's blood makes direct contact with another person's blood there is potentially an issue of virus transmission. This can be avoided through good hygiene and the wearing of gloves.

> ## Key Term
> **Cross-infection** – the transferral of germs from one person to another.

## Routines

K4H978

Routines are important as they help children to know what to expect and give them a sense of belonging. There should be a degree of flexibility in them, as any routine should focus on meeting both individual and group needs. This may include eating meals at different times, or needing to sleep at different times.

## Case Study: Changing the routine

At Jack in the Box Day Nursery, the children have outside play before going into lunch. Staff have noticed that the children always seem to be quite energetic at lunch time and this was brought up in a team meeting. They discussed sitting the children down for a short story before going into lunch, and decided to try this strategy out over the following week. Staff noticed immediately that the children were calmer and less active and lunchtime became much less stressful for the staff involved.

- Why was it important to try to change the routine?
- How has this change to routine benefited the children?
- Why is it important that routines are flexible and can be adapted?

You may find that the children in your care are showing signs of unwanted behaviour at certain times of the day. You should consider if this is because the routine they are following does not meet their needs, and also consider how it can be adapted. It is always worthwhile reviewing the routine to see if the needs of staff and children have changed, and considering how best to adapt it if needed.

## 412.3 Lead a process of change and improvement for the environment for children and families

### Identify improvements

K4H979

Once you have carried out your evaluation you will be in a position to identify any issues for improvement. It is important that you consult with others as part of this process. If change is to be successful, colleagues, children and families must be able to understand the reason for it and recognise the benefits of it. They may also have ideas that you may not have previously considered and that may be of benefit to the setting. It is worth taking the time to ask staff if they have any ideas and to take them seriously and discuss them fully.

As a manager, you are able to organise training for staff in order to develop their skills and give them a greater understanding of the areas you wish to improve. You will also be able to have discussions on the areas for improvement at staff meetings. You will need to be sensitive to the needs of others and be prepared to listen to their ideas and answer their questions, and perhaps overcome some resistance.

All changes should be reviewed and evaluated after a period of time to see if they are working or not, and to see what effect they are having.

## Work with colleagues

Change can be difficult for staff who are used to following the same routine and using the same ideas. It is important to promote the positive aspect of any improvements and to be enthusiastic and supportive when introducing them. Seeing you act in a positive manner will encourage staff to do the same, and it will also help to motivate them to carry through any improvements.

You will also need to listen to the opinions of staff as they implement the improvements, this is because they will have firsthand experience of the effect the changes are having.

## Case Study: Promoting improvements

Aisha has been working at the nursery for the past 7 years. She enjoys her job and is happy with the way things are in the nursery. Recently, a new manager has joined the setting and has made a few changes. Aisha has gone along with them, but when the manager tries to implement a new routine she gets quite cross and complains to other staff, saying that she doesn't see why everything has to be changed. She makes little effort to implement the new routine, and when asked to feedback to her manager says that she doesn't think it is working very well.

A few days later Aisha has her monthly appraisal. The manager asks her how she is feeling and Aisha says that she is becoming frustrated with all these constant changes, especially the change to the routine. The manager spends some time explaining why she has changed the routine and what she hopes the children will gain from it. Aisha thinks that actually, it does sound like a good idea and she is surprised the manager is so enthusiastic. She agrees to give it another go and they also agree that the manager will spend time with her and the other staff helping to implement it.

- Why should you explain proposed changes clearly?
- How can you help to implement changes?
- Why is it important to support staff to carry out changes?

# Unit 416   Assess quality assurance schemes against agreed criteria

This Unit is about assessing quality against the agreed criteria. It covers planning for visits to childcare providers, carrying out the visit and giving feedback. It also looks at the role of the National Quality Improvement Network.

The elements in this Unit are:

| | |
|---|---|
| 416.1 | Identify quality assurance requirements. |
| 416.2 | Examine initial evidence against requirements. |
| 416.3 | Assess provision and provide feedback. |

## 416.1 Identify quality assurance requirements

### Quality assurance schemes

High quality early education and a good learning environment at home have a big effect on children's learning and development. It is important that all settings offer high quality care and education and are prepared to undertake continuous quality improvement.

The National Quality Improvement Network replaces the Investors in Children scheme. Individual **quality assurance** schemes endorsed by Investors in Children have helped settings to raise the quality of childcare and learning that they provide. The individual quality assurance schemes continue to operate, but are no longer endorsed by central government.

Changes to the inspection regime, including the new outstanding grading from Ofsted and the emphasis on the learning and development requirements in settings, mean that the inspection system performs a stronger quality assurance function.

Local authorities are also required to follow a set of good practice principles, as shown in Table I.

## Key Term

Quality assurance – activities involving a review of the quality of services and the taking of any corrective actions to remove any deficiencies.

## Find it out

For more information about Quality Assurance, look at: www.surestart.gov.uk/improvingquality/guidance/nqin/ and www.ncb.org.uk/Page.asp?originx6689ut_3045064l604l3s32j5703270400.

**Table I:** Good practice principles

| | Good practice principles (Local Authority) | What this means for settings |
|---|---|---|
| I | Guide and support settings to improve outcomes | Listening to children, young people and parents so you know what they would like |
| 2 | Encourage settings to be inclusive and reduce inequalities | Welcoming all children and young people so that they feel that they belong |
| 3 | Strengthen values and principles in settings | Promoting your values and principles in all you do |
| 4 | Promote effective practice and its delivery in settings | All staff working together and sharing knowledge and experience |
| 5 | Increase the capacity of settings to improve quality | Reflecting on practice and always seeking to improve what you do and how you do it |
| 6 | Promote integrated working within and among settings | Working in partnership with all professionals so that you know where to go for support for a child, young person or parent |
| 7 | Challenge and support key people in settings to lead quality improvement | Making sure your childcare is well led and managed |
| 8 | Build on settings' proven workforce development strategies | Having training and professional development so that you are skilled and knowledgeable about meeting children and young people's needs |
| 9 | Support settings through the self-evaluation and improvement processes | Making sure you have time to monitor your progress |
| 10 | Local authorities and national organisations monitor quality improvements and communicate achievements | Celebrating your successes |
| II | Local authorities and national organisations ensure quality improvement is achievable, continuous and sustainable | Working with the local authority to help provide the best quality experience for children and young people |
| 12 | Schemes operate fair, inclusive and transparent accreditation processes | Making sure you meet more than the minimum Ofsted standards |

# Planning a visit

When arranging to meet a childcare provider, you should ensure that any time arranged is convenient and does not cause a disruption to the children's day. It is also a good idea to have a plan for the visit, so you know what you want to achieve and make good use of the time. When visiting settings, you must remain non-judgemental, making sure that you value the diversity of the different types of setting and encourage cultural differences. It is likely that the setting will want to know what evidence they are required to produce to meet the 12 principles.

# Providing evidence

**Principle One** is about how settings meet the five Every Child Matters outcomes, and about how well they are delivered. Evidence they could provide includes:

- showing they have good play provision
- undergoing training and self-assessment
- providing a statement of what they wish to achieve
- providing examples of records of the children's development and achievement.

**Principle Two** is about promoting inclusion and equality and creating an environment that is supportive and respectful to all. Evidence they could provide includes:

- listing obstacles and how they will challenge them
- undertaking training and reflective practice
- making links with the local communities.

**Principle Three** is about promoting the values and principles of the setting. Evidence they could provide includes:

- draw up a statement of vision and values
- link these to law and guidance
- show how these are expressed in practice.

**Principle Four** is about supporting and developing effective practice. Evidence they could provide includes:

- undertaking training on effective practice
- sharing good practice with other settings
- keeping up to date with new developments.

**Principle Five** is about helping settings to improve on quality through reflective practice, peer observation and working with children and families. Evidence they could provide includes:

- accessing training and guidance
- actively reflecting on practice
- developing support networks
- undertaking self evaluation.

**Principle Six** is about integrated working with other services and settings. Evidence they could provide includes:

- developing support networks.

**Principle Seven** is about developing strong management and leadership. Evidence they could provide includes:

- creating long-term goals for the setting.
- attending training.

**Principle Eight** is about developing the workforce and their practice. Evidence they could provide includes:

- attending training and updating
- training and development plans for staff
- monitoring staff turnover and staff satisfaction.

**Principle Nine** is about the process of quality improvement and assurance, and managing it effectively. Evidence they could provide includes:

- attending workshops and briefings
- accessing support materials
- undertaking continuous improvement.

**Principle Ten** is about making others aware of the improvements. Evidence they could provide includes:

- providing others with information about the achievements of the setting
- explaining why high quality is important.

**Principle Eleven** is about providing quality for children. Evidence they could provide includes:

- drawing up plans for improvement
- attending training and encouraging staff to gain qualifications.

**Principle Twelve** is about meeting the standards of independent assessment. Evidence they could provide includes:

- seeking guidance
- updating policies and procedures.

## 416.2 Examine initial evidence against requirements

### Making a visit

When you make a visit to a setting to examine the evidence they have provided, it will again be useful to have agreed a plan in advance with the manager/person responsible. One of the first things to do is ensure that all the evidence that you have requested is available for you to see. You will also need to ensure that the quality assurance criteria are available for reference. Without these things your visit may not be worthwhile and you may need to consider rescheduling.

Your next step is to assess whether the documents provided comply with the quality assurance criteria. If there are gaps, you should discuss with the setting what other pieces of evidence they may have that will be able to fill that gap. As part of your visit, you should also check that the policies and procedures of the setting meet the regulatory requirements and current best practice.

The final step in your visit will be to draw up and feedback a report about the assessment you have made. More detail on this is provided in the next section.

## 416.3 Assess provision and provide feedback

### Assess provision

K4P1024
K41022

Quality assurance is a type of quality improvement and it provides settings with recognition of the progress that has been made against a set of agreed standards, leading to gaining an accredited level or stage. In order for this to happen, an independent review of the setting's quality is carried out by a trained professional, who will follow procedures to ensure consistency, equality and objectivity. Undertaking and gaining quality assurance provides satisfaction for the setting and shows parents and others that the setting has raised its quality above minimum standards.

As that trained professional, you will need to assess all areas of the setting against the quality assurance criteria provided. It is important to remain objective and base your decision on what you have seen, and not what you think you know. There are different ways that the evaluation and assessment can be carried out. Ultimately, it will be down to you to decide if the setting complies or not. You may decide this by examining the evidence, asking for further evidence, observing the setting and speaking to staff, parents and families who attend the setting. The setting can support this process by carrying out the following activities, guided by you or another experienced professional.

- Self-assessment against standards.
- Self-appraisal of the setting's strengths and areas for improvement.
- Self-made plans to raise quality.
- Reflective practice and actions to improve.
- Self-review of progress made.

### Gaining the view of others

As part of your evaluation you should seek to gain the views of staff, children and other users of the setting. You will need to approach these groups in different ways. Any discussion with the children should be kept simple and short, whereas discussion with staff and other users may need to be planned, and carried out in a private room. You may also need to reassure them of confidentiality.

This is important as it will help you to gain a more rounded view of the setting, and you may find out information that you otherwise would not have. It is still important to remain objective, and to consider the validity of any extra information you gain.

### Providing feedback

As you complete your assessment you will no doubt have identified action points and areas for improvement. Make a note of these and ensure they are discussed in your feedback to the setting. You will also have identified areas of good practice, and these should also be fed back. Providing both positive and negative feedback helps the setting to feel the process is worthwhile, and helps to keep them motivated.

Feedback should always be supportive and constructive. Your role is to assist the setting in quality improvement, and they will need your support and practical advice to work through the improvements that need to be made.

You will also need to agree an action plan and timescale for making any identified improvements. This will need to be achievable for the setting. You should ensure that any action points are prioritised in order of urgency, so those that may affect the care and learning of the children should come before the action points that are quick and easy!

It is possible that there could be disagreement with your judgements. In this situation, it is important to remain calm and listen to the setting's opinion and reasons for disagreeing. If, after this discussion, you feel your judgement is unchanged, you will need to explain why and remind the setting that your role is to support them and assist them with any improvements.

# Unit 417   Establish and sustain relationships with providers of services to children and families

This Unit is about establishing relationships with providers of childcare services to encourage the development of networks and information sharing.

The elements in this Unit are:

**417.1**    Establish and sustain contact with providers of services to children and families.

**417.2**    Enable providers of services to children and families to access sources of information and support.

**417.3**    Contribute to the development and maintenance of support networks.

## 417.1 Establish and sustain contact with providers of services to children and families

### Prior to making contact

If you have chosen to take this Unit it is likely that you are working as a support or development worker, and will need to identify the childcare providers in your area of responsibility. Providers may include nurseries, childminders, crèches, holiday and play schemes, nursery schools, out of school care, preschool playgroups and toddler groups. There are various ways of doing this.

- Contact your local council for a list of providers.
- Visit www.childcarelink.gov.uk for an up-to-date list.
- Visit http://schoolsfinder.direct.gov.uk/.
- In Scotland go to www.scottishchildcare.gov.uk.
- In Wales visit www.childreninwales.org.uk.
- In Northern Ireland contact your local Sure Start centre.
- Contact your local Children's Information Service.
- Look through the Yellow Pages or www.yell.com.

Once you have identified which providers you are responsible for, you must consider how to make contact with them. This could be carried out individually, through a letter, phone call or visit, or you may be able to make contact in groups. Many local council Early Years teams run network support groups, and it is possible you could become involved in these.

All providers are likely to want information on the services that you provide. It will be helpful to have some information or promotional material that you can provide them with, and that you can use to explain your role. This could be in the form of a letter, leaflet, flyer or booklet, or you may have materials provided by the scheme you work for that you can use.

It is possible you will come across barriers when trying to make contact with providers. Some of these could include:

- missing providers from your list
- lack of understanding from providers of the service you offer
- information is not seen by the correct person or is discarded
- information provided is not clear, or not in a suitable language.

This list is not exhaustive and there may be other barriers that you identify or come across.

You will need to consider how you will overcome these barriers. If you think you are missing providers it may be worth going back over your original research to double check your records. You also need to make sure that any promotional information is clear, and begins by explaining exactly what you offer. Information that is sent by post should be addressed to the correct person.

## Making contact

When you make contact with the providers who you are responsible for you should re-iterate the service that you offer, to make sure providers understand and to give them the opportunity to ask any questions. Most providers will welcome extra support and advice. You will also need to agree how contact will be maintained, and at what intervals. These must be suitable for you and the provider.

# 417.2 Enable providers of services to children and families to access sources of information and support

## Providing information

Your first step when assisting a provider will be to find out exactly what information and support they need. This could be varied and is likely to include information on any new developments, for example government

initiatives, the Early Years Foundation Stage, any new research that has been carried out and so on. Information needs will depend very much on the individual setting and their aims and objectives.

Once this has been established, it will then be your responsibility to provide the information as far as you are able, or direct them to the right place to gain the information for themselves. Some useful sources of information are as follows:

- www.surestart.gov.uk
- www.standards.dfes.gov.uk
- www.4children.org.uk
- www.cwdcouncil.org.uk
- www.teachernet.gov.uk
- www.ndna.org.uk
- www.pre-school.org.uk
- www.everychildmatters.gov.uk
- www.dh.gov.uk

## Find it out

Look at the sites to find out what services they offer. How could this help your setting?

## Information and support

It will also be of help to you if you can encourage providers to share any information and information sources they have with you. This way you can provide more information to other settings in your area of responsibility. You can also help providers to identify other areas of support – if you are not able to help them with a particular topic you may be able to direct them to the person that can.

Providers should also be encouraged to share information between settings. There may be initial resistance if you suggest this, as many providers are not used to working with their 'competition', but there are a lot of benefits to doing so. Sharing practice and information can initiate new ideas, and can also help providers to work in partnership.

## 417.3 Contribute to the development and maintenance of support networks

### Networking

The providers in your area of responsibility may be able to join support networks that are already organised in the area. You may be able to give them details of these. If there are no networks available then you should try to encourage the providers to set up a network. This may be by organising something as simple as a one-off meeting of local providers to discuss the possibility of this, and to discuss if they would find it useful. If this is successful, then you should encourage providers to set a series of dates, and topics which they would like to discuss. You should also help them to organise who will be the chair at each meeting, who will minute the meetings and where the venue will be. You may also need to assist them in organising a contact list and perhaps setting up an online forum for them to keep in touch on a more ad-hoc basis. You can also encourage them to keep in touch through email. Providers may also feel happy to know that they can speak to others over the telephone for instant support!

### Continuous development

K4PI032
K4PI036
K4PI037

Some providers may be aware of the areas within their provision that they need to improve, and other providers may need your support to identify areas for development. As you will have provided them with information and guided them to the areas where they can seek further information, they should be able to carry this on to identify the information and resources they need in order to support their continuous development.

Providers should also be encouraged to share good practice. This could be through discussions, inviting others to look round their settings, showing videos or photographs or they could give a short presentation. This will help to give other providers ideas for how they can improve. Good practice in childcare is detailed within the Early Years Foundation Stage Practice Documents, or the relevant documents for your home country.

> You can find out more about EYFS Practice Documents in Unit 403.

## Unit 421 Provide information about children's and families' services

This Unit is about giving out information on the services available for children and families.

The elements in this Unit are:

421.1 Establish and maintain information about the full range of services available to children and families.

421.2 Provide information about children and family services in response to requests.

## 421.1 Establish and maintain information about the full range of services available to children and families

### Identify information

The children and families whom you are responsible for may require information about the services that are available to them, and will be likely to turn to you for this information. They will also need to know the details of the services on offer and in order for you to meet this need it would be worthwhile getting in touch with service providers to find out the details of what they offer. You will then be able to pass this on to others.

There are many services available to children and families, including public, private and voluntary. Some of these include:

- National Health Service (NHS)
  Provides health care for all those who need it, regardless of their ability to pay

- Social Services
  Responsible for providing benefits and personal social services

- National Society for the Protection of Children NSPCC
  Founded in 1884 to protect children. Offers training and a helpline

- ChildLine
  Telephone helpline to support children in distress

- Children's Society
  Works on areas such as fostering, adoption and community work

- National Childbirth Trust (NCT)
  Information and support for parents and parents to be

- Parentline Plus
  Provides support for parents having difficulties with their child

- National Council for One Parent Families
  Gives advice and campaigns to improve the position of lone parents

- Sure Start
  Is a government programme which aims to achieve better outcomes for children, parents and communities

- Cry-sis
  A charity that offers support for parents of babies who cry excessively

- Health visitor
  Offers advice regarding child development and carries out routine checks

- Educational psychologist
  Helps children or young people who are experiencing problems within an educational setting with the aim of enhancing their learning

- Speech therapist
  Assesses and treats speech, language and communication problems in people of all ages

- Play therapist
  Helps children to make sense of difficult life experiences or complex psychological issues through play

- Occupational therapists
  Assesses and treats physical and psychiatric conditions using specific, purposeful activity

- Parents centre
  Promotes links between school and home

- Disabled Parents Network
  Supports people with disabilities who are or who wish to become parents.

This list is by no means exhaustive and you should be able to find further information about services provided in your local area. These could also include childcare provision (including daycare and childminding, after-school clubs and holiday schemes), local support groups and leisure activities for children.

### Keys to Good Practice

Look at the list of services provided. How could you make this information available to the parents in your setting?

### Information systems

You are likely to gather a huge amount of information and will need to create a system that allows you to access the information you need quickly and conveniently. You may decide to keep this information on a computer database or as a paper-based system, such as a filing cabinet, index cards, a written list or in a ring binder.

If you choose to store your information on a computer database it would be worth considering the purchase of software that allows you to create a database, such as Microsoft Access, or using a Microsoft Excel spreadsheet. If you choose to keep a paper-based system then you are likely to need files, folders and dividers etc.

## Providing information

The information that you gather and give out will need to be in enough detail to allow parents to decide if it will be suitable. It will need to include exactly what the service provides, the age and ability it is suitable for or aimed at, contact details, and times, dates and cost.

Often, families who need help and advice do not receive the information they need. This could be for a variety of reasons:

- parents may not be able to read, or English may not be their first language
- parents do not have the time to access services
- parents may be afraid to contact other services
- parents may not be able to access information, for example they do not have time to find it, or do not have facilities such as Internet access
- information is not clear.

When providing information you must make sure it can be understood by all those who need it. This may mean you need to provide it in a different language, or take time to discuss it and explain it to parents. If you have regular contact with families this will be relatively easy to achieve, but you may need to change your approach if you do not have regular contact. In this case you may need to send information out by post, or make a visit to the family.

The information that you provide should not indicate any preference for a particular service, and you should take care to provide information that reflects all areas and groups in the community. This will ensure that no group feels discriminated against and they feel comfortable using a service where they are likely to meet others from their own community.

Figure 2: Why parents may not be able to access information

K4MI082

## Keeping information up to date

To ensure that the information you give to parents is accurate, you will need to monitor and update it on a regular basis. You may decide to include a date with the information about each service, so you and those using the information are aware of when it was last updated.

Try to encourage the providers of services to let you know if they make any changes to their provision. You should also maintain regular contact to find out if anything new is being offered or if any of the services have changed.

## 421.2 Provide information about children and family services in response to requests

### Dealing with requests

There may be occasions when you are approached with a request for information. You should ensure that you find out the reasons for the request in a friendly manner to ensure it is a genuine request and that you are giving the correct information. Using your systems, you should then be able to quickly identify the information needed. You should ensure that you give out information that is objective and does not

indicate a preference for a particular service or group. If there are several that may be suitable, you should give all the information and allow the person who submitted the request to decide which is most suitable for them. Be aware they may need assistance to do this. It is also worthwhile to set up a system of monitoring requests in order to ensure that children are protected.

## Providing information

In order to ensure that the information is accessible to as many families as possible, you should consider sharing it with a range of public and private organisations that are themselves easily accessible and frequently used by children and families. This will allow the information to be accessed more widely. This could include doctors' surgeries, libraries, childcare provisions or local council buildings. You may wish to present the information in a booklet for families to take away with them, or perhaps as leaflets. You should also leave contact details of your information service, to allow families to get in touch if they need more information.

## Feedback to providers

It is likely you will have built up a rapport with the providers of services. It is helpful if you can feedback any comments, compliments and complaints that you are given. This will help the providers to be aware of how their services are received by families, and will also help the families who are using the service.

# Unit 422   Coordinate work with families

This Unit is about coordinating work with families for the benefit of children, and dealing with complaints raised by families.

The elements in this Unit are:

422.1   Establish procedures and practices for work with families.

422.2   Implement policies and procedures for work with families.

422.3   Deal with family issues, grievances and complaints.

## 422.1 Establish procedures and practices for work with families

### Information needs

The setting you work in is likely to need some information about the children they are caring for and their families. Your setting will have a registration form to be completed when the children first start the setting, and this should contain all the information needed. There may also be permission slips that parents are asked to complete. You should clearly explain to the families why this information is needed and how it is likely to be used.

### Communicating with families

If parents regularly attend the setting to drop off and collect their children then you should have had the opportunity to build up a good relationship with them, and will have the opportunity to communicate at these times. If parents rarely attend the setting it may be worthwhile reminding them they can phone the setting if they have any concerns or worries, and consider setting up a home book communication system, so both parties can give feedback about the child progress. You can also involve parents as helpers in the setting, as they may have valuable skills and knowledge to share.

It is likely that you will need to adapt the way you communicate depending on the person you are talking to. Some people prefer to communicate using the written word, although some adults may have difficulty with reading and writing. Equally, some are comfortable using the telephone but others may prefer to communicate face-to-face. You may need to use pictures or a translator if the person you are speaking with does not have English as a first language. You should be able to find information about translating language from your local authority or Sure Start centre.

There is likely to be a wide range of family structures and backgrounds in your setting. It is important that you respect this variety and value the diversity that they offer. This is important because it will help all groups to feel welcome and it will enrich the children's experience at the setting.

**Figure 3:** It is important to keep parents and carers informed about their child's progress

## 422

K4DI084

# Involving parents

Most parents will probably welcome the chance to help at their child's setting. You could involve parents by asking them to come in and help, or by offering the opportunity to share a particular skill they may have. The Early Years Foundation Stage reminds us that families are important and should be welcomed and valued. It also states that: 'Parents are a child's first and most enduring educators. When parents and children work together in early years settings, the results have a positive impact on children's development and learning.'

## Policies and procedures

In order to check that the policies and procedures you have in place are suitable, you will first need to evaluate the needs of the children and families that attend your setting. From this, you can go on to either identify, develop or improve upon the following procedures:

■  involving families in the provision of the setting

■  security and safety arrangements for the collection of children

■  roles and responsibilities of all practitioners in relation to families

■  emergency contact details.

## Points for Reflective Practice

Think about the following when you are reviewing your policies.

■  Involving families in the provision of the setting. Consider how families are involved. Do families offer or do you ask? Do you have specific activities or times when you would like parents to be involved? How can you make families feel comfortable about being involved?

■  Security and safety arrangements for the collection of children.
How does this currently happen? What security is there for the entrance door? How do you ensure the correct person collects the correct child? How do you ensure unauthorised people do not enter the setting? Is there an area for these people to wait that is not inside the secure areas of the nursery?

■  Roles and responsibilities of all practitioners in relation to families.
Are all practitioners aware of their roles and responsibilities? Are they effectively carried out?

■  Emergency contact details.
Do you have the parents' contact details if there was an emergency? Do you have contact details for an emergency contact? Are they up to date and correct? How are these accessed?

# 422.2 Implement policies and procedures for work with families

## Observe practitioners

The practitioners who work in your setting are on the front line when dealing with parents. The way they communicate and behave gives the parents an impression of the setting and it is for this reason that you should ensure practitioners are welcoming and friendly. Practitioners should communicate with families in a way that can be clearly understood and shows respect. One way you can ensure that this is happening is by observing practitioners working with the parents in a variety of situations.

■  Liaising with parents.
Do practitioners listen carefully and answer any questions fully? Do they make good eye contact and put the parents at ease?

■  Involving families in activities.
Are families valued? Do practitioners clearly explain the aims of the activity and what they would like the families to do?

■  Informing families of the children's progress and any potential problems.
Are practitioners sensitive, and deal with any potential problems somewhere private? Do practitioners praise the children to their parents?

■  Dealing with families who are unhappy with any aspect of the provision.
Do practitioners listen carefully and check they have understood? Do they refer the families to the correct person if they are unable to deal with the concern?

# Making changes

As a result of this observation, you may require the practitioners to make some changes to their practice. You will need to discuss your observations with the practitioners involved and point out what they did well, as well as the improvements you would like to see. This may cause some conflict and you should try to remain positive and explain how the improvements will benefit their practice. Practitioners may require further training in diversity, equality and anti-discriminatory practice, and they may also require further training in working with parents. This is important for their professional development. This type of training may also help them to deal with families whose beliefs, attitudes and values are different to their own and help them to provide a professional and non-judgemental service.

The beliefs, attitudes and values held by families are likely to be different for everyone, and these should be respected. They may cause families to behave in ways that practitioners would not expect or that they do not agree with, but they need to learn to accept this and work with the parents regardless. The beliefs, attitudes and values held may also cause differences in self-reliance and identity, but again practitioners should accept these differences and work alongside them.

# 422.3 Deal with family issues, grievances and complaints

## Common problems

Your setting should have a policy and procedure that sets out what should happen if there is a complaint or a grievance from a family. You should follow this at all times. Common problems that may occur include parents not sharing the aims of the setting, parents who are unhappy about something they have seen in the setting, such as staff practice or an area they feel is unsafe, parents not understanding the activities that are carried out, or difficulties in the relationship between parents and practitioners.

## Dealing with incidents

It is important to ensure that you can be contacted easily by parents, that they feel comfortable speaking to you about any concerns, and able to talk to you about their grievances. If an incident does occur and a parent makes a complaint, you should listen carefully and make a note of what the problem seems to be and what the parent has said. You should reassure them that you will deal with the problem and get back to them within an agreed timeframe. You should then speak to the practitioner involved and make a note of the explanation given. Speaking to both parties means that you will have a full understanding of the perceived problem.

The steps that you take next will be dependent on what the complaint was, and the explanation given by the practitioner, and you should follow the guidance of your policy when deciding this. Either way, you will need to work with both the parents and the practitioners to resolve the issue. This should be carried out in a positive manner and it is extremely important to ensure that the care of the child is not affected, and that the child is not aware of what is happening. Once you have worked through the steps in your policy you will need to give feedback to both parties. This should be both calm and positive, and you should ensure that the steps you take are fair to both parties.

## Case Study: Dealing with parental concerns

A new member of staff has recently started and there have been some changes to the key worker groups to accommodate her. These changes have been communicated in the monthly newsletter. A parent asks to speak to you at the end of the day, and you both go into a quiet room. The parent explains that she is concerned because her child does not seem to like her new key person. The parent says that she has just spoken to the staff involved but has been told nothing can be done as the groups have all been decided. She is upset and concerned, and feels as though her concerns are not being taken seriously.

- What should you say to the parent?
- What will your next steps be?
- How will you discuss this with the staff members concerned?

# Unit 423 Manage multi-agency working arrangements

This Unit is about multi-agency working and how to manage the arrangements for this.

The elements in this Unit are:

**423.1** Establish and maintain relationships with other agencies.

**423.2** Share information with other agencies.

## 423.1 Establish and maintain relationships with other agencies

### Making contact

The idea of multi-agency working is that it brings together a range of services for the whole community, and that the practitioners involved work together to deliver integrated support to children and families. It is made up of a range of services and has a clear management structure. Normally, it is delivered from a school or other Early Years setting.

There are a whole range of practitioners who can contribute to multi-agency working. Some panels are open to anyone who feels they have an interest in a particular child or young person's welfare. Some panels, particularly those that are located in a school, are made up of practitioners who are already working in the school.

### Ground rules

When you are working with other agencies it is a good idea to set some initial ground rules and to clarify everyone's roles and responsibilities. Members of the panel or team often do so in addition to their normal work roles. There will be a coordinator or a chair of the group and they are responsible for the panel or team. It is likely that there will be regular meetings. It can be helpful to develop policies to ensure that everyone

is working towards the same aim. It is also useful to develop a purpose and vision statement.

### Building positive relationships

You are likely to encounter a range of different people across the agencies that you are working with. You are more likely to be able to work as a team if you can build up strong relationships with them. It is important to accept the views of others, and also listen to them as you may be able to learn by looking at things from a different angle. You should also recognise that others communicate in different ways and may have preferred ways of communicating. These include conversations held in person, over the telephone, written communication such as letters, or methods such as email, fax or text message. It is important to communicate clearly at all times, and to check if you are unsure.

### Maintaining contact

Regular contact is important, although the frequency of this is likely to depend on the aims of the group. As a group you will need to decide on how often you will meet, and how often you will make contact. It should be as easy as possible for members of the group to make contact and it will help to have a list of contact details and arrangements so everyone is clear.

## 423.2 Share information with other agencies

### Methods of sharing information

The methods you use to share information as a group will be dependent on the type of information involved and the location of the other agencies you are involved with. Sharing information when all the agencies are in the same building is likely to be much easier than when they are 20 or 30 miles apart. Different methods will suit different groups, and could include email, telephone conversations, fax, written information that is posted, or information saved to a memory stick. The main advantages of using ICT as a method of communication are that information is available 24 hours a day and large amounts of data can be stored. You are also able to work from anywhere, as long as you have computer and Internet access. The disadvantages include the

**Figure 4:** Communication – informal as well as formal – between professionals is vital to multi-agency working

importance of understanding how to keep information secure, though using passwords. You also have to be able to use the technology and accept that technology may fail or break down from time to time.

However information is shared, you will need to ensure that all users understand any specialist language used in the reports and information. You may need to include a glossary, or bring this up as a regular part of each meeting. All members should feel confident to ask if they are unsure.

## Confidentiality

There has been much discussion in previous Units around confidentiality. This also applies to multi-agency working arrangements. It is worthwhile taking some time to discuss the boundaries and limits of confidentiality before any information is shared. There will be some information that members need to keep

confidential and some that they may need permission before it is shared.

> You can find out more about data protection in Unit 403.

## Child welfare

K4SI094
K4MI096

Although confidentiality and data protection is extremely important, you must always put the needs of the child first. This is the main principle of the Children Act: 'The welfare of the child is paramount'. If you have information about a child that relates to their welfare, you need to consider if this should be shared or not. If it does, you should do so quickly so that the child is not put at any further risk. In this situation, welfare is more important that privacy.

## Points for Reflective Practice

- Can you think of a time when you had information about a child that related to their welfare? What did you do with this information?
- If you were in the same situation again, would you do the same thing?

One of the important benefits of multi-agency working is that it allows different organisations to work together and identify children who are at risk far quicker than was previously possible. The organisations can then work together to act upon this information and take on the responsibility for the welfare of the child, ensuring that they are safe and protected at all times.

## Benefits of multi-agency working

Prior to multi-agency working, problems were experienced by families who didn't understand the roles and responsibilities of the different agencies that they might be involved with and because of this were unsure about whom to go to for what advice and support. They may also have had conflicting information and found they were passed from one agency to another. Multi-agency working gives families a single point of contact with the services that they use and a named person to coordinate their needs.

Parents and carers should be informed of the information sharing policy of the agency. You should make it clear to them that you will ask for permission if you wish to share information, unless the welfare of the child is at stake, in which case they may not be consulted. Remember that all information you keep is covered by the Data Protection Act.

Figure 5: There are many benefits to multi-agency working

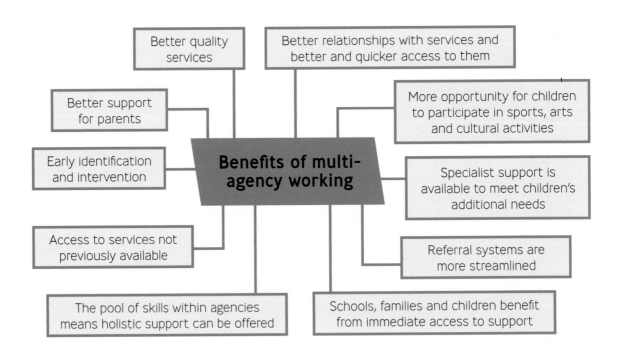

Better quality services

Better relationships with services and better and quicker access to them

Better support for parents

More opportunity for children to participate in sports, arts and cultural activities

Early identification and intervention

**Benefits of multi-agency working**

Specialist support is available to meet children's additional needs

Access to services not previously available

Referral systems are more streamlined

The pool of skills within agencies means holistic support can be offered

Schools, families and children benefit from immediate access to support

## Can't find what you are looking for?

| Level 4 KS Number | Knowledge Statement | Can be found in... |
| --- | --- | --- |
| K4M797 | Data protection | Unit 403 |
| K4MI092 | Legal frameworks | Throughout the book |
| K4MI097 | Record keeping and management of data | Unit 421 |
| K4MII00 | Knowledge management and information sharing | Unit 421 |

# Unit 431    Coordinate the leadership and management of integrated childcare provision

This Unit is about managing integrated childcare provision and covers both physical settings and services and facilities that support children and their families.

The elements in this Unit are:

**431.1**    Contribute to the leadership and management of a multi-disciplinary team.

**431.2**    Support integrated approaches to service delivery.

## 431.1 Contribute to the leadership and management of a multi-disciplinary team

### Building a team

The team that you lead is likely to be **multi-disciplinary** and all the members of your team will have different abilities, skills and strengths. It is important that you are aware of these, as this will allow you to allocate work to the best person and use their skills appropriately. It is also important that you value and respect all team members equally, remembering that they all have something different to offer. If you lead by example when doing this, it will encourage the other members of the team to do the same and lead to an atmosphere where each member is respected and valued for their contributions.

In order to find out each team member's strengths and area of expertise, it is worth taking the time to discuss this with them and find out what they think these may be. It may be useful to record this and discuss why they think so – have they got previous experience or qualifications, have they been on supplementary training courses, or do they have prior work experiences? You could then follow this up with discreet observation, to see if you agree, and if you feel that anything has been missed. You may also be able to talk to other managers or team leaders about each member and see if your views correspond to theirs.

It is also important to encourage good team relationships. A team that works well together achieves better outcomes. You should encourage each team member to respect each other and try to help them to find common ground.

> **Key Term**
> **Multi-disciplinary team** – team members from different disciplines and occupations working together.

### Encouraging innovation

K4PII05
K4PII07

Encouraging your team to be innovative can lead to some interesting and exciting new ideas. Encouraging innovation and creativity helps you stay ahead in your practice by ensuring that your provision remains up-to-date and in line with current guidelines, and you are likely to see changes coming before others do. Best practice in innovation involves looking at your existing processes and procedures to see what improvements can be made to keep them up-to-date.

There are several ways that you can encourage innovation.

- Involve your team from the planning stage.
  Ask them what they would like to see, and what changes they would like to happen. There are likely to be some good ideas and the team will be more enthusiastic about changes if they have played a part in making it happen.
- Ask for the team's help when solving problems.
  Asking your team is likely to lead to some good solutions.
- Encourage the team and individuals to explore and try out their ideas.
  Ideas should be tried, even if they seem as if they will not work. Sometimes the best innovations come from ridiculous ideas.

Innovative businesses often have strong leaders and management, and well-trained and motivated employees. The way that teams feel about their jobs often affects their motivation levels. You can motivate your teams by trying some of the following:

- providing varied and interesting work
- providing high-quality training and development
- encouraging individuals to study for professional qualifications
- practising an 'open door' culture where managers are approachable
- showing respect for work–life balance
- promoting fairness at work
- providing regular appraisals and positive feedback
- offering the chance to socialise with other team members.

## Leadership

K4P1106

If you are encouraging others to take on leadership, then you will need to recognise that there are different leadership styles. The main styles are identified below.

### Bureaucratic leader

- follows established procedures
- unwilling to find new ways to solve problems

- makes sure all the correct steps are followed
- good at ensuring quality.

### Charismatic leader

- energises and enthuses team
- normally looking for long-term commitment
- looks for recognition for the team.

### Autocratic leader

- has total authority
- makes decisions alone
- supervises closely.

### Democratic leader

- listens to team ideas
- makes the final decision
- happy to consider team input
- difficulty, making quick decisions.

### Laissez-faire leader

- gives little or no feedback and supervision
- can lack control.

### People-oriented leader

- supports and trains team members
- increases team members job satisfaction
- assigns specific tasks
- little involvement in team needs.

### Servant leader

- gives team members what they need so they can be productive
- not a 'commanding voice'
- achieves slow results.

### Transaction leader

- rewards and punishes team performance
- leads the groups to achieve the goals.

### Transformation leader

- motivates the team to be effective and efficient
- good communication
- highly visible leader
- focused on the big picture.

### Environment leader

- inspires individuals
- develops managers
- encourages team work.

## Points for Reflective Practice

Which type of leader do you think you are?

# 431.2 Support integrated approaches to service delivery

## SMART objectives

When considering your service delivery – which is basically the provision you are offering to the children and their parents and carers – you must first ensure that they are focused on the needs of the children.

> You can find out more about reviewing the provision you offer in Unit 419.

In order to help you do this you may consider setting **SMART** objectives (see also page 148).

SMART targets are the key to a successful action plan; they make it easier for you and others to identify action points.

## Specific

Your goals should be straightforward, well-defined and say exactly what you want to happen. It should be easy for others to understand. Being specific helps you to focus and define what you are going to do. You should use 'specific' to decide What, Why and How.

WHAT do you want to do? Action words are important here, such as direct, lead or develop.

WHY do you want to do it? Consider what you are you trying to achieve.

HOW are you going to do it? Use this section to explain.

## Measurable

If you are unable to measure it, then it is likely you won't be able to manage it. Your measure may be the achievement of the goal, or you may set several short term or small goals. Make sure you are able to see changes occur and know how you will measure progress made. This helps you to stay on track and reach any target dates you have set. You will also know when you have achieved your goal.

## Achievable

Any goal has to be within reach, no matter how good your intentions. If you know that something is too much for you then you are unlikely to commit to it. The feeling of success will help you to continue to be motivated. It also has to be agreed with all other team members.

## Relevant

This does not mean easy, but rather than you are able to do it. You should ensure that you have the skills and resources available, and that it fits in with your settings overall aims. You should not set goals that are too easy.

## Time-limited

Set a timeframe for your plan. This gives you a target to work towards. It you do not then it is likely that you will not achieve your goals. Ensure you give yourself enough time, but not too much time otherwise there will be no need for any sense of urgency.

### Key Term
SMART
S – Specific, M – Measurable, A – Achievable,
R – Relevant, T – Time-limited

## Can't find what you are looking for?

| Level 4 KS Number | Knowledge Statement | Can be found in... |
| --- | --- | --- |
| K4P1109 | Managing resources | Unit 412 |
| K4C1102 | Communicating with team members | Unit 401 |
| K4P1108 | Information exchange | Unit 401 |
| K4C1099 | Principles of effective communication | Unit 401 |

# Further references

www.childcarelink.gov.uk

www.childreninwales.org.uk

www.cwdcouncil.org.,uk

www.dh.gov.uk

www.direct.gov

www.everychildmatters.gov.uk

www.food.gov.uk

www.hse.gov.uk

www.ncb.org.uk

www.ndna.org.uk

www.pre-school.org.uk

www.schoolsfinder.direct.gov.uk

www.scottishchildcare.gov.uk

www.standards.dfes.gov.uk

www.surestart.gov.uk

www.teachernet.gov.uk

www.yell.com

www.4children.org.uk

# Coordinating special educational needs and safeguarding children

The following Units form part of the optional framework for NVQ CCLD Level 4.

These Units may be suitable if you are working in one of the following job roles:

- Individuals who have significant input and responsibility in meeting the individual needs of children who have been identified as requiring additional support.
- Practitioners who work in a setting supporting special educational needs.
- Practitioners who have an outside role in supporting and advising those who are involved in special educational needs.

Whilst you may undertake one of these Units of study, it may not be wholly appropriate for you to do both due to the nature of the role you are involved in and your ability to show sufficient competence and evidence for the performance and knowledge contained in each Unit.

The Units covered by this section are:

414    Coordinate and support provision for disabled children and those with special educational needs.

415    Coordinate special education needs for early education within a local area.

326    Safeguard children from harm. (This has been taken from the NVQ Level 3 CCLD.)

Because there is a significant amount of overlapping knowledge in Units 414 and 415, they are covered together in Section 1 below to avoid repetition. The main topics are Policies and Procedures, Assessment Frameworks and Working in Partnership with Families and other Agencies. Whether you are working towards 414 or 415, whether you are working in a setting, or whether your job is to support others, you will find the information you need in here. The Knowledge Specifications for both Units are clearly marked in the margin, next to the relevant areas of text; all the knowledge for both Units is either covered here or can be found in other Units within this book, in which case we have indicated where you can go to find more information.

All practitioners have some responsibility for safeguarding children and therefore Unit 326 will apply to almost any role. It covers information to enable practitioners to make contributions to safeguarding children by referring concerns about their welfare, participating in the assessment or planning process, and contributing to the review process. All this can be found in Section 2 below.

# Section 1

| 414 | Coordinate and support provision for disabled children and those with special educational needs. |

This Unit is about coordinating the support and provision for children with special educational needs in your setting, this can be suitable for individuals working in a community based capacity. As a lead practitioner or SENCO within the setting you will need to demonstrate and show you understand your obligations in meeting the needs of individual children in partnership with parents and other relevant agencies. Your role may include overseeing provision for all children in the setting with special educational needs or on a one to one basis; this is particularly relevant to childminders who are wholly responsible for the children in their care.

| 415 | Coordinate special educational needs for early education within a local area. |

This Unit is more specific to those who are not assigned to or based in one educational or daycare setting but who are more community-based in their role. This Unit may be undertaken by those of you who have considerable responsibility in coordinating services for children with special educational needs in a local area, including those of you who work on behalf of your local education authority or council. Your role may include advising, supporting and working with SENCO' in a variety of settings to ensure the needs of children with special educational needs are being met. You will need to demonstrate and show you understand your responsibilities within your role and effective working partnerships with a range of settings and professionals within the industry.

# Policies and procedures

To enable you to meet the needs of children with special educational needs it is firstly of great importance that you understand legislation relating to this. In Unit 402 you will have gathered vital information about SENDA and DDA, in addition to this you need to have a good understanding of the relevant codes of practice adopted by your country to ensure that you are compliant with regulatory policy.

You can find out more about children with special educational needs in Unit 402.

## England and Wales

In England and Wales the Special Educational Needs Code of Practice sets out the requirements for identifying and meeting the individual needs of children. The Code of Practice sets out its requirements in the following areas.

- Principles and policies.
- Working in partnership with parents.
- Pupil participation.
- Identification, assessment and provision in early education settings.
- Identification, assessment and provision in the primary phase.
- Identification, assessment and provision in the secondary sector.
- Statutory assessment of special educational needs.

- Statements of special educational needs.
- Annual review.
- Working in partnership with other agencies.

Whilst the main themes in the Code of Practice for England are identified in the Code of Practice for Wales it is important to note that there are some differences within its content which reflect the legislation and structure of Wales and the Welsh assembly.

## Scotland

In Scotland, the Education (Additional Support for Learning) (Scotland) Act 2004 identified key changes as the new act was enforced. These included the following.

- The replacement of the terminology Special Educational Needs (SEN) with Additional Support Needs.
- Measures to improve integrated working.
- Greater rights for parents and young people.
- Introduction of the coordinated support plan (CSP).

The Supporting Children's Learning Code of Practice outlines the requirements and obligations of individuals in meeting children's learning needs and should be followed in conjunction with the Education (Additional Support for Learning) (Scotland) Act 2004 and associated amendments of 2008.

## Keys to Good Practice

Take time to look at the relevant Acts, Bills and Codes of Practice associated with provision for children in your home country. You may have a discussion with your assessor to demonstrate your knowledge of relevant requirements.

At a local level, authorities have a duty to identify and meet the needs of those children who have been assessed to have special educational needs.

So how should special educational needs be defined?

Special Educational Needs are defined in the SEN Code of Practice as:

'Children have special educational needs if they have a learning difficulty which calls for special educational provision to be made for them.

Children have a learning difficulty if they:

a) have a significantly greater difficulty in learning than the majority of children of the same age; or

b) have a disability which prevents or hinders them from making use of educational facilities of a kind generally provided for children of the same age in schools within the area of the local education authority

c) are under compulsory school age and fall within the definition at (a) or (b) above or would do so if special educational provision was not made for them.'

(Taken from SEN Code of Practice, DFES, 2001.)

The Education (Additional Support for Learning) (Scotland) Act 2004 goes further in defining what Additional Support Needs are.

It states:

> 'A child or young person is said to have additional support needs where, for whatever reason, they need additional support with their education. This applies whether the need for additional support is temporary or ongoing.'

(Taken from www.additionalsupportneeds.org.uk.)

The Act recognises many factors that could be considered for giving rise to additional support needs being identified, including the learning environment, family circumstances, disability or health needs, social and emotional factors.

The guidance is keen to point out that this is not an exhaustive list and that children do not necessarily need additional support if these factors are identified. It emphasises that practitioners should focus on treating each child based on their individual needs.

## Northern Ireland

The Special Educational Needs and Disability (Northern Ireland) Order 2005 (SENDO) sets out its commitments in the Code of Practice.

> 'The Code of Practice addresses the identification, assessment and provision made for all children who may have special educational needs at sometime in their school careers, or even earlier.'

Special educational needs is defined as 'a learning difficulty which calls for special educational provision to be made'.

(Taken from www.deni.gov.uk.)

The code considers all types of learning difficulties, from situations where short-term measures are required, to more long-term needs where a statement of special educational needs is required.

Within its Principles and Essential Practices in the Code of Practice the Department of Education in Northern Ireland clearly states the need to identify children with special educational needs as early as possible and work with appropriate agencies to meet both their educational and non-educational needs.

## Find it out

Your local authority will have in place their own policies and procedures for working with settings, children and families in providing for special educational or additional learning needs.

■ Who is the point of contact in your local authority in supporting children with SEN?

■ How do they support SEN and Inclusion?

## Keys to Good Practice

To ensure compliance you must first understand what this is. Ensure your setting or service has available copies of Codes of Practice or regulatory documentation relevant to your country that practitioners can refer to regularly to build knowledge and understanding.

**K4SI002**
**K4D994**

# Assessment frameworks

All authorities within the UK have a responsibility as stated in the Codes of Practice or legislation adopted by their country to identify, assess and make adequate provision for children with special educational needs. Early recognition and intervention through assessment frameworks is important to prevent learning or other difficulties from developing. Authorities need to

consider short-term and long-term measures where applicable. For some children, consideration will need to be given to how their care needs will be met as they have additional needs reaching far beyond the learning environment.

Whilst it is important to understand that children with disabilities may require additional educational support, there may be no recognised need for them to be placed on an SEN register or have provision made within a school environment to access the curriculum.

In Scotland education authorities will usually assess the additional support needs of individuals if they have received a written request from a parent or person involved in the care and education of the child. Authorities will comply with requests unless they feel the request is not in the child's best interests or not relevant to the child's needs. In addition they may reject requests where this would repeat assessment processes already occurring. Coordinated support plans are then drawn up which stipulate the services and agencies involved in meeting the needs of the child.

Northern Ireland's Special Educational Needs Code of Practice adopts a five-stage approach to assessing a child's needs and making the necessary arrangements for those needs to be met. Stages 1 to 3 are based in the school or care environment. Stages 4 and 5 require input from a range of agencies and calls for a statutory assessment of needs to be made.

## The Common Assessment Framework (CAF)

Practitioners working in England and Wales will be familiar with the Common Assessment Framework. This framework has been developed to identify and respond to the needs of children who may not be achieving the outcomes of the Every Child Matters Agenda.

The groups and elements are as follows.

### Development of unborn baby, infant, child or young person

To include:

■ health

■ emotional and social development

- behavioural development
- identity, including self-esteem, self-image and social presentation
- family and social relationships
- self-care skills and independence
- learning.

## Parents and carers

To include:

- basic care, safety and protection
- emotional warmth and stability
- guidance, boundaries and stimulation.

## Family and environmental

To include:

- family history, functioning and well being
- wider family
- housing, employment and financial considerations
- social and community elements/resources including education.

Practitioners and professionals will need to complete a CAF form to record their concerns regarding a child's development and/or progress and share these with parents and other agencies relevant to meeting the needs of the child.

## Keys to Good Practice

Remember that effective working relationships with parents or the primary caregiver are crucial in achieving support for the child. Involve them in the assessment and explain fully the reasons you are doing this and what you can do to help. Their permission to share information must be sought and parents reserve the right to not share information with professionals from some agencies.

In addition to the CAF, practitioners in England and Wales should follow the SEN Code of Practice in relation to identification, assessment and provision in the primary phase.

When an early education practitioner who works day-to-day with the child, or the SENCO, identifies a child who has additional needs which may have

been identified through the CAF process, they need to provide interventions specific to the needs of the individual child.

Intervention can result in the following two processes occurring.

Early Years Action:
(SEN Code of Practice 4:21)
The triggers for intervention through early years action could be the practitioner's or parental concern, about a child who despite receiving early education experiences:

- makes little or no progress even when teaching approaches are particularly targeted to improve the child's identified area of weakness
- continues working at levels significantly below those expected for children of a similar age in certain areas
- presents persistent emotional or behavioural difficulties which are not ameliorated by the behaviour management techniques usually employed in the setting
- has sensory or physical problems, and continues to make little or no progress despite the provision of personal aids and equipment
- has communication and/or interaction difficulties, and requires specific individual interventions in order to access learning.

Early Years Action Plus:
(SEN Code of Practice 4:29)
Early Years Action Plus is characterised by the involvement of external support services who can help early education settings with advice on new IEPs and targets, provide more specialist assessment, give advice on the use of new or specialist strategies or materials, and in some cases provide support for particular activities.

The triggers for referral for seeking help from outside agencies could be that, despite receiving an individualised programme and/or concentrated support, the child:

- continues to make little or no progress in specific areas over a long period
- continues working at an early years curriculum substantially below that expected of children of a similar age
- has emotional or behavioural difficulties which substantially and regularly interfere with the child's

K4DI017

own learning or that of the class group, despite having an individualised behaviour management programme

■ has sensory or physical needs, and requires additional equipment or regular visits for direct intervention or advice by practitioners from a specialist service

■ has ongoing communication or interaction difficulties that impede the development of social relationships and cause substantial barriers to learning

## Find it out

Find out what opportunities exist in your local authority to give you more information about assessment and referral processes and the support you can get.

## The role of the Special Educational Needs Coordinator (SENCO)

All Early Years settings should have a designated team member whose main role and responsibilities include coordinating the provision for children with special needs. In addition their role may also be to support other practitioners in the setting in implementing action plans, differentiation strategies and procedures for ensuring inclusion and integration for service users.

Practitioners may seek advice and support from the SENCO about a child for whom they are the key person. Time should be allocated for SENCOs to talk to practitioners about the difficulties they face in daily practice and strategies they could employ to overcome these.

Managers of settings should recognise the role of the SENCO within the setting and in the context of the wider community. The role of SENCO should be designated to a practitioner with knowledge and understanding of

**Figure 1:** It is crucial for any practitioner to understand the particular needs of the child they are working with

special needs and a willingness to take on additional training to perform their duties to the best of their ability. SENCOs may need time away from the daily care of children to fulfil their record keeping requirements and may also need to spend time away from the setting at case reviews and Family Support meetings.

## Understanding disabilities

For any practitioner working with children who have disabilities or identified learning needs it is crucial they understand the needs of the child. This understanding is gained by having more knowledge about the disability or learning need itself.

The Internet has proven a very useful resource in recent years and can give practitioners an insight to the specifics of a condition or impairment and gain a greater understanding of the needs of the child they are caring for.

It would be unreasonable to suggest that any Early Years practitioner should have a wealth of knowledge regarding identified disabilities or special educational needs as there are many that have been researched and recognised. What is important, however, is that practitioners find out about conditions, disabilities and learning needs of children who they care for or are going to care for.

### Physical impairments

K4D988

Physical impairments can be short term or long term. A child who has a broken leg will need to have their needs identified and met for the immediate future but generally will not have long-term needs.

A child with a long-term physical disability such as paralysis, ataxia or cerebral palsy may need long-term measures put in place to enable them to participate in the setting.

**Figure 2:** Physical impairments, such as asthma, can carry long- or short-term consequences

Physical impairments/health problems can include the conditions given in Figure 3.

## Sensory impairments

Sensory impairments are those affecting an individual's use of hearing or sight. Sensory impairments often present themselves at birth and it is through thorough initial health checks that such impairments are detected. Sensory impairments include reduced or lost vision, deafness and speech impairments and impediments. In some cases sensory impairments can be the result of exposure to disease or illness which can cause immeasurable stress as, in addition to coping with the impairment, they have to cope with the sense of loss for something they once had and relied upon.

Sensory impairments can include the examples shown in Figure 4.

Figure 3: Examples of physical impairments

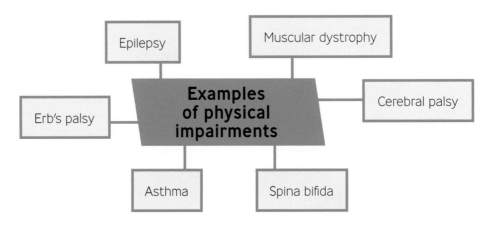

Figure 4: Examples of sensory impairments

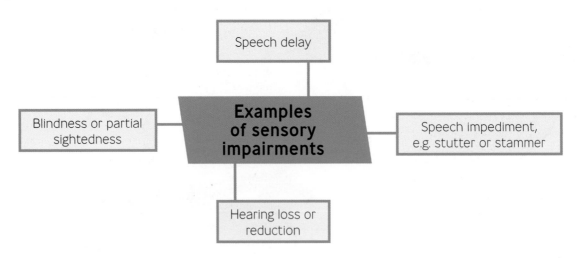

**Figure 5:** Examples of learning difficulties

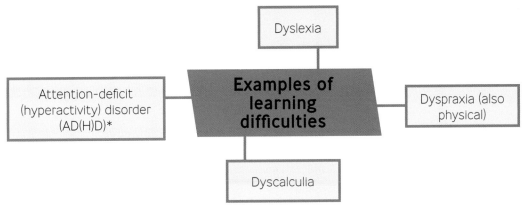

*This can exist with or without hyperactivity.

## Learning difficulties

Children who experience difficulty in learning may have a condition that affects only some elements of their learning, such as dyslexia which affects a child's ability to read and spell written symbols. This can prove to be quite a frustrating problem for children and can often be missed in the early years as children may not have any other significant learning need that can be brought to the attention of practitioners. Learning difficulties will readily present themselves in the classroom environment where it may be evident that a child is struggling to interpret what they have been asked to do or struggle to 'keep up'. Early identification and intervention is important so a child does not feel inadequate and suffer a loss of self-esteem and confidence as this can potentially affect their whole school life.

Learning difficulties can include those shown in Figure 5.

The Disability Discrimination Act recognises the need for settings to address access issues for disabled children and ensure that they are not treated less favourably than non-disabled children.

> Look back at Unit 402 for more information on the Disability Discrimination Act.

## Parents and families

It is extremely difficult for some families to accept their child has a disability or special educational need. Whether identification happens pre-birth, at birth or in early childhood it can overwhelm parents and families with a vast range of feelings and emotions. These can include:

■ sense of loss

■ anger

■ resentment

■ denial

■ loneliness

■ guilt

■ unable to cope

■ effects on siblings

■ effects on partner or spouse.

Practitioners should be sensitive to the feelings of parents and prepared to listen when they want to talk. Where appropriate, offer reassurance that it is ok to have these feelings; acceptance can often take time and requires a good support network to be available to the child, its parents and family.

K4D995

## Inclusion and integration

K4D990
K4D857

Regardless of the setting or service in which you work in the Early Years sector you must ensure that provision is inclusive and that children with additional needs are supported to access the setting or service.

**Inclusion** requires you to put in place strategies to promote the participation and access of those with disabilities or special educational needs.

## Key Term

**Inclusion** – is a process of identifying, understanding and breaking down barriers to participation and belonging.

## Individual Education/Action Plans

Having written documentation outlining objectives and intentions to support a child's identified need is good practice. So what should they include?

- Details of the child.
- Identified needs.
- Key objectives of the plan (e.g. realistic development and learning goals).
- How these needs can be met (e.g. differentiation strategies to play and learning opportunities).
- Who is taking the lead in making this happen (e.g. the child's key person).
- Other professionals that can support the child and the setting (e.g. speech and language therapist).
- Records of outcomes and/or achievements within the plan.
- Review date.

## Points for Reflective Practice

Look at the procedures currently followed within your setting or service to identify, assess and meet the individual needs of children in your care.

- Do they meet regulatory requirements for your home country?
- Are they clear and informative?
- Do they fit the purpose for which they have been designed?
- What needs changing (if anything) in your individual education/action plans?
- Is there anything missing from the list above or should anything be omitted?

Share your plans with your assessor and discuss how effective the strategies and resources have been in meeting the learning and development needs of children in your care.

## Resources and support

Any setting responsible for the care and education of a child or children with special educational needs or disabilities should ensure they are adequately equipped to provide for those needs.

So what does that entail?

- **Adequate knowledge:** to be able to provide for a child's needs you must first understand what those needs are. Practitioners who will be the key person in the child's life should be supported to gain further knowledge and understanding of their individual needs. This understanding may be gained through meeting with the child's parents and other key professionals or attending training and information events which can help you gain valuable information and knowledge regarding the specifics of particular needs as well as the associated language and terminology used that you may not have come across before.

- **Material resources:** you should ensure your provision has adequate facilities to meet their care and learning needs. For children with physical disabilities, this may include having access to tumble form chairs, standing frames and feeding equipment. For children who have a sensory impairment this will include access to resources and toys such as light and sound toys designed to stimulate the senses.

- **Human resources:** ensuring practitioners working with the children are confident in the role and understand the individual needs of the children. It is also important to recognise the human resources beyond the immediate environment and their role in supporting children in your setting on a peripatetic basis, such as speech therapists and physiotherapists.

## Find it out

Some local authorities will help Early Years settings with the cost and/or loan of equipment and resources for children's particular needs. Consider the advantages, disadvantages and associated costs related to purchasing specialist aids and equipment.

## Case Study: Specialist equipment

Kirstie is the SENCO in a pre-school setting and has to consider how she is going to meet the needs of children in the setting with communication difficulties. This includes a child with limited speech and a child who has impaired hearing. Kirstie is in the process of developing an individual education plan for each of the children in her care.

- What should the plan include?
- What strategies might Kirstie use for effective communication?
- What resources could help with the successful implementation of this plan?
- Where might Kirstie go for her resources?

# Working with families and other agencies

When working to identify and meet the needs of children with disabilities and/or special educational needs, it is important to recognise the role that other professionals play in this.

Legislation throughout the UK clearly identifies the need for collaborative working relationships between those professionals involved in identifying, assessing and meeting the needs of children.

Early Years practitioners play a crucial role within this system and those who work closely with the child in a setting play a key role in communicating the needs and abilities of the child to parents and other professionals.

Who the other professionals are (in addition to you) who play a key role in providing for a child's specific needs will depend on what those needs are; likewise the agencies involved will vary according to which are the most effective in meeting those needs.

Meetings between agencies, Early Years practitioners and parents should be arranged so that all parties involved can work collaboratively to ensure an

**Figure 6:** Some local authorities will help Early Years settings with the cost and/or loan of equipment and resources for children's particular needs

integrated approach in meeting a child's needs. Discussions can take place with everyone's viewpoint being heard and real progress can be gained by each agency or individual identifying their roles and responsibilities and the action that will be taken to meet the child's needs.

Ensure you have a record of what has been said during these meetings so you can refer to them later. Parents may also approach you for clarification on parts of the meeting which you can share with them. Records or minutes of meetings are of increased benefit to those unable to attend meetings and are a crucial form of communication between agencies.

Reviewing progress is an essential element in multi-agency work and can go some way to ascertain if current ways of working and communicating are of benefit to the child. The review process is often a way of ensuring that progress is being achieved, that key objectives are being met and that everyone involved in the process is happy with what they are doing and what is happening.

The parents and practitioner play a key role in reviewing progress as they have a detailed understanding of the child and their capabilities. Other agencies rely on this valuable information to help them and you provide for the child's needs.

## Models of disability
K4D987

By working alongside parents, practitioners and other professionals, you will inevitably encounter a range of opinions and viewpoints. These may be termed 'models' of disability. Two main models are the medical model and the social model.

- **Medical model.** This viewpoint looks at the child from a medical angle, perhaps labelling the child and seeing the disabled child as a problem. In this model, the disabled child is expected to fit into society as it is.
- **Social model.** This viewpoint looks at how society is disabling for children with impairments, arguing that disability is created by society and changes to society can make a child with an impairment fully included.

## Points for Reflective Practice

Discuss with your assessor the agencies involved in meeting the individual needs of your setting.

- What methods of communications are used to meet the information needs of the agencies with which you work?
- How does multi-agency working impact your setting?
- What other local or national support does your setting have?

## Can't find what you were looking for?

| Level 4 KS Number | Knowledge Statement | Can be found in... |
|---|---|---|
| K4D859 | Principles of partnership with parents and families | Unit 407 |
| K4D989 | Identification of barriers to access and participation and how these may be overcome | Unit 402 |
| K4D1010 | Detailed understanding of how to develop differentiated curricula based on children's individual needs | Unit 406 |
| K4D1122 | Specific issues for children's development and learning in multilingual or bilingual settings or where children are learning through an additional language | Unit 405 |

# Section 2

# Unit 326   Safeguard children from harm

This Unit is about working with others who have responsibility for safeguarding children and contributing to the process of keeping children safe.

The elements in this Unit are:

**326.1**   Refer concerns about the welfare of children.

**326.2**   Share information for the purpose of assessing children in need and their families.

**326.3**   Support plans, interventions and reviews that safeguard children and promote their welfare.

## Points for Reflective Practice

Take a few moments to read over your policies and procedures and make sure that you understand them.

K3S350

## 326.1 Refer concerns about the welfare of children

### Procedures for expressing concerns

Your setting will have policies and procedures in place that clearly show what your setting expects you to do if you have concerns about a **child in need** or a **child at risk of significant harm**. These should also state who the representative is within your setting for child protection, and it is this person who you will share your initial concerns with. If you are the representative for your setting, then you may like to share your concerns with the responsible person, and then take responsibility for making a report for social services.

### Discussion with children and parents

Once you have expressed your initial concerns and it has been agreed that these are valid, you will need to consider if you will discuss them with the child and parents. As a general rule, you should only discuss your concerns if by doing so you *do not* place the child at further risk of harm. It may be the case that the parents are unaware that there may be cause for concern, or are unwilling to ask for extra support, or do not realise that support and help is available to them.

The extent to which you discuss this with the children will also depend on their age and stage of understanding. It is obviously inappropriate to try to discuss your concerns with a small toddler, but as children become older you may be able to do so, ensuring that you do not prompt or 'put words in their mouths' and using simple language at all times. There is information on how to deal with a child's disclosure in Unit 402, and you should have regard to this when initiating any discussion. Remember to keep a record of this discussion.

If you chose to discuss your concerns with the parents then you should arrange a meeting in a private place to do so. You should ensure that you stress that the welfare of the child is your main concern, and do not reach premature conclusions about the suspected abuse. The parents may react with shock, and you will need to communicate in a way that is not threatening but is supportive. It is important to work in partnership at all times in order for the welfare of the child to be promoted. You will need to explain to the parents your decision to make a referral, and it is possible that this will cause upset and resentment. You should be clear about your reasons for making a referral and try to get parental agreement.

### Find it out

For more information about what to do if you are worried a child is being abused read www.everychildmatters.gov.uk/_files/34C39F24E7EF47FBA9I39FAOIC7B0370.pdf.

## Making a referral

You will need to decide which the most appropriate agency is to make a referral to. This may include children's social care, the police, the NSPCC, or the Local Child Safeguarding Boards. When you make the referral, ensure you agree with the recipient what the child and their parents will be told, by whom and when they will be told. If you have made your referral verbally or by telephone then it is very important that you confirm it in writing within 48 hours. You should then ensure that this written referral is acknowledged within one working day and chase it up if you have not heard back within three working days. All action you take should be recorded and kept in a secure place.

You can find out more about referral to appropriate agencies in Unit 402.

## 326.2 Share information for the purpose of assessing children in need and their families

### Sharing and providing information

K3S345
K3S355

Children's social care services will carry out an initial assessment to determine if there is a cause for concern. This will be completed within seven days. You

may be asked to provide information to assist this and you should ensure that you follow the procedures of your setting at all times. Any information that you provide should be clear and accurate. It is likely you will be asked about:

- the child's development and developmental needs
- if the parents/carers seem able to meet and respond to those needs
- any other factors, such as the relevance of the wider family and other environmental factors.

You should ensure that you clearly understand what information you are able to share with the parents and others and you will need to work with those who are carrying out the initial assessment to find this out.

## Keeping records

You should ensure that you maintain careful records and that you keep detailed, timed and signed **contemporary** and **retrospective notes** about anything that may be relevant to the welfare of the child or anything that seems unusual. These must all be kept in a secure place where unauthorised access cannot be gained.

### Key Terms

**Contemporary notes** – notes written immediately as an event has happened.

**Retrospective notes** – notes written after the event.

## 326.3 Support plans, interventions and reviews that safeguard children and promote their welfare

### Plans to promote welfare and safety

The result of the initial assessment will either lead to a core assessment being undertaken, or to the family being offered further services and support if necessary. You may be asked to participate in discussions and decisions with other professionals and parents in order to decide the best way to meet the needs of the child, and to ensure their welfare and future safety.

Another part of this planning process is the Children's Assessment Framework.

## Written reports

It is possible that a case conference may be held and the role of this conference is to decide if the child is at continuing risk of significant harm and whether or not the child requires a child protection plan to be put in place. You may be asked to contribute a written report for this. It is important that you discuss and agree with any relevant professionals whether your conference report can be shared with the parents or not.

## Case conference

If you are invited to the case conference then it is very important that you attend and participate as fully as you can in the decision-making process of the conference. A child protection plan may be drawn up and you should support this and use it within your setting with the child. The processes involved in a case conference may include the following.

- **Core assessment:** an in-depth assessment where detailed information is gathered, looking at the child's needs in the context of their family and wider community. This involves meetings with parents and the child as well as others who may be involved in the child's care. `K3S356`

- **Strategy discussion:** this will take place if there is reason to suspect a child is suffering or is at risk of suffering significant harm. The aim of the discussion is to plan a strategy about what should happen next. It can be held with members of the social care team and others who are involved with the case and the child's care. `K3S357`

- **Child protection conference:** the role of this conference is to decide if the child is at continuing risk of significant harm and whether or not the child requires a child protection plan to be put in place. `K3S360`

## Reviewing plans `K3S361`

The case conference will be held every six months until the child is no longer at risk. In this time you should continue to keep your normal records on the child and any others that are requested by social care. You may be asked to produce a report on the child. It is important to review plans and interventions regularly to ensure that the child continues to be safeguarded from harm, and to ensure that the plans in place are meeting their needs.

## Can't find what you were looking for?

| Level 3 KS Number | Knowledge Statement | Can be found in... |
|---|---|---|
| K3S344 | The legislation, guidelines and policies which form the basis for action to safeguard children | Unit 402: K4SII2O |
| K3S346 | The procedures and protocols in your setting for safeguarding and protecting children and expressing concerns about children's welfare | Unit 402: K4H776 and K4S779 |
| K3S348 | The nature and forms of abuse | Unit 402: K4S795 and K4S796 |
| K3S349 | The nature and forms of neglect | Unit 402: K4S795, K4S796 and K4S780 |

| Level 3 KS Number | Knowledge Statement | Can be found in... |
|---|---|---|
| K3D358 | The factors that influence parents' capacity to meet children's needs | Unit 402: K4S794 |
| K3D359 | The influence of environment and wider family on children's development | Unit 403 |
| K3S353 | The roles and responsibilities of all those involved in safeguarding children and promoting their welfare | Unit 402: K4S780 and K4M787 |
| K3M351 | The legal and organisational responsibilities regarding confidentiality, limits and boundaries and why these are important | Unit 403: K4M797 |
| K3M354 | Methods of recording and storing information, including the importance of contemporary notes in cases of protection and safeguarding | Unit403: K4M797 |

# Further references

Griffin, S. (2008) *Inclusion, Equality & Diversity in Working with Children*, Heinemann

Pugh, G. & Duffy, B. (2006) *Contemporary Issues in the Early Years*, Sage Publications

Wall, K. (2006) *Special Needs and Early Years: A Practitioners Guide*, 2nd edition, Sage Publications

Special Educational Needs: Code of Practice, DfES, 2001

# Index

## A

abuse 71-3
  possible indicators 73-4
  *see also* safeguarding
access 219, 239, 251
  barriers to 61
active listening 50
activities 219-20, 221-22, 229-31
  intellectual development 228-9
  physical 227-8
  resources 223-4
age discrimination 60
aggressive behaviour, adult 36
allergies, children's 87
anti-discriminatory practice 6, 29, 59
APL (accreditation of prior learning)
  13
appraisals 139, 200, 203
Argyle, M. 111
art therapy 238
assertiveness 36
assessment of practitioners 7-16
  direct observation 7-9, 14
  e-portfolios 15-16
  professional discussion 9-11
  reflective accounts 12-13
  witness testimonies 11-12
  work products 13
assessments of children 92, 220
  confidentiality 127, 128
  data protection 128-9
  evaluating records 127-30
  physical development 226
assessor visits 14
attachment 109, 110

## B

balance, development of 228
balance sheet 174-5
Bandura, Albert 126
behaviour 120-28
  factors affecting 120-1
  goals and boundaries 121
  inappropriate 120, 122, 125
  learning theories 125-7
  policies 63, 125
  time out 125
behavioural development 108-11
behaviourism 111, 112-13
best practice 214-15
bilingual settings 216, 252
body awareness 228
body language 50
Bowlby, John 109-10
Bruner, Jerome 115
budget 174-8
  variances 176-7
bullying 64
  in workplace 39
business plan 159
  policies and procedures 161
  *see also* planning

## C

cash flow forecast 175-6
changes to practice 181
child development 100-7, 115-19
  communication 103-4, 111
  creative development 236-40
  dealing with concerns 129-30
  emotional intelligence 110-11
  influences on 100-102
  intellectual 105-7, 228-9, 233
  learning/cognitive 112-15
  personal, social and emotional
    229-31
  physical 103-4, 111-12, 226-8
  role of play 231
  social, emotional, behavioural 106-7,
    108-11
  stages of 102-7
  theories of 107-15
Childcare Act (2006) 143, 144-5, 146,
  171
childcare registers 165
childminders 149, 166, 276
Children Act (1989)(2004) 59, 115, 250
Children's Workforce Development
  Council 202
choices, respecting others' 47-8
Chomsky, N.A. 111
cognitive development 111, 112-15
Common Assessment Framework 56,
  278-9
communication 42-3, 45, 48, 77-8
  adapting 49
  and conflict 38
  development 103-4, 111, 232-5
  with families 265
  methods 35, 50
  styles 35-6
  in team 30, 34-5, 189
complaints from parents 41
concentration, children's 229
conditioning 112-13
confidence, children's 111, 226, 230, 234
confidentiality 6, 28, 36, 47, 128, 269
conflict management 38-39, 40-41
constructivist theories 112, 113-15
continuous professional development
  148-55, 216, 235, 240, 261
  mathematical skills 244
Convention on the Rights of the Child,
  UN 56, 57, 147
cooperation, children's 111, 120
COSHH Regulations 83, 182, 251
creative development 236-40
  creative play 239
  imagination 237-8
Criminal Justice and Court Services
  Act (2000) 68, 148
Criminal Records Bureau 68
cross-infection 253
cross-referencing 8
culture 82, 231

  of team 188, 188
curiosity in children 111
curriculum 222
  evaluating delivery 245, 246
  frameworks 119, 218
curriculum planning 226, 247
  evaluating 224-5

## D

data collection *see* information
Data Protection Act (1998) 28, 70,
  128-9, 180
delegation 164, 189
development: defined 100
  *see also* child development
Dewey, J. 133, 134
diet, healthy 78-80
dietary needs information 87
direct observation 14
disabilities 60, 61, 82, 281-3
  Early Support 146
Disability Discrimination Act (1995)
  (2005) 58-9, 147, 220, 251
disclosure 75
discrimination 56, 60
diversity 6, 224, 265
DWCL (Disqualified from Working with
  Children List) 145, 146

## E

e-portfolios 15-16
Early Learning Goals 117
eatwell plate 79
Education and Inspections Act (2006)
  144
educational provision 245-7
  improvement strategies 246-7
  resources 245-6
egocentrism 113-14
Electricity at Work Regulations (1989)
  84-5, 182
emotional abuse 74
emotional environment 215
emotional intelligence 110-11
empathy 110
Employers Liability (Compulsory
  Insurance) Act (1969) 85
employment policies 209
employment process 30-31, 32
empowering children 72-3
empowering team 188-90
environment 83, 101, 252-52, 254-5
  and early learning 218-19
  stable and consistent 214-15
equal opportunities 6, 47, 62
  and resources 64-5, 224
Erikson, Erik 108-9
ethics of practice 47
ethnicity 82
event sample 96
Every Child Matters 68, 78, 146
  outcomes 115

  evidence-based practice 130
  evidence-gathering 7-16
  exercise and health 81-2
  exit interviews 205
  expert witness evidence 11-12
  exploration skills 241-42
  eye contact 50
  EYFS 92, 93, 117-19, 144, 222
    principles 115, 116, 117-18

## F

facial expressions 50, 125
families 264-7
  *see also* parents
feedback 258
  appraisals 203
  from colleagues 38, 51
  on performance 197, 198
finance 171-73, 174-8
  applying for 174
  budget 174-8
fine motor skills 102, 227
Fire Precautions (Workplace)
  Regulations (1997) 84, 251
food groups 79
food intolerances 87
food safety 251, 253
formative assessment 93, 99
Freud, Sigmund 108, 238
fun days 192, 194
funding *see* finance

## G

Gardner, Howard 110
gender 60, 82
genes and development 101
Gessel, Arnold 111-12
Getting it Right for Every Child 146, 147
good practice 256-7, 261
grievances, dealing with 267
gross motor skills 102, 227
growth: defined 100

## H

hand-eye coordination 227, 228
harassment and bullying 39
hazards 86, 183
health and safety 82, 181, 195
  audits 184
  legislation 84-5, 181-82
  policies 64, 182-3
  resources 183
Health and Safety at Work Act (1974)
  83, 182, 195, 251
Health and Safety (First Aid)
  Regulations (1981) 84, 251
health and well being 78, 253
  healthy diet 79-81
  and physical exercise 82-3
Healthy Schools Programme 78
HIV/AIDS awareness 253
holistic assessment 7

Human Rights Act (1998) 59, 147
hygiene 253

**I**
ICT, use of 246
impairments
    physical 281-82
    sensory 48, 282
in-house training 42-3, 202
incidents, dealing with 267
inclusion 29, 56, 61-5, 219-20
    and additional needs 283-4
inclusive practice, 29-30, 54
independence 230
Individual Education/Action Plans 284
induction 31
information 36, 87, 213-14
    sharing 27, 37, 49, 88, 128, 268-9,
        288
    storage of 28, 88, 129
information about services 261-63
    information systems 260-1
innovation in workplace 191-94
    in team 271-72
inspection 166-70
integrated provision 271-73
intellectual development 104-6, 228-9,
    233
interagency working 42-7
    safeguarding 77-8

**J**
jargon 48
job advertisements 207-8, 209
job descriptions 31, 206

**K**
Keeping Children Safe 78
key person system 92, 214
Kohlberg, L. 127
Kolb, David 133, 134-5

**L**
Laming Report 68, 78
language 60, 82, 111, 233, 234
Language Acquisition Device 111
law of effect 113
leadership 186-90
    styles 186-8, 272
learning, children's 217-20, 222
    achieving high-quality, 223
    and cognitive development 112-15
    Piaget's stages 114
    role of play 222-3
learning diaries 93, 97
learning difficulties 277, 283
learning, practitioners' 199-203
    from colleagues 51
    identifying needs 200-201
    Kolb's learning cycle 134-5
    see also training
learning styles 135-6, 153
learning theories 114, 125-7
legislation 143, 160, 203, 250-51
    health and safety 84-5, 181-2
    inclusion 219-20
    see also individual Acts
listening to colleagues 50
literacy 233-4
Local Safeguarding Children Boards
    68, 69, 76
locomotion skills 228

**M**
manipulative skills 227
Manual Handling Operations (1992)
    (2002) 84, 182
mathematical learning 240, 242-4
medication 63, 87, 88
mentoring 31
modelling behaviour 126
mood management 110
moral development 127
motivation of children 229

motivation of team 190, 272
multi-agency working 129-30, 268-70
    sharing information 268-9
multi-disciplinary team 271-71
multilingual settings 216, 252
music, use of 234, 238

**N**
National Curriculum Key Stages 218
National Occupational Standards for
    CCLD 3, 4-22
    assessment 7-16
    units and elements 4-5, 18-22
nature vs nurture debate 127
needs of children 136, 251-52
    information on 87-8
neglect 74
networking 261
non-participant observation 94
non-verbal communication 50
Northern Ireland 119, 202, 277-8
nutrition 79-80, 101

**O**
obesity 81
object permanence 113, 114
observation of practitioner 7-9, 14
observational learning 126
observations of children 92-8, 99, 100
    parental permission 92
    and reflection 141
Ofsted 143, 144, 165-6
    gradings 170
Ofsted Childcare Register 144-5
operant conditioning 112-13
operational plans 160, 161-5
outdoor environment 215, 227

**P**
paperwork 33-4
parents 47, 212-13, 222
    concerns of 267
    involving 213-14, 233, 235, 266
    see also families
participant observation 94
partnership with parents 47, 222
Pavlov, Ivan 112
performance issues 197-8
persistence 229
person specification 206
personal development plan 148-9,
    150-51
personal, social and emotional
    development 229-30
personality development 108-9
physical abuse 74
physical care 253
physical development 102-3, 111-12
    facilitating, 226-7
physical exercise 81-2
physical impairments 281-82
Piaget, Jean 113-14, 127
planning 148-9, 161-64
    contingencies 164
    for work allocation 195-6
    see also business plan
planning cycle 67, 247
play 118, 222-3, 231
Police Act (1997) 147
policies and procedures 27-8, 47, 61-4,
    66-7, 146-7
    business plan 161
    health and safety 64, 182-3
    keeping up to date 143
    whistleblowing 69, 71
PPE Regulations (1992) 84, 182
praise 123
principles 6, 115, 116, 256-7
problem-solving skills, 241-42
    improvements to support 244
product evidence 8
professional boundaries 44-5
professional development 216
professional discussion 9-11

professionals, liaising with 42-3, 44-5,
    46-7
profit and loss account 175-6
Protection of Children Act (1999) 68
Protection of Children (Scotland) Act
    (2003) 145-6
providers of services 259-61
    identifying 259-60
    networking 261
punishment 127
PUWER (1998) 84

**Q**
quality assurance schemes 255-7
    examining evidence 258-9

**R**
Race Relations Acts (1975)(2000) 56,
    146, 251
records: Ofsted requirements 167
recruitment and selection 30-31,
    204-11
    exit interviews 205
    job descriptions 206
    person specification 206
    recruitment methods 207-9
    staff leaving 204-5
referencing your work 17
reflective accounts 12-13
reflective analysis 140-1
reflective practice 51, 133-42
    benefits of 136-7
    curriculum planning 225
    ethics 47
    Kolb's learning cycle 134-5
reflective practitioner 133, 216
registration and inspection 165-9
Rehabilitation of Offenders Act (1974)
    67-8, 147
reinforcement 112-13
relationships, children's 110
    developing positive 230-1
relationships with service providers
    259-61
research 16-17
researching area of practice 178-80,
    181
    ethics 179-80
    literature search 178
    reliability and validity 180
resilience 230
resources 223-4, 242, 243, 253-4
    creative development 238
    stock control 223, 245-6
respecting others 47-8
responsive practitioners 216
retention of staff 211
RIDDOR (1995) 84, 182, 251
risk assessment 63, 86, 183, 195
risk and physical activities 228
role modelling 123
role as practitioner 51
    limits of expertise 44, 45, 46,
        51-2
routines 253-4

**S**
safeguarding 67, 68-70, 287-9
    case conference 289
    disclosure 75
    empowering children 72-3
    making referral 288
    policy 61, 69, 83
    support agencies 76-7
safety 82-3
scaffolding 114
schemas 113
Schon, Donald 133, 134
Scotland 119, 202, 277
self-assessment 169-70
self-awareness 110
self-concept 111
self-esteem 6, 122, 230
self-motivation 110

SENCO 62, 65, 280-81
SENDA (2001) 146, 220, 251
sensory impairment 48, 282
separation anxiety 109-10
service provision 213, 214, 273
sexual abuse 74
sexuality discrimination 60
shadowing 31-2
sharing information 27, 37, 49, 88, 128,
    268-9, 288
simulation 13
Skinner, B.F. 111, 112-13
SMART objectives 149, 162, 273
social background 82
social and emotional development
    106-11
social learning theory 126
social skills 230
socialisation theory 126-7
spatial awareness 228
special educational needs 59, 251, 276,
    284-5
    assessment frameworks 278-80
    Code of Practice 93, 220, 276-7, 279
    Coordinator 62, 66, 280-81
    intervention triggers 279
    multi-agency approach 285-6
    policies and procedures 276-8
    referral triggers 279-80
studies, planning 16-17
summative assessment 99
Sure Start 59, 146

**T**
teacher, role of 217-18
team 30, 32-3, 188-90
    communication 30, 34-5
    multi-disciplinary 271-72
    staff shortfalls 205
    supporting 31, 32-3, 41
teamwork 30, 43
Ten Year Strategy for Childcare 115,
    146
thinking, modes of 115
Thorndike, Edward 113
time sample 96
training and development 98, 139,
    151-5, 200
    events 33, 138
    in-house training 202
    plans 149, 201
    sharing learning 49, 52, 154-6
    venues 151-2
transitions, supporting 127-8

**U**
Units and Elements CCLD4 18-22

**V**
values 6, 46, 142
vision, creating 186
visiting settings 256-7, 258-9
Vygotsky, Lev 114

**W**
Wales 119, 202
waste disposal 253
welfare of children 250, 269-70
    concerns 70, 75, 287-8
    see also abuse; safeguarding
whistleblowing policy 69, 71
witness testimonies 11-12
work plan 195-7
work products 13
working relationships 24, 137
    other professionals 42-3, 44-5
'Working Together to Safeguard
    Children' 76
workloads, allocation of 195-8
Workplace (Health, Safety and Welfare)
    Regulation (1992) 85

**Z**
zone of proximal development 114